The Comic Worlds of Peter Arno, William Steig,
Charles Addams, and Saul Steinberg

Iain Topliss

THE COMIC WORLDS OF

PETER ARNO

WILLIAM STEIG

CHARLES ADDAMS

AND SAUL STEINBERG

The Johns Hopkins University Press

Baltimore and London

© 2005 The Johns Hopkins University Press
All rights reserved. Published 2005
Printed in the United States of America on acid-free paper

Johns Hopkins Paperback edition, 2007

9 8 7 6 5 4 3 2 1

The Johns Hopkins University Press
2715 North Charles Street
Baltimore, Maryland 21218-4363
www.press.jhu.edu

*The Library of Congress has catalogued the hardcover edition
of this book as follows:*
Topliss, Iain, 1944–
The comic worlds of Peter Arno, William Steig, Charles
Addams, and Saul Steinberg / Iain Topliss.
    p.   cm.
Includes bibliographical references and index.
Contents: Peter Arno : the last days of Cabaret—William
Steig : art, armor, and amour—Charles Addams : comic
American Gothic—Saul Steinberg : the lifeline from
A to B—Conclusion : laughing with *The New Yorker.*
ISBN 0-8018-8044-0 (hardcover : alk. paper)
    1. Caricatures and cartoons—United States. 2. American
wit and humor, Pictorial. 3. New Yorker (New York, N.Y. :
1925) I. Title.
NC1428.N47T66   2005
741.5'0973'0904—dc22   2004017270

ISBN 13: 978-0-8018-8753-6
ISBN 10: 0-8018-8753-4

A catalog record for this book is available from the British
Library.

This publication has been supported by La Trobe
University.

To Nadia

More Things to Come

Just think what fun a Ph.D.
Will be to win in future ages,
When knowing facts on you and me
Will bulge the brows of crusty sages;
When tabloid art and headline prose
(Not tribal paintings in a cavern)
Shall rate the student, and Major Bowes*
Dims the bright name of Mermaid Tavern.

Researchers then, between mild benders,
Will ponder what a lifted face meant,
Study inspired streamline fenders
And fossils of the bargain basement;
They'll dig in the Valley of Hollywood Kings
And find what time cannot destroy,
Queens in celluloid, priceless things
Like Donald Duck and Myrna of Loy.

They'll waste their youth in going, coming,
To trace the growth of the paper towel,
Write longer footnotes on neo-plumbing
Than we can write on a Saxon vowel;
Food will get cold and their bosoms swell
Over vacuum cleaners, synthetic fur—
But oh, how I wish I could hear them tell
What a race of supermen we were!
—Hortense Flexner, *The New Yorker*,
October 3, 1936, 38.

*Edward Bowes (1874–1946) was a real estate entrepreneur and popular radio entertainer. He built the Capitol Theatre in New York and was the host of the "Original Amateur Hour," broadcast on NBC in the thirties. The military title derived from a reserve commission given to him as an entertainer during the First World War. Edward Bowes is buried in Sleepy Hollow Cemetery, Tarrytown, New York. For these and further details see the entry by James E. Mooney in Kenneth T. Jackson, ed., *The Encyclopedia of New York City* (New Haven: Yale University Press; New York: New-York Historical Society, 1995), 132.

CONTENTS

ACKNOWLEDGMENTS

Ian Catchlove was the first person to make me appreciate cartoons in *The New Yorker*. His favorite drawing, by Donald Reilly, showed a Renaissance patron confronting an artist who was painting an already elaborate portrait of him: "Give me more angels and make them gladder to see me." (The cartoon appeared in the December 31, 1966, issue.) Ian is the real inspiration for this book, although he would have demurred at any such suggestion. The following people offered invaluable help and information over the years: Delinda S. Buie, the late Israel Chernow and Ruth Chernow, Ron Chernow and Valerie Stern, Jessica Milner Davis, Graeme Duncan, Ken Gelder, the late Brendan Gill, Alec Hyslop, Lizzie Hutton, the late Warwick Hutton, Ed Koren, Harold Love, Patrick McCaughey, Patricia Arno Maxwell, Frank Modell, Peter Otto, the late George Price, Alison Ravenscroft, Marilyn Richmond, Maggie Steig, Jeanne Steig, the late William Steig, the late Saul Steinberg, and Duncan Topliss. I am especially grateful to Denise Bethell for keeping me abreast of the latest developments at *The New Yorker* with a regular stream of newspaper clippings, and for her interest in my work and friendship. To Barbara Nicholls, for many years the assistant to James Geraghty when he was art editor at *The New Yorker,* I owe a debt of gratitude that cannot be repaid. Ms. Nicholls granted me unrestricted access to her library of cartoon art and also to her clipping file on *New Yorker* cartoonists. She put me in touch with helpful sources and went out of her way to offer advice, information, and hospitality. She was the first to make me think this could be a real book. I would have never started it without her encouragement.

For assistance in securing permission to reproduce drawings and cartoons originally published in *The New Yorker* I am grateful to following people: Merrideth Miller (Cartoonbank) Kevin Miserrochi (Tee and Charles Addams Foundation), Sheila Schwartz (The Saul Steinberg Foundation) in conjunction with Sarah Balcomb (ARS) and Anne Plummer (Viscopy), Maggie Steig (estate of William Steig), Adrian Nivola (Chermayeff and Geismar Associates, New York City), Lisa Digernes (Cowan, DeBaets, Abrahams and Sheppard LLP), Leigh Montville (Condé Nast), John Benicewicz (SCALA Art Resource), and Steven Higgins (Museum of Modern Art, New York City).

Preparing a book of this kind is a costly exercise. I acknowledge generous financial support provided by the School of Humanities and Social Sciences at La Trobe University, including two periods of sabbatical leave. In particular, I am grateful for specific grants toward the cost of meeting copyright permission fees from the Publications Committee, the School of Communications, Arts and Critical Enquiry, and the English Program at La Trobe University. I was also the recipient of a generous grant, once again for copyright fees, from the Australian Academy of the Humanities. Without such backing it would have been impossible to publish a book of this kind.

It is a special pleasure to record my good fortune at being a member of the English Program in the School of Communications, Arts and Critical Enquiry at La Trobe University. The collegiality I have enjoyed there is as remarkable as it is precious. Its existence at La Trobe is a tribute to those who have headed the program over the years, especially Lucy Frost, John Barnes, Sue Thomas, and Greg Kratzmann. I have especially benefited from the enthusiasm and example as well as the friendship of Paul Salzman. I am grateful to three of my colleagues in particular. Richard Freadman devoted the greater part of one summer to reading an earlier version of the manuscript. He made painstaking comments on that draft and more than once in subsequent years renewed my faith in the possibilities of this study. John Wiltshire read a later version of the text. An exacting and inspiring critic, he made countless suggestions that I have done my best to adopt. Much of the book was rewritten in the light of his comments. Finally, Christopher Palmer undertook to read the manuscript on very short notice when it was close to completion. I hope I have made good use of his many characteristically penetrating comments.

At the Johns Hopkins University Press I am grateful to Maura Burnett for first seeing that my proposal had possibilities. Melody Herr gave welcome support and advice during initial work on the manuscript, and Amy Zezula expertly guided it through its final stages. I am particularly indebted to Alice Bennett: as copyeditor, Alice improved this book to an extent that only I am in a position to truly appreciate. Any remaining errors are attributable to me alone. Robert Brugger's faith in a manuscript that, considering its subject, arrived on his desk from an unlikely source has been especially important to me, and I am pleased to have the opportunity to thank him properly. He shepherded this book through all its stages with tact, care, and wisdom, steadily turning it into a much better book than it would otherwise have been. From the start I saw my good fortune in having such editors; my consciousness of that good fortune continues to increase.

Finally, I want to thank Richard Johnstone, not just for his many indispensable and instructive telephone calls, but also for his loyalty and friendship. If this book has any merit, he is at least partly responsible. I also hope that my parents, Jake and Elsa Topliss, will find here some compensation for the sacrifices they have made and the opportunities they gave me over the years. Julia Topliss and Maggie Topliss have always encouraged me even when my interests distracted me from paying them the attention they deserved, for which I hope they will forgive me. My greatest debt is to my wife, Nadia, who along with our children, Gemma and Harriet, has sustained me in my work with patience, good humor, and love.

The Comic Worlds of Peter Arno, William Steig, Charles Addams, and Saul Steinberg

INTRODUCTION

The Scope of the Cartoon

Instantly enjoyable and instantly disposable, the single-panel comic cartoon is also instantly forgettable. Frank Modell relates the following party dialogue:

"What do you do?"
"I'm a cartoonist."
"I love cartoons. Where do you publish?"
"*The New Yorker.*"
"I love *The New Yorker.* What's your name?"
"Frank Modell."
"Yes? [Pause.] I've never heard of you."

Despite its obvious importance as a popular form, the art of graphic humor—unlike films, television, or popular music—is only beginning to establish itself as worthy of sustained analysis by anyone interested in popular culture.[1] Cartooning is, as one commentator says, "a noble but limited form, which always seems on the verge of greatness, but which, because of its ephemerality, is finally condemned to the wastepaper basket."[2] These are hard words but, in the main, true. The art of single-panel comic drawings—whatever the fate of a few individual examples (the refrigerator door is usually mentioned at this point)—has never quite emerged as a freestanding, independent genre, just as comic artists have rarely emerged as culture heroes, celebrities, or national treasures.[3] As Modell's anecdote suggests, the cartoonist's invisibility to the popular eye is the norm. But it is an invisibility that arouses curiosity. Why should this be so? One explanation is that people do not usually pause to identify artists whose work they like because they are enjoying them too much. "I explain to people that they are too busy laughing to notice my name," Modell says, not entirely in jest. Laughter cancels thought and substitutes a moment of rapture outside cognition.

The lack of interest among academics charged with getting beyond the way popular culture is taken for granted is another matter. This dearth is partly explained by the institutional history of cultural studies, which generally has interested itself in powerless groups in the dominant culture and explored the way they have dealt with whatever was served up to them.[4] Scholars have less often thought interestingly about the inner history of the dominant class itself, the class that produces whatever it is that everyone else is busy resisting. This indifference to the cultural habits of the middle and upper-middle classes is especially odd given their importance in shaping both the forms of popular culture in modern times and the general character of the age. The lack has not gone unnoticed. When he announced that the story of American culture was largely "the story of the middle class," the pioneering cultural historian Warren Susman added that it was a story more often ignored than attended to.[5] This was back in the seventies, and not a lot has changed. Of course, redressing an imbalance of that magnitude is a large task, and since the obvious place to start would probably not be cartooning at *The New Yorker,* I emphasize that this work is modest in its aims, forming only the smallest part of the larger narrative Susman asked for. Yet *The New Yorker* and its cartoons are certainly a part of that story. This book, then, invites readers to think about the comic worlds of Peter Arno (1904–68), William Steig (1907–2003), Charles Addams (1912–88), and Saul Steinberg (1914–99), four brilliant cartoonists whose careers flourished in *The New Yorker* under the editorship first of Harold Ross (from his founding of the magazine in February 1925 to his death in December 1951), and then William Shawn (from January 1952 to February 1987), four artists who were popular, acclaimed, and critically recognized well beyond the magazine's pages. None of them has yet had anything like the extended attention and assessment he deserves. I take the cartoons and drawings of these artists as forming four distinct oeuvres, which I discuss in detail, aiming to give a clear account of the development of their art and the nature of their achievement. I work into this a sketch of the wider cultural and social situation within which their work appeared and from which it derives some of its meaning. In the conclusion I also offer suggestions about the place of humor in the modern world, especially in relation to the saturation of our media—including *The New Yorker*—by advertising.

As I worked on *The Comic Worlds of Peter Arno, William Steig, Charles Addams, and Saul Steinberg,* a more general argument began to emerge. Nearly all the cartoons of Peter Arno and Charles Addams first appeared in *The New Yorker,* and this is also true of a large part of the work of William Steig and Saul Steinberg. As it happens, it is truer for Steig than for Steinberg; but even Steinberg, in calling *The New Yorker* "my political world," conceded that he had been able to establish a taste for his very unusual art only through the magazine. This was the situation of all these artists—and of every artist who published consistently with *The New Yorker*. Their long-sustained link with the magazine put them in touch, week after week, with a stable, comparatively unified reading public whose goodwill, intelligence, and responsiveness could be relied on. This relationship led me to frame the following proposition: Whatever cultural power or influence *The New Yorker* possesses, in the humorous drawings of Arno, Steig, Addams, and Steinberg an unpredictable, undermining, and countervailing attitude evinces a profound middle-class attachment to humor, irony, and self-criticism, encouraging us to rethink the inner history of the middle class.

In pursuing this idea I nonetheless let those four oeuvres themselves dictate where the discussion would go. A formal feature of humor, Freud once suggested, is condensation—a compressed, disguised, indirect way of representing things. If this is true, it follows that the discussion of humor always has to be grounded in the opposite, the careful laying out in some detail of what the joke itself compacts into a small, dense space. Accordingly, my approach is historical and interpretive. As I hope this book will show, such an approach is especially useful when breaking into a new field. I am not aware of any other book that treats single-panel cartoon art in this way. The nearest is Lee Lorenz's *The Art of "The New Yorker"* (1995). But Lorenz's work is an insider's history of graphic humor at *The New Yorker* and, valuable as it is, offers only the most general of hints about the broader significance of each artist's work, an inevitable consequence of the synoptic view. Other books on *The New Yorker,* such as Thomas Kunkel's *Genius in Disguise: Harold Ross of "The New Yorker"* (1995), Mary Corey's *The World through a Monocle: "The New Yorker" at Midcentury* (1999), and Ben Yagoda's indispensable *About Town: "The New Yorker" and the World It Made* (2000), on occasion discuss the cartoons, sometimes in detail and usually in pertinent ways.[6] What they do not do (not surprisingly, given that their interests do not lie primarily with the cartoons) is develop any systematic understanding of a particular cartoonist's career with attention to the artistic and comic nuances of that particular oeuvre.[7]

In preparing *The Comic Worlds of Peter Arno, William Steig, Charles Addams, and Saul Steinberg* I looked at nearly 69,000 cartoons as they appeared in weekly issues of *The New Yorker* between 1925 and 2004. Of those cartoons, between four and five thousand were drawn by the artists I am interested in. I consider 250 cartoons by those artists in this book and reprint about 50 of the most important. These figures give a good idea of the difficulties involved when the material is so extensive, so rich, and so varied. All the cartoons I discuss that appeared in *The New Yorker* are dated, most for the first time since their original publication in a book of this kind.[8] It is understandable but regrettable that in all collections of these cartoons published in the previous century they are not dated.[9] Nothing has hindered the proper discussion of the *New Yorker* cartoons so much as this habit. Context is forgotten (that a certain Arno cartoon is published in the Valentine's Day issue), as is the larger historical situation (that a certain Addams cartoon appears shortly after an important State of the Union address), and allusions to other cartoons go unnoticed (*The New Yorker* often ran cartoons based on similar situations—people climbing mountains, cartoons about the Horn of Plenty, or erupting volcanoes—expecting at least some readers to respond to one treatment with an earlier one in mind). Not just the pattern of a cartoonist's career but the way an artist's work develops and changes over time, sometimes very slowly, is obscured. One of the many remarkable things about a magazine like *The New Yorker* is that its back issues give a ready-made outline of the careers of all its contributors, and especially of those artists—like Arno, Steig, Addams, and Steinberg—whose careers the magazine sponsored and enabled. The recent publication of *The Complete Cartoons of "The New Yorker"* makes the researcher's task a lot easier. But even that remarkable collection will not relieve the serious student of the genre of the need to look at the cartoons in the actual issue in which they originally appeared.[10]

As a magazine for the middle classes, *The New Yorker* is an almost embarrassingly hegemonic document. It might be described as the house organ of a key fraction of the American middle class. For most of the period covered by this book its readership—whether ideal, implied, or default—was largely thought of by *The New Yorker*'s business and editorial departments as white, Anglo-Saxon or Jewish, affluent professionals or businesspeople with higher education, socially well established, living in one of the great metropolitan centers.[11] From the mid-1960s onward, as the occasional cartoon, article, and advertisement testifies, the readership was tentatively extended to include middle-class blacks and perhaps other minority groups. Whatever its precise composition, the actual readership was derived from a segment of the middle class that had a strong influence over the rest of the middle class in America and hence over middle classes elsewhere in the developed world. This is an elite demographic group for which consumption is lifestyle and lifestyle is self-fashioning. A certain cultural tone of sophistication and exclusiveness is an essential part of the class mystique. In different ways and with different degrees of success, it is this class that has set the tone for sophisticated high living, for self-fulfillment through wealth, and consumption-based identity formation over the past seventy years. It is this more than anything else that has undermined

The Comic Worlds of Arno, Steig, Addams, and Steinberg

the credibility of *The New Yorker*, for all its undoubted success and prestige, for many people, especially on the left. It is this, rather than any specific instance, that Dwight Macdonald had in mind when he spoke many years ago of the magazine's "honeymoon with the oligarchy"—a honeymoon that according to some has never really ended, as we see in complaints voiced in the decades since by (for example) Seymour Krim in the sixties, Josephine Hendin in the eighties, and most recently Mary Corey.[12] *The New Yorker* has always been a prosperous general magazine[13] aimed at subscribers who (in the words of the brochures it distributed to advertisers from the 1930s onward) would be "intelligent and discriminating men and women who appreciate fine things and can afford them."[14] While *The New Yorker* inevitably reflects the interests and epitomizes the cultural style of an ascendant (if latterly assailed) American middle class, particularly a well-to-do East Coast white upper-middle class with strong cultural pretensions, it also reinforces that group's sense of cohesiveness and ratifies its worldview. So where do the cartoons fit into this?

The cartoons are an important but tricky part of *The New Yorker* archive, and a consideration of their nature complicates the notion of the middle-class *New Yorker* reader who is too frequently imagined as existing in a state of hypnotic suggestibility, conformity, and inertia. If it is true that comic incongruity is social contradiction,[15] then the typical cartoon in *The New Yorker* in effect offers a small-scale comic epiphany centering on a revelatory conflict in someone's experience. A cartoon offers a releasing insight into those events, mundane and nonheroic, self-divided and confronting, that punctuate the drama of our daily lives. In the single-panel cartoon the big stories of twentieth-century social history are scaled down to fragmentary, minuscule narratives that are also microconflicts in the fraught biography of the modern subject. Not any or every "modern subject," of course. The subject here is, as we have already noted, typically white, urban, and middle class, and in that class position lies all the interest. *The New Yorker*, as an exemplary American middle-class magazine, offers itself as a site of peculiar richness for an exploration of the contradictory, sometimes rebellious and self-aware inner history of the middle-class subject.

Cartoons have been a defining element in *The New Yorker* since Harold Ross founded it in 1925. Even in the prospectus Ross had expressed the hope that his new magazine would be "distinguished for its illustrations," and the cartoons, more than anything else in the early years of the magazine, set its tone, established its look, and offered anchorage for readers navigating the vast ocean of its text. The magazine's editors understood from the very start how important to its success the cartoons were going to be.[16] The cartoons provide special opportunities to anyone interested in the interpretation of middle-class experience because they do not fit easily into any version of an influential idea in modern cultural theory—the one that hinges on the role of art and image making in the construction of subjectivity.[17] One of the assumptions of this book is that the cartoon—a marginal form never completely under editorial control, waywardly idiosyncratic and involving the release of laughter—is too anarchic to square with theories of docile, obedient formation of self and identity. The cartoon inevitably stands in an unusual relation to the cultural power systems of which a magazine like *The New Yorker* is often thought to be a part.

Cartoons are difficult to discuss because although they "reflect their times" it is not always clear how they do this or even what this phrase really means. Great cartoonists are obviously great image makers, and this is important. Peter Arno's man drowning in the shower (fig. 1.2), Steig's petrified sheeplike underling (fig. 2.11), Addams's diabolical family pouring boiling oil on a group of carol singers (fig. 3.2), and Steinberg's trembling, fluffy rabbit ego peering out nervously through the boiler-plated carapace of the skin (fig. 4.12) are all immediately apprehensible, witty metaphors for one or another predicament of a harassed modern self. Such cartoons are valuable because they create memorable images that speak intimately of how things are for their readers. This much is apparent. But can we go further? It is useful to pause at this point and notice a general characteristic of the cartoons I am interested in.

Cartoons tend to direct our attention to events that, for both the participant and the observer, fall between private experiences that are merely accidental and personal and public experiences in which everyone within a certain group has a share and that therefore possess a commonly recognized and well-understood importance and even "universality." (Not all cartoons, of course, but certainly the cartoon of character and situation that *The New Yorker* made its staple.) We can call these events "midway" experiences. In general terms one could argue that the aesthetic, committed as it is to concrete, individual experience, is the mode of representation in which we try to make sense of just these kinds of experiences. The most important midway experiences are what the British cultural critic Raymond Williams once described as "new social experiences." They are very much of their time. They are registered powerfully and disturbingly within the individual psyche. They are often typical of a particular group, although the group hasn't yet identified or recognized them as group experiences. They lack an accepted vocabulary that would make them generally intelligible.[18] Experiences like these do not easily fit into whatever established interpretive frameworks are around, and even though they hint at an extrapersonal significance, the nature of that significance is often elusive and mysterious. In such experiences the pressure and form of the age is felt

6   The Comic Worlds of Arno, Steig, Addams, and Steinberg

in a personal destiny, and the future is glimpsed in a way that individuals are only just beginning to recognize.[19] One of the things imaginative creation of all kinds does is to name and dramatize just such an emerging and collective sense of how things stand, of understandings not yet fully explicit or formulated, not yet precipitated but awaiting systematic categorization and classification and hence apprehensible only in an intuitive and concrete mode.[20] All this is a matter of something as nebulous as a "feeling" (say) rather than an "issue." Certainly it is not really a matter of "worldview" or "ideology." Such experiences are lived through and felt, not grasped in formal discourse. They are located at the "very edge of semantic availability." [21] And although such experiences may in actuality be widely shared, because they are still at the stage when they are thought to be private, personal, and idiosyncratic they make the people they happen to feel isolated, powerless, and anxious. Among many other things they do, cartoons ask us to pay attention to just these kinds of experiences.

Obviously, not all cartoons fit the schema. But I am suggesting that the cartoon, because of its ephemeral, secretarial, and informal nature, is the form we have devised to make sense of situations that fall into the midway category, experiences at once both meaningful and meaningless, trivial and significant, that leave us feeling isolated, powerless, and anxious. In treating such experiences comically, the cartoon isolates them from the flux of experience. It makes something memorable out of them, enlarges our understanding of them, and, in getting us to laugh at them, frees us a little from their hold over us. Popularity is an inevitable concomitant of a form that shows an interest in midway events.[22] Popularity implies just that broad, communal recognition of the greater than personal nature of midway experiences and alerts us to the existence of the largely intuitive and yet to be articulated understandings and insights within a community to which the cartoon speaks. Every joke calls for a public of its own, Freud observes in one of those suggestive asides that pepper the pages of *Jokes and Their Relation to the Unconscious,* and laughing at the same joke is good evidence of a "wide-reaching psychic conformity." [23] The cartoon resonates within some such network of emerging, half-grasped, unvoiced understandings. Cartoons—like jokes in general—"reflect the age" in this sense: allusive in nature, they depend for their effect on the sense they make within an unacknowledged network of understandings about the common experiences and larger tendencies of an epoch. But in stabilizing such otherwise transient understandings, it is possible to say that jokes help "create the age" as well.

Consider two examples from *The New Yorker* at either end of the 1930s. Helen Hokinson and James Thurber both specialized in cartoons that stage what we might call minute and ephemeral crises of gender identity linked to a loss of social role. (That such a formula immediately seems to claim too much illustrates the difficulty of talking about humor.) They are typically about (Hokinson) comfortably-off, socially useless upper-middle-class matrons and (Thurber) anxious and sexually precarious lower-middle-class men—the problems of the large woman and the little man, to adopt the iconography of each artist. The term "gender identity" had not been coined in the 1930s, of course, and that is in a way my point: the cartoonists got there first.

In Hokinson's cartoon an ample East Coast matron, fanning herself as she sits under an umbrella on a terrace with a view of the ocean between her lolling, bespectacled son and a formally dressed friend, says, "His father wants him to be a lawyer, but I want him to go into a bank. It's always so nice and cool in a bank" (fig. I.1). This is one of those midway experiences described above, even though it is, as it were, witnessed and overheard by us rather than happening to someone who is our surrogate or representative. Both drawing and caption are full of implication, and for all its particularity we would hesitate to describe what is going on here as a merely private drama. The listless pose of the pampered son (looking at his mother rather than at the limitless expanse of the ocean), the complacency and self-indulgence of the adoring mother, the loving foolishness of her remark about her son's future, projecting her present discomfort into the coolness of his imagined workplace, the friend's tense body, suggesting a protest that will never be voiced—these are the elements of the situation. The mother's failure to grasp even the simplest of realities in her comment points up her isolation from the world of work and purposive activity, her innocence of the reality of a country sliding into the Depression, and her infantilism. But it also says something about women of her class and—given that the conversation is about the nerveless scion of the family and his career in 1930—something about the future of that class too.

In Thurber's cartoon a pliant, meek, besuited little man, hat in hand, tells a smartly dressed woman in a hotel lobby, "You wait here and I'll bring the etchings down" (fig. I.2). Here is yet another midway experience, this time from the other side of the gender divide. Once again, despite the extreme unusualness of the situation shown, we would not call this merely a private moment: its very popularity tells us something important about masculinity in the late 1930s. Thurber's style is striking; its amateurishness is very different from Hokinson's professionalism. But Thurber's untrained draftsmanship has great descriptive power, even as it rejects the studied art-school realism of Hokinson, a devotee even in her cartoons of Hambidge's theory of dynamic symmetry (the idea that the composition of a painting could be reduced to a series of converging straight lines). It is in the style that the essential is caught. We notice how summarily the artist handles the extraneous details (the clumsy

The Comic Worlds of Arno, Steig, Addams, and Steinberg

Fig. I.1.
Helen Hokinson.

"His father wants him to be a lawyer, but I want him to go into a bank. It's always so nice and cool in a bank."

Helen Hokinson was one of the most brilliant cartoonists recruited into *The New Yorker* by Harold Ross. Originally the supplier of captionless spot drawings, she later worked mainly in collaboration with James Reid Parker, who thought up most of the ideas and captions. This cartoon shows the high degree of sophistication and subtlety Reid and Hokinson achieved. Seemingly gentle, the cartoon is an example of the cold, anti-sentimental gaze of the typical *New Yorker* joke. The first effect is of the capture of a passing incident so slight as not to register as an incident at all. But as the implications deepen, we realize that it says something essential about women of this class, and indeed about her class itself and its destiny. The drawing is the perfect example of how the cartoon as a form works simultaneously at the level of both microcosm and macrocosm.

treatment of the figures in the elevator, the badly drawn ornamental palm, the simplified background figures). But the hasty way Thurber describes his people is still fresh and remarkable. Careless but immediate, inept yet expressive, the form of pictorial notation catches something nerveless and deenergized in the male figure who is the drawing's subject: style and vision are one. Look at the man's pinched-in waist and tensed pelvic region—his posture in

The Scope of the Cartoon

a sense pictorializes what the caption implies. The caption—turning upside down the seducer's cliché, "Come up and see my etchings!"—has a wonderfully secure hold on matters of seemingly unreachable psychological subtlety. What *is* going on here? Has the seduction technique been badly learned? Inexpertly applied? Stupidly literalized? It is not quite any of these. The man is so determined to show that the etchings have nothing to do with seduction that whatever libidinous drive has propelled him to this point and compelled him to deploy this terrible line has so completely turned back on itself (his pose, again) as to neutralize the original impulse: it now appears only as its meaningless, self-defeating, polite opposite. ("You might think I've asked you to see my etchings so that I can seduce you, but to show you that this is not at all the case—even though I secretly admit it is—I will produce the etchings in a public space in which seduction is quite impossible, such a tamed and civilized creature am I.") Thurber's genius above all is perhaps to have found a way to draw such complicated, concealed, unconscious, self-defeating maneuvers of the overanxious little man, crushed by a cruel superego.

Thurber and Hokinson were very popular cartoonists. That popularity implies more than mere recognition—it is self-identification and even self-understanding. Who, looking at such drawings, can doubt that these cartoons register a profound dissatisfaction with the way things are for a certain class of both men and women? Who can doubt that they promote a kind of laughing, critical self-detachment? Moreover, the stories these cartoons tell are at once individual, contingent, and deeply personal, yet at the same time social and general—symbolically a comment on the fate of a gender, a community, and a class at a particular historical moment. Of course, describing the cartoon as a form in such terms runs a serious risk of overstatement. Crucial to the effectiveness of the cartoon is its very modesty. The principal critic of book illustration in the nineteenth century, John Harvey, writing about the *Punch* cartoonist George du Maurier, rightly points out that "when one is dealing with the small vices that loom large in life, a constant return to the attack within the tight limits of a cartoon may be a better tactic than a sustained prose onslaught." The cartoon gives moments like those caught by Hokinson and Thurber "just the amount of attention they deserve and no more" and strikes "just the right balance of seriousness and satiric amusement."[24]

I am trying here to frame a defense of the cartoon as a form, along with a liberationist account of humor, that will not be too excessive in its claims. I don't want to suggest, for instance, that the kind of humor one finds in *The New Yorker* is "transgressive" or "subversive" or even "carnivalesque." Words like these have been emptied of meaning over recent years, but they always promised far too much to catch what *The New Yorker* characteristically offers,

The Comic Worlds of Arno, Steig, Addams, and Steinberg

"You wait here and I'll bring the etchings down."

James Thurber introduced into The New Yorker an untrained, informal, and abbreviated form of draftsmanship that cleared the way for the tradition of modern cartooning. The distinct comic persona of the artist is strongly discernible in the line itself. In Thurber's case the line—clumsy, tentative, and approximate—is essential to the piquancy of the comic effect. But Thurber also had an unerring feel for the essentials of composition—grouping, posture, gesture. Expression—the line of a mouth, or the slant of an eyebrow—is caught by an unrepeatable accident of line. The drawings were dashed off, so Thurber once wrote, in "approximately thirteen seconds." As a humorist, Thurber was never a realist like Hokinson: his figures were notional and naive, and his ideas and captions reminiscent of the Dada, absurdist tradition in The New Yorker of Joseph Fulling Fishman, Robert Benchley, and S. J. Perelman. And yet, no less than Hokinson's, the cartoon suggests the bigger picture: it speaks volumes about the gender predicament of the little man at the end of the thirties, a man whose libido has driven him to point of seduction, who has mastered the appropriate cliché, but in whom something—ineptitude, cowardice, decency—brings about a self-defeat that is also, in the words of one admirer, a "fragile health." In collections of his work Thurber liked to have initial capitals for each word of the caption, a practice The New Yorker might well have followed as it generalizes the burden of the joke but at the same time gives it a comic overemphasis.

as the Hokinson and Thurber examples show. My point is a more modest and (I hope) subtler one. It is that the mind that detours through the mazes and blind alleys created by the jokework of such drawings, the mind that recognizes some part of its own world in them—for just those fleeting seconds that its attention is caught—is unlikely to end up merely acquiescing and accommodating. In such drawings a gap is opened up between the world and one's consciousness of it, and that gap encourages detachment and disengagement, which in the long run might well modify one's inner sense of the state of the outer world in beneficial ways. Certainly, when the comic habit of mind is adopted, the familiar never looks quite the same.

Much of the humor one finds in *The New Yorker* is what one might call benign. The word is important. Humor, as we know, is not necessarily benign at all and can indeed be used malignantly to define and privilege a group and to attack some denigrated other. But benign laughter is directed back into the group that is the subject of that humor. Humor has, as one theorist has put it, no automatic global politics—whether of liberation or domination, though it can clearly serve both these ends. This may be true, but if so, how do we account for the fact that humor is often experienced as liberating? Although I don't like the neologism, it does make sense here to speak of "humors" rather than "humor"—on the understanding that humor is often associated closely with one social group or another: the middle class, gays, the working class, blacks, the aristocracy, the French, the English, the Poles, and so on. When the humor emerges from one group (often socially dominant) and is directed against another group (often socially inferior or oppressed), talk of "benign" laughter is ridiculous and even offensive—this is indeed humor as social control, as domination.[25] *The New Yorker* is not entirely innocent of this kind of humor, and there is an unmistakable racist character to a few of its cartoons, especially in the first two decades of its existence, such as the pernicious drawing (by Perry Barlow, alas) of a man of Asian appearance talking on a telephone and saying "Listen, Grandma, Helga and I want you to come over for Thanksgiving dinner" (November 19, 1932, 18).[26] But this kind of conscious racism is rare in *The New Yorker*. The humor is predominantly directed back into the social group it emerges from, and it is this—an intraclass form of humor, benign and liberating—that is both interesting and difficult to write about.[27] (Even though it remains true that, as John Updike has pointed out, there is more pervasive and subtle unconscious racism in the erasure of ethnicity in the cartoons and covers in the years between the 1940s and the mid-1980s.)

The laughter that is excited by benign humor implies self-doubt, liberation from habitual modes of thought, a relaxed freeing up of governing attitudes, and a self-distancing stance. Benign laughter of this kind produces a very spe-

The Comic Worlds of Arno, Steig, Addams, and Steinberg

cial, exquisite pleasure. It binds people together in a momentary, powerful, but not necessarily sinister or smug group consciousness, creating a special solidarity born of self-awareness and manageable self-doubt, especially when the humor that provokes it is elusive, sophisticated, skeptical, and intelligent. If laughter implies the presence of unconscious materials, it can in these circumstances also imply insight and understanding. The subversive links it forges compromise the acceptance of what Plato called *doxa*. The word is usually translated as "opinion," but it means something more momentous in our lives than adopting casual attitudes. *Doxa* is that set of commonly agreed-on, socially enforced, group-defining, and to some extent coercive values in terms of which much ordinary life is conducted within a particular social group— both public, sectional, and private. Humor does many things, but one thing it does very well is to combat received and automatic opinion, which it seeks to unsettle or disturb, producing a state of mind that is temporary but intensely vivifying. So Frank Modell liked to quote Charles Addams's definition of a cartoon as "violence done to the cliché."[28] Participating in that struggle is a bracing, liberating, and above all consciousness-enlarging experience, one that I associate in this book with the function of humor in *The New Yorker*. It is, incidentally, a struggle that I hope may be entered into as legitimately through rational reflection as through laughter itself.

Hokinson and Thurber are both considerable humorists, and this brief discussion of their work raises the question of the selectivity I have shown in limiting my discussion to four artists. There are reasons why neither Hokinson nor Thurber appears. Hokinson drew too much and never seemed interested in developing her art. Her work, brilliant at its best, is more than a little repetitive. Moreover, her close collaboration with James Reid Parker is so crucial to her success that her drawings cannot be considered apart from his captions, requiring discussion of Parker's own extensive contributions to *The New Yorker*.[29] Thurber's career as a cartoonist was comparatively short, and his art cannot be adequately discussed without bringing in his journalism, his humorous pieces, and his more ambitious literary works. Even so, Hokinson and Thurber, along with many other cartoonists who published in *The New Yorker,* would repay sustained attention, and I regret having to ignore them.[30] Among many examples I could mention, Perry Barlow seems to me a completely underrated cartoonist whose work would repay careful study; Charles Saxon was an unrivaled recorder of the manners, mores, and look of his age; and James Stevenson was one of the most inventive, funny, and imaginative of all modern American humorists. Looking beyond my period a little, Roz Chast is a true comic genius whose large and complicated oeuvre offers a perfect opportunity to investigate the madness of late twentieth-century life. But if we are to grasp what *The New Yorker* characteristically offers its readers in its comic art, attention to a few individual careers is unavoidable. To take a parallel example, a critic can easily suggest succinctly the qualities of Joseph Mitchell's journalism. But to truly show how Mitchell expands and enlarges readers' sense of what the city is like—the richness of its social history, the density of its experiential texture, its incalculable, unpredictable, teeming variety as displayed in a remarkable piece like "The Bottom of the Harbor" (January 6, 1951, 36–52)— is going to require more than a few pages. The same is true of the magazine's cartoonists. My aim is to make a particular cartoonist's comic world available for discussion and appreciation in depth, and depth of analysis is incompatible with breadth of scope, not to mention a manageable number of pages.

The artists I have chosen to concentrate on are highly original practitioners who would merit an extended place in any discussion of graphic humor at *The New Yorker*. Their work stands out in the pages of the magazine, and each one adds something original and surprising to its stock of humorous drawings. Their work is distinctive, diverse, and substantial, expressing an assertively personal vision of life.[31] They are funny, inventive, witty, and inspired, and each shows an energetic comic curiosity about the world. The way they draw is completely individual and marked by an urge to extend the comic mode and by stylistic experimentation. (Stylistic experimentation is of the highest importance because style and form, the principal bearers of meaning in any art form, go to the heart of the cartoonist's achievement.) In each case what strikes us is the freshness and immediacy of the drawing itself, qualities that made their work irresistible to their original readers and, I suspect, to anyone who encounters it for the first time today. Arno, Steig, Addams, and Steinberg are cartoonists whose work stimulates the laughter and humorous appreciation that sustains a sense of the complexity of things, as opposed to humor that flattens out complexity. Furthermore, for reasons I have already given, I wanted to look at artists who were popular beyond the pages of *The New Yorker* itself, who struck some kind of general public nerve. Unlike many other cartoonists who published at *The New Yorker*, the artists I have chosen to concentrate on produced work that resonated with a larger public. The kind of popularity— even celebrity—they enjoyed makes their work doubly interesting.

The cartoons of Arno, Steig, Addams, and Steinberg disclose their importance when they are linked, as I link them in the chapters that follow, to a particular passage of time—the ethos of a decade or two, the mood of a particular generation. The cartoons of my chosen artists tap into various emergent and anxiety-provoking situations prevalent between 1925 and 1975, and they offer insights into the unconscious and unacknowledged drama of middle-class consciousness in this period. Peter Arno, a significant popular figure in his day, gives us a comic account of the rejection of puritanism and pursuit of hedonism in the twenties and thirties—and of the subsequent emergence of a mood of rueful discontent with modern life. William Steig, whose cartoons early attracted the attention of serious cultural commentators like Diana Trilling, tells the story of the transformation of lower-middle-class identity in the thirties and forties and the struggle of a blue-collar/lower-middle-class psyche to remain integrated under the intense pressures of modern living. Charles Addams, whose cult status continues to grow, invents a comic solution to the projective, gothic drama of paranoia and suspicion of the forties and fifties. Saul Steinberg, profiled in *Life* as an artist whose unique visual commentary on America was especially timely, investigates the strange, conformist, and yet exuberantly individualistic "new" America of the late fifties through the early seventies as experienced by an immigrant consciousness. The popularity of these four artists suggests that in their work a personal paradigm may indeed be interpreted as being culturally paradigmatic.[32]

That a study of cartooning in a citadel of American middle-class culture like *The New Yorker* should be taken up by someone living half a world away requires a brief word of explanation if not justification. My interest in *The New Yorker* is no doubt a trickle-down effect of the worldwide saturation with American culture that began with the rise of film and popular music in the early part of the previous century and has continued unabated ever since. As I was growing up in Australia in the fifties, American popular culture meant to me just that: film and popular music with the addition of television (which began in Australia in 1956, in time for the Melbourne Olympic Games). I usually inspected these for evidence of the material superiority of American culture—something inseparable from its mystique—as much as for their actual content. I was mesmerized by the lavish domestic interiors (white telephones on very long cords with soft ringing tones), alien teenage social habits (friendship rings and junior proms), and big bouncy American cars with low-geared steering (which teenagers only a few years older than me appeared not only to drive but sometimes to own). The story of American postwar cultural hegemony of which my personal experience is a tiny but not unrepresentative chapter is often presented negatively as the homogenizing process of a postwar and imperial Pax Americana. In such accounts the very thing that excited people and drew them to American culture in the first place—its mythic but immediate contact with the experience of modern living—gets left out, leaving in place of the excitement a malevolent cultural brainwashing (to use a term suggestive of the period). As the child of British migrants, I was drawn to the alternative that American popular culture offered and to its freshness, vigor, and originality. It was magical, enchanting, and enriching, and I cannot imagine how life in innocent, staid, boring Melbourne in the late fifties could have been endured without it. Living in a society that seemed a raw, distant backwater neglected by history and doomed to remain so because of the distances involved, to me American popular culture seemed anything but standardizing.[33]

In fact, Melbourne wasn't a stagnant backwater. The forces of change, the beginnings of a globalized, multicultural world, were already at work—in the world, within Australia, and even in my own city. At age thirteen I could see none of this but—as I discovered while writing this book—to an outsider, with a broad experience of Australia and the world beyond, it was all very obvious. John Lardner, in Australia for the Olympic Games at the end of 1956, reported back to *The New Yorker* describing a Melbourne very different from the one I thought I was living in.[34] He was enthusiastic about my city and thought that Australia was then "enjoying almost a world monopoly of peace, harmony, civility, understanding and other such symptoms of civilization and good breeding, while Europe is behaving like someone you would think twice about before introducing to your sister." With considerable prescience, Lardner went on to draw attention to the decline of Australia's traditional xenophobia, mentioning especially "the Australian public's enthusiasm for the [Olympic] village and its exotic contents," an enthusiasm that, twenty tears later, would bear fruit in a highly successful form of social multiculturalism.[35]

By the end of the fifties I was an avid reader of American magazines— mainly *National Geographic* and *Scientific American*. I had also persuaded my parents to subscribe to *Life* and *Look*. I was well aware of how good these publications were: not just the articles or the photographs, but the design, the quality of reproduction, and even the luxurious paper—glossy yet soft, soft yet durable, durable yet refined. They had no Australian equivalent, and I had to acknowledge their superiority over local productions. I was also an admirer of Charles Addams, and a taste for his cartoons was an in-group marker in my circle. His humor, saturnine and macabre, was just what you needed to complicate and combat the blandness of the suburban world that seemed likely to be our fate.[36] At the university I encountered Saul Steinberg's *The New World*. The effect of this book was very powerful—a genuine epiphany—and I can still remember the dank room in a student house where I first handled it. I wondered at the jacket for a long time, unable to place it in any idea I had of the development of modern art. Its marbled decorative ground (which you might expect to find as the endpapers of a musty nineteenth-century edition of Tennyson), the way the author and title were confined to what looked like

The Comic Worlds of Arno, Steig, Addams, and Steinberg

a stick-on office label, the red panel along the spine, and the blue triangular corners all produced discordant effects of antiquity and modernity. Once I'd gotten past the cover I was reduced to speechless admiration by the book's contents—such eloquent, puzzling, uncategorizable things they seemed: drawings that were so full of meaning and yet so opaque; drawings that fitted in with nothing I knew about cartooning, illustration, or modern art. They were so *American* and yet at the same time so impossible to place. They demanded to be imitated yet were clearly inimitable. (This I soon found out when I tried to learn from them—I had pretensions toward cartooning myself.) In my enthusiasm, basic questions went unasked. Where had drawings like Addams's and Steinberg's first appeared? Had the artists always drawn like this? What sort of artistic culture had supported them? Who had paid them for drawing? I would have laughed in disbelief if anybody had told me they had both originally been published in the same magazine.

I was to be enlightened on some of these matters in due course. A friend who read *The New Yorker* thought I ought to look at it because it was so very, very good: literary, cultural, and humorous, worldly and sophisticated, full of droll cartoons I would surely like, about priapic captains of industry, dyspeptic stockbrokers, and harassed clerks—Peter Arno's cartoon world, in fact. That was a road not taken until many years later, by which stage I had come across William Steig, but as an author and illustrator of children's books, not as a cartoonist. I also had a brief experience of New York itself. One cold morning in February 1986 I stood at the corner of Fulton Street and Broadway. It was my first week in this baffling, exhilarating, and overstimulating city, a city that, rather like the cover of Steinberg's *New World*, was puzzling because of its antiquity as much as for its modernity. Acres upon acres of brownstones, buildings made out of cast iron, still intact, the noisy street life of Chinatown, and a few miles away, extraordinary architecture like Philip Johnson's AT&T Tower, the irresistible vulgarity of Trump Tower, the Gothic-modern detailing and breathtaking simplicity of the World Trade Center. I had heard Jonathan Miller describe New York as a nineteenth-century version of what a twentieth-century city should be, and I saw what he meant on my first day there: it was all straight lines and steam and iron feverishly striving into futurity, old and new at the same time. In this mood I saw with disbelief—because of the cover—the anniversary issue of *The New Yorker* on a newsstand. There it was again, antiquity and modernity all over again, a Regency dandy on the cover of a magazine published at the height of greedy 1980s America. I bought it and instantly felt I was a New Yorker myself, not just a visitor.

I still have the copy I bought that day, with cartoons by Addams and Steig, among other artists that I knew of, like Charles Saxon, Bud Handelsman, and

Frank Modell, as well as cartoons by unfamiliar artists whose brilliance struck me instantly—wonderful creations by Jack Ziegler, James Stevenson, Arnie Levin, and Roz Chast. There were articles and reviews and stories by other familiar writers such as Raymond Carver, Peter De Vries, Pauline Kael, and John Updike—as well as unlikely pieces by writers of whom I am ashamed to say I knew nothing. "Annals of a Former World (Geology—Part I)" by John McPhee sticks in my mind. One Sunday I sat down and read McPhee's piece. It must have been 25,000 words long. I had never in my life read a magazine article that was as demanding, as literary, as informative, as compelling. When I finished it I stood up and looked out my window, reeling not from the perspective before me, astonishing as it was—dusk, flurries of snow, a vista running from Brooklyn Bridge with the lights coming on to the southern tip of Brooklyn Heights, a tugboat navigating through the ice floes on the East River—but from the dizzying vista now opened up to me, the continent's geological past brought into contact with the tragic struggles of the pioneer families of the Midwest. It is hard to sum up how crucial buying that copy of *The New Yorker* was to my experience of New York, how much more rewarding than (say) buying a copy of a magazine like *New York* that would have done the job just as well from a utilitarian perspective. When I returned to Melbourne I subscribed to *The New Yorker* and started to read everything I could find about it. A New World, indeed.

Unlike many Americans I met, for whom *The New Yorker* was a fixture of their parents' lives and the symbol of a cultural ethos they believed they had to overcome and sometimes repudiate, *The New Yorker* in the last year of William Shawn's editorship was for me the entrance to a realm at once richer, more various, more unexpected, and more rewarding than anything comparable I had encountered or imagined. It was adult, intelligent, imaginative, informative, respectful, critical, humorous, and entertaining all at the same time. It was full of surprises, open to the extraordinary richness of the world beyond the ego. Once introduced, I felt I could never do without its companionship. To write adequately about what *The New Yorker* represented, as a fragment of a uniquely American achievement (that kind of high-popular culture typical of New York, of which the Broadway musical would be another example), was clearly a noble if (given my background) difficult ambition. But every viewpoint has its possibilities as well as its limitations, and perhaps along with certain disadvantages my outsider's status accords me at least one advantage— that of a clarified enthusiasm for a subject with no personal history to dull its effect. My "discovery" of comic art at *The New Yorker* introduced me to one of the great achievements of popular culture in twentieth-century America. It is undervalued within the society that produced it, and perhaps it is the lack of

The Comic Worlds of Arno, Steig, Addams, and Steinberg

a similarly various tradition in Australia that has encouraged my investigation into the work of four of its chief practitioners. John Lardner, an outsider, had written illuminatingly about a place that I, an insider, thought I knew well. As he belatedly showed me, Melbourne's very familiarity had blinded me to what it was and to the ways it was changing. I hope that just as I find Lardner a valuable commentator on my own city's history, readers of this book will find me a helpful commentator on the tradition of cartooning at *The New Yorker*.

I · PETER ARNO

The Last Days of Cabaret

"The balloting is all over with at Princeton and the results are public. The favorite beverage of the senior class is whiskey. The favorite actress is Lynn Fontanne. The favorite artist is Arno, with Titian second and Leonardo third. The favorite poem is 'If.' The greatest benefit derived from college is 'contacts.'" So reported E. B. White, with due sarcasm, in "The Talk of the Town" for May 31, 1930.[1] By that date Peter Arno (1904–68) was the most celebrated and influential cartoonist working at *The New Yorker*—and perhaps in America—a position he consolidated over the next twenty years.[2] His drawings of clubmen and chorines, dowagers and doormen, lushes and lechers,[3] comically compromised in the cabaret world of hotel lobbies, gentlemen's clubs, theaters and speakeasies of a New York City that was the very capital of capitalism, had made him the most famous cartoonist of his day. The first collection of his drawings, *Peter Arno's Parade,* with an enthusiastic introduction by William Bolitho, was issued in 1929 by the libertarian publisher Horace Liveright (of Boni and Liveright fame) and was so successful it was reprinted twice within a month of its appearance.[4] Arno was the cartoonist as dandy, a New World Honoré Daumier, Constantin Guys, and (for good measure) Georg Grosz all rolled into one, with the addition of something they lacked—a piquant sense of humor that was sharp and knowing but also genial and sometimes warmly sympathetic.[5] Both as an artist and as a man-about-town, Arno lived at the very center of the Jazz Age and its untidy aftermath. His career amply demonstrates why it was he, of all artists, who set the tone for a new kind of magazine that was sophisticated, adult, and antisentimental: *The New Yorker.*

An early cartoon epitomizes his achievement. It shows a fancy-dress party in full swing in the background and, in the foreground an irate middle-aged stockbrokerish guest dressed in a rabbit suit expostulating to his host and some puzzled guests, "This has gone a bit too far, Remson! Someone purloined my Burberry!" (fig. 1.1). The drawing is notable for evoking character and place in a few effortless, scrolling brushstrokes (Arno knew exactly how such people dressed, posed, and relaxed, but he also knew how to draw them without being too literal). It is notable, too, for the artist's appreciation of the comic drama of public self-exposure. And yet in the revelation of the fluffy rabbit inside (or around) the angry man there is a quality not reducible to either satire or wit, something—perhaps affectionate and certainly sympathetic—that responds to the unprotected unselfconsciousness of the man and his not contemptible quest for pleasure. It is wry as well as cutting.

An East Coast aristocrat by birth,[6] the scion of an established New York family whose father was a New York State Supreme Court justice, Arno was educated at Hotchkiss and Yale, showing the path he was supposed to take: a safe, predictable journey ending in the law or Wall Street. But the twenties was not a decade when much could be taken for granted, and there was too much on offer for someone like Arno. No sooner had he entered Yale in the autumn of 1922 than he began to stray. He gave up his studies. He caroused. He painted (the Bulldog Grille in New Haven was for a long time decorated with murals by the young Arno). And he played jazz. It was as a musician that he left Yale in 1924 without a degree, heading back to New York to make a living in the cabarets, jazz clubs, and speakeasies. Renting rooms in a Greenwich Village that contained, according to *The New Yorker* for April 17, 1926, "about everything but artists," Arno sponged off his mother, who was by now divorced from his father, and eventually found a job playing piano with Rudy Vallee's band. But he also began sending out drawings to the humorous weeklies of the day—*Judge* and the pre-Luce *Life*. Eventually, and unexpectedly, *The New Yorker*—itself only a few months old—took a small drawing, and with that chance acceptance Arno's life was set on course.

Arno's aristocratic pedigree was important to Harold Ross, who had hired Ralph McAllister Ingersoll on the spot, partly on the grounds of a tenuous link to the Ward McAllister of the Social Register, but also because of a more realistic sense of Ingersoll's familiarity with the upper reaches of New York society.[7] The elite viewpoint that came naturally to someone of Arno's background was as essential to his art as it was to the ethos of the magazine whose tone he helped create. Like *The New Yorker* itself, Arno grew to be so familiar with Manhattan high life that the knowingness of the participant was rapidly transmuted into the detachment of the observer. Arno plunged so deeply, and so cleanly, into the river of New York high life that he surfaced on the far side. Disengaged intimacy, the hallmark of his humor, was the basis of *The New Yorker*'s famous sophistication.

The Comic Worlds of Arno, Steig, Addams, and Steinberg

"This has gone a bit too far, Remson! Someone purloined my Burberry!"

The end of the decade of decadence brings with it the collapse of the authority of the older generation and the puzzled
indifference of the younger. Arno shows a connoisseur's relish
for the older man's unawareness of his lack of dignity, but the
cartoon is not entirely pitiless: for a start, the rabbit is lovable,
even cute, and the drawing maintains a wry sympathy with the
man's loss of an expensive raincoat, a loss so momentous that
it drives out any sense of how absurd he is. There is fellowship
here as well as satire. Noticeable is Arno's impeccable sense
of how to pose and group his figures for maximum dramatic
effect. It is daring to show the principal actor with his back to
us, so that everything has to depend on his crouching, minatory posture, the angrily gesturing arm, and the erect rabbit
ears. The harsh lighting from a single source that picks out the
action is also important, with the people looking startled, as if
caught in a society photographer's flashlight, as Arno once put
it. Admirable, too, is the evocation of setting as seen in the
economical depiction of the party in the background and the
suggestion of the chandelier and the pattern on the drapes in
a few eloquent scrolling lines.

Personally, Arno was egotistical, avaricious, and abrasive, a man-about-town with a luxurious Park Avenue apartment, vague plans for shows on Broadway, and a completely impractical automobile expensively built to his own design. He embodied everything New York could offer the successful young man in the twenties and thirties. Inevitably there was another side to this picture. Nagging inner doubts about the value of his gift troubled him throughout his life. He was plagued by unresolved feelings toward a father who had never acknowledged his achievements. And he lived an emotionally chaotic, debt-ridden personal life tinged with a tendency to violence. He knew the discontents of Manhattan high life as well as its pleasures. Triumphantly hedonistic as it often is (celebrating the freedoms of privilege, booze, and sex), Arno's humor becomes deeply anxious and pessimistic, a chronicle of the many ways the quest for indulgence can fail, misfire, or disappoint.

Although at first glance Arno's early work has a celebratory cast, on closer inspection the satiric underlining becomes obvious. His enthusiasm for the social revolt of the young in the late twenties implies a dislike of the reign of the elders of his own class. Powerful men of his father's generation long remained a favorite target. But the immense popularity he gained as his career developed from the mid-1930s onward is due to the appreciative, genial, and rueful cynicism that modifies his sense of humor, a cynicism he shows toward any situation in which actuality can subvert even the most modest of personal goals. This is the burden of "Man in the Shower" (fig. 1.2), which discovers a catastrophe in one of the most banal moments of everyday life. In his best later work Arno creates an alarmingly capacious comic world of disillusionment, failed purposes, and actuality's falling short of expectation. Importantly, for this is one function of the true humorist, he teaches us to savor and appreciate such a world rather than to protest against it. All this pinpoints an important shift in American middle-class character and values. On one level, Arno's drawings reflect a move away from a dour, inner-directed, hypocritical puritanism toward a frenetic, other-directed, open hedonism characteristic not just of the twenties but of the modern consumerist world in general. At a deeper level, Arno is the great comic chronicler of the emerging discontents of industrial, urban civilization.

Peter Arno first walked into the office of Harold Ross shortly after *The New Yorker* initially appeared in February 1925. Ever the one to dress to type, he was wearing "paint-smeared canvas pants, a turtleneck sweater, and ragged sneakers."[8] He left a folder of drawings with Philip Wylie, the prototype of the magazine's "Jesuses" and at that time third man in the weekly art meetings with Ross and Rea Irvin, and returned to the nightclub on West Fifty-seventh Street where he was playing the piano for shimmy girl Gilda Gray. Gilda Gray

The predicament of the male at the beginning of the forties? But it is debatable how far we should see the joke as gendered, since the drawing is really an image of Arno's feeling for the universal imminence of disaster: how it can, and inevitably will, strike anyone, anywhere, even in the most ordinary and everyday circumstances. Even so, and for all his interest in men as powerful figures, Arno was drawn to situations that showed them as defenseless and disaster prone. He liked to undermine their competence, social position, or dignity. This drawing, which supplied the title of one of his most successful collections, spoke to a whole generation of bemused males. The banality of the setting, replacing the exotic cabarets, speakeasies, and society balls that he drew a decade earlier, shows Arno adjusting to wartime social realities. The style has changed, too: his line is tighter, more abbreviated, and a good deal less decorative, corresponding to the diminished note of celebration in his later drawings—although he can't help eroticizing the wife just a little. Harold Ross was reportedly worried about the plausibility of anyone's being trapped in a shower like this.

was a free-spirited, uninhibited bohemian, the popularizer of a highly suggestive dance whose performances were routinely raided by the police. It was Gray who had carried a statue of Bacchus into Rector's nightclub on the evening of January 15, 1920, the last night for thirteen years when alcoholic drinks could be legally bought in America: at the end of the evening the five hundred guests tore the god apart and placed him in a coffin thoughtfully provided by the management.[9] For Ross, Arno's association with Gray must have completed a perfect résumé. He accepted Arno's work and mailed him a check. His first drawing—a small atmospheric, effortlessly drawn letter-box format spot showing a night scene in which a sinister pair of low-lifes, one of them black, watch a topped-hatted and mink-coated couple strut across the street to a speakeasy—appeared in the eighteenth issue of *The New Yorker,* June 20, 1925, on page 6 under an article by Owen P. White called "Better Banditry."[10]

From then on Arno's contributions and destiny became inseparably linked with the new magazine. His work immediately began to appear every week: mainly small spot drawings, vignettes of Manhattan high life, decorating suitably appropriate pieces, but also the occasional caricature like the one in the June 18, 1927, issue of Dr. Harry Emerson Fosdick, the progressive Baptist and pastor of the still unfinished Riverside Church in Morningside. His first "idea" drawing appeared on September 5, 1925, a quarter-pager showing a top-hatted upper-class drunk being helped past a black cat by a shady friend who is saying, "'s All Right, Bill Has a White Ear." (It was printed on page 2: thenceforth Arno never relinquished his place at the front of the magazine.) These early contributions were done either in ink or in charcoal with some shading. His first ink-and-wash drawing, showing the stylistic path forward, appeared in the January 23, 1926, issue (page 11), again a quarter-pager. His first full-page idea drawing came on July 3, 1926 (page 12), titled "The Ruined Weekend." (A disgruntled guest complains to his host, "What! No archery butts?")

There is something tentative and exploratory about these early pieces, but by the following year, 1927, Arno hit his stride. Along with countless smaller pieces, he had twenty-nine major cartoons published that year, many of them outstanding. Although there were already some brilliant artists working for *The New Yorker* to whom Ross accorded the privilege of a full page—Helen Hokinson, Rea Irvin, Ralph Barton, and later Al Frueh—Arno is the standout figure, and the vitality of his work makes 1927 a remarkable year in the history of comic art. It is given to few artists to leave their stamp on a new magazine in quite this way, to make their tone and character its tone and character. Arno's bold, brilliantly lit full-page tableaux with their sharp, knowing, contemporary captions show how confidently he seized his opportunity. To complete a hugely successful year, he married Lois Long, who as "Lipstick" and the author

The Comic Worlds of Arno, Steig, Addams, and Steinberg

of the "On and Off the Avenue" department was one of *The New Yorker*'s most important staff contributors. Arno and Long's tempestuous and nondomestic marriage sums up the age's rejection of conventional norms and sealed the image of Arno as the playboy of the Manhattan demimonde. One small recorded incident encapsulates their relationship: Arno first learned that his wife was pregnant through Walter Winchell's gossip column, "On Broadway," in the *Daily Mirror*. The couple divorced in 1931 after only four years of marriage.

Born in 1904, Arno was sixteen when Prohibition began, twenty-one when *The New Yorker* was founded, and twenty-five in the year of the Great Crash. The dates are telling. What makes a person someone of his or her time is usually the seven-year passage between ages eighteen and twenty-five. This is when one disengages from the family and encounters life as an independent and unprotected individual. It is now that the psyche takes into itself the conditions of its social milieu and historical moment. Arno belonged completely to the postwar twenties generation that embraced a bohemian, libertine way of life and revolted against its parents' puritanism and hypocrisy. The era may have passed, and sometimes Arno's humor is dated, but with most of his early cartoons we are confronted by an art that vividly conjures up a vanished epoch. In drawing after drawing the Jazz Age comes to life, and we feel ourselves at the turbulent center of the powerful forces—monetary, social, and sexual—that surged through the New York of the period.

The character of the social revolt of the twenties that Arno was a part of can be approached through Ellin Mackay's "Why We Go to Cabarets: A Postdebutante Explains," published in *The New Yorker* for November 14, 1925.[11] Mackay holds up the cabaret as a new social space typical of the era, where the obligations of society are replaced by individual freedoms—dancing with everyone on the stag line replaced by the liberty to chose one's own companions, for example. Not that Mackay is a rebel. Going to the cabaret does not entail completely abandoning old social principles, nor is it an anarchic form of social intercourse.[12] The repeated and betraying word in her article is "fastidious." "We go to cabarets because of the very fastidiousness that Our Elders find so admirable a quality. We have privacy in a cabaret. . . . we go with people we find attractive. . . . we go, because like our Elders, we are fastidious. . . . we go because we prefer rubbing elbows in a cabaret to dancing at an exclusive party with all sorts and kinds of people."[13] Far from abandoning the code of the older generation, Mackay maintains that her generation's ability to discriminate is so nice that the social rituals of established society have themselves come to seem crude. And so she turns the charge back on her parents' generation. The fastidiousness of the elders is hollow. The social rituals they cling to fail to perform the very function they are supposed to have. The stag line, a petrified survival of the prewar world, is wrong because it makes the group defenseless against outsiders. Far from abandoning the fastidiousness of their parents, the new generation's fastidiousness is so acute that its members see through all established forms, understand how they fail, and find in their new freedoms a better way to preserve an exclusivity they continue to value. The key value of the group is thus preserved, even though the enveloping social ritual is drastically modified in character.

In retrospect, Mackay's arguments cannot be accepted without qualification. The special pleading from the twenty-three-year-old daughter of a Catholic tycoon (her father owned the Postal Telegraph and Cable Company), shortly to elope with the widowed Irving Berlin, fourteen years her senior and Jewish to boot, is understandable.[14] But she is on to something. If the new customs signal a break with the past, they also restate old values in a form better adjusted to new social realities; these customs are more flexible and in the end more truly chic. Her article is a good pointer to Arno's own rebellion, which involves a much franker recasting of "aristocratic" social practice in a bohemian mold. A crucial element in all forms of cool and chic is to free up existing social customs in the direction of greater personal expressiveness but at the same time to install new rules recognized only by insiders. Arno's humor in the late twenties depended on precisely these kinds of new social niceties, and it functioned as an "understanding test" that separated an in-group from an out-group.[15] A core value—the need to exclude people—remained. Indeed, Arno's own work—louche, suggestive, but never crude—was part of the test. If you got Arno, you got everything. If you got Arno, you belonged. A taste for Arno signaled your membership in a new imaginary community created by the magazine, a virtual community founded on the mere fact of common readership by chic insiders.

Arno's humor of the first decade is socially liberationist in a manner that has clear links to Mackay. Generally, he endorses the new social and sexual freedoms of the young. The tone is one of a comic-romantic celebration of their world, if not outright idealization. In an exemplary cartoon like the one captioned, "You do give such perfect parties, Alice. Is there anyone here you'd like to meet?" (January 12, 1929, 12), the drawing savors the serpentine, glossily clad bodies of both the man and the woman. It also delights in the sumptuousness of the setting: those rich floral drapes that Arno was able to suggest with the barest touch of wash and scrolled line, the luxuriant fern, the Empire settee, and the atmosphere of a privileged, vivacious, buzzing social scene in the chandelier-lit room beyond. The caption embraces informality and antistructure. But the joke's relation to Mackay's inverse snobbism is complicated. What the man says is partly a self-betraying line, of course, and to that extent we might read it as satire. But it is also a boast, a celebration of the collapse of social form, a snub aimed at the social niceties of an older generation, a welcoming of the new. It chimes in with Mackay's case only to the extent that it illustrates her point that the old customs are ineffective as social filters. But Arno, unlike Mackay, relishes this kind of social anarchy—a party at which the most interesting guests are the gate-crashers. There is a similar cheerfulness about collapsing social forms in many other drawings of the period. "Charmed" (March 9, 1929, 13) shows an actor being presented to a society matron in his dressing room with his trousers around his ankles. In an untitled drawing used as the cover for *The New Yorker* of April 11, 1931, an effete young man in running shorts and spikes unconcernedly forces his way through a group of formally dressed elders strolling along Fifth Avenue (they are offended as much by the obscurity of the insult as by anything else). In a sketch captioned, "Oh Lord, there they are now! You entertain them while I get dressed!" (from *Peter Arno's Circus,* his second collection, published in 1931), a half-naked wife issues the command to a husband emerging from the shower with only a towel around his waist. In all these drawings Arno sides with the young and the new, and the joke is at base a declaration of loyalty to his generation.

Arno's cabaret world is decadent, faster than Mackay's; his insight into its excesses is savage. Abandoning her attempt at justification, he simply enjoys the destructured, irresponsible world of the nightclub, the speakeasy, and society dances, all of which have become infected by the new freedoms. Arno's eye is usually caught by some minute betrayal of social embarrassment or gaffe: the all but undetectable guilt of the couples hunched over their drinks in a speakeasy (*Peter Arno's Parade,* 1929); the bluffing overconfidence of a man trying to talk his party's way into a club where he is not known (January 21, 1928, 11); the troublesome enthusiasm of the businessman, new to New York and hooch alike, who joins in a chorus line (November 14, 1931, 16–17).

Inevitably, the focus is on matters sexual. One thing you needed to get Arno was a hold on the new knowingness about sex that by the end of the twenties had completely replaced received sentimental notions of romantic love in the common consciousness of the sophisticated. Many of Arno's early cartoons presuppose readers' understanding of just how things really are between men and women. The paramountcy of the sexual drive is frankly admitted. Declarations of romantic love are presented as no more than idealization, euphemism, or pretext (all those drawings in which seedy-looking men haul gorgeous young women before dubious "marriage" celebrants). The couple in "You're like a lovely flower tonight, darling—everyone's looking at you" (fig. 1.3), the first really striking Arno cartoon to be published in *The New Yorker,* and the one that initiates his annus mirabilis of 1927, are still caught up in the old dream world of romance. The man particularly (his head is the work of a major caricaturist), with his talk of the woman's looking "like a lovely flower," but the swan-necked woman too, are both lost in a romantic swoon. A residual sympathy surrounds this fact, but while it is important to recognize this, it is hardly the point of the drawing, which is that the man's hand has accidentally caught the woman's loose-fitting gown and lifted it to reveal her underwear. The underwear is the real flower, just as its exposure is the real event for everyone else in the ballroom. The expressions in the eyes of the onlookers, both male and female—leering, lustful, triumphant—contrast with the look in the eyes of the lovers. Both the men and the women openly share curiosity and excitement. The joke is not particularly about the couple's embarrassment or shame. It is about the unreality of their sentimental and romantic attitudes (an unreality that Arno doesn't completely scorn). Those attitudes once shaped the mold in which male-female relationships were cast, but no longer: hence the collision between the remnants of that unreal vocabulary and the unembarrassed, voyeuristic behavior of everyone else in the room. The observers share an openly acknowledged interest in exposure. How well the new Freudianism, translated into English in the decades before, accounts for what is going on in this cartoon. The hand lifting the dress is a perfect example of the Freudian symptomatic action—the "accident" that shows what the man really wants to do behind the screen of his flowery talk. And the word "flower" is clearly an example of the condensation and displacement of meaning that Freud thought essential to a joke—an "empty" metaphor suddenly "filled" with literal content, since the woman's underwear does indeed look like a flower.

The cartoon implies that women not only have caught up with male frankness about sex but have surpassed it. This was an additional truth Arno's readers needed to understand. Of the thirty or so cartoons about sex in his first collection, *Peter Arno's Parade* (1929), more than half show sexually knowing women in a situation involving sexually innocent men. Hortense (the name is itself a joke, used often by Arno in his cartoons of the twenties, inappropriately suggestive of the proprieties of an earlier epoch) in the cartoon captioned, "Oh, Hortense! Do you think you could ever learn to love me?" (November 12, 1927, 21), clearly has nothing to learn about anything. Hortense is a lithe young woman in a gossamer-thin flapper dress, flinging her arms around a reluctant male and pulling him down onto a sofa. It is the man who is trying to contain the outbreak of passion within the clichés and sentimentalities of romantic love. Arno's Hortense is a minor triumph of draftsmanship and a pointer to what lay ahead for him. He conveys both the androgyny of the flapper's dress and the sensuousness of the body beneath it. We see the emergence here of what is Arno's most obvious contribution to cartoon art, a stylized eroticizing of the female body that has immense implications for both mainstream and subculture publications. Out of his example grew not just the cartooning

Fig. 1.3.
Peter Arno.

The New Yorker,
February 19, 1927, 29.
© *The New Yorker* Col-
lection 1927 Peter Arno
from cartoonbank.com.

"You're like a lovely flower tonight, darling—everyone's looking at you."

The nightclub, a sexual joke and (for the Valentine's Day issue of *The New Yorker*) a sentimental occasion ready for demolition. Arno could not ask for anything more. He was the first cartoonist to draw women as both comic and erotic—really comic and really erotic. Even Arno's flappers, while being true to type (flat-chested, willowy, androgynous), are sexy. This joke responds well to a Freudian treatment, and not just because it is a sexual joke. The "lovely flower" is one of Freud's crossover points in a joking utterance, a set of ambiguous words through which run colliding and opposing meanings: here the romantic idealization of the lover (she is like a lovely flower) and the voyeurism of the onlookers (the flower is her panties). And the young man's hand, rucking up the woman's dress to expose her underwear, is unconsciously perform- ing one of Freud's symptomatic actions. But the drawing is complicated. The looks in the eyes of the dancing couples may be leering and pitiless, but what about the lovers? They are extraordinary creations: the masklike, swooning face of the young man, the woman's distorted, elongated, Alice in Wonderland neck, give them an otherworldly quality. They are truly lost in a romantic dream, as the drawing acknowledges and values.

style we associate with a wide range of popular strip and single-panel cartoons from *Playboy* and *Esquire* (and thence other more openly pornographic magazines) but the long line of semieroticized children's characters from the *Archie* comics to Lara Croft. More generally, what is apparent from a comparison between Arno's women in the period 1925 to 1930 and women in advertisements and fashion photographs of the same period is that his comic drawings eroticize the female body far more vividly than contemporary photographs (see, among countless examples, the self-consciously erotic but also tastefully "artistic" photographic advertisements for underwear by B. Altman and Company, *The New Yorker,* July 31, 1926, 1, and Van Raalte Company, *The New Yorker,* May 12, 1928, 64).

In the same vein as the "Hortense" couple, but in a marvelous drawing fraught with significance, are the two figures in "Good God, woman! Think of the social structure!" (fig. 1.4). Here, at a Christmas ball, is the definitive confrontation between the New Woman and the old order. The woman, lithe and sensuous, her diaphanous dress so flimsy that she appears to be wearing nothing at all, presses her body up against the older man: she melts into him. The man struggles to disengage himself from her embrace, speaking the words of the caption. We feel the pressure of the resisting hand on her encircling arm, and there is outrage and alarm on his face and in his awkward posture. The setting evokes both a milieu and the forces undermining it. This is a society dance in one of the great Manhattan ballrooms. There is a huge chandelier and tall swaths of drapes, but the music is by a jazz band, and the saxophonist is casually playing while sitting down. Also important is the double meaning of the caption. This was a cartoon that, according to Thurber, Ross was reluctant to publish, on the grounds that "social structure" might imply "social [i.e., sexually transmitted] disease" and therefore, possibly, "erection."[16] Thurber thinks that Ross is too suspicious here, but he is spot-on, as ever: "social structure" is one of those ambiguous phrasal conduits in a joke through which several meanings can simultaneously flow, one of which here must certainly be "erection." If there was a problem for Ross, it must lie in the drawing, not the caption. The line work on the material of the trousers around the man's crotch sketchily describes the erect penis, and the way he has retracted his pelvis is exactly the posture of a man trying to hide an erection.[17] What the woman asserts with her body the man rejects with his—to little avail. The man's protest sums up the great battle of the Jazz Age. The behavior of the new generation is sweeping away the social structure of the prewar world.

Janet Flanner once noted that "something visibly and communicatively new" was taking place in Manhattan in the years after the First World War. As we see from these cartoons, Arno was the visual historian of that newness, of chaotic postwar modernity.[18] He gave it form, visibility, and memorableness.

Fig. 1.4. Peter Arno.

"Good God, woman! Think of the social structure!"

The New Yorker, December 17, 1927, 22.

One of Arno's eroticized flappers, whose body, barely covered by her diaphanous dress, melts alarmingly into that of the indignant and resisting older male. The indulgent, moneyed, upper-class setting is beautifully suggested: the deep shadows of the sumptuous drapes, a few scrolled lines to suggest the chandelier, the bright light flooding in from the dance floor. Amid this there is one little sign of rebellious informality, a straw in the wind that is blowing away the old ways—the sitting saxophonist. But there is a big sign of change as well. The joke is a socially disruptive one: the man pulls back his pelvis to disguise his erection, the phrase "social structure" may well have the sinister implications Harold Ross thought it had, and the man's general anxiety is well founded. Society was indeed receiving seismic shocks from the hedonism of the young, and things would never be the same again. As in many of the cartoons of the twenties, Arno draws as a propagandist for the new, against the stuffiness and hypocrisy of the old. This positive inflection in his cartoons would not survive the Depression.

One of Arno's earliest and most perceptive critics, William Bolitho, understood that Arno's willowy flappers and elegant, sinuous men expressed not just the body image of the age but its very ethos: "some composite of expressions, poises, walks, smiles, sittings" that added up to "the very plasticity of our flesh."[19] Without the descriptive power of Arno's draftsmanship, which enabled him to place on the page week after week an authentic image of the object of attack and exposure, his satire would mean nothing. What underwrote the satire was the immediate recognition the drawings prompted.

How important style was to his success is apparent from comparable work by other artists of the same period, for example from *Life* (fig. 1.5).[20] In this drawing ("The Bedtime Story. 'I am somewhat reminded of the two Irishmen, Pat and Mike, who—'") the artist is drawing the same milieu as Arno and is a not unaccomplished draftsman. But the style derives from a tired nineteenth-century school of caricature, owing much to the example of Charles Dana Gibson, and the drawing lacks immediate contact with contemporary reality. A comparison with figure 1.3 ("You're like a lovely flower tonight, darling—everyone's looking at you") shows what Arno brought to similar subjects—a racy, vibrant, and stylish line that conveys an inwardness of understanding, an intensity of sexual consciousness, a heightened awareness of the demonic element in people, and a feel for the essential energy of the period.

Arno's drawings create their meaning first stylistically, in the way they are drawn, and only secondarily in their paraphrasable content (whether of drawing or caption). Arno's trademark thick, black line and those dramatic effects in which the figures are picked out by an intense light flooding in from a single source, producing stark highlights and deep shadows, are both essential to his success.

In the 1920s the line is made in charcoal (probably a Woolf pencil) and has just a little of Daumier's uncommitted, exploratory quality. From the mid-1930s Arno works in ink, painting with a thick brush over a pencil underdrawing, but the effect is the same. The line is always bold, confident, elegant, and stylish. It has weight and presence and yet—when Arno is at his best—is never mechanical or dead. Arno wrote feelingly about this process, the central moment of an Arno composition, his stylistic signature:

> It's a long tough grind, with endless penciling, erasing, rectifying, to recapture the effect and mood produced in the original rough. This penciling is the invisible framework that's later erased so the viewer will never suspect it was there—the labor and sweat which enable it to look as if no labor or sweat had been spent on it. . . . Sometimes this pencil layout won't come right, no matter how I wrestle with it. It lacks the life and movement it should have. When this

The Comic Worlds of Arno, Steig, Addams, and Steinberg

Fig. 1.5. [Artist's name undecipherable.]

Life, January 31, 1924.

"The Bedtime Story. 'I am somewhat reminded of the two Irishmen, Pat and Mike, who—.'"

Arno's milieu, as seen by a nearly contemporary artist whose pictorial language derives from *Punch* in the nineteenth century. The insertion of a title sends too obvious a signal to the reader and damages any effect the caption might have. The figures seem separate, not part of a group; hence the group is dramatically inert. They seem English rather than American. The women have little sexual presence. There is also a suggestion of snobbishness in the joke, as if the artist has no time at all for the embarrassed young man. Arno is much more sympathetic to his wimps and nerds. But what really makes it feel old-fashioned, and distant from the world it is satirizing, is the way it is drawn, the hint of art-school training, the wooden poses, the too finicky cross-hatching. Compared with this, the superiority of Arno's technique for anatomizing a similar world—his bold, suggestive lines, his dramatic use of chiaroscuro, and his powerful groupings of characters—is obvious.

happens I start all over again on a new piece of gleaming white board. Sometimes I make five and six beginnings, reworking faces and postures, striving for the exact comic quality the idea calls for. . . . But finally I think I've hit it, and am ready to continue. . . . Now you—let's suppose, here, that you're the artist—you dip a fine pointed sable brush into India ink and start laying in the heavy black strokes that will be the skeleton of your drawing. You keep the line rough, jagged, spontaneous-looking. That's your god (or mine): spontaneity. You move fast, with immense nervous tension, encouraging the accidentals that will add flavor to the finished drawing. . . . When the ink is dry, if it still looks right to you, you start that awfullest of chores, the erasing of the maze of penciling that lies beneath the ink, till nothing is left on the board but crisp, clean black-and-white.[21]

It is a dramatic account, taking us inside the very act of drawing. Arno's words have the ring of authenticity and hint at the essential integrity of his work as cartoonist, his daily wrestling with the uncompromising demands of the line itself.[22]

For his characteristic lighting effects Arno, a dedicated amateur photographer, imitated the flashlight snap as taken by the society gossip photographer. "I like the people in my drawings to have the startled looks on their faces you sometimes see in the flashlight photo," he said—hence the look of surprise in his cartoons as people are caught unprepared and off balance.[23] The laying-in of the washes required to produce this effect was the part of the drawing he liked most.

> The drudgery is over, the framework is up. You pick up a fat red-sable brush, the kind that used to cost six dollars and today costs seventy-five, and dip it into one of the washes you've mixed. All you have to do now is swim luxuriously in rich grays, startling blacks, and brilliant whites, while you build up lighting effects that will make your characters stand out like actors on a stage— or so you hope. (To tell the truth, before I reach this stage I seldom have more than a general idea of what these lighting effects are going to be. Sometimes, in the middle of things, I find I've unconsciously switched the imaginary light source from the left side to the right, or from behind the characters to in front of them, seeking, without thinking, for a better effect.)

The stark chiaroscuro thus created separates the comic moment of unmasking from the routine moment of ordinary living and signals the scene's importance as an epiphany. Arno transferred this lighting effect from the cabaret to the daylit world: nearly all his cartoons are heightened, brilliantly lit tableaux in this vein.

Pictorial technique is important in an assessment of Arno's work, then, and its relation to his success is clear and unambiguous. But this consideration of technique leads to the more vexed issue of the collaborative nature of Arno's ideas and captions. In common with many artists who published cartoons in the early *New Yorker*, Arno rarely supplied his own ideas or captions once he became an established artist.[24] The situation was a complicated one and varied from artist to artist. Helen Hokinson relied so much on ideas brought to her by James Reid Parker that the two must be considered collaborators.[25] E. B. White is generally thought to have had a key behind-the-scenes role in pol-

The Comic Worlds of Arno, Steig, Addams, and Steinberg

ishing many captions even where he did not devise them. The comic novelist Peter De Vries also had a spell as caption editor and inventor. Moreover, the job of gag writer was often a route into cartooning proper. This was the case with Frank Modell, who began supplying ideas in 1941 (particularly for Whitney Darrow Jr.), then worked for some years as an editorial assistant to the *New Yorker*'s art editor, James Geraghty. Ross liked Modell's ideas from the start but felt that his style had to develop.[26] Consequently Modell published his first cartoon only in 1946. The practice of gag writing was well established, with special fees paid to writers who supplied usable ideas. Richard McCallister is reputed to have contributed over four thousand "ideas"—five thousand in some accounts—and made a handsome living from it. Arno first relied on suggestions generated by Philip Wylie and later by McCallister, who supplied the famous line for Arno's drawing of a group of elderly Manhattan patricians saying to a group of friends, "Come along. We're going to the Trans-Lux to hiss Roosevelt" (September 19, 1936, 16). By the late thirties many of Arno's ideas were thought up by Geraghty himself, who was paid $50 for each published cartoon.[27]

The practice has not gone unnoticed, but its workings have not always been properly understood, and it is easy to draw the wrong inference—that the artist is somehow not the true "author" of the joke and that the drawing "merely" illustrates a joke that has already been created. In fact, the system was administered with a care typical of *The New Yorker*. A close editorial liaison between artist and writer, which included matching a particular cartoonist to a particular writer, and a careful editing of the cartoon from preliminary sketch to accepted drawing, including polishing the caption itself,[28] ensured that raw ideas received the best possible pictorial realization. It also made sure that imaginative priority lay with the artist, not the ideas man. A fascinating undated letter written by Harold Ross to the cartoonist Alice Harvey, unearthed by Ben Yagoda and quoted at length in his *About Town: "The New Yorker" and the World It Made*, shows how complicated the situation was. Harvey had written to Ross asking if she could "illustrate" some jokes. The word angered Ross:

> For years and years before the *New Yorker* came into existence, the humorous magazines of this country weren't very funny, or meritorious in any way. The reason was this: the editors bought jokes, or gags, or whatever you want to call them, for five dollars or ten dollars, mailed these out to artists, the artists drew them up, mailed them back and were paid. The result was completely wooden art. . . . Now this practice led to all humorous drawings being "illustrations." It also resulted in their being wooden, run of the mill products. The artists never thought for themselves and never learned to think. They weren't humorous

artists; they were dull witted illustrators. A humorous artist is a creative person, an illustrator isn't. At least they're not creative as far as the idea is concerned. . . .

And now you speak of "illustrating" jokes! The very words in your letter to me. I always see red when an artist talks of "illustrating" a joke because I know that such a practice means the end of the *New Yorker,* the new school of humor, and all. Unless an artist takes ahold of an idea and does more than "illustrate" it he's (she's) not going to make a humorous drawing.[29]

The letter illustrates Ross's mastery of detail, a mastery carried to such a pitch that it deserves Thomas Kunkel's word "genius." Ross had a sure grasp, comparatively rare in editors, of the precedence of visual realization over abstract conception in a cartoon.[30] The joke lies in what the drawing shows, in the realization of the conception, not in the idea or in what the caption says.[31] The difference between what Geraghty was paid for an Arno idea in the late thirties ($50) and what Arno was paid to draw it (at least $500 at that time) tells its own story.

One way of testing the truth of this is to read a few captions and ideas without the drawings and then compare them with the drawings: "Gad, it's good to be alive!" (February 2, 1929, 21), or "How am I—amusing?" (December 8, 1928, 30), or "I was discussing the Mexican situation with Bottomly today. It seems fraught with interest" (September 15, 1928, 26). None of these is especially promising even if we add in the idea: a thin man stretches in the morning; a weedy fellow in fancy dress addresses an elegant woman; the same man is in bed with a voluptuous and bored wife. But Arno makes something piquant, distinctive, and funny out of all of them. (Compare the third example with the finished cartoon, fig. 1.8 below.)

Even more helpful is a comparison of two versions of the same idea by artists as unlike each other as possible, Arno and George Price.[32] It's a comparison that isn't entirely to Arno's advantage, but it clearly shows how an "idea" is funny or not depending entirely on the realization of the drawing. The joke works around the idea of a hospital visitor in bed with the patient and the caption "Visiting hours are over, Mr. (or Mrs.) X." Arno does one of his "boss and secretary" drawings, in which the male visitor is middle-aged and unprepossessing, the woman patient is young, voluptuous, and empty-headed, and the nurse (who speaks the words of the caption, "Visiting hours are over, Mr. Kugelman") shows a degree of prurient complicity with the situation (*Peter Arno's Man in the Shower,* 1944). The cartoon is not funny, is in bad taste (the man's hands are beneath the blankets), and discloses Arno's sexist streak at its worst. Twenty years or so later, George Price is given the same idea ("*The New Yorker" Album of Drawings, 1925–1975,* 1975). Price draws one of his grotesque but completely sympathetic old couples, making the woman the visitor (she hasn't removed her hat, Price's equivalent of Arno's fully dressed man) and the man the patient. Man and wife sit bolt upright in the hospital bed (itself carefully observed and beautifully drawn, in the best Price manner) with knobby hands folded on the crisp sheets in front of them, toothless mouths clamped shut, staring at the nurse with eyes that are at once piercing, resentful, defiant, and bewildered. (Once again the nurse, but now a completely neutral figure is saying the words of the caption: "Visiting hours are over, Mrs. Glenhorn.") The drawing is a funny, moving tribute to the survival of a companionable marriage. Price gets something fresh out of the idea: for Arno it simply stirs a tired, stock response. After looking at these two drawings we see for ourselves what Ross had always understood—the primacy of the presentation of the joke in pictorial terms—and why Ross worked so exasperatingly hard at getting drawings right in those weekly art meetings.

Every cartoonist answers to some general category: William Steig, as we shall see, is the comic diagnostician of modern ills, Charles Addams the diabolical jokester, and Steinberg the investigative pedagogue. Arno is the dandy. It is not just that his willowy, elegantly dressed men are often shown in top hats and tails, wearing cravats or high collars and bow ties, boutonnieres, waistcoats, and cummerbunds. Nor is it that his drawings of the contemporary city are interspersed with period studies like "The Parade" that depict an indefinite nineteenth-century Manhattan—anything from the 1820s to the 1870s. (In an untitled drawing of a couple in *Peter Arno's Circus* the woman might well be a 1920s bride, but the man looks more like a contemporary of Beau Brummell.) Arno's dandyism is a matter of style and approach rather than subject matter. In drawing after drawing in the first six or seven years of his career, Arno's drawings have both a distinct Regency feel and the dandy's viewpoint of disdainful, knowing superiority. This kind of sensibility mirrors a superficial fascination in twenties Manhattan with the Regency period (which owed some of its currency to the revival of dandyism in the 1880s by the London *Vanity Fair,* replicated in Frank Crowninshield's New York magazine of the same name, founded in 1913). But it also reflects a much deeper contemporary interest in the dandy as a special kind of artist figure, uniquely positioned to grasp the complexities of life in a modern city. The idea of the dandy underpins both Arno's work and the ethos of the early *New Yorker.*

New Yorkers were attracted to the dandy, and to his close relatives the *flâneur* and the loiterer, because they felt, following hints dropped by Charles Baudelaire and picked up by Walt Whitman, that the complicated and puzzling life of the modern city, indeed of "modernity" itself, could be truly grasped only by a disengaged, promiscuous, peripatetic consciousness. For Baudelaire, the *flâneur* is the "passionate spectator" who, disdaining bourgeois domesticity, sets up house "in the heart of the multitude, amid the ebb and flow of movement, in the midst of the fugitive and the infinite": the "lover of life," says Baudelaire, "makes the whole world his home." In merging with the crowd he becomes "a kaleidoscope gifted with consciousness," responding to each one of the crowd's movements and reproducing both "the multiplicity of all life and the flickering grace of all the elements of life." He is "an 'I' with an insatiable appetite for the 'not-I,'" rendering the passing events of the city "in pictures more living than life itself." [33]

How much of *The New Yorker*'s program is anticipated here is evident when we recall the example of E. B. White. White, who gave *The New Yorker* its heart and soul and was the model countless contributors drew on, specialized in the early years of the magazine in informal, reflective vignettes of city life, like "Defense of the Bronx River" (May 9, 1925, 14); the anecdote about snow in the city that opens "The Talk of the Town" for February 4, 1928, 9; or "Dance Halls at Midday," a paragraph in "The Talk of the Town," February 11, 1928, 9–10, (as retitled for White's 1934 collection *Every Day Is Saturday*). In "Dance Halls at Midday" White imagines not the nightlife of the city in daytime but the "heavy day silences" of its night places: "a hundred theatre auditoriums, empty and hushed; beer places east of Third Avenue, breathing heavily; dance floors, darkly dreaming by the side of still drums" (10). It is a remarkable piece, a genuine prose poem, and a meditative exploration of the more concrete observations of Baudelaire's disengaged but passionate spectator. White was aware of what he was doing. Looking back in the 1940s on his achievements, he drew a comparison between the open mind of the loiterer in the city and the focused mind of the office worker. The office worker "is desk-bound." Unlike the *flâneur*, "he has never, idly roaming . . . stumbled suddenly on the Belvedere Tower in the Park, seen . . . boys along the shore fishing . . . girls stretched negligently on the shelves of the rocks; he has never come suddenly on anything in New York as a loiterer because he has no time between trains." [34] Without adopting the pose of the disengaged consciousness one could never, according to White, come to terms with a city that is "like poetry"—a place that "compresses all life . . . into a small island and adds music and the accompaniment of internal engines . . . the greatest human concentrate on earth, the poem whose magic is comprehensible to millions . . . but whose meaning will always be elusive." White's register is hardly Baudelaire's, or even Arno's for that matter, but the connections are clear.

Baudelaire's hero had been the artist Constantin Guys, whose life, Baudelaire thought, might appear one of "absolute idleness" but who made idleness artistically serviceable: "He is the stroller and onlooker, the dandy as passionate observer and perfect *flâneur*. His place is not in the studio but out on the boulevards, among the crowds of the modern city."[35] Arno, who had experienced Paris, deeply admired Guys. And it was to Guys that his contemporaries sometimes compared him.[36] Arno transfers the dandy's loitering observations from the street to the cabaret, the society party, or the bedroom, but the justification remains the same. It is only in casual, normally unregarded moments, registered by the disengaged but passionate spectator, that the life of the great city can be caught. Implicit in this was the idea that the city was so infinitely varied that it could never be summed up. All one could hope for was a wandering consciousness sampling fragments of experience that would gesture toward the unimaginable totality. To which Arno added a rider: it is particularly in moments of comic catastrophe that such a possibility is opened up. The tessellated work of a cartoonist could therefore legitimately suggest, if not actually embrace, a whole way of life. Arno was adept at making a passing moment imply the complete dissolution of the old ways, as in the drawing in which a bellhop is shown leaving a hotel room and saying to the naked young woman he has left in bed, "By golly, Miss Eppis, I forgot to give you the telegram!" (*Peter Arno's Circus*, 1931). What is held out as important is not the mere fact of casual sex involving a well-to-do hotel guest and a lowly employee but something that a more outraged and moralized consciousness might miss: the reversion to type, social function, and proper form now completely empty ("Miss Eppis") that follows the seduction. This is the new, piquant, sophisticated, and suggestive comedy of the dandy.

Whether in England, France, or the United States, the dandy is a simulated aristocratic figure who exists in an ambivalent, but symbiotic, relation to middle-class life. As a kind of recognized fool, the dandy rejects just those forms of seriousness that people in the years leading up to the First World War could not think of unless dignified by capital letters—Work, Character, Self-Denial, and Thrift: the values of the titanic accumulators of money in post–Gilded Age, progressive, and industrial America. The dandy embraces play, pleasure, and consumption. Nonetheless, his audience is typically a middle-class one, just the sort of people who are supposed to take work, character, self-denial, and thrift seriously—readers of the early *New Yorker*, for instance. If members of the middle class are fascinated by the dandy, it is because they see him as that part of themselves they are cruelly called upon to deny. The dandy embraces just those material and hedonistic pursuits that are the reward for middle-class abstinence. In his over-the-top fascination with clothes and material possessions, in his life of idleness and pleasure, in his care for the empty rituals of good form, the dandy is what the responsible citizen can only dream of being. The dandy speaks to middle-class desire and discontent, saying that there is so much more than work, self-discipline, deferral of gratification, character, and family. There is excitement, pleasure, and living for the moment. Excitement, pleasure, and living for the moment underpin the dandy's aesthetic pose, his wit, and his fondness for display. ("What brings you up to town?" asks Oscar Wilde's Algernon. "Oh, pleasure, pleasure! What else should bring one anywhere?" replies Jack.) If the dandy makes any criticism of middle-class life, it is necessarily an indirect criticism, of a sort that rarely alienates. For this reason the dandy is suspect for the left intelligentsia. The parasitic relationship of the dandy with middle-class life, the easy habit of going with the flow, the outright refusal of direct critique are thought to imply collaboration and compromise—charges often laid at Arno's door. But the dandy has a purpose that, in the last instance, involves anything but complicity. His aloofness and disdain amount to a studied disregard of the key ideals of the host culture and a refusal to take seriously its foundational values. And this, especially as it wells up within the dominant culture, is a profoundly undermining impulse.

In the humor of Oscar Wilde, the most famous dandy of them all and the person who brought dandyism to the pitch of perfection, all received ideas are turned inside out to reveal a lining of antithetical truthfulness. Triviality is more useful than earnestness, style more important than substance, nonsense more valuable than reason. In the humor of Peter Arno, which works at a lower level of intensity, we find a similar transvaluation of values: in his cartoon world idleness, play, and dissipation replace work, self-discipline, and moral rectitude as the focus of living. Arno's dandylike fascination with the flux of daily life makes him the witness of just those moments in middle-class life, off-guard and seemingly trivial, when a whole way of life betrays itself. The tone is one of a bemused, nonserious, sardonic enjoyment at the way nothing ever falls rightly into place. The technique is to undercut whatever a society takes seriously by hingeing the joke on some detail that betrays the underlying quest for pleasure, as in the drawing showing two stockbrokers, one predictably saying to other, "Well, I cleaned up a lot o' jack on Radio Electric common today" (February 18, 1928, 14): less predictably, these two beefy men are cross-dressers at a fancy-dress ball. The dandy's comic tactics have been well described as the opposite of the strategy of countercultural revolt. He opposes nothing but seriousness, accepts everything that produces pleasure. In going deeper into the reigning culture, as Arno does here, and in taking notice of something that would ordinarily be dismissed as too trivial to be noticed, the dandy arrives at a point where a society's working values contradict themselves, collapse under their own weight, or reveal themselves as empty forms that no one can take seriously. This is how "unsettling a social order from within" happens.[37] If this is virtually a description of the method of Peter Arno's art, it is also a description of the method of Ross's *The New Yorker*. It is hardly an accident that, as Eustace Tilley, the dandy was the icon of *The New Yorker* itself.[38]

The dandy's prime virtue is sophistication. And as Janet Flanner noticed, Arno was *The New Yorker*'s "first success in sophistication." "Sophistication" was a word *The New Yorker* had annexed to itself in an early advertisement, saying with sophisticated understatement that it implied "a reasonable degree of intelligence or enlightenment on the part of its readers." Flanner meant sophistication in matters of sex, although this was only part of a larger shift in comic feeling that Arno's drawings exemplify. Sophistication is the signature not only of Arno but of all the magazine's important artists and writers, defining *The New Yorker* itself. Already implied in Arno's man-about-town role, sophistication for *The New Yorker* meant taking as understood the social and cultural world of Manhattan in all its intricacy and judging exactly how far your readers or viewers would also take all this as understood. Many of Arno's best cartoons are extremely subtle and carry their freight of meaning almost entirely through the most understated of visual clues. For instance, the meaning of the drawing of a bejeweled, mink-swathed woman tearing her hair out as she screams at her dull-looking, paunchy, and unmoved companion, "You're so kind to me, and I'm so tired of it all" (September 29, 1928, 20) is completed only when we take into account the elegant, sexually charged figure of the chauffeur—the third point of a potential sexual triangle, whom Arno leaves almost out of the frame.

For Arno the opportunities for sophisticated humor arose most often in the speakeasy (until Prohibition ended, *The New Yorker* regularly ran pieces on speakeasies such as the one by Niven Busch Jr. called "Speakeasy Nights," in the issue for October 6, 1928, 66–67),[39] the nightclub, the restaurant, and the bar—public places of pleasure, much frequented by the dandy, that can be gathered together under the general heading of "cabaret."[40] In cabaret the disciplined endeavor needed to accumulate wealth receives the payoff of intoxicated pleasure. The lives of the fashionable, the wealthy, the criminal, and the bohemian intersect; alcohol (Prohibition alcohol) lowers inhibitions; and people's underlying drives—lust, competitiveness, aggression, ambition—are on display, as are the inevitable moments of disappointment. Cabaret, in various manifestations typical of New York in the years between 1890 and the mid-1930s, is the symbolic center of Arno's comic universe.

Why should this be so? What the inhabitants of modern industrial societies demand for their recreation is what the historian of Manhattan cabaret, Lewis A. Erenberg, calls an "action environment."[41] An action environment is a place where a populace dulled by the routine demands of work, in a period of increasing social and corporate order, can find amusement, excitement, and hedged personal risk.[42] Urban populations have a great need for action in this sense, action that the happenstance of everyday life rarely provides. Early in the twentieth century, a new phenomenon emerges to cater to it—"commercialized action." Cabaret is a commercialized action environment: a destructured leisure space set apart from the main business of life where excitement and stimulation can be purchased, a place where men and women meet as equals, with no boundaries between performers and spectators (everyone eats, drinks, dances, performs in the same arena), where the respectable bourgeois can mingle with louche bohemians (dancers, gangsters, prostitutes, singers, gamblers, artistes, con men, drunks, actors), where exciting, dangerous (but not too dangerous) action can be expected. The dandy and the cabaret go well together: as a humorist, Arno contributes an appreciation of what inevitably goes wrong in such situations.

In his drawings of the twenties Arno returned again and again to the cabaret and similar places—bars, speakeasies, dance floors, restaurants. In one cartoon, set in a society dance and drawn from the low vantage point Arno liked, two men wistfully survey a woman dancing seductively with a third man. One says to the other, "She was wearing that dress the night we got engaged" (fig. 1.6). There is so much to take in: the self-satisfaction of the man dancing with the woman (winning is everything), the overacting of the woman as she plays enraptured seductress, the envy on the face of the onlooker as he leans forward to catch his companion's sotto voce confidence. The subtlest touch of all is that we are shown nothing of the speaker except the back of his head. His anguish is conveyed simply by the way he tries to set his body square to the table while his head swivels around, tilted at a pathetic angle, drawn to the sight of his humiliation. The woman's dress, onto which all the churning emotions of the speaker have been displaced, is a marvel—the hem is attached to a ribbon looped around her arm so that it reveals her leg and garter. The caption works because Arno could draw that dress so well. The whole history of a quartet of destinies, marked by yearning, exploitation, betrayal, triumph, and defeat, is effortlessly evoked. The joke exemplifies something typically Arno: a fleeting moment is fished out of the time stream, a tableau in which a pose, a grouping, and a throwaway line that implies a before or after action spotlight a complex imbroglio and a tangle of intentions, motives, and sentiments that are at base sexual. But finally, the "suffering" itself makes the speaker feel alive. Where else could all this be caught except in the cabaret world?

On either side of the public space of the cabaret are two favorite Arno locations—the bedroom and the automobile, important for his dramas of seduction, infidelity, and betrayal, action environments in their own right. Bedroom scenes—there were many of them—now seem an obvious choice for humor,

The Comic Worlds of Arno, Steig, Addams, and Steinberg

Fig. 1.6. Peter Arno.

Peter Arno's Circus (New
York: Liveright, 1931).
© 1931 Peter Arno.
Illustration reprinted by
permission of the Estate
of Peter Arno.

"She was wearing that dress the night we got engaged."

The painful comedy of the cabaret in one of Arno's best cartoons from the late twenties. The drawing conveys so much:
the self-satisfaction of the man dancing with the woman; her
falsity as she overacts the part of enraptured lover; the envy
on the onlooker's face as he leans ever so slightly forward to
capture his companion's sotto voce confidence. The subtlest
touch of all is that we see nothing of the central character,
the jilted lover, except his back. We don't need to: everything
is conveyed by his awkward, tense pose as he sets his body
square to the table to suggest indifference but swivels around
nonetheless, drawn to the sight of his humiliation. "That
dress" is one of Arno's marvels: the caption, comically neutral if considered apart from the image, would be meaningless
unless Arno could show that the dress was, indeed, a very
special piece of equipment in the woman's *batterie de séduc-
tion*. That is exactly what the drawing does show. As a result,
a chapter in the history of a quartet of destinies, crisscrossed
by yearning, exploitation, betrayal, defeat, and triumph, is
effortlessly evoked.

but only because Arno made them so. In directing the comic gaze at places and activities (especially those before, after, and in place of sex) that cartoonists had never previously been bold enough to entertain, Arno is something of a pathfinder. *Peter Arno's Circus* opens with one such cartoon—two pairs of legs at the foot of a bed, the crescent moon showing though the window, and the routinely anti-Semitic caption, "Haf you had any previous experience in pictures?"[43] (Arno was quick to make jokes about a burgeoning motion picture industry.) In such cartoons Arno is particularly aware of moments of sexual disaster, often involving the Remson figure (though he appears to have no fixed name).[44] In the little drama captioned, "See, darling, I told you we couldn't have a Platonic friendship" (*Peter Arno,* 1979) the man, rolling on his socks as the woman, unseen, dresses behind a screen, is rendered as a blank, passionless face and a loose collection of scrawny arms and legs, which makes it impossible not to conclude that despite the bravado nothing much has happened. Indeed, a particular theme running through a lot of Arno's bedroom cartoons is the idea that despite the sexual revolution of the Jazz Age, women are unlikely to get much in the way of sexual satisfaction.

The automobile was probably a less obvious setting for humor (though F. Scott Fitzgerald had made it the centerpiece of Gatsby's tragedy in 1925), but once again Arno was quick to see the possibilities. It offers new opportunities both for sexual liaison (for example, "I adore driving at night. Once I caught my foot in a bear trap, though," where the words are spoken by a young woman to a pleased-looking man who is driving her down a moonlit country road [September 15, 1934, 33])[45] and for sexual betrayal ("Er—is that you, Gwendolyn? I believe this is our dance, Gwendolyn," spoken by Arno's weedy Remson character to some legs and arms wrapped around a male body in a parked car [June 14, 1930, 14]). If Ross felt some qualms—even puzzlement, if you believe Thurber—about the cartoon that showed a man and a woman outside a lonely country gas station late at night, the man holding the backseat of an automobile and saying to policeman, "We want to report a stolen car" (December 7, 1929, 31), he had enough sense of its timeliness and sophistication to see that it had to be published.[46] The cartoon is justly famous and catches the spirit of the age much as jokes about cybersex would seventy years later. (Sophistication here means that the joke works as a prompt to a fantasy reconstruction of the events that have already happened.) As all these examples suggest, Arno's mise-en-scène was rarely domestic. A few precocious upper-class children in patrician mansions are depicted in the drawings of the 1920s, but Arno almost never shows a middle-class family in his first ten years, and the middle-class home doesn't appear until the late 1940s. The responsibilities of home and hearth never interested him compared with the dramas of a twenties culture of hedonistic revelry.

Sexual desire lies at the heart of Arno's work, and he represented female desire in popular culture long before the liberationist feminism of the 1970s made this generally acceptable. In Manhattan in the 1920s and 1930s sexual liberation for both sexes was, among the young, openly permissible for the first time after the long reign of Victorian puritanism and prewar hypocrisy. For the previous generation, that of Arno's father, sexual freedom was a clandestine male privilege, controlled by the application of the double standard to maintain the facade of middle-class rectitude and ensure the proper distribution of property via inheritance. The women involved were, with some bohemian exceptions, either social victims or pariahs. The cases of Stanford White— murdered by the new husband of an old lover—and more notoriously, J. Pierpont Morgan—who made his yacht a love nest—are well known.[47] The chosen launching places of these relationships were very likely the so-called lobster palaces, essentially male preserves and not generally frequented by middle-class women who aimed to retain their respectability.[48] But the 1920s saw the emergence of new varieties of the New Woman, the citified feminist (like Ross's wife, Jane Grant), the consciousness-raised debutante (like Ellin Mackay), and the pleasure-seeking, sophisticated career woman (like Arno's wife, Lois Long) as well as the flapper. Between them they claimed new and unconventional liberties of speech, movement, and behavior (especially in sexual matters). They wore bold new fashions. They smoked and drank. And they sought careers and an independent life in the city. With their appearance, the end of the double standard was in sight. Women could now legitimately claim to be the equals of men in the pursuit of pleasure. Early *New Yorker* cartoons that exploited the appearance of this changed view of femininity were often drawn by women. One from the late twenties by Alice Harvey shows a couple engaged in earnest conversation while an adoring mother comments to a friend: "They're discussing sex—isn't that cute?" ("*The New Yorker*" *Twenty-fifth Anniversary Album, 1925–1950,* 1950). An early Helen Hokinson drawing is based on the following exchange between a mother and her daughter: "Couldn't you let that skirt down a little, Mary Louise? It's only an inch below your garters." "For heaven's sake, mother! Do you want me to look like a monk?" (May 1, 1926, 14).[49] *The New Yorker,* which had made its name by printing Mackay's protest against strict social codes, understood from the start that it had to make an appeal to women readers.[50] Many of Arno's cartoons feature the 1920s New Woman—she is, in effect, the precondition for many of his risqué jokes.[51]

The cabaret scene with its typical duo of characters (a young woman with a vacant, or excited, expression as the sexual object of an older, priapic male) raises the question of Arno's portrayal of women. There is an obvious sense in which Arno, with his penchant for scenes of sexual victimization, is a sexist artist. Yet when his work is dismissed as "misogynist," as one art historian has done, something is wrong: what should be a starting point is made a moment of dismissal.[52] Take a typical example: a secretary with disheveled hair is being chased around a desk by her elderly employer, who is saying, "Young woman, do you realize my time is worth thirty dollars a minute?" (fig. 1.7). It would be pointless to deny the element of sexism in this drawing. But as in all Arno's best cartoons, there is a surplus of meaning unaccounted for by such an explanation, so to dismiss it as simply misogynistic, as if such a description ended the drawing's interest for us, is overhasty. Tendentious jokes may well offend, but in doing so they free up repressed material that would otherwise go unnoticed.[53] This cartoon certainly makes visible workplace sexual harassment, long before anyone had identified, named, or proscribed it. The anger the cartoon provokes is completely dependent on the vividness with which Arno has drawn the scene. The drawing's offensiveness owes everything to its clarity—the horror on the secretary's face; the power implicit in the old man's body; the claustrophobic quality of the disturbed room. This much is made clear by a later unequivocally sexist treatment of the same theme by Whitney Darrow Jr. (July 10, 1954, 20). Darrow has a teacher in a secretarial school instructing class members on how to keep the desk between them and the boss— "Notice, class, how Angela circles, always keeping the desk between them. . . ." In this cartoon the intention is to normalize the aggressiveness of male sexuality and to routinize intimidation. What takes place is a ritual to which the secretary has given her assent, as is confirmed by the absence of extreme emotion in either of the participants (the secretary actually looks quite happy) and the classroom setting. Arno, who shows terror and lust, is very far from such complacency. The difference is between a cartoon that knowingly and cynically endorses male predatoriness and a cartoon that unmasks it and makes it look truly frightening.

What is unnerving about Arno's drawing is the old man's singleness of focus, the brutality suggested by the body about to pounce, the spread fingers. In drawing after drawing, he shows an acute awareness of the coldness of sexual motive, which he finds a matter for anxiety as much as for laughter. The man with his hands thrust down in his pockets, once again a pose meant to conceal an erection, standing behind the impossibly wasp-waisted, full-breasted woman and saying, "And now, Miss Evans, I wonder if I could take a small liberty?" (March 29, 1947, 30) wears an extraordinary expression—one of demonic excitement, barely under control. Arno often sees this look on men's faces (those in fig. 1.3, for instance), and it implies the very reverse of a celebration of sexual liberation. What is unmasked in Arno's cartoon (fig. 1.7) is not just the man's unselfconsciousness about the base peremptoriness of his

Fig. 1.7.
Peter Arno.

"Young woman, do you realize my time is worth thirty dollars a minute?"

The kind of cartoon that would give Arno the reputation of being sexist. But is this completely fair? It is true that the woman is objectified, made a little too available to the way-ward fantasies of the male gaze (see the next illustration). But the cartoon also makes visible workplace sexual harassment—long before it was identified, named, and proscribed. If the cartoon provokes anger, it is only because Arno renders so objectively the essentials of the scene in the first place: the distress and horror on the face of the trapped woman; the peremptory, predatory cruelty of the old man. The joke itself is really an example of comic unmasking. The businessman is so used to quantifying and calculating everything that even the time spent on assault has a monetary value attached to it.

demands. It is really a joke about commodification, underscoring a deeply ingrained professional habit that compels the man, even in the grip of violent lust, to quantify the exact exchange values that might be involved. This account of male sexuality shows it to be both predatory and calculating and is anything but flattering. Arno's undoubted commitment to hedonist self-gratification never quite forgets the destructive aggressiveness of the sexual drive, especially the father's, as we see from the countless old satyrs who appear in his drawings.

And yet it is perhaps the many cartoons enacting this revenge upon the father that show most clearly the deeper sense in which Arno's drawings *are* sexist. This is not just because of the erotic stylizing of the women's bodies, drawn to excite male fantasies, but because Arno's implied observer is always male and because the drawings often try to pull the viewer into the scenario presented. Here Arno's cartoons about sex imply a comic repetition of the child's fascination with the primal scene, based as they are on a voyeuristic optics that panders to the male gaze. Arno's cartoons often seem to encourage the male viewer to become not just a spectator but an imaginary participant in the action of the drawing. The dramatis personae in these cartoons include not just the couple (man and woman, or woman and group of males) in the cartoon but also the male observer of the cartoon. In some drawings this is obvious. In figure 1.8, "I was discussing the Mexican situation with Bottomly today. It seems fraught with interest," the woman stares wistfully out of the frame as if to connect with a male observer who would be interested in something other than politics.[54] But it controls male response in many other cartoons as well. The two older men in fancy dress (one is dressed as a rabbit and the other as a little girl) quarreling over a drowsy and scantily dressed young woman ("Look here, Grenville, this isn't getting either of us anywhere." [July 9, 1938, 12]) are so distracted that they leave the woman, shown in a state of unprotected sexual arousal, freely available to the gaze of the reader. The stylization of the women's sexualized body simply serves to make her more completely the unresisting object of the male gaze. Arno's style is phallographic—if the neologism can be permitted—because for him the sexual drive, the will to knowledge, and the urge to draw were one and the same. Sexual curiosity and social curiosity about the pulsating life of Manhattan merge in his work. Arno's masculine drawing style is fueled by a powerful scopic drive—voyeuristic, aggressive, and aiming at total possession and control of the subject. This is legitimately a matter of feminist complaint, but it is important to recognize that Arno's considerable achievement is built on it.

Arno's relationship with his own father, an intemperate, cruel man who constantly denigrated his son's talents, throws much light on his career. Biogra-

The Comic Worlds of Arno, Steig, Addams, and Steinberg

Fig. 1.8.
Peter Arno.

*"I was discussing the Mexican situation with Bottomly
today. It seems fraught with interest."*

The sexist optics of Arno's cartoons are made explicit in this
cartoon. The asexual male drones on. Meanwhile the voluptuous woman looks dreamily out of the cartoon frame as if
to connect with the male viewer. For all his fascination with
sexually aggressive men, Arno often drew scenes of sexual
humiliation and disaster, and he had a special affection for this
character, sometimes called Remson. Like all great comic characters he exists powerfully because of, rather than despite,
his folly and ineptitude.

phy sits congruent with social history here. The son's quarrel with his father
represents in miniature the much larger quarrel between the generations that
played itself out in Manhattan after the First World War.[55] Some commentators have ignored the intensity of Arno's engagement with this material.
They speak of his "pompous but unthreatening Depression-era plutocrats,"
say that he "regretted their passing," and call him the "gentle" lampooner of
his age, doubting whether any real indignation fuels his humor: "Today, his

stuff hardly looks angry, much less satirical. It is apolitical, utterly lacking in reformist intent; in fact it looks gentle." [56] Arno's work might have been apolitical, but otherwise these remarks are completely wrong. Justice Curtis Arnoux Peters Sr. personified for Arno the respectable (but hypocritical), traditional, moneyed oligarchy that ruled East Coast society, against which his own generation rebelled. Throughout his life Arno was engaged in a fierce quarrel with his father's generation, a generation that held power until the 1930s and beyond, and he was bitterly (if somewhat enviously) opposed to its values, privileges, and hypocrisy.

Arno's own words as recorded by Joseph Mitchell in 1937 are worth recalling:

> At no time in the history of the world have there been so many damned morons gathered together in one place as here in New York right now. The town squirms with them. Vain little girls with more alcohol in their brains than sense. Take a look in any nightclub or the fancy restaurants around lunchtime. . . . Yes, those people make me mad, the young ones more than the old ones. You don't do good work of this sort unless you're mad at something. I'm sure that's true. I've always rebelled against the social order, if you get what I mean. . . . [F]atuous ridiculous people. . . . I had a really hot impulse to go and exaggerate their ridiculous aspects. That anger, if you like, gave my stuff punch and made it live. [57]

Much of this is not worth taking seriously, either as social commentary or as aesthetic manifesto. But if it is short on understanding (one feels, for example, that Arno is not fully aware of how much self-betrayal there is in what he says), the anger is real enough, and we need not doubt that these negative feelings are what truly fueled his art. If Arno never rose above anger to indignation, this is perhaps because he lacked a certain intellectual and even moral awareness. But indignation might have robbed Arno's satire of its characteristic mixture of repulsion and attraction, its ability to identify with, and unsettle, Manhattan life in its most dizzying and self-confident phase. More damaging, indignation would have robbed his drawings of the drollness and sense of absurdity that characterize his best work. The humor works because the humorist is fully implicated in what he satirizes yet able to stand back from it (Arno's special talent). Over his drawing career he brought to the highest pitch his appreciation of his social milieu's fundamental lack of nobility and dignity and its excess of hypocrisy.

The Manhattan where Arno conducted his own revolt against his father's values was a city of extraordinary promise and romance. "There is no place like it," Thomas Wolfe had written, in terms Arno would surely have approved

The Comic Worlds of Arno, Steig, Addams, and Steinberg

of, "no place with an atom of its glory, pride and exultancy. . . . it lays its hand upon a man's bowels, he grows drunk with ecstasy; he grows young and full of glory; he feels he can never die."[58] Returning there after a barren stint in the movie studios of Hollywood early in the thirties, Arno had felt afresh this seductive allure. "Return to N.Y. and sanity. . . . Waking first morning in Biltmore, looking out window and breathing in the wonderful city."[59] This profound capacity to enliven, excite, and uplift was based on the fact that New York was now *the* world city. Long a financial center, it was now a powerhouse of many new forms of popular culture—in music (popular song and jazz), theater (including the musical and the revue), and publishing. It was the city where modern consumer culture was being born and the art of modern consumerist hedonism was being perfected. It was above all enormously rich, a city of rapacious appetite and greed. In New York, in H. L. Mencken's sardonic words, "all the aspirations of the Western world meet to form one master aspiration."[60]

The moral legitimacy of this heady mixture remained a constant anxiety that Mencken summed up in the notion of "harlotry." "At no time and place in modern times," Mencken wrote, "has harlotry reached so delicate and so effusive a development: it becomes in one form or another, one of the leading industries of the town."[61] "Harlotry" is a word that has literal relevance for many an Arno drawing—for example, the late drawing showing a resplendently dressed and bedizened young woman draped over a sofa explaining to a friend, "Of course I still have my room at the 'Y'—a girl can do that much to keep her mother happy" (April 2, 1960, 41).[62] But "harlotry" in a broader sense—decency and integrity sold out for money—is everywhere in Arno's world. Even *The New Yorker,* devoted to a luxurious *douceur de vivre,* was through its advertisements not as distant from this harlotry as the constant editorial protestations of innocence insisted.[63] Certainly the great river of commerce had unexpected tributaries. As Malcolm Cowley had argued, the new ethic of hedonistic consumption that characterized the twenties—and went on to characterize the rest of the century—was first legitimized by the bohemians of Greenwich Village, where Arno himself had lived as a young man: "It happened that many of the Greenwich Village ideas proved useful in the altered situation. Thus, *self-expression* and *paganism* encouraged a demand for all sorts of products. . . . *Living for the moment* meant buying an automobile, radio, or house, using it now and paying for it tomorrow. *Female equality* was capable of doubling the consumption of products formerly used by men alone. Even *changing place* would help stimulate business. . . . Everything fitted into the business picture."[64] Cowley's example of the old business ethic was *The Saturday Evening Post.* A perfect example of the new business principle might well be Harold Ross's *New Yorker*. And in that *New Yorker* the person who set the tone for the twenties and the decades that followed was Peter Arno, to whom Ross had once written a note saying, "You're the greatest artist in the world."[65]

Arno's own career is a perfect example of someone's cutting a successful path through harlotry in the modern Babylon. As a cartoonist he himself was a supremely successful creator of commodities. He became famous at a time when cartoonists were able to command considerable fees for their work (which suggests how necessary to the period the work of the humorist once was—the demand is far less now, as most practicing cartoonists report). As one of Ross's three favorite artists, Arno was someone whom, according to Thomas Kunkel, Ross tried to publish in each issue,[66] and he usually had a full page allotted to his work.[67] For this he was paid at least $500 a drawing (at a time when the going rate for a full-page cartoon was about $200).[68] Later the fee rose to $1,000.[69] Arno could hope to get $2,000 for a cover (and he averaged five covers every two years over his professional life). With these figures as a guide, we can arrive at a conservative estimate of Arno's income in some typical years. In 1934 Arno was working in Hollywood on contract to Paramount Pictures.[70] Nonetheless he contributed nineteen cartoons to *The New Yorker* that year, fifteen of them full page (but no covers), worth about $9,000 in all, in addition to whatever Paramount was paying him. In 1935 Arno was back in New York, lured by an advertising contract for billboards, among other things. That year Arno contributed twenty-three cartoons to *The New Yorker,* including nineteen full-page drawings and one cover: these must have been worth about $13,000 all told. The following year Arno contributed thirty-six drawings, including two covers, all worth about $20,000. Arno's basic income over these three not untypical years averaged at least $14,000 a year and probably was much higher. To put this into perspective, according to Ralph Ingersoll key *New Yorker* staffers at this time, such as E. B. White and James Thurber, received annual salaries of $12,000 and $11,000, respectively, while Ross denied receiving $40,000 a year.[71] In later years Arno was even more successful. In 1942 he had forty-one drawings accepted by the magazine, including an astonishing five covers: if we allow that by then Arno was getting $1,000 for a cartoon and $2,000 for a cover, he must have had an income of at least $51,000 that year. Yet in 1945 *The New Yorker* reported that Norman Rockwell, the most successful of all U.S. illustrators, actually earned only a little less—$50,000 in 1944 (and $40,000 a year over the previous twenty years)—from his work with *The Saturday Evening Post*. Rockwell was truly unique, an artist who could easily have doubled those sums had he exploited the market for his paintings more ruthlessly, but it is revealing that Arno was earning a comparable income for his drawings alone.[72]

Like many *New Yorker* artists including Thurber, Steig, and Richard Decker,

The Comic Worlds of Arno, Steig, Addams, and Steinberg

Arno was also taking on advertising commissions. He had been drawing for advertisers from as early as 1926 when *The New Yorker* carried an advertisement for Miltiades cigarettes with one of his illustrations (January 23, 1926, 48). A few years later he drew illustrations for Log Cabin Syrup (February 17, 1933, 34) and Old Gold cigarettes (August 27, 1932, 27). By the early thirties he was so much in demand, and presumably so expensive, that several artists began specializing in Arno knockoffs—as shown by advertisements for Johnson and Johnson (March 11, 1933, 60) and the *New York American* (August 8, 1931, 56). The advertisement for the latter includes a full-page drawing by an artist signing himself "Roese," plagiarizing Arno's "The Ruined Weekend" cartoon of 1926 with inexpertly drawn Arno figures circa 1930 (the men are done better than the women). In 1942 Arno was commissioned to draw ten cartoons for publication in *The New Yorker* as Pepsi-Cola advertisements. If we conservatively reckon that the work for *The New Yorker* in 1942 was worth $51,000, the work for Pepsi-Cola must have brought in (at a rough estimate of $1,000 a drawing) no less than $10,000, giving an income of $61,000 for that year.[73] Advertising was very lucrative for cartoonists in the forties and fifties. Arno frequently boasted about how much money he had forgone by refusing advertising commissions, including one for Chesterfield cigarettes ("$32,000 net to me") and Formica ("$1,000's"), yet the work continued.[74] In 1953 Arno drawings appeared in advertisements for Bourbon de Luxe (October 10, 1953, 75), and later Arno drew advertisements for Noilly Prat liquors (September 22, 1956, 35).

Whatever his true income, Peter Arno, dandy, playboy, and man-about-town, certainly lived like a very wealthy man. He rented a succession of large apartments in fashionable midtown locations, with the full complement of domestic help including butler, maid, cook, and chauffeur. In the late thirties he designed and had built his own car, the Albatross, which reputedly cost him $75,000.[75] He was voted the best-dressed man in the United States in 1941 and the most eligible bachelor in the country by *Mademoiselle* in the late forties, when he was photographed perched on a high shelf in his closet surveying his huge wardrobe.[76] He was seen in the city's most fashionable nightspots escorting famous debutantes whose names appeared in the Social Register (a well-known photograph shows Arno with Brenda Duff Frazier at the World's Fair in 1939).[77] When this all became too much, he took long recuperative cruises or sought spiritual renewal in the desert.

The life of glamour and fashionable ease inevitably had its other side. Avaricious, with an eye for the quick buck, Arno was often tempted into litigation. In November 1929 he sued the Packard Motor Company on the grounds that the company had misled him about the top speed of a car he had bought. Arno demanded that the company take the car back and refund his money. When the matter went to court, Packard countered that Arno had bought the car on a deposit of $21 cash, a trade-in, and a series of monthly promissory notes, only one of which he had honored. Counsel also pointed out that Arno had made no complaint about the car until the company sought to compel him to pay two overdue notes. The judge denied Arno's application. (Arno's penchant for speed was genuine, however: a few years later Rhode Island banned him as a driver for speeding.) Touchingly hopeful, Arno then sued Irving Berlin on the grounds that Berlin had plagiarized an idea from one of his cartoons (combining Gandhi and Aimee Semple McPherson) for his 1933 Broadway musical revue, *As Thousands Cheer*. Arno lost.[78]

In 1931 Arno made the long journey to Reno to be divorced from Lois Long (or "reno-vated," in Winchellese).[79] Rumors immediately started hinting at Arno's involvement with the wife of Cornelius Vanderbilt Jr. On June 17, 1931, Arno accused Vanderbilt of attempting to shoot him. Two days later Vanderbilt filed for divorce from his wife on the unspecific grounds of "extreme cruelty," and Mrs. Vanderbilt counterfiled, denying to the press that she had any involvement with Arno, whom, she said, she had known for only ten days. Given Arno's reputation, this was perhaps not the strongest argument she could have made, but Arno insisted he had never paid any attention to Mrs. Vanderbilt and promised to sue Vanderbilt for slander. Vanderbilt was undeterred. The two men met by accident at the Reno railroad station shortly afterward; Arno descended from a railway carriage "retaining an insulting grin." Vanderbilt knocked him down. Shortly afterward Arno left, accompanied by an unnamed "female friend," and went into hiding. Vanderbilt set off in pursuit, darkly refusing to tell reporters what he would do to Arno once he found him.[80]

One way or another, Arno must have escaped Vanderbilt's wrath. In 1933 he was still in one piece, fending off accusations that he had helped the confidence trickster Harry Gerguson (who passed himself off as the improbable "Prince Michael Alexandrovitch Dmitry Obolensky Romanoff") enter the country illegally.[81] A year later the Waldorf-Astoria successfully sued Arno for an unpaid bill for a party Arno had held there some years before.[82] In the forties his janitor attempted to blackmail him over pornographic photographs that had turned up in the cartoonist's garbage can. In 1947 Arno was himself arraigned for threatening someone with a pistol (the case was later dropped).[83] These are scattered examples, and no doubt Arno's life was often more mundane that the impression they create. But despite his large earnings there is a constant sense of income overspent, of financial precariousness, and above all, of a chaotic and unhappy personal life.

Arno's anxieties were brought to a head by the death of his father in December 1933. Curtis Arnoux Peters Sr. had divorced Arno's mother in the early 1920s and had subsequently remarried. His father's death was a release for Arno, but it also opened up the inevitable drama of inheritance. Details of the will were first disclosed in February 1934. Justice Peters left his widow $25,000 in cash, the life income from half the residual estate, and a remainder interest in half a trust fund of $30,000. His daughter by the second marriage received the other half of the residue in trust and a remainder interest in the other half of the $30,000 fund. Arno's mother received $25,000, and Arno got $20,000. In November of that year it was confirmed what Arno must have long ago guessed. The residual estate was very large, consisting mainly of securities worth over $600,000.[84] All of this was to pass to the justice's second wife and the child of that marriage. Whatever Arno had hoped for, he must have been disappointed. His father's will brought to the surface long-standing grievances and resentments. Arno later commented: "To be known as an artist was always more important to me than to be a millionaire. . . . My father was a millionaire a few times over. He never gave me instructions on how to become one, and there was no aspect of his life or work I envied. The greatest favor he did me was not to leave me a sizeable inheritance. I was a little sore about it at the time (broke in Hollywood), but the years have proved that a lot of money would probably have destroyed the incentive to work."[85] Arno then adds, speaking of his own professional life: "It started, after boyhood and adolescent days of compulsive, incessant drawing on my own, with the relentless drive to excel. This was undoubtedly to show my father that I could be greater than he. Eventually I was."[86]

Arno's fraught relationship with his father is summed up by his nom de plume. As Curtis Arnoux Peters Jr., Arno was named after his father. But his first drawing, that small spot showing the night scene with a high-society couple stepping out in a low part of town, was already signed "Arno." By the issue of October 10, 1925, the signature became "Peter Arno" (it fluctuated between this and "Arno" for another eighteen months or so before settling down as "Peter Arno"). This new identity is a typical example of the twentieth-century invented self. But why did Arno bother? One explanation is that he adopted his pseudonym to protect his father's dignity. But any pseudonym would have done that.[87] The one he chose sums up the drama of Arno's rejection of his father's world, on which his humor is based. Its invention suggests how difficult and even imperfect that revolt was, and how necessary a tangled, compromised loyalty was to his life's work. Arno dropped his first given name, "Curtis," also his father's first name. Then he lopped off two extraneous letters from his middle name so that "Arnoux" became plain "Arno." Finally he dropped the *s* from his surname, "Peters," and reversed what was left: "Peter

Arno." Despite the felicitousness of the new name and the visual confidence of the famous signature (it becomes more and more forcefully inscribed as Arno's own success as an artist increases), it is not really a new beginning in the way so many twentieth-century celebrity names are—John Wayne, Cary Grant, Marilyn Monroe; the list could be extended indefinitely. It is a conflicted invention, preserving, even as it denies, the existence of the father who brutalized the son as a child and denigrated his artistic talent as an adult. It records a minor crisis of subjectivity and its tortuous, not entirely successful, negotiation. Curtis Arnoux Peters Sr. exists in a mutilated and caricatured form within the invented name "Peter Arno," just as Peter Arno's cartoons preserve in a mutilated and caricatured form the upper-class Manhattan world to which Curtis Arnoux Peters Sr. belonged and against which the son defined his talent.

Arno was always aware of the oedipal nature of the origins of his art (he had been in analysis toward the end of his life). He was perhaps less aware of how the question of money became so easily mixed up in it. In a memoir, Arno reports a conversation he had once had with "Bill Stern." (Probably the commercial artist Bert Stern, whose work had appeared in a notable series of advertisements for Nettleton shoes in *The New Yorker* in the early fifties.)[88] Stern had said, flatteringly, "Pete, you've turned down so much loot (mostly in advertising) because you've insisted on integrity in your work. I've always done anything that there was money in; I guess I'm just a whore." After assuring Stern that he (Stern) was certainly not a whore, Arno fell to wondering "whether I'd ever done anything whore-like."[89] The only answer he could come up with was that he had once played the piano in a Paris brothel to pay a hotel bill—but that, he thought, "doesn't make one a whore." ("Does it?" he added, as if not quite sure.) But the truth was that like many cartoonists Arno was haunted by the unreasonable feeling that he had prostituted his talent and that his "real" work was not done for sale or publication. In fact those paintings—for instance the pastiches of Georges Rouault—are of little value. But a sense of Menckian "harlotry" seems an inevitable concomitant of all careers in professional and commercial art—particularly so in the middle years of this century when cartoonist were paid so much.[90] In the case of Arno those rewards, as well as stirring anxieties about his integrity, became entangled with the resentment he felt against his father, who had treated him badly when he was a child ("My father would . . . 'box my ears' so thoroughly that I sometimes couldn't hear for *three days afterwards*," Arno reported).[91] He had never recognized his son's talent. He had slighted him in his will. Understandably, Arno felt he had to best his father in his own life. To that end he confronted him in countless drawings, some of them the best he ever did, like the wonderful one of the ancient man, with scrawny neck and long talons gripping his

Fig. 1.9. Peter Arno. Untitled. [Illustration for Elmer Rice, "A Voyage to Purilia."]

The New Yorker, October 12, 1929, 25. © 1929 Peter Arno. Illustration reprinted by permission of the Estate of Peter Arno.

A beautifully drawn and composed title illustration that shows how Arno's style was changing by the end of the twenties. The drawing is done in ink and wash, giving greater definition and sharpness than the charcoal and wash Arno was commonly using at this time. But all the characters are observed with a satirical eye: the dastardly villain, the lovable old woman, the ingenue, the dopey hayseed, and the handsome, narcissistic, juvenile lead. This was a way of drawing, and a way of looking at the world, that Arno would polish and perfect in the coming decade.

armchair, who is shown saying gleefully to his attorney, "Now read me that part where I disinherit everybody" (December 7, 1940, 29).

The character of Arno's first period derives from the boom of the late twenties: the period of the "economy of abundance," with the businessman and stockbroker as its prophets.[92] It was his close engagement with the social experience of this era that gave his work punch and relevance. But in the first half of the thirties, following that initial success, Arno's work often gives the impression of being a technique in search of a subject. Although the drawing can be strong, many of the actual jokes are flat. There are far too many cartoons on uninventive sexual themes. There is the distinct sense of an artist drawing at a distance from his material and even resting on his laurels. In some of his less studied pieces, like the brilliant title illustrations he drew to accompany Elmer Rice's "A Voyage to Purilia," which ran in *The New Yorker* between October 12 and December 21, 1929, Arno can be observed developing his line and wash technique and carving out a new, confident sharpness of form, at once satiric and erotic (see fig. 1.9). But in his featured cartoons Arno often repeats himself. "Er—do you still want an ice, Miss Charteris?" (May 5, 1934, 20) is simply a new version of "Er—Is that you Gwendolyn? I believe this is our dance, Gwendolyn" (June 14, 1930, 14), just as "Dad says if I buy more pastels he'll cut me off" (February 6, 1932, 14) redraws with minimal alteration the characters and situation of "I was discussing the Mexican situation with Bottomly today. It seems fraught with interest" (September 15, 1928, 26). It is possible that Ross had decided that the winning formula devised by a successful cartoonist could bear repetition and consolidation. A sign of how far the magazine was willing to rely on a stock response from its readers was the experiment the editors conducted through the early thirties—reprinting exactly the same drawing week after week but with a new caption each time. (Ross was fond of running gags.) Richard Decker supplied a drawing of a convict reading a letter in his cell (the letter changes from week to week), and George Price did the same with a man levitating above his bed (with a series of useless visits from the doctor). Arno, who seems to have initiated the practice, drew a man and a woman embracing on a porch swing, first with the caption, "And you really don't mind my being a college girl?" (July 12, 1930, 21), then with "Petunias would look nice" (July 19, 1930, 18), and a week and a half "You know, Mrs. Creighton, you do give rather dull parties" (August 2, 1930, 22). The series was continued long past the point of being cheeky and amusing. Fortunately the magazine is buoyed through these years by the likes of Hokinson, Frueh, and Thurber, along with the first appearances of William Steig. For at least part of this time Arno was working in Hollywood, and he had domestic problems as well, all of which may explain the flatness of much of his work in these five years. Yet Ross continued to give him a full page, almost invariably the prominent one after "The Talk of the Town" that preceded the week's main casual piece.

These are also, of course, the years in which the effect of the Depression was most felt. The pre-Christmas issue of the 1929 *New Yorker* had run to 132 pages; the same issue in 1933 had shrunk to a mere 60 pages. And yet though the effect of stock market crash of 1929 on the consumer hedonism of the epoch was severe, it was never evenly distributed. Compared with many other businesses, *The New Yorker* did well during the Depression, and well-paid, regularly published contributors like Arno were insulated from the social trauma that affected many other Americans. The very rich, as Brendan Gill once observed, were little affected by the Depression and even benefited from it—if you had money, you could now get everything much more cheaply, and there was no reason for the party not to roll on. What closed off the twenties for Arno was not the Crash, not the Depression, not even the election of Roosevelt in 1932, but the end of Prohibition, the death of his father the following year, and the failure of his Hollywood career. From Arno's return to New York in 1935, his art assumes a different character. His attachment to the younger generation (now no longer young) weakens, and his humor develops a more

The Comic Worlds of Arno, Steig, Addams, and Steinberg

unequivocally satiric thrust. Up to the end of the twenties there are two impulses driving Arno's art—utopian hedonism and sardonic skepticism. After the long interval between 1930 and 1935, the latter drives out the former, and Arno's art gains punch and confidence, finds new directions and bearings.

Accompanying this change of emphasis is a modified graphic style that is uniquely Arno's. Even in the lesser works of the early thirties Arno is steadily purging his drawing of all traces of dandified elegance and is beginning to exploit the more openly masculine character of his drawing style—always there, but now set to become its defining characteristic. It takes about five years for this to complete itself, from about 1931 to 1936. A more solid, expressionistic line in india ink applied by brush over a pencil underdrawing replaces the free-flowing, sketchy charcoal line. The difference is to be seen in the contrast between the women in figures 1.3 (done in 1927) and 1.12 (done in 1954). In the earlier drawing ("You're like a lovely flower tonight . . .") the woman's body— she is long-necked, flat-chested, sinuous, and willowy—is treated in a spirit of disinterested aesthetic pleasure, even though the joke itself centers on a sexual theme. In the later drawing ("Cette . . . and cette . . . and cette . . . and cette") the woman is full-breasted, voluptuous, and possesses a strong sexual aura, even though here the erotic and sexual element is irrelevant to the joke. In the former drawing the charcoal line is still exploratory and even a little tentative; in the latter the inked line is definite, quite certain of what it wants to capture.

Up to the end of the twenties Arno is absorbed in the task of finding a way to draw his milieu adequately, to convey its characteristic look as well as its charm and attraction. A typical example is "You do give such perfect parties, Alice. Is there anyone here you'd like to meet?" (January 12, 1929, 12), which, as we have seen, is really an endorsement of the age rather than a satire at its expense. The artist is all for the collapse of formality and etiquette in which a truly charming party is one populated by gate-crashers. But after Arno returns to New York from Hollywood in 1935, realizing that his true vocation is that of a cartoonist rather than a set designer, after the death of his father and the decline of the cabaret world, the character of his cartoons changes. His eye becomes sharper, the note of celebration and justification disappears, and the draftsmanship is more direct. A powerful drawing like "Hello, Edmund. Hello, Warwick. Hello, Teddy. Hello, Poodgie. Hello, Kip. Hello, Freddie . . ." (fig. 1.10) is one of the first in which we see Arno displaying this new comic sensibility. The litany of names is provocatively spoken by a bride as she passes along a guard of honor of Royal Lifeguards, and the effect is typical in manner, matter, and the unkindness of the humor. Arno revels in the priapic geometry of greatcoats, upraised arms and swords, in the phallic connotations of the bearskin hats, and in the sexiness of the woman (not to mention the unconscious symbolism of the receding line of arms and swords). The overtly eroticized, betraying female, set to become Arno's signature, has ousted the androgynous, covertly sexualized flapper.

Eventually, in Arno's classic phase (the late thirties to the early fifties), the line acquires a taut, geometric discipline. In the best drawings the line simplifies without reducing complexity; it caricatures without courting superficiality; it stylizes, but not at the cost of vitality or vivacity. Drawing after drawing demonstrates a true satirist's confidence as the area of attack and comment widens across the whole social field. We see this in some typical drawings from the early 1940s. "Please stand aside, sir. There's a gentleman coming out" (June 12, 1943, 23) shows two waiters wheeling a drunk diner out past a bemused couple waiting for a table. "Now who shall say grace?" (December 18, 1943, 23) depicts fifteen clergymen, each vying for the privilege while taking care to preserve an expression suitably humble and meek. "Ready, Marcel! You're on next" (March 21, 1942, 18) has a maître d'hôtel marshaling his underlings as they prepare to wheel carts laden with spirit stoves and covered fowl out into a crowded restaurant for a piece of grand culinary theater. The delineation of both mise-en-scène and character in such drawings is masterly. Caption and drawing are fully integrated. The comment is adroit and unforced, and it administers a shock of genuine recognition. There are no extraneous, exploitative elements here: the woman in the first drawing is glamorous but not excessively sexualized; the unmasking of the clergymen's self-interest and ambition is not aggressive but remains deeply cutting; the observation of the theatrics of restaurant management is subtle and appreciative even while it is mocking. Cartoons like these work because of the subtlest disjunction between caption and illustration: the idea of the "gentleman" as opposed to the drunken sot being dragged out; the connotations of "grace" as opposed to the gentle but urgent competitiveness of the assembled clergymen; the theatrical slang and the edginess of the performer as opposed to the routine of serving the next course. Implicit in all these is a comedy of letdown or anticlimax, the classic comic trope of the gap between expectation and reality. Toward the end of the thirties Arno had perfected both the style and the comic mode, and his art was ready to hand as the ideal tool for dissecting a world altogether more banal and less Dionysian than that of the twenties.

A good place to inspect Arno's achievement in the late thirties and after is in the covers he supplied for *The New Yorker* at this time. Arno published thirty-three covers between March 1935 and March 1950, and fifteen of them are among the strongest work he ever did.[93] Four are of particular interest for their assuredness of draftsmanship and execution, effectiveness of composition, and transparency of meaning. In the cover for November 7, 1936, a man advances

Fig. 1.10. **Peter Arno.**

The New Yorker, July 25, 1936, 14. © *The New Yorker* Collection 1936 Peter Arno from cartoonbank.com. All rights reserved.

"Hello Edmund. Hello, Warwick. Hello, Teddy. Hello, Poodgie. Hello, Kip. Hello, Freddie . . ."

By the mid-1930s the note of celebration found in the cartoons of the twenties has vanished, to be replaced by an altogether colder tone. The style has changed, as epitomized by this drawing: it is geometrical and hard edged rather than fluid and suggestive. This cartoon has an unkind glance for both the bridegroom (we are made to laugh at the way the man's puzzlement is about to break into enlightenment) and the bride (the cartoonist emphasizes that she is unable to give up playing the field). Arno revels in the sexual imagery: the priapic suggestions of the upraised arms and swords (receding into a dizzying infinity that has its own unconscious symbolism), the phallic bearskin hats, the seductive coyness of the voluptuous woman. Arno's flappers, although sexualized, were often treated sympathetically. This woman is presented more straightforwardly as the betraying, unreliable female. Sexual immorality, once a sign of his generation's freedom, has become a matter for disquiet. The response of the male viewer, for example, is divided: he may feel like projecting himself into the sexual opportunism of the other men, but he is just as likely to end up feeling sympathy for the betrayed husband.

menacingly upon a woman, who lifts her arm to protect herself from the anticipated blow. The woman has sunk to the floor, one leg stretched before her, the other folded behind: her torso, which is slender but by no means boyish, half turns away, and her loosely draped, semitransparent dress falls over her legs and off her full breasts. The unsettling effect of sadomasochistic eroticism[94] is controlled partly by the fact that this, we realize, is only a cabaret act, and also by the comedy of the man behind her—a member of the audience, Arno's archetypal wimp and alter ego, Remson—rising in an act of gallantry to defend her from her "attacker." One of the remarkable things about this painting is that it is done entirely in monochrome except for certain details—the man's scarf, the woman's dress, lips, and hair—which are picked out in a vivid red. (The combination of monochrome with a restricted color palette was something Arno was later to use to great effect, and perhaps it answered Ross's reported objection to the use of color in cartoons: "What's funny about red?")[95] The other remarkable thing is that it is so unsettling—comic, yet verging on a kind of comic book soft porn. It is memorable because it switches from the lurid world of the cabaret to the mundane world of the Remson character, from erotic involvement to comic imbroglio. More than anything else, that crossover indicates the difference between the Arno of the twenties and the Arno of the thirties. The risky action environment of the Jazz Age has now dwindled to a place of safe playacting, funny because there is no real action there anymore.

The cover for February 1, 1941, is a simpler work, close to pure pictorialism, and an example of the sympathetic attitude that often underlies Arno's best work. Here a chauffeur, huddled under a Fifth Avenue awning while a snowstorm rages, is handed a demitasse of coffee by the headwaiter of a restaurant. The cold, the driving snow, the small comfort gratefully accepted, are vividly depicted. The contrast between the two figures—one huge and hulking but warm in his chauffeur's greatcoat, in whose hand the coffee cup shrinks to the size of a thimble, the other thin, red-cheeked, hunched against the cold in his uniform—establishes an immediate sense of the fellowship between members of the classes serving the Manhattan social elite. Arno often evokes place by choosing a narrow, closeup field of vision. Here we see only a short stretch of snow-covered sidewalk, part of an awning, a fragment of wall with the restaurant's barely legible plaque, and a doorway. But these details evoke a New York that is both romantic and real. A scene like this is uniquely available to Baudelaire's "passionate observer" or White's "loiterer" in the city, the detached person who alone has time and opportunity to witness the city's true life.[96] Once glimpsed, however, such details suggest the entire life of the snowbound city.

This cover highlights a particular Arno trope, the life of the Manhattan upper class as seen from the perspective of the servant. (Although he was an extremely selfish and rude man, Arno was nonetheless interested in framing the life of the rich through the duties of those who served them.) The wonderful cover for October 24, 1942, is one such illustration (fig. 1.11). A well-fed middle-aged couple sit back at their restaurant table (Le Pavillon? Lutèce? Le Cirque?) as a group of five attentive waiters prepares crêpes suzette. The only source of light comes from a huge flaring flame in the pan over a spirit stove that fills the center of the painting. The same qualities that distinguish the previous drawing are apparent here—a limited palette, faultless draftsmanship, perfect composition. (The central table is framed by the sides of two tables closer to the viewer, giving the picture depth and lateral movement, but composition disposes everything along two strong diagonal axes, created by the group of waiters and shadows in the background and the two figures at the foreground tables, that cross in the middle of the picture.) The wit is entirely in the characters themselves—the waiters applying themselves to their duties with expressions of undivided attention while the portly couple sit back with looks of fatuous complacency and self-satisfaction. The social revolt of the thirties may as well not have happened. The satire is given additional bite by the wartime dateline. Arno's cartoons of wartime indulgence have to be set against his drawings of the very different conditions then being endured by men serving in the armed forces, like the cover for December 26 of the same year. This shows an orderly bringing out a tray of coffee and neatly wrapped Christmas presents for two officers on watch on the bridge of a destroyer, heeling over in sleet and heavy seas.

The final cover is for December 25, 1948, and a companion to figure 1.11. It takes place in the kitchen of a large house or apartment and shows a butler fulfilling his key professional task of lighting the Christmas pudding, under the watchful eye of the cook who made it and maid who will serve it. As with the chauffeur and the headwaiter, the artist narrows his vision to isolate the most minute and ephemeral of all the moments in the life of a great city. Yet out of this he evokes the contradiction of the season—without whimsy or sentimentality, without resort to cliché, and pinned down to a few exact seconds. The subtle hierarchies of backstairs power relations (the subservience of the women is clearly shown), the privileged lives of Manhattan's wealthy (offstage), and the slightly absurd but real enough sense of professional skill are brought together to unmask a moment of Christmas festivity.

In Arno's best drawings from this period the draftsmanship is breathtakingly assured: something of the free-flowing, improvisational quality of the early period is retained, but the effect is now less dependent on accidental felicities. From the late thirties onward Arno achieves expressive simplification without fudging of effect, crispness of definition without rigidity.[97] A dramatic handling of light and shadow (owing something to Hollywood lighting effects, perhaps) gives the figures added weight and solidity. Philip Herrera rightly emphasizes Arno's "somber, expressionistic lines" and "powerful groupings." The fin de siècle fluidity of body shape has vanished, replaced by figures less aesthetic, more sculptural, statuesque, tactile—but, as we have seen, far more satiric and comic in conception. Crucially, bodies lose their androgynous shape and become more overtly sexualized—the men more masculine, priapic or impotent, the women more womanly, erotic or matronly. There are new discoveries in physiognomy, body posture, and gesture. The interiors become less sumptuous for their own sake and more utilitarian. It is tempting to say that the drawings are deglamorized, but this is not quite true. Arno still shows the mystique of glamour as few cartoonists have ever been able to do. But the effect is of glamour itself displayed, objectified, and only because of this detour, *de*glamorized in the last instance. We see this, for example, in "You cad! You're not fit to touch the hem of her skirt," a cartoon with yet another powerfully eroticized female at its center (March 20, 1943, 17). Here the two men quarreling at the door of the woman's dressing room (she is a performer of some kind) are locked in a contest that has its origins in a complete misunderstanding of the woman they are both obsessed with. While they fight, she is shown, half-naked, making herself up at her mirror, absorbed in a narcissistic dream. They glare at each other. Indifferent to their anger, she looks at her-

---

Fig. 1.11. *(facing page)* Peter Arno. Untitled. [Upper-class couple being fussed over in a restaurant.]

Cover illustration, *The New Yorker*, October 24, 1942. © *The New Yorker* Collection 1942 Peter Arno from cartoonbank.com. All rights reserved.

The world of the expensive, midtown restaurant (Le Pavillon? Lutèce? Le Cirque?), lovingly created, in which two diners are fussed over by no fewer than five staff members. The action is framed by two envious onlookers (dining out in such a place is essentially about show, not food). In the center of the picture sit a well-fed, dewlapped, middle-aged couple with expressions of fatuous complacency and self-satisfaction as a cadre of waiters, sous-chefs, and sommeliers ply their trade. The drawing shows Arno at the height of his powers—faultless draftsmanship (the line work is crisp and economical but in no sense mechanical), perfect composition (everything is arranged along those strong diagonals intersecting the flare from the pan), and a dramatic, restricted palette (black, blue, and flesh tones with highlights of yellow and orange). The satire of this brilliant drawing is given extra bite by the wartime dateline.

self. In nearly all cases what informs such drawings (in contrast with the note of celebration that accompanied the drawings of the earlier period) is a wry, clear-eyed, sardonic, comic realism. This, the 1940s, is Arno's classic period.

Arno's treatment of the face also develops in the thirties and after. Arno was a true caricaturist, able to show the individual and delineate the type in one figure. In his first eight years or so at *The New Yorker,* he experimented with various ways of rendering the face. Initially he was drawn to stylized, generic faces, like that of the young woman with little round circles for eyes in "Oh, Freddie, play that ma-a-arvellous classical piece again—the one that sounds just like 'Don't Bring Lulu'" (published without a caption in *The New Yorker* for December 21, 1929, 22). He maintained a similar simplification and impressionistic typifying when he was drawing young people for some years, but with the faces of older people (who, as the possessors of real social power, increasingly fascinated him) Arno started to aim for a high degree of individuation while preserving typicality. In "Did you think I was going to eat you, little girl?" (February 21, 1931, 14), the svelte young woman with her clownlike face is basically a version of the flapper (wonderfully but schematically drawn), but the old man draping diamonds around her neck, though a representative type (priapic captain of industry), is a highly individualized figure. This was the direction Arno's art was pointing, and he went on, after the early thirties, to develop as a truly great caricaturist, one of whose primary achievements was to invent, in a manner worthy of Daumier, a whole galaxy of comic individuals truly representative of their society. In his mature cartoons the joke is often focused through a keenly observed registration of expression backed up with posture and gesture.

An example is the drawing from the early fifties (by which time the social milieu has changed completely) in which a young man struggles to order from a menu and is reduced to saying "Cette . . . and cette . . . and cette . . . and cette" (fig. 1.12). The joke, charming in itself, requires for its full effect the beautifully individualized faces and body poses of the waiter, the young man, and the young woman. Arno gives each one of the trio due attention. The waiter, who has seen this all before, displays an easy superiority yet holds back destructive insolence. The young man shows performance anxiety, bravely overcome. The young woman radiates a receptive, contained innocence, drinking it all in. Without our being able to read the status of the participants so confidently—especially that of the young couple as suburbanites visiting the city— the joke loses both its charm and its meaning. And as in so many Arno drawings, the eroticizing (not excessive) of the woman spins a fragment of the humor off into some other orbit. The joke is a good example of what one finds

Fig. 1.12. Peter Arno.

"Cette . . . and cette . . . and cette . . . and cette."

The New Yorker,
January 23, 1954, 31.
© *The New Yorker* Col-
lection 1954 Peter Arno
from cartoonbank.com.
All rights reserved.

A sympathetic, observational cartoon from the fifties. As is
often the case in Arno's work, the caption, and even the idea,
is nothing apart from the drawing. Arno pays due attention to
each member of the trio, and the comedy is partly a matter of
the way each one's mood fails to intersect with the others':
they are all lost in a world of their own. The waiter is on
automatic pilot, and his superiority over someone in a situation he has seen many times before does not develop into
destructive insolence. The young man displays performance
anxiety doggedly and bravely overcome. The young woman is
so innocent that all she can do is sit there and drink in the
situation, a model of unguarded, unselfconscious receptiveness. Arno being Arno, the woman is lovingly drawn, but there
is a poignancy about her that makes one hesitate to say she is
objectified in the way that many similar Arno women are.

often in cartoons in *The New Yorker*—the sympathetic, warm joke dependent on character rather than comic predicament.

Although there is an undoubted aggressive masculine quality in much of Arno's work, there is another contrasting (perhaps complementary) thematic strand. It treats of sexual inadequacy, a subcategory of Arno's growing awareness of frustrated expectation as the great comic subject. Arno was frequently drawn to the subject of male impotence and inadequacy, mainly through the Remson character. In many instances the joke is at the expense of his low level of libido, as we have seen in "I was discussing the Mexican situation with Bottomly today. It seems fraught with interest" (fig. 1.8). A later version of this joke, the cover for the issue of January 1, 1944, shows him seated next to a baffled-looking woman, inspecting his watch as midnight, New Year's Eve, approaches and everyone else is embracing passionately (this in effect redraws his cover for December 28, 1929). There are many slurs on this character's masculinity: for example, "Please, Mr. Winney, don't be a gorilla" (*Peter Arno's Circus,* 1931).[98] Here is a striking contrast between a drooping, pathetic male, folded up like an abandoned marionette and even though dressed as a caveman as unlike a gorilla as it is possible to be, and a vibrant, seductive woman, one of Arno's most extraordinary creations, whose contained, vivid sexual elegance is really quite remarkable.[99] Other cartoons are about cuckoldry, a subject that becomes far more significant when they show an older man cuckolding a younger husband. An early cartoon with an older man (the boss) comfortably bedding down between a husband and his wife and declaring, "awfully nice of you to ask me to stay" epitomizes the theme (March 26, 1932, 14). A young woman pursued by a much older man is a closely related trope, one that Arno drew and redrew obsessively throughout his career. The theme appears in the early thirties, as in "Did you think I was going to eat you, little girl?" (February 21, 1931, 14), where the old man is shown fastening a diamond necklace around a younger woman's throat. It crops up often in the late thirties with examples like "I keep wanting to put you on a pedestal" (June 24, 1939, 20), in which a comically short and stout millionaire is shown dancing in the garden of his mansion with a tall, full-breasted young woman, with statues of naked women in the background—the two strongly contrasting figures are wonderfully caught. And it continues into the forties and fifties and beyond with countless boss-and-secretary cartoons such as "I used to see your expense accounts at the office, Mr. Hofstetter, but gee, I never dreamed I'd be in them" (September 27, 1952, 33), where a leering middle-aged man woos a young employee in an expensive restaurant. Arno's sexual jealousy of the older man, whose money, position, and power entitled him to the bodies of younger women, is a constant throughout his career—an area, perhaps, in which he never did prove himself entirely free of some fantasy version of his father.

Lee Lorenz, James Geraghty's successor as cartoon editor of *The New Yorker*, says that something mechanical comes into Arno's work in his last phase, the early 1950s to Arno's death in 1968, and there is some justice to this charge.[100] What in the earlier period was a bold and hard-won simplification now regresses, on occasion, into mere formula. Nonetheless there are some outstanding cartoons from the late period. One shows a man saying to a completely uninterested man next to him, "I love this old place and everything it stands for" (December 13, 1958, 41). His posture (he sits hunched on a stool with one hand resting on the bar clutching a glass and the other thrust down between his legs) and his brightness of eye signal that state of drunkenness in which banality passes for insight. The dreary, democratic neighborhood bar is one of the several 1950s stand-ins for the vanished world of twenties hedonism, the cabaret of an earlier decade. But everything that made that world exciting has gone: all that is left is a drunken illusion that no one else cares about. Out of such banal locations Arno produced some wonderful work. A striking example is his cover for June 5, 1954 (fig. 1.13), which returns to the cabaret of the twenties, but in a totally unromantic and disillusioned way. The painting shows a man seated alone at a table halfway through a meal and about to take a mouthful of food, being interrupted by an imploring chanteuse. Although the singer is merely dramatizing her song, the effect—and it is beautifully wry and comic—is that she is begging the man to give her some of his meal. Food —the middle-aged indulgence—replaces sex; the man, no longer the hunter, becomes the hunted. This is where the rebellious action environment of the twenties, the cabaret world and all its promise, has ended up.

It may seem that one of the most famous and funniest of Arno's cartoons, "Man in the Shower" (fig. 1.2), fits into none of the categories that this account of his career has used. But it epitomizes something essentially Arno, the way his jokes entail a wry connoisseurship of everyday disaster—of purposes frustrated, expectations dashed, and illusions shattered. The recurrence of these motifs throughout his career forms a kind of bass figure in Arno's humor, but it is in the 1940s that these kinds of cartoons start to appear in abundance. Arno's 1956 collection *Peter Arno's Hell of a Way to Run a Railroad* has some wonderful examples, all of them subtly different in tone and tendency. One shows a thin, nerdy, anxious man, uncomfortably perched half-naked on a chair in a doctor's office. The doctor is taking a call from his wife and is saying to her, "By all means, dear—buy it if you really want it. We'll find the money for it somehow" (ca. 1954, reproduced in *Peter Arno's Hell of a Way to Run a Railroad*,

1956). The drawing gets perfectly the contrast between the roles of doctor and patient. The doctor is well fed, secure in his professional role, patronizingly and pleasantly dispensing private benevolence to a wife whom we can only imagine, the invisible third person of the trio; the patient is nervous, embarrassingly exposed, uncertain whether what the doctor is saying applies to him. The doctor is beautifully drawn, his eyes the most striking feature: it is impossible to tell if what one sees is the top of the eyelids as the eyes look down to the desk or eyes narrowed to mere slits that frighteningly display only the whites, no pupils. Either alternative makes him a figure of menace. From the same period there is "I just can't wait to see your work, old fellow" (December 26, 1953, 21). Here an enthusiastic collector rushes into an artist's studio unaware that he has tossed his hat onto the artist's latest sculpture. That the enthusiasm of the speaker is genuine is the foundation of an insult all the more galling for being unintended. Finally, there is one of Arno's small masterpieces, another Valentine's Day comment, the drawing captioned, "This giblet gravy is lumpy!" (February 13, 1954, 36). It returns us for the last time to the cabaret—now transformed, by the long historical process that turned the 1920s into the 1950s, into a sedate, middle-class restaurant with musical entertainment, a tame Gypsy fiddler. The bright young things have been transformed as well: the willowy young man has become the woman's husband, his flabby, jowled face illuminated from below by the candle on the table (he is superbly done in three or four lines and a wash); the sensuous flapper is now the wattled, portly, and querulous matron bearding the fiddler, paid to entertain with ren-

---

Fig. 1.13. *(facing page)* Peter Arno. Untitled. [A cabaret chanteuse implores a diner.]

Cover illustration, *The New Yorker,* June 5, 1954. © *The New Yorker* Collection 1954 Peter Arno from cartoonbank.com. All rights reserved.

A solitary diner in a nightclub is beseeched by an over-the-top and over-the-hill chanteuse. But what does she really want? Whatever the romantic words of the song, it seems to be food not love, let alone sex. The drawing is magnificent—both characters are wonderful creations; their poses sum up their intentions and desires completely. The dramatic contrast of light (she in spotlight, he in the shadow) shifts readers' attention meaningfully about the drawing (first we look at her, then at him, then at her again). There is a fractional delay before we get the joke—what she is actually looking at (as the diner has realized with dismay) is not him but what is on his fork. For Arno, the triumph of antisentimentalism in his comedy is complete. It is June 1954, the fulcrum of the Eisenhower equilibrium and the decade degree zero of the American century. This is where the rebellious action environment of the twenties cabaret and all its promise has ended up.

The Comic Worlds of Arno, Steig, Addams, and Steinberg

June 5, 1954 · THE NEW YORKER · Price 20 cents

ditions of "Gypsy Nights," who is suddenly brought to book for the failures of the kitchen. In each case in these three cartoons the crux of the joke is the slight but impossible to ignore comic reversal suffered by the central character—the patient, the artist, the fiddler. Their expressions imply is that this is the last thing they ever expected: "her fur coat at the cost of my appendix," "my work is indistinguishable from a hatrack," "I'm supposed to fix this gravy?" No wonder the stunned, bewildered, perplexed looks. These characters demand—and get—the viewer's profound sympathy. They are stumped, nonplussed, and unable to answer back. The patient is pathetically vulnerable, perched on his chair as if on display. The artist with his middle-aged paunch, comically stereotyped clothes (the silly beret), and grizzled beard, can only frame the lineaments of an anger he dare not show for fear of the even deeper humiliation of a lost sale. The fiddler, a comically portly figure despite the romantic accoutrements, is reduced to complete silence—he can neither play (he has been interrupted in midflight) nor speak. What can you say?

All these characters have run up against an unexpected right-angle turn in the expected straightforward flow of events. In their different ways they are all metaphors for the disillusionment of the tranquilized fifties and the Eisenhower equilibrium. This is what it has all come down to. (Hence the way cultural historians now read the fifties as the seedbed of the countercultural revolt of the sixties.)[101] The "Man in the Shower" of 1943 is the metaphor of metaphors here, with its banal domestic setting and powerful image, comic and yet frightening, of death by drowning in the middle of suburban plenty. Arno's men are often shown as powerful, predatory, and violent, but perhaps this man, vulnerable, ungainly, out-of-control, frightened, desperate, and dependent on a woman for his life at the very moment when the daily grind begins, is Arno's true and sad epiphany of maleness at midcentury? Certainly an overwhelming sadness now possessed Arno. Although he produced some good covers in the late fifties and after, most of the cartoons of this time are lackluster. In his last years he lived as an embittered recluse on his farm at Harrison, outside New York City, seldom visiting town. His sole companion was his housekeeper, a woman her employer called "the doormat."[102] Arno died of lung cancer complicated by emphysema on February 22, 1968, only three weeks after the death of his mother. When the fun-loving, fast-living, sociable epitome of the Jazz Age was buried, only a handful of people showed up at his funeral.

2 · WILLIAM *S*TEIG

Art, Armor, and Amour

William Steig's first drawing in *The New Yorker* showed two convicts sharing a cell. One is saying to the other, "My youngest is a terror. We can't do a thing with 'im" (August 9, 1930, 18). Unexpectedly, work like this struck a note with readers of the magazine that would resonate down the decades to come. Steig was a man of strong liberal sympathies. He was drawn to ordinary people, street life, and small lower-class dramas of success and failure.[1] These preferences made him the antithesis of the aristocratic, anarchic-conservative Arno — the antithesis, indeed, of all those *New Yorker* contributors whose interests and sympathies lay with high society.[2] Whereas Arno was the type of the boom decade of the twenties, Steig, who turned twenty-five a few days after Roosevelt's landslide victory in November 1932, was the artist of the New Deal. His rapid ascent through the ranks of *New Yorker* artists, along with the appearance of figures like George Price and Syd Hoff,[3] was a signal that as the Depression gripped America tighter and tighter the magazine's honeymoon with the oligarchy was well and truly over.[4] Recognition of this parting of the ways is stylishly conveyed in an unusual joint drawing published in the mid-1930s. It is set in the Metropolitan Museum of Art and shows a guided tour in progress. On one side of the frame, gathered around a sarcophagus, stands a group of docile middle-class children. They have been drawn by Helen Hokinson, whose signature is in the lower right-hand corner. On the other side of the frame, glaring angrily and defiantly, stands the outsider, a pugnacious working-class teenager. He has been drawn by William Steig, whose signature is in the lower left-hand corner. The tour leader is saying, "Pardon me, young man, are you a member of this Study Group?" (fig. 2.1). Henceforth the outsider had indeed to be welcomed as a member of the group.

A liberal individualist and radical moralist, Steig professed a lifelong belief in human innocence. "People are basically good and beautiful," Steig announced in the 1950s. Accordingly, his indignation is directed against whatever undermines that goodness—generally what Christopher Lasch called the principal targets of old-style radicalism: the family, repressive sexual morality, respectability, routine, censorship, the work ethic—everything, in short, that middle-class society is built on and everything it yearns to escape.[5] It is a stance summed up by a midcareer cartoon of a little boy sticking his tongue out at a policeman's back (May 10, 1952, 32). When the counterculture arrived in the sixties, Steig was a late-middle-aged supporter: he was against the war in Vietnam, sympathetic to the drug culture, and in favor of the new, liberated sexual morality.[6] Underlying his intuitive dislike of various forms of social discipline is the great, tragic story of the way freedom, innocence, and natural goodness are restricted, corrupted, and undermined by society. Like Jean-Jacques Rousseau, Steig believed that people were born free but everywhere lived in chains. Like William Blake, he thought their manacles were essentially mind forged. That first drawing of the convicts says it all, with its twin motifs of childhood and imprisonment and a tonality that we ought to call sentimental but probably don't. It went further than this, however. He insisted to one interviewer in the 1950s that "neurosis is the biggest obstacle to peace and happiness."[7] Even by that date "neurosis" was a capacious term, and in using it Steig no doubt meant it to cover many kinds of psychic disturbances.[8] But fifteen years before, for two psychoanalysts with whom Steig had been in close contact, "neurosis" had meant something quite specific. For Karen Horney and Wilhelm Reich, neurosis was the harried individual's response to the pressures of a materialistic, competitive, overdisciplined market economy, and the ramifications of this position help us understand many of Steig's more difficult drawings of the 1940s. This is not to suggest that Steig ever set out to "illustrate" in a deliberate way the thinking of people like Horney and Reich.[9] Equally, like most *New Yorker* staff contributors, Steig was a small businessman, a player in the market economy, and if not an acquisitive man, hardly averse to making money out of his work. But Steig's imagination was unconsciously influenced by the writings of Horney and Reich, and there is no better way to appreciate the discontents of a market system, as outlined by them both, than to have to earn one's living within it.

It is true, nonetheless, that few artists could be less ideological in the way they work. Steig was an intuitive humorist who was always fascinated to see what he would draw next. He fixes his eye steadily on the contemporary reality of life, he is a wry connoisseur of behavioral oddity, he observes the principle of the sacred importance of detail, and above all, he sees character as most revealingly displayed in small, unpredictable, but defining traits.[10] Steig's con-

"Pardon me, young man, are you a member of this Study Group?"

An unusual collaborative venture between Helen Hokinson (who drew the lady and her young charges) and William Steig (who drew the boy on the left). As the Depression sets in, *The New Yorker*'s honeymoon with the oligarchy is over. This cartoon shows the magazine wittily admitting the parting of the ways. Hokinson's genteel gallery guide and her group of privileged youngsters recall the comfortable world of the Manhattan elite—quiet drawing rooms in elegant apartments off the Avenue, ladies' clubs, holidays on private Long Island beaches, prep schools, and pony clubs. Steig's impudent teenager (the word "teenager" would not be invented for another six or seven years, but looking at this drawing one wonders why not) evokes the life of the Lower East Side, the Bronx, or Brooklyn—the brownstone stoop, the sandlot baseball game, the noisy street. Henceforth these two worlds would live much closer together in the pages of *The New Yorker*. The drawing leaves us with a burning question: Why shouldn't the "young man" be part of the study group? The coiled energy of his body, his bold expression, and his aggressive stance suggest he cannot be kept out much longer.

vict, whatever he has done, is in the toils of a crisis, all too familiar and conventional, typical of the middle-class parent. The peculiarity of his concern is what catches Steig's attention. Comic drawings, he once said, were a pictorial equivalent of the haiku, "a special moment, fleetingly observed."[11] Whatever his beliefs, that moment—of betraying contradiction, epiphany, and revelation—was what he always pursued.

An exquisite example is the twelve-panel sequence titled "The Accident in the Street" (fig. 2.2). Here a woman looks out at the goings-on in the street with mild curiosity passing quickly into boredom. Suddenly she is shocked by the sight of a terrible accident. She calls her husband, and then her daughter appears. They look at what has happened and at each other, first with stunned interest and then with dismay. In the last two panels the mother and father's attention passes from the accident to their daughter, and in the final panel the family members embrace in relief. The accident itself happens out of frame. We see nothing except how the offstage event is registered by the family, although at the end we realize that the accident has involved a child. The whole drama is a finely managed balance of humor and sympathy, entirely dependent on the sureness with which Steig understands his true subject—the slowly aroused sympathy of the family, the anxiety and protectiveness of the parents. It also depends on his skill as an artist, particularly his uncanny ability to register the finest shades of expression and posture, and through them to suggest what is going on in people's minds.

This drawing takes us a huge distance from Arno's nightclubs and speakeasies. The way of life is not affluent. It is blue collar or lower middle class—reassuringly dowdy. It is neither uncomfortable nor insecure. We see a community preoccupied with the ordinary dramas of life suddenly faced with something that merges into the tragic, to which they respond with unguarded receptiveness. The drawing celebrates the strength of this culture. People are decent and warm. They back each other up. They lack the bitter, competitive, self-seeking individualism that drives so many characters in Arno's drawings, whose motives are self-interested, exploitative, and unworthy. The only anger in Steig's early cartoons is found in the occasional outburst of egalitarian self-assertion. But Steig's characters represent not an angry proletariat (there is no sense of exclusion or exploitation) but a comfortable blue-collar class being won over to a decent, unostentatious lower-middle-class prosperity.[12] The democratic self-confidence that Steig's characters of the early thirties possess is so impressive that to account for its power and popularity we have to refer it to some grand abstraction such as "the people." In William Steig Harold Ross had found an artist whose work added something previously missing in his magazine. Arno might have summed up high-living Manhat-

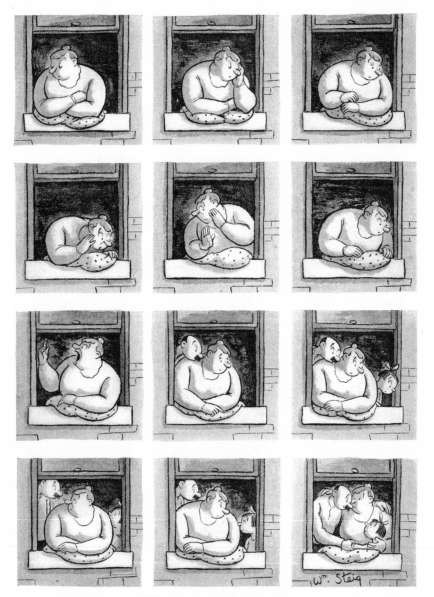

Fig. 2.2. William Steig. *"The Accident in the Street."*

The New Yorker,
May 26, 1934, 18. © *The New Yorker* Collection
1934 William Steig from
cartoonbank.com. All
rights reserved.

A brilliant and affecting example of Steig as the humorist of everyday life. The various members of the family look out their apartment window at the accident (not shown), first with mild curiosity, then with mounting interest, and finally with dismay. The sequence is a finely balanced blend of humor and sympathy. Steig understands that his true subject is the slowly aroused fellow feeling of the watchers, and he demonstrates his genius as an artist able to depict the finest shades of emotion on faces and in bodies. The viewer's contribution comes with the slow realization that the accident has involved a child.

tan nightlife, Hokinson the perils of East Coast upper-class clubwomen, and Thurber the tribulations of the urban little man, but what Steig captured, with a vivid humanity, was something much more central: the experience of ordinary people and, through them, of the nation itself. Steig, who within a year of his first appearance in the magazine often had two drawings an issue (in this rivaled only by Helen Hokinson), illustrated no fewer than four Independence Day covers in his first nine years at *The New Yorker.*

William Steig was born into an immigrant family in Brooklyn on November 14, 1907, the third of four boys. His parents, Polish Jews, had come to America early in the century. His father, Joseph, was a housepainter; his mother, Laura (née Ebel), was a seamstress. The parents held left-wing political views. "My father," Steig said many years later, "was a socialist—an advanced thinker—and he felt that business was degrading. But he didn't want his children to be laborers." There was an interest in high culture, and the children were all encouraged "to go into music or art."[13] Steig later recalled: "My mother, though physically tiny, was more formidable, although my father was no nebbish. . . . One of my motives for being a good artist was to get my mother's admiration. My mother thought she was a superior being and she was in many ways. She admired all her sons and said 'I have given birth to four geniuses.' We were all artists, and she said we were all fantastic, so we never believed anything she said. My father's approval, when it was forthcoming, seemed genuine."[14] The voice of many such immigrants was *The Jewish Daily Forward,* whose masthead motto quoted the *Communist Manifesto* and that once published a letter including the words, "My heart bounded with joy when I saw New York in the distance. It was like coming to the world city where everything breathed in freedom and where I can become a proletarian."[15] For his part, and more typically, Joseph Steig became not a proletarian but a lower-middle-class small businessman.

The family lived first in Brooklyn and then in the Bronx, where Joseph's business prospered.[16] Later in life, after he had been ruined by the crash of 1929, both Joseph Steig and his wife became exhibiting artists. Joseph's work was described in *The New York Times* as having a distinctively American feel,[17] high praise to people who valued assimilation as highly as the Steigs. In later years Steig proudly insisted he grew up to be an "all-American boy." The parents were not religious, and Steig himself, while remaining culturally Jewish, also rejected Judaism. They spoke Polish and Yiddish at home, especially when they did not want the children to understand. Steig, like his brothers, came to understand most of what was being said, but as he grew up he did not as a matter of course speak Yiddish or Polish. Being an artist was a family ideal.

The Comic Worlds of Arno, Steig, Addams, and Steinberg

Joseph and Laura Steig encouraged all their children to live creatively. Arthur, who ran a very successful ink and paint company called Steig Products, also wrote poetry and painted (and contributed introductions to several of his brother's collections of drawings). Irwin, also a successful businessman, was a poker and bridge tournament champion who wrote several well-respected instruction books on these subjects. Henry, deflected from a no doubt profitable career in dentistry, was in turn a jazz musician, a cartoonist, an essayist (his work appeared in *The New Yorker*), a photographer, and latterly a jewelry designer.[18] In the early forties Henry also published a novel titled *Send Me Down*, loosely based on his experiences as a jazz musician. Although it is not a roman à clef, it offers a glimpse into a household no doubt very similar to the Steigs' and includes a telling portrait of the mother—a compelling, dominating character "with a pale, oval face, black hair and black eyes."[19] Steig was very close to this charismatic person.

After leaving high school, Steig studied art at City College of New York for two years (he joked that he majored in water polo—throughout his life he excelled as an athlete), and in 1925 went on to the National Academy of Design, where he spent the next three years. (He also put in five days at the Yale School of Fine Arts.) It was while Steig was a student at the National Academy of Design that he began selling drawings to *Judge* and the pre-Luce *Life*.[20]

At this time Steig cherished dreams of escape in which fantasies of eroticism and creativity, familiar motifs in his later work, were intertwined: "to go to sea, live with native girls in Hawaii, and become a writer." But his career as a cartoonist was starting to bear fruit. As early as 1930 Steig reported earning $4,500 for the year, a handsome, if not huge, sum well above the national average family income.[21] Since his first drawing for *The New Yorker* appeared only in August of that year, he must already have been widely published in other magazines.[22] Steig had already approached *The New Yorker* with completed cartoons, but the editors, as was often the case with unknowns, wanted to buy only the ideas for some other artist to illustrate. Steig's mother insisted that her son sell both the idea and the drawing or nothing. Eventually the editors—probably Rea Irvin—relented. Once accepted by *The New Yorker,* Steig rapidly became a fixture. In 1931 it published forty-six of his drawings, on several occasions two in the same issue (for example, in the issues for September 12 and November 28). In his first six years at *The New Yorker,* 1931–36, Steig's annual publishing strike rate (the ratio of published drawings to the number of issues in a year and counting full-page series like "Small Fry" as one drawing) averaged about 80 percent, not including covers—an astonishingly high figure.[23] The income generated ought to have set him free, but because his father had been financially ruined in the Depression Steig stayed at home to support his parents and his seventeen-year-old brother.[24] "I flew out of the nest with my parents on my back," he said later (it is a characteristically charming image).[25]

In 1934 Ralph Ingersoll compiled the following thumbnail sketch of the artist:

> Age: twenty-six. Habitat: Manhattan's West Ninety-ninth Street. Education: High School. National Academy of Design. Looking even younger than he is, Steig has thick, wavy, black hair, a shy engaging smile, no conceit whatever. When *The New Yorker* turned down the first pictures he ever offered for sale, wanted to buy his ideas alone, he refused, kept on drawing and submitting, checked several months later. Art Director Irvin proved the infallibility of his rule by taking exception to Small Fry, has never been enthusiastic over them. The rest of the staff overruled him. Steig enjoys watching kids, but insists he is not fond of them.[26]

By the middle of the decade, and despite Irvin's determined hostility, Steig had become one of *The New Yorker*'s most celebrated artists. But even though he attracted some enthusiastic patronage, he remained an independent figure. Steig saw himself as a serious artist as much as a cartoonist (no other *New Yorker* artist has published quite so many cartoons about artists as Steig has, with the possible exception of Steinberg), and he was much more ready than either Arno or Addams to venture beyond the pages of *The New Yorker* when the occasion demanded. This gave his driven talent the freedom to develop in ways that few other *New Yorker* artists ever did. When at the end of the thirties his art took a direction that Ross found hard to follow, Steig simply published his drawings as collections in books and worked on commission for advertisers. When in the seventies he began a new career as the author and illustrator of children's books, he pursued it with vigor and dedication and was soon hugely successful.

Steig's background readily accounts for the preoccupation with blue-collar and lower-middle-class life in his early work. Many of these drawings are celebrations of the vibrant life of the still intact neighborhoods of the city boroughs: the Lower East Side, the Bronx, and Brooklyn, before expressways, the automobile, the rise of the suburb, the triumph of television, urban decay, overcrowding, black and Hispanic poverty, and drugs changed them forever. *Man About Town,* published in 1932, is a representative early collection, drawing on Steig's early contributions to *The New Yorker* but including drawings selected from *Life, Judge, Collier's,* and *The Gentle Reader,* magazines that were on occasion less genteel than Ross's. The title offers an ironic comment on the ethos of *The New Yorker* of the 1920s—Steig's man-about-town is neither Corey Ford's dandyish Eustace Tilley on Park Avenue nor Arno's perennial nightclubber at "21" but an unshaven, overweight, balding blue-collar worker in an undershirt, living on the Lower East Side. The frontispiece drags in a portly, Hokinson-like matron from the avenues and shows her inspecting the book of his exploits with dismay. And indeed in the drawings published outside the pages of *The New Yorker* Steig treats sexual themes with a directness that even Arno was never to match. A man with a cloth cap resting on his knee explains to a disbelieving doctor, "I don't know *where* I could have caught it!" Gazing amorously at his wife in bed, he is told, "You only think of one thing!" Much of this is a calculated assault on the hypothetical reader of *The New Yorker*—cultivated, moneyed, sophisticated. In the unaccustomed circumstance of being served at the table in a diner, Steig's man-about-town lays a brawny fist on the table and barks at the waiter through a brush mustache, "I don't want no flunkies fussing over me!" Fashionable ennui and neurasthenia are mocked as one street sweeper throws up his hands and tells another, "I can't go on with this farce any longer!" Even when a cartoon is drawn from the point of view of the upper classes, the advantage remains with the lower orders. In one drawing a little boy (hands in his pockets and wearing a flower, necktie, and hat) inquires patronizingly of the elevator attendant, "And how are *you* this morning, Charles?" but the attendant more than matches him, supercilious glance for supercilious glance.

In the years before Steig appeared, the typical *New Yorker* cartoon about lower-class life tended to be facetious in tone and superior in attitude. A drawing by I. Klein (August 31, 1929, 29) shows a man whose face is a mess of adhesive tape staggering out of a building with "Barber College" over the door and saying to a friend, "Just my luck! Shaved by a freshman again." (Both men appear to be lower-class Jews.) Another by Gus Peck (September 7, 1929, 32) shows two workers raiding a trash can, with one of them sniffing an empty perfume bottle and exclaiming, "M-m-m, Ybry's Femme de Paris." Steig's cartoons in *The New Yorker* never put lower-class characters down like this, nor are they presented as such distant, objectified comic objects, even when the joke is at their expense. His humor springs naturally from a lower-class viewpoint, and when it criticizes it does so with understanding, validating what it finds amusing. Moreover, there is strong element of lower-class self-assertion in his cartoons, like that shown by the street sweeper who yells after a couple of haughty women in a chauffeur-driven car who have tossed a banana skin overboard, "After all, who the hell are *you*?" (August 1, 1931, 16). Similarly, two working-class men on a fishing trip encounter a snooty, expensively outfitted canoeist, and one says to the other, in exasperation, "Out here I thought we'd got away from all that" (August 15, 1931, 44)—a drawing that was tellingly printed on the largely upper-class "The Tennis Courts" page. At their best Steig's lower-class cartoons express an unsentimental sympathy for the view from the bottom of the social hierarchy.

Examples in the early thirties proliferate. Two men in top hats and bow ties who have the temerity to address a short-order cook (who looks alarmingly like W. C. Fields) as "garçon" receive a completely devastating glance in return (December 17, 1932, 11). A man in the dock roars at the judge, "Do you think I *like* to steal?" (February 4, 1933, 8) and clearly means it. A news vendor confidently recommends a magazine called *Zowie* to a derby-hatted customer: "Very clever, sir. Brilliant satire" (November 5, 1932, 17). The jokes at the expense of women are far less hostile and antagonistic than those by many other artists then publishing in *The New Yorker*—Arno's, once again, or Addams's.[27] A besotted husband gazes at his very substantial wife parading around their bedroom in a slip and begs, "Now turn around" (May 21, 1932, 11). A bedraggled housewife in a forlorn apartment with an unpromising baby in her arms tells a friend, "And suddenly you got something to live for" (February 18, 1933, 11). Exasperated beyond patience, an angry woman yells at her husband, "I hate you! Do you hear me? Hate you, hate you, hate you!" (August 8, 1931, 14). These drawings, whether mocking the attitudes and pretensions of a moneyed world or registering the pleasures and agonies of the less privileged members of society, carry a subtle freight of social consciousness into *The New Yorker*'s pages.[28]

The anthropologist Margaret Mead, Steig's sister-in-law at this time, spoke of Steig as a "compassionate humorist."[29] The humor is warm, and this feels new. Steig's early characters are ebullient, self-confident, and integrated, qualities that come through particularly in the solid, well-upholstered figures with their comfortable presence and robust, pugnacious body language. The humor is a mixture of pathos, frustration, and pleasure, as in the highly characteristic occasional series that Steig drew for *The New Yorker* from the mid-1930s onward. This consists of multiple-panel vignettes of life in the lower-class neighborhoods: "Bronx Park" (July 14, 1934, 22–23), "Election Day" (November 2, 1935, 18–19), or "The Barber Shop" (March 28, 1936, 28–29). In drawing to a general theme in this way, Steig was following the example of Helen Hokinson, who had drawn place- or activity-based series with titles like "So, You Want to Get Your Hair Cut Short?" But somewhere in the background was the more complex example of Harold Tucker Webster. Webster was a phenomenally successful cartoonist of the day who published humorous drawings in the Chicago *Daily News* and later in the New York *World* under such general headings as "The Timid Soul," "The Thrill That Comes Once in a Lifetime," and "Life's Darkest Moments." Webster moved the focus of the thematic draw-

The Comic Worlds of Arno, Steig, Addams, and Steinberg

ing from a location and an activity to a general existential condition, something Steig obviously took careful note of. Steig understood that because such a heading sets a general framework or context, each drawing could then be extremely subtle, since the heading guides and shapes readers' responses. Steig, who had perhaps seen the value of this format when developing his own "Small Fry" series, uses it more and more from the late thirties onward, with thematically grouped drawings like "Stream of Consciousness" (June 5, 1937, 25), "Spleen" (March 6, 1937, 26–27), and "Medical Manners" (December 31, 1938, 22–23). Under these general headings the individual drawings illustrate a particular mood or state of mind characteristic of everyday life, like the thoughts of the young woman on the subway in "Stream of Consciousness": ". . . I should say not I wouldn't! Who does he think I am? What does he think? I should say not! Some nerve! . . . ." In a similar vein, in "Boiling Anger" the boss has a violent tantrum ("Spleen"), and in "Medical Manners" a doctor delivers a well-worn pleasantry to a sick patient ("The Stock in Trade Joke").[30] The title of one group of drawings, "Emotional Crises" (November 12, 1938, 30–31), sums up what Steig is getting at here and is one of several pointers in the thirties to the direction his art was to take in the following decade.

Steig made his mark in the thirties with his "Small Fry," humorous observations of the everyday life of children, in an adultless world. "Small Fry" continued into the 1950s, well past its author's disenchantment with it. The first "Small Fry" drawing appeared in the April 2, 1932, issue of *The New Yorker* as a single image (13). It showed a little boy sitting in an armchair and was captioned "Spring—and that strange pounding in the breast." Others followed, usually every two weeks or so: the tiny paper seller calling out "Libiddy!" (April 9, 1932, 25), the batter being intimidated by the catcher's calling to the pitcher, "C'mon, Georgie old kid, dis man's pie for you!" (May 14, 1932, 24). These readily merged with more conventional cartoons about children, like the drawing that showed a half-naked youngster, shoes in hand, cautioning his out-of-sight parents, "Shh, you'll wake the kid" (March 18, 1933, 13). In the same year the Small Fry moved onto the front cover for the issue of September 2, 1933.[31] Then, starting in the issue of December 30, 1933 (17), with a group of images titled "The Day after Christmas," they turned into multiple vignettes of four, five, or even more thematically linked drawings ("Misery" of May 5, 1934, "Little Women" of December 1, 1934, "Criminal Types" of April 27, 1935). By the time Ralph Ingersoll profiled *The New Yorker* in *Fortune* in 1934, the series was legendary. Steig's general feelings about children are summed up in words that cast an interesting light over the "Small Fry" series. Asserting his belief in the fundamental goodness of human beings, Steig added, "Since they [children] are still so full of life, the conflict between life and social insanity is more dramatic in them (Society has not yet won)."[32]

The "Small Fry" drawings fall into two groups that illustrate an important transition in Steig's vision at this time. First there are those that celebrate childhood pure and simple, such as the set of drawings titled "Phenomena" (fig. 2.3). Here the children are drawn at a moment of discovery, perplexity, or at worst anxiety. The children are completely sympathetic. What propels the situation forward is essentially their innocence. The drawings show the artist's ability to empathize with children, his understanding of the tiny dramas that enliven their existence (the moment when one's toes are of absorbing interest, for instance). Second, there are those drawings that mark the moment when the adult world impinges, often disturbingly, on the innocence of childhood. Sexuality is often the focus. An example is the drawing "Startin' kinda early, ain't we?" (November 10, 1934, 66) in which a father catches a preteen girl putting on lipstick. In another drawing a little girl yells at a small boy with an unbearably smug expression, "You beast!" (August 13, 1932, 17). In yet another an "artist" is shown painting a nude "model"—both are aged five or six (fig. 2.4). None of these drawings is simple or uncomplicated: the children, shown imitating adult sexual maneuvers, are disturbingly precocious.

Violence also attracts Steig's attention, especially in a related series about older children called "Dreams of Glory" that Steig developed from the war years onward. In a midcareer drawing, "Captain Blood" (August 30, 1952, 18), a boy of about ten captures a pirate ship and singlehandedly saves a damsel in distress. The heroism is spoiled a little when we look at the realistic dead bodies on the deck, one with a sword sticking out of his chest. Steig's interest in the child's fascination with violence grows out of the "Dreams of Glory" drawings done during wartime, which are often very dark. In one of the less complicated examples a little boy in a cowboy suit arrests Hitler (February 19, 1944, 24), a drawing that suggests a simple enough conflict between American idealism and German wickedness. But other drawings are morally ambiguous. They show scenes of violence in which children take over the conflict with the Germans or the Japanese in bloodthirsty ways, as in the cover for July 17, 1943, where a little boy dreams of shooting down German planes and the falling aircraft, trailing smoke, are turned into decorative motifs for the magazine's spine. Steig draws children engaged in "hand-to-hand fighting" (August 7, 1943, 23), mounting a "tank attack" (August 21, 1943, 21), and, with umbrellas, acting as "parachute troops" (September 11, 1943, 34). In one drawing a little boy heroically saves his mother from being raped by a Japanese soldier (March 18, 1944, 27). Two weeks later the same boy has captured the soldier

Toes

Worm

SMALL FRY
PHENOMENA

• •

The boiling pot

Lightning

What makes it go?

Fig. 2.3. William Steig.   *"Small Fry: Phenomena."*

Steig as the completely sympathetic observer of young children. These are innocent, untouched in any serious way by the adult world, something Steig responds to warmly. Like the adults in the previous drawing the children impress us with the solidity of their presence: they are well fed, secure, self-absorbed. He shows them at a moment of discovery, anxiety, or perplexity—but he goes no further in this drawing. Yet there is a difference between the upper three and the lower two. The upper vignettes depict moments of absorbed enlargement of the child's experience the child can easily cope with—toes, worms, and boiling pots present no real challenge. The lower vignettes show more open-ended moments that suggest a larger cosmos—the mysteries of lightning and clockworks.

and stands triumphant over his bound body while the soldier's wife pleads for her husband's life (April 1, 1944, 22). Most disturbing of all are drawings like "Chemical Warfare," in which the children shower each other with flyspray (December 19, 1942, 22), and "Bombing of Civilians," in which little boys are shown bombarding a group of little girls with water balloons (fig. 2.5). What Steig's drawings stress over and over is the enthusiastic participation of the little boys. That the world conflict should invade children's play is inevitable,

Fig. 2.4. William Steig. Untitled. ["'Artist' and 'model.'"]

As the "Small Fry" grow up they lose their innocence. Steig is especially aware of a prepubertal interest in sexuality, which is partly a genuine instinct and partly a precocious imitation of adult ways. This is an odd drawing, not quite right, but prophetic of the late-twentieth-century sexualization of young children. The little boy parodies one of Steig's artist figures (he has the air of congratulating himself on his own pose), who are often shown with a nude model. Steig, one feels, is not quite aware that this is itself a cliché. He takes it at face value, though here the little boy's concentration also seems something of a mask. (His painting does not seem to have been noticeably improved by his having a live model.) The little girl, too, wears a face of false modesty, though she is also a little smug at the idea of the perpetuation of her beauty. Both children are playing a role. Diana Trilling spoke of something a little too knowing in many of Steig's "Small Fry." The drawing shows what she meant.

The Comic Worlds of Arno, Steig, Addams, and Steinberg

Fig. 2.5. William Steig.   *"Small Fry: Bombing of Civilians."*

The Second World War was the daily modern conflict between individualism and fascism writ large on the world
historical stage. Consequently, many of the "Small Fry" panels
that show children acting out the global conflict have heroic
implications, like the little boy who arrests Hitler. This one is
more ambiguous. Germany had blitzed London in 1940, but by
1943 the bombing of German civilians by the RAF had begun.
Are the little boys the Germans or the Allies? Are the little
girls the inhabitants of London or Hamburg? In drawings like
this we see that the "Small Fry" series is Steig's version of
William Blake's *Songs of Innocence and Experience.*

no doubt, and hardly unusual, but these drawings are a powerful indication of innocence corrupted.

When these various tendencies are finely balanced, as in "Andante! Andante!" which shows a crabby music teacher bawling the command at a startled young violinist, the result is subtle, original, and charming (January 31, 1953, 55). In such a drawing Steig hauntingly evokes the mixed quality of childhood experience—its simple delights and sensual pleasures, its pains and tribulations, its fall from innocence, its thraldom to adult demands and expectations. For Steig as an heir of the romantic movement, childhood is health. But for Steig as a product of his own era, childhood is compromised and under attack. The "Small Fry" and related series are Steig's updated version of Blake's *Songs of Innocence and Experience.* In his seventies Steig told an interviewer that he had never felt grown up: "I carry a lot of the functions of an adult but I have to force myself," he said.

More than one commentator noticed that the children in the "Small Fry" series are rarely unequivocally innocent but are poised between childhood innocence and adult knowingness. Steig often pinpoints the moment when children mimic corrupt adult manners and begin to embrace a false sophistication—something that can be glimpsed even in the vignettes that form the often anthologized "Sandlot Baseball" (September 6, 1941, 24–25). The most cogent expression of this case comes from Diana Trilling in a review published in *The New Republic* in 1943. Trilling notes that "beside the lunacies of Thurber or Price," Steig's children seem to "shine . . . with a beguiling normality"; but "even while we smile we are vaguely disquieted by something that lurks behind the cockiness of Mr. Steig's youngsters; their innocence is paraded, but not convincing; whatever they are up to they leave us grown-ups holding the bag."[33] Trilling continues: "Of course, all children have a secret, but surely the Small Fry know more than is good for them. When they are pleased, they smirk, and when they are bad they roll evil about on their little tongues as if they had long ago had it out with Original Sin. Can an adult possibly have a comfortable relationship with children who sail through life with their nose held so high: can you imagine, for instance, daring to cuddle a Small Fry, for all that these kids cry out to be loved?" "Smirk" is exactly the right word for many of Steig's children, and Trilling makes an essential point. It is tempting to argue that "Small Fry" was such a huge success because the series was a fantasy, at once wishful and skeptical, about the diminishing of childhood at the end of the first third of the twentieth century. Childhood, sometimes said to be an invention of the Enlightenment and romanticism, shrinks under the onslaught of modernity. Children are no longer simply innocent. It is not that they now know more about the adult world—children have always had that knowledge. It is that now they know that adults know that they know.[34] The "Small Fry" series darkens the activities of young children with the shadow of an adult society seen as knowing, possessive, authoritarian, violent, or oppressive—something that becomes especially marked at the end of the decade and with the advent of war.

Steig's early career at *The New Yorker* is remarkable. By 1930 Ross had assembled a stable of artists—the likes of Peter Arno, Ralph Barton, Al Frueh, Alice Harvey, Helen Hokinson, Rea Irvin, and Barbara Shermund—whose work he could rely on completely. They made *The New Yorker* the upper-class magazine it was. In the thirties a number of new, highly individual artists joined the magazine whose contribution, in retrospect, was important in continuing and extending this tradition—James Thurber, most obviously if eccentrically, but also artists like Charles Addams (also eccentric), the underrated Perry Barlow (one of the drollest of all humorists in *The New Yorker*), Robert Day, Richard Decker, George Price (who gradually drew on his own lower-class origins), Garrett Price, and Gardner Rea, among others. Many of them found it hard to break into the magazine, and their contributions initially appeared at infrequent intervals, as in the case of Addams. What makes Steig different among all these second-generation artists is that Ross clearly felt he did something more than carry the magazine's ethos forward—he added to it, he modified it, he supplied something essential that had been missing. Consequently, Steig is rapidly absorbed into *The New Yorker*. In the thirties his work appears consistently, with more than sixty cartoons in 1932, sometimes two an issue, over forty in 1933 and seventy in 1934, and twenty-four covers in the decade. Steig also changes the form itself. He ambitiously enlarges the single-panel cartoon, modifying it into multiple images, series, sequences, and subgenres; he shifts the cartoon away from the gag and toward acute pictorial social observation; he is drawn to occasions when the national pulse is most strongly felt (Independence Day, Election Day, Thanksgiving), and in his concentration on children he is in touch with both the threatened innocence of the country and its tremulous future. There was an element in Steig's work that vibrated in deepest sympathy with Ross's own respectable, lower-class, provincial origins: a feeling for the way American identity was rooted in ordinary people and in the decencies, the tribulations, the triumphs of the experience of ordinary folk. Steig's genius lay in his receptiveness to that kind of experience.

But having discovered this milieu, Steig did not stay there. Toward the middle thirties the working-class locales and characters that figure in his early drawings start to disappear. His characters edge their way up the social ladder; the settings become more middle class, and the people look settled, prosperous, and complacent. The family shown in "Here's *one* family, Mr. Gillis, that goes right through the winter without catching cold" (fig. 2.6) is typical: looking distinctly middle class, they are robust, self-centered, very pleased with themselves, rather irritating even though still innocent in their enjoyment of a small moment of social assertiveness and neighborhood triumph — a success so inoffensive that even the neighbor is pleased for them. But as this cartoon shows, the rivalry, anger, and conflict that Steig later associated with the competitive market economy of the post-Depression years is starting to emerge.

The typical formula for a Steig cartoon at this time consists of having someone making an inane, but supremely confident, assertion that marks a pointless social victory. Steig rarely demands a big laugh. He is dryly attentive to those moments that betray small but decisive occasions of one-upmanship (boastfulness, self-satisfaction, pleasure, shock, surprise, putting the other person at a disadvantage). The wry accuracy of this kind of observation reminds us how much of ordinary life is transacted in just such terms. When such moments occur, we may feel that they block the flow of everyday social interplay, but we rarely pause to bring such situations into distinct consciousness. Steig's cartoons perform exactly this task. Still a realist at this stage of his career, Steig avoids stylized faces, just as he avoids extreme expressions of emotion or states of mind. Of the four cartoonists discussed in this book, it is the early Steig who prefers a pure, uninflected realism as against the possibilities of conventionalizing. Steig draws people who tend to resemble one another from drawing to drawing, whereas Arno, while drawing obvious social types, also produces a gallery of distinct individuals. The faces of Steig's people are human, very much of "the people," in keeping with the naturalistic ethic of his art, whereas Addams's faces, also of ordinary people, are subtly made monstrous.[35] Steig sides with the democratic commonness of his characters, an attitude Steinberg does not share when he draws his mass Americans a few decades later.

The fate of the original working-class community in Steig's work is summed up by two drawings. One, a cover for *The New Yorker* of August 7, 1937 (fig. 2.7), is a collage based on a road map of the tri-state area (not yet crisscrossed by Robert Moses's network of expressways and parkways), over which is drawn in much larger scale a convertible family coupé heading down into Manhattan and bearing a typical Steig family: a mustached father with astonished eyes; a complacent, portly mother holding an infant; and in the rear two highly self-confident and poised children — far more comfortable in the luxury of car ownership than the parents who actually own it. Ownership of private motorcars was booming in this period, and Steig has identified a crucial moment in the emergence of modern American society. The second drawing dates from the early thirties (December 16, 1933, 18) and is a more complicated and pro-

Fig. 2.6.
William Steig.

The New Yorker,
January 27, 1934, 25.

"Here's <u>one</u> family, Mr. Gillis, that goes right through the winter without catching cold."

A typical Steig lower-middle-class family in full flight. They display an astonishing security of being, as if not the merest shadow of self-doubt had ever fallen across their lives.
Mr. Gillis endures the pointless and irritating boast with an equanimity that rivals, if this is possible, that of the woman making it. Like all Steig's figures of the thirties, they are solid, chunky creatures. They have big shoulders, full, impervious faces bursting with pride and not a little smug, chubby hands that point and gesture or lie folded like well-fed lapdogs ready to perform at their owner's command. The drawing possesses so much in the way of tactile values that you fear you might sink into the page. Steig houses his people in comfortable but claustrophobic rooms, closed off from the outside by dark drapes (though sometimes the apartment opposite is seen at arm's length) and crammed with solid thirties furniture that swallows up the people. Although the mood is generally cele-bratory, there is a sense that things will go wrong with this way of life. It is all so suffocating.

phetic joke. It shows a well-dressed, smug man chatting to some friends and announcing, "I'll admit, under certain circumstances, I could commit murder." It is an unusually dark and ambiguous joke for Steig. Is it about a Prufrock figure, pathetically imagining a major transgression? Or is it about the darker side of even the most ordinary, inoffensive-looking person? Whatever the answer, the drawing is disquieting and points toward the more disturbed drawings of the forties.

Certainly, as the thirties draw to a close things start to come unstuck in Steig's cartoon world—perhaps because the artist's own unprotected receptivity to the stresses of modern life makes him aware of discord and conflict. He publishes far less: a mere six cartoons in 1938 and around ten a year in the following four years. Cheerful and ebullient working-class self-assertion, fundamental to Steig's early cartoons, tends to disappear. His cast of characters is now mainly middle class. The emphasis is on negative emotions, conflict, and, with gathering emphasis, neurosis, as in a sequence like "Holy Wedlock" (begun in 1936 and particularly interesting in the light of Steig's later anatomy of modern marriage). In one drawing, "Indefatigable Wife" (March 21, 1936, 22), a woman is shown dragging a reluctant, top-hatted husband out for a night's merriment; in another, "New Chapeau" (March 7, 1936, 23), a man is shown laughing derisively at his wife as she models a hat for him; in a third, "Joint Bank Account," a husband watches in frustration as his wife tries hope-

---

Fig. 2.7. William Steig. Untitled. [Family in new car drawn in large scale over map of New York, Connecticut, and Massachusetts.]

Cover for *The New Yorker*, August 7, 1937. © *The New Yorker* Collection 1937 William Steig from cartoonbank.com. All rights reserved.

The machine that changed the world changing the Steigian family. This is one of the first examples of *The New Yorker's* using a collage on its cover—there had been two earlier, in 1932. Disregarding scale, Steig lays his gouache of a lower-middle-class family returning from their summer vacation over a map of the tri-state area, as yet unimproved by Robert Moses's network of parkways and freeways. The father seems amazed by the power of the automobile to transform his life and not quite comfortable with owning it. The mother is contained but apprehensive. The children, even the baby, take it in stride. Most cover drawings featuring the automobile had, to date, concentrated on upper-class owners with luxury vehicles. Rea Irvin had even drawn a millionaire in a fantastically streamlined limousine being chauffeured with police escort vertically toward the Pearly Gates. Steig is one of the first to put his finger on the real potential for social change of the mass-produced car, cheaply available to the ordinary family. Ironically, the car would bring about the end of the old Bronx.

The Comic Worlds of Arno, Steig, Addams, and Steinberg

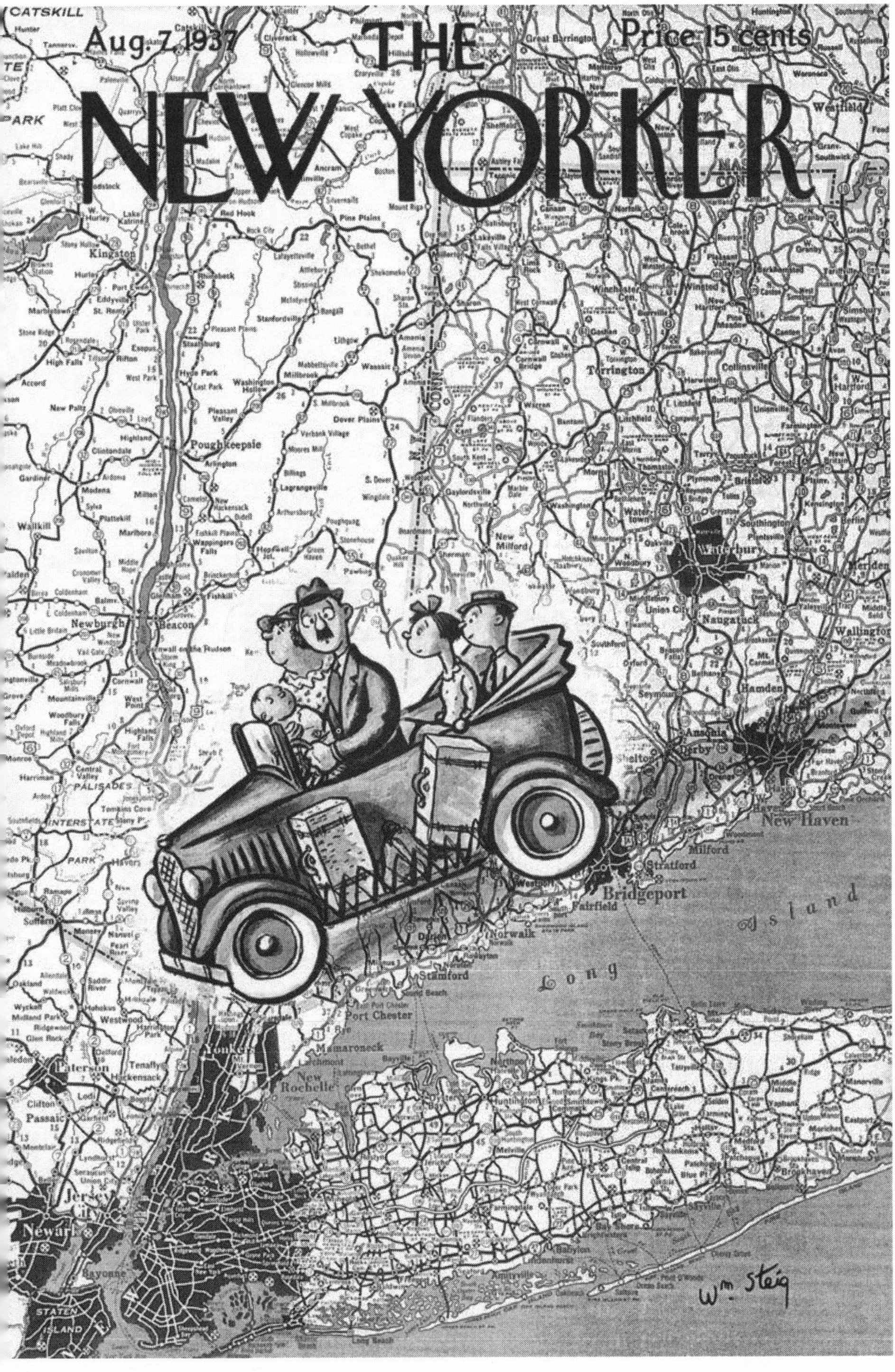
Aug. 7, 1937
THE NEW YORKER
Price 15 cents
CATSKILL
Kingston
Poughkeepsie
Newburgh
Beacon
Torrington
Waterbury
Naugatuck
Hamden
New Haven
Milford
Stratford
Bridgeport
Fairfield
Norwalk
Stamford
Port Chester
Mamaroneck
New Rochelle
Yonkers
Paterson
Passaic
Newark
Long Island
Wm. Steig

lessly to reconcile her checking stubs with his (June 13, 1936, 17). The drawings in this series bring to our attention a small incident in married life onto which a larger incompatibility or conflict has been displaced. Neither the small incident itself nor the underlying conflict can be dealt with directly. Such is the predicament of the husband in "Triangle" (August 22, 1936, 19), which consists of the man, his wife, and their son. Such drawings are observational, not disguised autobiographical confession: Steig had married only in 1936 and did not have children until the early 1940s. They suggest principally the artist's impersonal registering of the social world around him and its characteristic ills and discontents.

In a similar vein are the other series that Steig drew in the years leading up to the Second World War: the six vignettes of "Holiday Trials" (December 26, 1936, 22–23), the seven portraits of oddities in "Strange People" (November 28, 1936, 18–19), and the six case studies in "Woe" (September 26, 1936, 16–17). Such drawings are visual diagnoses of how the individual psyche is wounded —and worse—by the everyday tensions of ordinary life, exemplified by the single-panel drawing of a middle-class husband standing on a chair in his sitting room, declaiming to his alarmed family, "Do you realize who I am? I am Morton P. Ipplehart, the only Morton P. Ipplehart in the entire universe!" (July 9, 1938, 15). The situation of this man verges on the pathological, and the borderline pathological was set to become a leading motif in Steig's work for the next decade.

If, in such drawings, Steig's conviction of the innate goodness of human beings remains, especially as found in the ordinary "little" person, it does so only as a negative charge. Society is increasingly presented as a place of constriction and corruption. Trilling says that Steig's "Small Fry" grow up into the "Lonely People" he drew in the forties. The various series that Steig drew in the late thirties confirm this observation. But the transition is hardly a gradual one. Steig's career was approaching a fork in the road, a split between the more routine (but infrequent) work he drew for *The New Yorker* in the forties and the more savage drawings he published outside the magazine, mainly in books of his own drawings. These collections—*About People* (1939), *The Lonely Ones* (1942), *All Embarrassed* (1944), *Persistent Faces* (1945), *Till Death Do Us Part* (1947), and *The Rejected Lovers* (1951)—are savage and pessimistic. They are quite unlike anything Steig drew earlier, and they are often difficult to interpret. It is not surprising that these drawings by an artist who was in many ways as essential to *The New Yorker* as Arno or Hokinson or Thurber would never appear in the magazine he had helped to build. It would be nearly twenty years before the experimentalism of the early forties found its way into the pages of *The New Yorker* (in, for example, the untitled series published on May 14,

1960, of restaurant-goers). Steig's career in the 1940s eventually runs on two parallel tracks: the drawings he published in *The New Yorker* (far fewer than in the 1930s) and the more personal drawings he published in various collections of his work.

Because the drawings in these collections of the forties never appeared in *The New Yorker,* they represent an interesting limit case for what the magazine was prepared to publish in the 1940s and for the kind of art Steig felt he could offer it at that time. Harold Ross thought the drawings were interesting and that the time might well come when Steig would be hailed as a genius for drawing them, but that they were not right for *The New Yorker.*[36] The drawings are indeed so strange that it is hard to see any sort of continuity between them and those that had made Steig so popular in the thirties. What accounts for this stylistic rupture? An obvious answer is Steig's personal anguish. And yet many drawings of the thirties are about personal unhappiness and frustration, and Steig was well able to cope with those themes without its involving any severe internal modification of his art. A more probable answer is given by Steig's direct acquaintance with two analysts of the plight of the individual in midcentury America, Karen Horney and Wilhelm Reich—although that acquaintance would have meant nothing in either case had not Steig already been receptive to what they had to say. By the end of the thirties Steig certainly felt he had entered the age of anxiety: "I began to feel neurotic when I was grown up," Steig told an interviewer many years later: "I began to feel impure and everyone I knew felt the same way."[37]

William Steig had married Elizabeth Mead, a painter and art teacher, on January 2, 1936. Steig was twenty-eight and by now a well-established cartoonist, and although the marriage lasted until the late forties and ended amicably, it must have had its difficulties. Steig has confessed that when he was introduced to Wilhelm Reich in the mid-1940s he was "just about dead."[38] When Charles Poore interviewed Steig for the *New York Times* in 1947 he evidently suspected that the deeply pessimistic *Till Death Do Us Part* (Steig's visual report card on modern marriage) was based on something more than mere observation and quizzed Steig. But the artist was uncommunicative: "All appearances to the contrary notwithstanding, William Steig thinks marriage as an institution is here to stay. 'I like it,' he says. 'I'm glad to endorse it.'"[39] Yet while it may not be a direct portrait of the Steigs' marriage, the prose appendix to *Till Death Do Us Part,* "Theme for an Animated Cartoon," certainly shows the problems of private life generalized to represent a wider predicament. Husband and wife are at loggerheads even before the story opens. The narrative builds through a series of trivial but heavily freighted quarrels to a "reconciliation" in which the initial problems have merely been buried and the wife, as the persecuted member of the couple, regains the upper hand. The repeated physical metamorphoses of the couple as they act out their petty domestic conflicts symbolize both individual psychological states and the hidden dynamics of the marriage. At one point the husband knocks the wife down. But no sooner has this happened than her neck extends so that she can watch her husband from above, demonstrating how she can turn her misfortune to advantage. (Steig anticipates here the gamelike nature of ritualized family quarrels familiar to us from popular proponents of transactional analysis.) At the climax the husband throws the wife through the apartment window. While he is overcome with remorse, "his wife is returning to the apartment, rising majestically on the elevator like an orchestra about to perform." She appears in the doorway as "the Winged Victory of Samothrace in profile, the door-slammer."

The despair and pessimism manifest in the drawings of this period are due to more than personal unhappiness. They are the consequence of an apprehension of the tragic fate of the individual as worker and consumer in a conformist society. That Steig's work should now emphasize the demands of marriage is no accident. For Steig, as for many radicals of the time, marriage, a pivotal institution of capitalism, is a straitjacket that generates conflict and destroys spontaneity. Equally, that his work should so often lay the blame on the woman rather than the man is not simply personal misogyny. Steig follows common views about marriage and the conservative role of women within marriage, often promulgated by women we would now think of as feminists. Steig had a direct link with one such thinker. Elizabeth Steig's elder sister was the anthropologist Margaret Mead, who was a colleague and close friend of the psychoanalyst Karen Horney. It may well have been through Margaret Mead that Steig became acquainted with Horney's best-selling diagnosis of the plight of the modern individual, *The Neurotic Personality of Our Time,* published in 1937. There is no evidence that Steig read Horney's book, but her views may have been discussed at family and other gatherings and were widely enough known for Steig to have come across them independently. In any event, Steig did have one analytic session with Horney, from which he emerged, according to family tradition, feeling uplifted and liberated.[40] Whether Horney directly influenced Steig is, in the end, unimportant. What is indisputable is that her writings, like Reich's a few years later, supply a vocabulary that helps make sense of some of Steig's most puzzling drawings.[41]

The Neurotic Personality of Our Time was a key work of the Freudian revisionist left. The author had been a socialist before leaving Europe for America, and her book rejects family determinants of character in favor of societal ones. Margaret Mead had no doubt about the importance of Horney's book. On its pub-

The Comic Worlds of Arno, Steig, Addams, and Steinberg

lication she wrote to Horney that its "creative hypothesis" would "inevitably lead to more and better thinking, like a road that leads out from a confined little walled town to an open plain, where there are many possible paths."[42] Horney's "creative hypothesis" is that neurosis is an intensifying (often to the point of disablement) of an ordinary, "well-adjusted" mental state. Neurosis has its roots not in the family history of the psyche but in the psyche's interaction with its environment. The neurotic personality suffers more, suffers more intensely, and pays a higher price for defending itself against anxieties and conflicts typical of a competitive and individualistic society than do more resilient and less vulnerable people. This, indeed, is the situation of many of Steig's characters in his series in the late thirties: the excessively downcast figure suffering from "Rejection" in the series "Woe," for example (September 26, 1936, 17). According to Horney, the anxieties and conflicts that dog the neurotic are what everyone feels to a greater or lesser extent.[43] As a diagnostic category, the neurotic state therefore applies not just to the individual but also to the general fate of the personality in a competitive free-market society.[44] Horney is adamant that there is a special kind of modern neurosis that is specifically a consequence of contemporary social conditions. Because capitalism is based on competition, it makes people stand alone and then pits them against one another in a Darwinian struggle for survival: "The isolated individual has to fight with other individuals of the same group, has to surpass them and, frequently, thrust them aside."[45] From the outset, opposing categories of "success" and "failure" are built into a social system in which "the advantage of the one is frequently the disadvantage of the other." And since failure is much more likely than success, the fear of failure is realistic. (Success is generally more a matter of luck, or sheer unscrupulousness, than of merit.) As a final, bitter twist, the internal logic of a competitive economic system affects both the successes and the failures. If successful, "even the most normal person is constrained to feel he amounts to something." If a failure, he will think himself "worthless." To fail is to suffer material deprivation, which is bad enough. But failure is made worse because according to the puritan work ethic, success is "a visible sign of the grace of God." Failure thus strikes a double blow at the core of a person's self-esteem.

From this general analysis Horney outlines the symptomatology of the modern personality: shaky self-esteem; potential hostile tensions toward other individuals; competitiveness; and to allay the resulting uncertainty, an intensified need for affection (a useful insight even today, given the overvaluation of romantic love in popular culture). The neurotic person displays exactly the same symptoms but in an exaggerated form: crushed self-esteem, destructiveness, anxiety, and enhanced competitiveness, along with an exaggerated need for affection and the peremptory and destructive demand for love.[46] This general state is further complicated by two sets of contradictions also endemic to capitalism—between "competitiveness and brotherly love" on the one hand, and on the other, between the stimulation of needs and the frustration usually experienced in satisfying such needs. In the case of the former the individual must decide either to discard one value or the other (a difficult choice) or to take both seriously and be caught in the clash between them. Horney makes it clear that she regards these alternatives as presenting an impossible decision. In the case of the latter Horney sees that capitalism, with its emphasis on desire, especially for material satisfaction (the lure of advertising, "keeping up with the Joneses," "conspicuous consumption," the equation of happiness with material possessions), presents the individual with "a constant discrepancy between his desires and their fulfilment."[47] As a result, many everyday social interactions bring forth little dramas of ruthless competitiveness (sometimes disguised by politeness) or enact the bitter frustration of powerful material "needs." Even the most trivial of daily contretemps will bear the displaced weight of larger social conflicts, conflicts that are "structural" in the sense that they are entailed by the economic system. It was situations like these that Steig had frequently drawn in his early cartoons.

Horney offers a persuasive general picture of the plight of the individual in midcentury America, and in an intuitive way Steig's early cartoons had foreshadowed much of what Horney said. But Horney's "creative hypothesis" perhaps permitted Steig to venture upon a much more ambitious attempt to pictorialize the range of personality types typical of his era—neurotic and near neurotic. This is the goal he steadily pursued throughout the forties, and it produced an impressive black comedy of hysteria. A key example is the series of drawings collected under the title *The Lonely Ones,* published in 1942.[48] In these drawings Steig significantly extended the range of modern comic art and made powerful—albeit implicit—claims for its essential seriousness. Lee Lorenz goes so far as to claim that "as character studies, they are both wider ranging and more penetrating than anything attempted by Leonardo da Vinci or Hogarth."[49] This is extravagant, but Lorenz is surely right to insist on the importance of Steig's bringing together high art and low art in his new work. In fact the drawing style, while borrowing a little from each of expressionism, primitivism, and Picasso, is sui generis. (Picasso was particularly current in New York in the forties: his first exhibition in Manhattan was held in 1939, and as "Gênet," Janet Flanner had written a profile of him in *The New Yorker* of December 9, 1939. He became a more direct influence on Steig later on.)[50] *The Lonely Ones* rapidly established itself as a classic drama of forties angst, alienation, and hysteria, and for all its difficulty it met with huge popular success:

The Comic Worlds of Arno, Steig, Addams, and Steinberg

the volume went through ten printings in the three years following publication.[51]

A few examples will show how Horney's writings clarify many of the problems that commentators have had with the Steig's new work. Horney had noticed four ways people dealt with anxiety: affection, submissiveness, power, and withdrawal.[52] These aim not at pleasure or happiness but at reassurance— and reassurance becomes the subtext of many modern social transactions, in a world in which inferiority feelings are "the most common evil of our time."[53] There are, says Horney, five typical areas in which modern anxiety manifests itself: these are the need for affection, low evaluation of self, excessive self-assertion, aggression, and sexuality.[54] Steig's drawings pictorialize various combinations of these insights, intertwining them into a set of visual variations on Horneyan themes. Steig's female acrobat, "MY TRUE LOVE WILL COME SOME DAY" (fig. 2.8), shows not merely a familiar compensatory romantic daydream, for instance, but withdrawal (symbolized by her superior height on the rope as well as by a caption, capitalized by Steig himself, that emphasizes her unattainability) along with the desire for affection. The strange, toylike figure stuck on a pole, titled "IT PAYS TO CONFORM" (The Lonely Ones, 34–35), demonstrates both self-assertion (the rigid body and the smug facial expression) and submission to the social order and its values. The kneeling figure in "REVENGE IS SWEET" (44–45), face convulsed in anger, suggests power and aggression but also the luxurious pleasure of rage (he is kneeling on a comfortable cushion or a rich prayer rug). "I WANT YOUR LOVE BUT DON'T DESERVE IT" (82–83) shows desire for affection accompanied by manipulative low self-esteem: the man retains an inane, clownlike expression meant to please, but the body has regressed into an earlier, amphibian form, as shown by the finlike projections on the legs. The burly but narcissistic bodybuilder in "I RECREATED MYSELF" (76–77) depicts the ultimate vanity of self-assertion. Steig's point in all these drawings remains the same: that many common forms of both "strength" and "weakness" are in fact anxious ways of warding off contact with others.

In an uneasy foreword to The Lonely Ones, The New Yorker's Wolcott Gibbs praised the drawings, noting that they abandoned pictorial literalism in favor of "a pure investigation of the spirit." But he also voiced a number of reservations (as he often did where New Yorker artists were concerned): "It would be excessive to say that I'm always precisely sure what was going on in the artist's mind"; the book, is "not for everybody"; many people will find it "obscure and, consequently, exasperating."[55] Seen in the light of Horney's arguments, the drawings are less obscure—though it is true that the displacement of psychic anguish onto the hysteric's body produces a visual language that is sometimes perplexing. But even to the casual observer it is plain that the range of character portraits offers a gallery of modern, neurotic alienation in which portraiture pushes beyond mere representation toward analysis. The mood is somber. There are no genuinely happy or contented people here, only various forms of dis-ease: defensiveness, anguish, acedia, pathos, aggressiveness, and anomie. All are presented alone, recalling, along with the title, Horney's view of the atomistic state of the individual in modern America. The capitalized caption that accompanies each portrait is invariably a phrase that defines the individual life pattern—"I DO NOT GIVE IN TO MYSELF"; "MOTHER LOVED ME BUT SHE DIED"; "I CAN LAUGH AT MYSELF"—indicating the general strategy by which the individual copes with life. Lapidary, concentrated, evocative statements, they remind us of Steig's poetic gifts. Steig is drawing not people but, as he

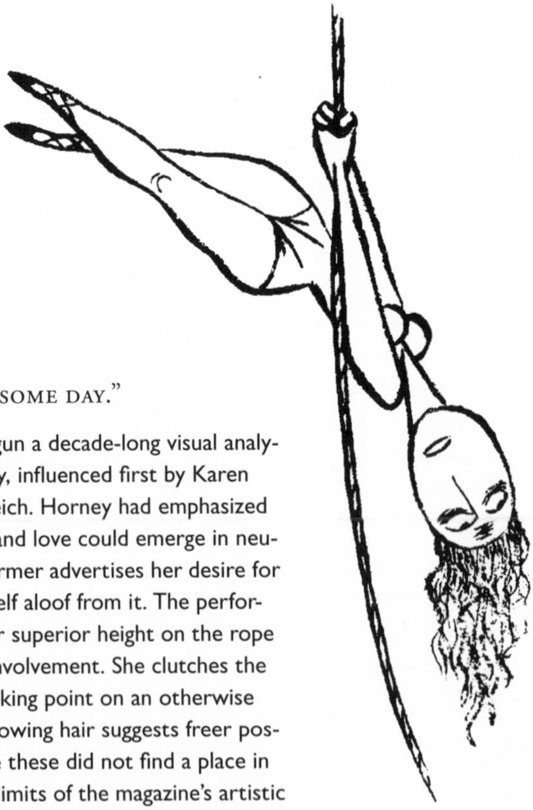

Fig. 2.8. William Steig.

William Steig, *The Lonely Ones* (New York: Duell, Sloan and Pearce, 1942), 28–29. © 1942 William Steig. Reproduced by permission of the Estate of William Steig.

"MY TRUE LOVE WILL COME SOME DAY."

By the late thirties Steig had begun a decade-long visual analysis of neurosis in modern society, influenced first by Karen Horney and then by Wilhelm Reich. Horney had emphasized the way the quest for affection and love could emerge in neurotic forms. Steig's female performer advertises her desire for affection even as she holds herself aloof from it. The performance implies exhibitionism; her superior height on the rope underscores her fear of actual involvement. She clutches the rope tenaciously, her grip a blocking point on an otherwise streamlined composition. Her flowing hair suggests freer possibilities, however. Drawings like these did not find a place in *The New Yorker*, pointing to the limits of the magazine's artistic policy at the time, perhaps, but also marking how far it was prepared to criticize contemporary society.

The Comic Worlds of Arno, Steig, Addams, and Steinberg

himself insisted, states of mind—and these drawings offer something as ambitious as a survey of personality types in midcentury America. W. H. Auden, who was interested in cartooning, was right to take these drawings in "The Icon and the Portrait" (1940), a famous essay, as an indication of a general psychic malaise. But what is pertinent is the sexual element in Steig's work: it could never be said of Steig's figures, as Auden wrote of Thurber's in "New Year Letter" about the same time, that they were "the neuter outline that's the plan / And icon of industrial man." "Industrial man," yes—but not "neuter."[56]

Steig's belief in free love, and his broader sense that bourgeois life was unduly antagonistic to hedonist gratification, was confirmed from mid-1940s onward by the teachings of yet another Freudian revisionist, the charismatic Wilhelm Reich. Steig first met Reich about 1944 and came to know him well.[57] Reich's unconventionality and the rebellious inventiveness of his thought were irresistible to Steig. Drawn to Reich, as were other Jewish intellectuals like Saul Bellow, Paul Goodman, and Norman Mailer, Steig actually became a patient.[58] His analysis, which lasted forty sessions, was "a wonderful experience."[59] He was also a collaborator (illustrating Reich's *Listen, Little Man! What Now?*). When Reich was investigated by the Food and Drug Administration and prosecuted by the FBI in the mid-1950s, Steig joined the committee formed to organize his legal defense.[60] Steig retained warm feelings for Reich—"the most amazing, most insightful, deepest, strongest, most manly, most beautiful human being I ever met."[61] He maintained a sense of outrage at his fate, declaring that "the way he was treated is one of the disgraces of modern times"[62]—a judgment that history has surely vindicated. In his studio in rural Connecticut in the 1990s, Steig still had an orgone accumulator, into which he retreated for recuperation. "It looks like a crock of crap," he told one interviewer, "but it cured my mother of cancer."[63] Steig himself—who was ninety-five when he died and had remained vital, energetic, and productive well into his nineties—was testimony to the benefits of Reich's creed.

Reich's psychology mixes a generous dash of libertarianism into equal parts of Marx and Freud.[64] Rebarbative though this may sound, there was something in it highly attractive to anyone intuitively discontented with marketplace capitalism and competitive individualism, as Steig was in the 1940s. Philip Rieff has noted Reich's importance for those countless modern artists at midcentury who believed they had to live and work in opposition to society or go down in defeat. Reich's gift to such people was a psychoanalytic theory of opposition and revolt.[65] Horney's understanding of the social basis of neuroses certainly anticipated Reich, but Reich's account, as it progressively unfolded, modified itself, and developed in surprising (not to say bizarre) ways through the 1930s, was undoubtedly more exciting than Horney's. It had a speculative depth and reach that Horney's lacked, as can be seen in Reich's notion of "character." There is, he argues, a necessary connection between the typical character structure and the social order of a particular era. Each character type in a given society at a given epoch is to be understood as a "congelation" of the social order—an early form of the Althusserian argument in which individuals become "bearers" of the social structure. Every form of economic and social organization "produces those character types which it needs to exist,"[66] and the character types so produced will perform, among other things, the task of reproducing the social order. Character in all its variety and guises ("character structure") represents nothing other than the social order as required by those in power. Character structure is thus fitted to the economic and productive operations of a particular society—the social order as it has been internalized and stabilized as a psychic structure. According to Reich, this production of character is "a matter [not] of indoctrinating attitudes and opinions, but of a far-reaching process in every new generation of a given society, the purpose of which is to effect a change in and [to] mold psychic structures . . . in conformity with the social order," a social order bent upon its own reproduction.[67] The implication for an artist, in particular a cartoonist given to caricature like Steig, is that character depiction becomes a form of sociological analysis.

For Reich, character structures do not merely mirror the social system, they also have an active role in maintaining it from moment to moment. They reproduce it or "represent its anchoring," in Reich's phrase.[68] The key institution is "the patriarchal family," which, says Reich, "lays in its children the character groundwork for the later influencing by the authoritarian order."[69] For its efficient operation, the social order requires reliable, efficient, docile functionaries. These qualities entail self-discipline, self-control, and above all self-repression, especially the repression of libidinal energy. Horney had made no special claims about the value of libidinal energy (she was suspicious of many of its manifestations), but for Reich the suppression of the sexual drive is the most characteristic feature of capitalist society. Capitalism positively requires sublimation—"the utilization and transformation of the instinctual apparatus"—if its main purpose, the efficient production and distribution of the commodity, is to be performed. Reich argued against the Freudian idea that sublimation deflects instinctual satisfaction toward a higher cultural good, that civilization is built upon instinctual renunciation.[70] For Reich this idea was false and pernicious. The truth was that "releasing sexual tensions liberates energy for higher achievements."[71]

Reich's basic ideas offer little that many other radical programs—pure Marxism, for example—could not also offer. But there was one aspect of

The Comic Worlds of Arno, Steig, Addams, and Steinberg

Reich's teaching that made it particularly attractive to artists, and this was his emphasis on the body. If the characteristic dynamic of a capitalist psychic economy is the transformation of the free, libidinal energy of the psyche into blocked, neurotic forms of character, then the key Reichian claim was that all this was typically expressed in and through the body. Here Reich bypassed the Cartesian dualism still present in a shadowy form in Freudianism and stressed the indivisibility of the embodied self—one of the most original and enduring aspects of his work. Manner, look, way of speaking, countenance, habitual expression, posture, muscular tension, handshake, and dress were to be understood as more than just symptomatic gestures. They were both the person and the illness, and at the same time they were society itself. The manifestation of the psychogenic in the body Reich called "character armoring." Character armor had a double aspect. It was both the bodily stabilization of people's triumph over (more accurately, their defeat of) their instinctual and libidinal drives and their bodily defense against the outside world. Character armor was the permanent record on the body of people's negotiations and compromises with the forces—internal and external—acting upon them. The particular operation of character armoring, the modes of behavior in specific situations (not *whether* one was polite or aggressive, but "*how* one is polite and *how* one is aggressive," and so on),[72] Reich called "character resistance." Reich conceded that some kind of armoring was unavoidable, indeed necessary. But there was a difference between the "reality-oriented character" and the "neurotic character." The "reality-oriented character" can respond positively to "pleasurable situations." Its armor is flexible, and such a character has "the ability to open . . . [itself] to the outside world."[73] The neurotic character, by contrast, is inflexible, literally trapped by the rigidity of its character armoring and closed to pleasurable stimuli.

Reich was convinced that the analyst had to understand his patients by attending not to what they said about themselves, but to what they revealed indirectly in the most ordinary and innocent aspects of their embodied being. As the importance of the embodied nature of psychic life dawned on Reich, he became convinced that therapy itself should be directed to the body. Clinically this led Reich to invent an analytic process that reversed the flow of orthodox Freudian psychoanalysis. Whereas Freud used the analysis of symptoms to work back into the psyche and then to perform his talking cure upon the inner psyche that in due course would result in the relief of any physical symptoms, Reich worked from the outward embodied manifestations of character back into the inner self. He eventually came to believe that analysis could be conducted somatically, by working entirely on physical symptoms.

The last phase in Reich's controversial career opened in 1934 with a notorious lecture on the relation between psyche and soma and a controversial holistic therapy he called "vegetotherapy" (unaware at this stage of its comic implications). The lecture resulted in Reich's expulsion from the International Psychoanalytic Association. The name "vegetotherapy" becomes less strange when we understand that it refers to what was then called the vegetative nervous system but is now known as the autonomic nervous system. Unhappily, the problem was not just with the name. "Vegetotherapy" was founded on certain highly contentious assumptions—not the least of which was Reich's conviction that the unconscious was actually situated in the parasympathetic part of the autonomic nervous system. It was for this reason that Reich believed that "the psychic grows out of the vegetative."[74] In Reich's view it was the positive energies of "vegetative" life, rather than their sublimation in the name of "culture," that truly underpinned human achievements. Reich's notion of bodily therapy was greatly strengthened by the idea of vegetotherapy, for if the psychic truly grew out of the vegetative, then there was theoretical warrant for working exclusively on bodily symptoms.

In 1939 Reich discovered (to use his term) the existence of the orgone—a cosmic particle of libidinal energy, a particle that Reich claimed to have observed and that he believed could be gathered and beneficially transmitted to a suitably receptive patient in an orgone accumulator.[75] This ushered in the era of "orgone biophysics." Physical symptoms revealed their true importance within the framework of orgone biophysics: the body—its characteristic postures and distortions, its muscular seizures and rigidities—became, quite literally, a form of armor. "We discover," wrote Reich, "the armor functioning in the form of chronic, frozen, muscular-like bearing."[76] This "armoring of the periphery of the biophysic system" and, indeed, "every increase of muscular forms and rigidification" is a clear indication that "a vegetative excitation, anxiety, or sexual sensation has been blocked or bound."[77] Part of the object of Reichian therapy was to loosen up the body's armor so that orgone energy could penetrate the chinks between the various armored segments of the body. With the discovery of the orgone, Reich believed that problems of terminology associated with older forms of psychotherapy and psychoanalysis were banished forever: the exact denotative language of the physical sciences would replace the inexact metaphorical language of psychiatry. Reich now decided that a healthy emotional energy could be reactivated by attacking directly a physical muscular armoring that was "identical" to character armoring, thus making the body receptive to the influx of cosmic, orgone energy (an influx assisted by the use of the orgone accumulator).

Finally, Reich turns to the idea that dominates *Listen, Little Man!* the book he commissioned Steig to illustrate: the idea of "the emotional plague." This

The Comic Worlds of Arno, Steig, Addams, and Steinberg

was Reich's summing up the totalitarian features of modern life (fascism being for Reich this tendency carried to its logical extreme). The emotional plague manifested itself in coercive behavior: "The person afflicted with the emotional plague makes his demands of life not only on himself, but, *above all, on his environment*. . . . [He] imposes his mode of life upon others *by force*."[78] The list of such traits (Reich was a past master of the art of the list) is a litany of complaints against the deadening tendencies of modern urban life. "Passive and active thirst for authority; moralism; biopathies of autonomic nervous system; party politicking; familial plague . . . ; sadistic methods of education; masochistic toleration of such methods or criminal rebellion against them; gossip and defamation; authoritarian bureaucracy; imperialistic war ideologies; . . . the American concept of 'racket'; antisocial criminality; pornography; profiteering; racial hatred."[79] This rant has a substantial vein of truth running through it, but it also shows the omnivority of Reich's theories, how paranoia overcame him in his later years, and the imprecision that dominated the thought of a man who believed he had refounded psychotherapy on a scientific footing. Reich, in his rages, is reminiscent of Lear—a great man, a prophetic man, a tormented man, a defeated man. Ironically, he himself was a compulsive, rigid character (at least in his writings—people who were in analysis with him speak of him in extraordinarily positive terms), someone whose own energy seems blocked and bound. Yet the extraordinary influence that Reich exerted over certain sections of the literary and artistic communities of New York in the 1940s is undeniable—and probably not yet fully understood.

Principles akin to Reich's had long been shaping Steig's cartoon world, and the foregoing account is intended for clarification, not to suggest that Steig was necessarily or consciously drawing to Reich's program. Steig had arrived at an intuitive and experiential understanding of the stresses of modern life without the aid of any theory, and these understandings had been articulated by him before his encounter with Reich. Obviously enough, Steig's cartoons had always postulated a world shaped by some of Reich's fundamental principles, among them the idea that the natural human being is "kindly, helpful, giving"; that whatever is living is "naively kindly" and, under prevailing conditions, "endangered." Equally, the seminal Reichian distinction between the "kindly individual" and the "plague individual" had long been there in Steig's work.[80] Steig had always seen people and comprehended their characters as a revelation of a type within an individual. He had had a long-standing general interest in neurotic character as an index of social ills. And he was always determined to forge a drawing style commensurate with such convictions. But all this could only have been strengthened by his encounter with Reich, who ordered and made explicit Steig's more intuitive grasp of such matters. Reich's particular taxonomy of neurosis has a direct bearing on Steig's difficult drawings from the mid-1940s onward. In any case, as with Horney, the important thing is the way Reich's thought helps clarify our understanding of these extraordinary drawings and their importance for us.

At least two of Reich's suppositions have direct relevance for Steig's drawings in the forties. One is that "the living organism functions autonomously, beyond the sphere of language, intellect and volition." Here was the warrant (or at least a justification) not just for Steig's drawings of people as bodily symptoms but, more important, for his abandoning underdrawing in pencil preparatory to inking in a drawing. Lorenz notes that few artists have the confidence to do this,[81] and it is true that a turning point in any artist's career comes when he or she abandons underdrawing. At this point the artist draws into the blankness of the paper, committing to whatever the hand produces, and the line becomes the permanent record of those spontaneous movements of the body.[82] Drawing approaches the dance. The image survives as the trace of purified gesture. This kind of drawing is well described as a "living functioning" of the organism "beyond the sphere of language [and] intellect." Many (if not all) of Steig's psychological drawings in the forties appear to have been done without underdrawing, although it was not until the sixties that, under the influence of his son, Jeremy, he finally gave up underdrawing altogether.[83]

The other supposition is Reich's notion that the unarmored body shapes itself like a crescent—that "the organism unceasingly attempts to bring together the two embryonically important zones, the mouth and the anus"[84] (see fig. 2.9, from Reich's *Character Analysis*). Looking at Reich's sketch of "armored" and "unarmored" organisms, we start to understand the basic grammar of Steig's representation of the body: "hard," rigid, linear "armored" types as opposed to "soft," fluid, crescent-shaped "unarmored" types. Reich thought that muscular armor was arranged in a series of circular segments around the body—the bands of the eyes, mouth, neck, chest, diaphragm, abdomen, and pelvis. Reich's somatic therapy involved freeing up each of these circles, one by one, for "the orgastic pulsation can function only after all the segmented armor rings have been loosened." Steig typically pays particular attention to the manifestation of tension in just these zones. Such gnomic pronouncements offer, if not the key to the mysterious and difficult figures Steig drew in the forties, then at least some help in locating the lock (see figs. 2.13a and 2.13b).

The immediate consequences of Steig's contact with Reich can be examined in the collection of ninety-one portraits published in 1945 as *Persistent Faces*. The word "portraits" must be immediately withdrawn, however. As Steig explained many years later, he has aimed to draw "not actual people" but "charac-

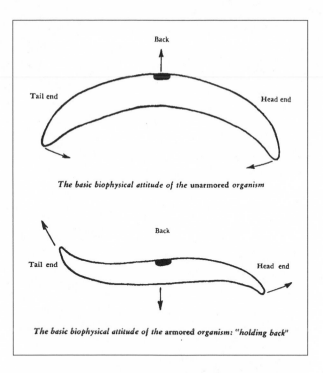

Fig. 2.9. "The basic biophysical attitude of the *unarmored* organism" and "The basic biophysical attitude of the *armored* organism: 'holding back.'"

Wilhelm Reich, showing why Philip Reiff called him an "unconscious cartoonist." The unintentionally comic drawing makes clear the tendency of the body language in many of Steig's drawings from the forties. (See fig. 2.13b.)

ter traits" or "psychological states" that would illustrate "the psychopathology of everyday life."[85] But whatever the artist's intention, the misfits, neurotics, and tormented souls of *Persistent Faces* can be readily interpreted as generalized instances of the individual bearers of capitalism as Reich would see them: the kind of character types society requires in order to function and to perpetuate itself, people who bear in their faces and on their bodies signs of the resultant strain. Thus drawings such as "MASTER" (fig. 2.10), where the obvious tension in the eye, mouth, and neck bands is the sign of self-discipline, and "SHEEP" (fig. 2.11), in whose face these zones are unintegrated and chaotic. Whether one succeeds as "CHAIRMAN OF THE BOARD," or fails as a "FALL GUY," the result is much the same. In these tormented and distorted faces we see either the effort required to make the "free and natural self" conform (Steig's phrase)[86] or the failure to come up to the mark. Here the demands of the social order, positively or negatively expressed in professional, familial, and personal spheres, are all too plain.

William Steig: Art, Armor, and Amour

Fig. 2.10. William Steig.

From William Steig, *Persistent Faces* (New York: Duell, Sloan and Pearce, 1945). © 1945 William Steig. Reproduced by permission of the Estate of William Steig.

"MASTER."

Persistent Faces (1945) is the first collection of drawings to show the influence of Reich, whom Steig met in the mid-1940s, and it concentrates on the character types that capitalism requires, and indeed produces, in order to work efficiently. The book is a comic visual encyclopedia of city faces. In the drawings Steig concentrates on the top three segments of the body, the eye, mouth, and neck zones, those parts of the body in which, so Reich taught, the symptomatic freezing of spontaneity and life was most plainly to be found. "MASTER" shows an unblinking, fixed stare, clamped mouth, and rigid, set neck. The carriage of the head is pushed back, as if retracting from engagement with others, in accordance with Reich's sketch of the "*armored* organism" (see fig. 2.9) in the "holding back" posture.

The types collected in *Persistent Faces* outline a psychological taxonomy of New York City life, ranging from the intellectuals of the Village ("LIBERAL" and "INTELLECTUAL'S GIRL"), to Wall Street ("INVESTOR," "KEEPER OF ACCOUNTS," and "CONFORMIST"), to Madison Avenue ("THE MAN WITH THE BRIEFCASE"), to Audenesque dives off Fifty-seventh Street ("BARFLY"), to the Upper East Side and fashionable Midtown ("HOSTESS" and "PARK AVENUE CAPON"). New categories of behavior are thrown up ("AMBULANCE CHASER," "STUFFED OLIVE," and "COMMERCIAL VISIONARY"). Not a single "affirming" face appears in this universe of damaged souls. Taken together, the portraits exemplify Reich's argument that character types ("hard . . . soft . . . noble . . . base . . . proud . . . servile . . . cold . . . warm . . .") are merely "various forms of an *armoring of the ego* against the demands of the outside world and the repressed

The Comic Worlds of Arno, Steig, Addams, and Steinberg

Fig. 2.11. William Steig.

From William Steig, *Persistent Faces* (New York: Duell, Sloan and Pearce, 1945). © 1945 William Steig. Reproduced by permission of the Estate of William Steig.

"SHEEP."

"SHEEP" is the antithesis of "MASTER." Here the treatment of the "ocular zone" is complicated: it must be looked at sideways in order to see the man's fear and despair. His lips are slack and flabby (compared with the firm, sculpted lines of "MASTER"), suggesting vulnerability. The man's head is nothing but a chaotic, unintegrated trio of body segments. Moreover, the carriage of the head reminds us of Reich's "*unarmored organism.*" But he maintains a rigid neck, part of his necessary self-armoring for the daily battle. "SHEEP" is one of Steig's "little men"—naive, gentle, kindly, but fundamentally oppressed, a victim of Reich's "emotional plague."

instinctual demands of the id."[87] Steig restricts himself to head-and-shoulders portraits: the three topmost segments of the Reichian body armor—the eye, mouth, and neck zones—are the segments in which the "orgone blockage" starts.

Technique in these drawings abandons established standards of caricature. Instead, the drawings show a free-form distortion derived from expressionism and cubism. But the distortion is more than a stylistic quirk. The effort to conform to authority, to command or ingratiate, to attract love or attention, to wield or placate the petty power of office, pushes and molds these faces into strange and disturbing forms. Features collapse along fault lines and reassemble unconvincingly as in "CONFORMIST," where eyes (each on a separate level), nose, mouth, and neck are all misaligned. They distend under pressure

William Steig: Art, Armor, and Amour

("OVERSEER") and swell like hideous balloons. The contours of "ALLEY CAT" and "LIAR" are angular and jagged and repelling. Eyes spin unseeingly in their sockets as in "HOSTESS," start out menacingly ("FAMILY HEAD"), or swim aimlessly around the pool of the face ("SQUAW"). In some cases the attempt to hold the self together fails completely and only a notional identity is achieved: the face of the "STOOL PIGEON" is just a series of intersecting circles and lines, yet the eyes and mouth express great pathos behind the mask. Much of the work is done by the line itself—which has traveled a long way from the confident, solid, substantial line of the 1930s, enamored as it was of the shape and outline of worldly things, intent on describing a world of intact people. In the drawings done outside *The New Yorker* in the 1940s, Steig abandons his earlier "fine draftsmanship." The new line is savage, clumsy, lacking in finesse, even violent. It is a release to draw in this way, like a child with the expressive directness of vision young children possess but lose once they pass age five.[88] To draw like a child is to regain the presocialized innocence of the child's vision.

If, in many drawings done at this time, the line is ugly and negative, this is because even the ugly line has a therapeutic benefit. It unblocks, it lets go, it does not hold back. Steig now draws in a manner freed from the twin constraints of good taste and mimetic realism. So if the drawings *depict* blocked energy, they *imply* released energy—a drawing practice free of that very same pressure to conform, adapt, and maintain discipline that dogs and defeats so many of the types depicted. At some level this can be brought home to Reich with his insistence on freeing up the body: drawing, the permanent trace on blank paper of the body's gestures, is really a way of trusting the embodied language of unconscious gesture over the socialized ratiocinative language of the symbolic order. Steig appears to draw first and title afterward—a procedure that gives priority to the "automatic" insights of the drawing over the programmatic insights of the conscious mind.[89] To this extent, at least, the drawings are a kind of self-analysis in the Reichian mode.

Steig's subsequent volume of collected drawings, *Till Death Do Us Part* (1947), recapitulates the themes of the earlier works. It stresses the way society promotes an excessive, "neurotic" need for love; it further insists that marriage, with its suppression of free libidinal energy, is an institution with the definite social function of anchoring character and securing its role within the social order. (The title draws attention to the way the marriage service discordantly but pertinently links Eros and Thanatos.) Once again it seems as if the drawings come first, the categorization after—an impression confirmed by the way the drawings are printed in only the loosest narrative sequence. The series begins with the title drawing, "TILL DEATH DO US PART," but after the first dozen or so vignettes any pretense at linkage is abandoned and the sequence of drawings becomes more random: the book ends with "OLIVIA STILL HAS MYSTERY FOR ME" rather than the more obvious "WHOM GOD HATH JOINED LET NO MAN PUT ASUNDER."

In these drawings attention is called to the whole body rather than the face and to the couple rather than to the atomized individual (the collection is subtitled *Some Ballet Notes on Marriage*). Pose, posture, body shape, the gestalt of the couple now become the vehicles of meaning. In the first drawing, "TILL DEATH DO US PART," the married couple march purposefully into the future: the militaristic image recalls not just Horney's emphasis on the competitive nature of marriage (here the struggle for dominance has been won by the wife, and the husband "marches" only by standing on her feet, propelled from behind by her greater force, his purposefulness nothing more than an illusion) but also Reich's notion of emotional fascism. The two torsos mirror exactly Reich's drawing of the armored body: the heads erect and pushing up and backward, the stomachs drawn in and the bottoms pushed out. Other drawings offer variations on the internal dynamics of apparently successful couples. In "OUR MARRIAGE WILL BE DIFFERENT," where husband and wife are shown capering on a stage, the apparent "harmony" is merely an act, an inane vaudeville turn put on for public show. In "WE'VE GOT TO MAKE A GO OF IT," husband and wife are shown facing one another other but also holding back, and the upright carriage of the two bodies, the husband's pointing finger, and the muscular strain about the neck and shoulders in both figures signal the discipline required to will compatibility.

In choosing marriage as his theme Steig was taking up something Reich saw as the pivotal institution of capitalism—the patriarchal family was "the first and most important organ for the reproduction of the social order," Reich endlessly insisted.[90] In Steig's hands the implications of such raw pronouncements are subtle and intriguing even though he preserves the essentials of the Reichian critique. A drawing like "I'M THE LUCKIEST MAN IN THE WORLD" (fig. 2.12), which shows a proud, upright male gazing with admiration at a lissome, floating female, is anything but simple, for instance. Both figures wear happy expressions. And yet something does not seem quite right. The woman hardly suggests excessive binding of energy, since her body is free and supple. But for Reich such flexibility was ambiguous, implying both "the ability to open oneself to the outside world" and a tendency "to close oneself, depending on the situation." The woman, floating or leaping so high above the ground, is too weightless. On a second glance her unseeing eyes are narcissistic, her face characterless and emptily pretty. There are hints of coquettishness. (Reich identified a hysteric type characterized by undisguised sexual coquetry and excessive softness, leading to suggestibility and fickleness.)[91] For the man's part, the upper Reichian zones are locked, his torso is too rigid (hands protecting his genitals), and his leg muscles are tensed. He displays aspects of the phallic narcissistic character—self-assured, elastic, sometimes arrogant, a leader, tending to attitudes toward the beloved infused with sadism. As his look of self-satisfaction implies, the woman has become a spectacle for him. This sort of relationship is redrawn in a more advanced and exaggerated form in "MEET THE WIFE." Here both the wife's hysterical character and the husband's phallic narcissism are more pronounced. The volume abounds in instances of "hard" male and "soft" female pairings, but contrary examples are also given. In "I LET HIM DO JUST AS HE PLEASES," the woman is composed, ordered (she is shown arranging flowers in a vase), with a disciplined body, while the man is a regressive, oversupple hysteric (slightly off balance, idiotic masklike face, hat awry). Even when a couple seems to have reached some sort of equality, as in "RECONCILIATION," where the body language is relaxed and the couple are mirror images of each other, gesture balanced by gesture, there is something that compromises the image of stability. The eyes in this drawing, intent on the footsteps (the bound ocular zone), betray the effort of will required to maintain the pose. One drawing, "HE KEEPS ME IN STITCHES ALL DAY" (fig. 2.13b), is a remarkable example of how far Steig was prepared, on occasion, to follow Reich. As we can see when we compare Steig's drawing with Reich's sketch, the male adopts the classic defensive position (the "holding back" of the armored organism), suggesting how his supposedly amusing and spontaneous behavior is in fact calculated and even manipulative, while the woman, genuinely and innocently receptive, spontaneously adopts the unarmored posture.

Persistent Faces and *Till Death Do Us Part* are impressive collections, groundbreaking as examples of occasional comic art and interesting as examples of the gradual fusing of high and low art that will eventually define postmodern aesthetics in twentieth-century culture. Yet even the strongest admirer of Steig's work in the forties would have to confess than his drawings from this period make for depressing and difficult viewing. This must not be taken as an irrelevant demand for comedy in a situation in which comedy is impossible. Humor in Steig is often rather dry, reduced to a bare minimum. In *Till Death Do Us Part,* for example, the humor lies in something as elusive as the friction between caption and image, where the clichés of married life (going about their appointed task of blunting an awareness of misery and thwarted potential and of suppressing personal revolt) are exposed in all their fatuity by being brought into conjunction with a drawing that wonderfully exceeds the readymade wisdom of the hand-me-down phrase. (To say this is not to minimize Steig's extraordinary sensitivity—the sensitivity of a poet—to just those banal, seemingly empty phrases that in their very insignificance are full of content.)

Fig. 2.12. William Steig.

From William Steig,
*Till Death Do Us Part:
Some Ballet Notes on
Marriage* (New York:
Duell, Sloan and Pearce,
1947). © 1947 William
Steig. Reproduced by
permission of the Estate
of William Steig.

"I'M THE LUCKIEST MAN IN THE WORLD."

In *Till Death Do Us Part* (1947), Steig considers the institution of marriage, for Reich the pivotal institution of fascism-capitalism, the enemy of libidinous freedom and spontaneity (code for free love). The book is a collection of penetrating, mordant images of some familiar marital performances. Here a proud, upright, but armored man (look at his neat but overassertive bow tie) gazes with admiration at his lissome, weightless, unarmored wife. Both figures wear happy expressions, but something about the couple doesn't seem right. His expression is too goofy. Her expression is too vacant. What we witness is probably the simulation of harmony and felicity. The caption, spoken by the man, is certainly self-deluding (a woman as light as she is might well just blow away) and even controlling (designed to obligate the woman to him).

But for all that, in these books Steig appears defeated by his own pessimism about ordinary life under capitalism. As Diana Trilling said in her review of *The Lonely Ones,* Steig is himself the loneliest of all: "Unlike an artist like Daumier, who knew all the things Mr. Steig knows, the author of *The Lonely Ones* lacks the compassion that would spare him so much cruelty of insight."[92]

The reduction of the comic element to a bare minimum is matched in the other major arena for Steig's work, *The New Yorker.* During the 1940s he contributed far less to the magazine than in the thirties. In 1940 he published only five cartoons and four feature pages. This rose to nine (and another three feature pages) in 1941, then fell to a mere seven in 1942. After a return to more respectable figures (eleven and fifteen) in the following two years, when the "Dreams of Glory" series commenced, Steig's contributions tailed off completely: he published only one cartoon in 1945, one in 1946, and none at all in 1947. Thereafter the figures slowly start to mount again: eleven in 1948 (with one feature page) and twenty-five in 1949. All in all, Steig had an average publishing strike rate of 23 percent (including feature pages, but not covers) in the forties, a quarter of the rate for the thirties. Over the same period Steig published only four cover illustrations (compared with twenty-four in the thirties). No doubt there are many reasons for this, including that Steig was now the father of two small children within a marriage that was steadily falling apart, but among them must be that he was enduring some kind of personal crisis throughout the historically traumatic war decade, a crisis that steered him away from humor and *The New Yorker* and toward grim psychological satire and alternative publishing venues. Certainly the two middecade cartoons—one showing a man sleepwalking into a bar (April 6, 1946, 23), the other a man saying "Swell" to a barber holding up a mirror to show him his new short back and sides (December 18, 1945, 37)—are not among his most memorable.[93] The humor of the kind Steig had specialized in at the start of his career, the kind of sly observation that provokes laughter, perhaps required a poise, distance, and self-possession—in a word, equilibrium—that Steig found hard to achieve in the forties.

Steig's cover for the pre-Christmas edition of *The New Yorker,* December 16, 1950, hints at a welcome recovery of the lost equilibrium of the thirties, the return of an artist entirely at peace with himself. It shows a host of children as Christmas angels, and the irony (all children are angels close to Christmas, but only then) is balanced by the obvious pleasure the drawing gives in its image of seasonal joy. And there is a change, too, in the last collection of overtly psychological drawings, *The Rejected Lovers* (1951). If the book is a recapitulation of the Horneyan and Reichian themes of the previous decade, it is also a valediction to them. It is far more approachable than any of the previ-

The Comic Worlds of Arno, Steig, Addams, and Steinberg

Fig. 2.13a. "The basic biophysical attitude of the *unarmored* organism" and "The basic biophysical attitude of the *armored* organism: "holding back."

Illustration from *Character Analysis* by Wilhelm Reich, translated by Vincent R. Carfagno (New York: Farrar, Straus and Giroux, 1972), 364. © 1945, 1949, 1972 by the Wilhelm Reich Infant Trust. Reprinted and cropped by permission of Farrar, Straus and Giroux, LLC.

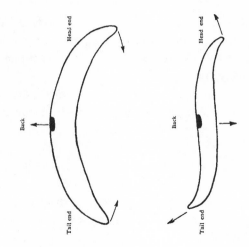

Fig. 2.13b. William Steig.

From William Steig, *Till Death Do Us Part: Some Ballet Notes on Marriage* (New York: Duell, Sloan and Pearce, 1947). © 1947 William Steig. Reproduced by permission of the Estate of William Steig.

"HE KEEPS ME IN STITCHES ALL DAY."

There are suggestive similarities between Reich's view of the symptomatology of posture and bearing (2.13a) and Steig's treatment of body language (2.13b). In the drawing below the man adopts the classic defensive position (the "holding back" of the "armored" organism), suggesting that his apparently amused and appreciative behavior is calculated and even manipulative. The woman, genuinely receptive and spontaneous, adopts the "unarmored" posture. Both figures are lovestruck. Once again Steig has his eye on the way a married couple often performs, codependently, as a double act. Such a parallel may not represent a conscious intention, but that Steig was unconsciously influenced by Reich during this phase of his career can hardly be doubted.

ous volumes (leaving aside the collections of "Small Fry" drawings also published in the 1940s) and, since the wartime restrictions on book production were now relaxed, a much handsomer volume in a generous octavo format, printed on a luxurious uncut cream stock, with careful layout and typesetting.[94] The book seems loosely organized, but the text is closely worked: the triadic arrangement on each double-page spread of quotation on the left-hand page and epigrammatic title and image on the right is full of interest. There is a welcome reappearance of a warm comedy as in "WAIT TILL SHE SEES ME WITH THOSE OTHER GIRLS" (73), which shows a perky Steig man dressed in medieval costume complacently looking at himself in a cheval mirror. And in focusing entirely on the character of the male rejected lover, the work possesses an essential unity. The figure of the rejected lover recalls Horney, as Steig hints: "The behavior of the typical jilted lover is one symptom of a general world-craziness that has prevailed for a long time. . . . Here we see a man shaken out of what proves to have been a phony composure and in full possession of a neurosis that, always there, is suddenly made manifest."[95] If Horney had long ago alerted Steig that the cry for love was merely a defense against a hostile social climate, Steig now only required Reich to point out the most obvious instance of that mechanism. Mentioning his gratitude to Reich, Steig adds: "I am indebted [to him] for much of my insight into the sickness described in the following pages, as well as for the phrase 'Mama, mama!' which I heard him use in characterizing infantile attitudes of 'love.'"[96] There are no fewer that ten drawings (out of a total of seventy-six) in which this plaintive cry is used, including the final image.[97]

The Rejected Lovers presents a variety of typical reactions to rejection and in doing so builds up a compelling picture of the insecure male ego in the decade before women's liberation and feminism, a period in which men are supposed to have enjoyed their patriarchal entitlements to the full. The reactions run the Reichian gamut from the masochistic to the hysterical to phallic narcissism. But the drawings hardly require any scaffolding, courtesy of either Horney or Reich. There is a genuine playfulness and wit at work here—and even warmth—and the inventiveness and play of insight is striking. "LOOK WHAT I'VE BROUGHT YOU, DARLING," in which the "gift" is the man himself, served up in a gesture of self-abasement, is typical (fig. 2.14). The real meaning of gift giving (which sociologists tell us is a way of controlling someone) is adroitly exposed in a drawing of remarkable lucidity. The memorable image directs a searching light back onto the anonymous poem chosen as the epigraph: "See, my own sweet jewel, / What I have for my darling: / A robin red breast and a starling. / These I give both, in hope to move thee /—Yet thou say'st I do not love thee!" In his foreword Steig apologizes for the stylistic unevenness of the collection.

The Comic Worlds of Arno, Steig, Addams, and Steinberg

Fig. 2.14. William Steig.   "LOOK WHAT I'VE BROUGHT YOU, DARLING."

From William Steig, *The Rejected Lovers* (1951) is the last of Steig's explicitly
The Rejected Lovers psychological collections. It is far less programmatic than the
(New York: Alfred A. previous volumes (one of the ironies of being a follower of
Knopf, 1951), 20–21. Reich was that in some people it induced a rigidity of intellec-
© 1951 William Steig. tual bearing). In this collection we see the return of a genuine
Reproduced by permis- pictorial wit, as in this drawing of a man making a present of
sion of the Estate of himself. After inspecting it no lover can, perhaps, remain en-
William Steig. tirely innocent about his (or her) acts of generosity. (All gift
giving, sociologists tell us, is a form of control.) The trouble is
that the cold, suspicious, consciousness-raised gaze, whether
sociological or psychoanalytic, can easily become the enemy
of spontaneous feeling and behavior, as Steig well understood.
His answer in the coming decades was to return to children
and childhood themes—as seen in his *New Yorker* covers of
the fifties—and, more generally, to produce drawings that
gave simple pleasure.

He is right to do so, since some drawings appear to date from the mid-1940s
when Steig was savagely distorting and dismembering his images.[98] But we see
also signs of the artist's reintegration of his draftsmanship, a foreshadowing
of the more pleasure-giving aesthetic of the fifties and beyond, as in drawings
like "WHAT MAKES HER THINK SHE CAN REPLACE ME SO EASILY?" (89), with
its decidedly cheeky, not say demonic faun, or "AH, HOW SHE USED TO LOVE
ME!" (127) where the "she" is luscious, full-bosomed, and oversized compared

with the tiny swooning male she has swept up in her arms, or "WHO THE HELL DOES HE THINK HE IS?" (129), in which an angry Steig little man clutching a rapier apprehensively views his rival, a tall, handsome, club-wielding Greek god in neck-to-knee bathing costume. There is finally one very significant drawing—the single truly optimistic and positive drawing in all Steig's collections on modern neurosis—and this is the penultimate drawing titled "WE COULD HAVE BEEN SO HAPPY TOGETHER" (151). It shows a composite figure made from the upper torsos of a man and a woman in the sky above the sea. The drawing can be linked either to the epigraph on the left-hand page or to the caption beneath it. The caption ("WE COULD HAVE BEEN SO HAPPY TOGETHER") voices the rejected lover's yearning, but it is a legitimate yearning, the voice of real (not neurotic) loss, a yearning for the transcendence of real love, about which W. H. Auden had, a decade before, noted that Steig was too pessimistic.[99] For what the drawing pictures, with its childlike image of the two lovers, blissful but calm, joined at the waist and spinning in a star-studded sky above a heaving ocean, is the union of real lovers, the union celebrated in Kari Homestead's poem used as the epigraph ("Let our fire / join together / and burst into / an orange sun / melting / let us become one"). It comes as no surprise to learn that William Steig was now married to Kari Homestead.

"Man dreams, stirred by dark 'oceanic' feelings, instead of mastering his existence, and he is destroyed in dreams." So wrote Wilhelm Reich in the later editions of *Character Analysis*.[100] Reich's negative view of daydreaming as an uncreative escape from real relations with external objects foreshadows the more sustained attack on daydreaming conducted by many psychoanalysts a decade or so later.[101] Nonetheless, there is a productive link between daydreams and other forms of visionary transcendence—including art. (In the context of *The New Yorker,* the classic example of the uncertain border between destructive daydream and sanative fantasy is James Thurber's Walter Mitty.) At the other end of daydreaming lies a romanticism that places its faith in the dream and the imagination. The implication here is that art, unlike the daydream, is more than a substitute or compensation: art offers a "world elsewhere," beyond the deadening routines of everyday life, a world of feeling and understanding that strengthens the ego, restores a sense of mastery, and makes life endurable and enjoyable. (The special promise of humor is that it effects a reconciliation of two contradictory principles in the Freudian metapsychology—the pleasure principle and the reality principle—and does so with particular intensity and efficacy.)

These matters are crucial to any understanding of the later Steig. There is no doubt that he had once been in complete agreement with Reich as to the

The Comic Worlds of Arno, Steig, Addams, and Steinberg

deceptiveness of the oceanic feeling and the unreality of the dream. The man with a blissful smile on his face, hurtling through the air toward the earth, captioned "I AM AT ONE WITH THE UNIVERSE" (*The Lonely Ones*, 18) pictorializes Reich's insight: it shows a man happy but fatally deluded (he is not flying but plunging toward the earth and certain destruction). But "WE COULD HAVE BEEN SO HAPPY TOGETHER" challenges Reich's confident assertion with an ambiguous reprise of the same motifs of sea and flight. Although it does not directly affirm the possibility of transcendence (the caption strikes a discordant note), both the drawing and the epigraph celebrate romantic *ecstasis*. Steig is perhaps repositioning himself here vis-à-vis Reich's skepticism. The oceanic feeling, all mystical notions of transcendence, may well invite suspicion—but Steig now seems hesitant about the value of suspicion itself. The particular dream in question, however, is not so much the oceanic feeling of religious at-oneness with the universe as the Apollonian dream of art, and it is in the transcendental capacities of the artist that Steig finally reposes his trust. Hence the new sources of inspiration in Steig's later career—myth, literature, and memory. But those interests in themselves signal a turning away from the more engaged, implicitly political, work of the forties.

In the history of cartooning and comic drawing few things are as remarkable as the efflorescence of William Steig's art, which, beginning at the end of 1950s, blossomed and bloomed into his old age. Steig turned fifty-two in November 1959, at the end of the "tranquilized fifties." He had behind him a career of nearly thirty years as a published artist. At this age many artists—commercial, comic artists especially—are repeating themselves. But for Steig over forty years of extraordinary creativity lay ahead, and for the commentator even the simple task of outlining the third phase of his career is a daunting one. Throughout the 1950s Steig seems to have grown more and more impatient with the narrowness of much comic art, and he was obviously wondering what new direction his own work might take. *The New Yorker* cartoons of the period—whether of children ("Andante! Andante!" [January 31, 1953, 55]), adolescents (the two teenagers sitting at opposite ends of a sofa practicing their newly acquired, unidiomatic French, "Je vous aime. Je vous adore" [December 19, 1964, 33]), or adults (the self-satisfied husband tilting his chair back, arms and legs crossed, interrogating his crabby-looking wife, "And why *don't* you love me, if I might ask?" [May 30, 1953, 25])—do not lack freshness, charm, or dry humor. The problem is that in many ways Steig is repeating himself, and he has not yet found a way to incorporate into his art the possibilities opened up by the experimental drawings of the 1940s.

There was, as it happened, a sharp spur toward experimentation in the pages of *The New Yorker* and an object lesson in what could be done with comic drawings. Saul Steinberg had been publishing cartoons and spot drawings since the early 1940s, and from the start it was obvious that his work was that of a highly original master draftsman. But from the mid-1950s Steinberg (seven years Steig's junior) began a dizzying and ambitious expansion of the possibilities of pictorial wit in drawings of astonishing virtuosity, daring, and intelligence, such as his drawings of the sounds made by musical instruments (February 12, 1955, 32–33); his visual essays on his travels in the Soviet Union (May 12, 1956, 45–48, and June 9, 1956, 30–31); his riddling rebuses (August 20, 1960, 28–31); or the cover of March 20, 1954. This last example takes a subject that Steig might well have relished—a smug middle-class man showing off his three children. But it transforms it into something pictorially and intellectually challenging, where the games played with representation intensify the interest of the literal content of the image: the "family members" are actually cats; the "drawing" is really a drawing not of the group but of an old-fashioned family photograph of the group; and while the figures are rendered in a simple line, the flowers in the vase on the flower stand to the right of the group are a pasted-in clipping of a photograph of daisies and roses and hence seem far more "real" than the figures themselves. Steinberg's example could hardly have been lost on Steig.

Brendan Gill noted the rivalry between the two in *Here at "The New Yorker."*

> If one were to ask Steinberg which of the artists on the magazine, himself excepted, was the greatest, I suspect he would answer, "Steig." And if one were to put the same question, with the same exception, to Steig, I suspect he would answer, "Steinberg." They are certainly the two who have gone the furthest in producing works of art that are not jokes. . . . They have escaped the bounds of weekly topical journalism, and in doing so they invite being judged by standards of criticism not usually associated with popular magazines. The fact is that by now they are not so much *New Yorker* artists as artists whose work happens to appear . . . in *The New Yorker*.[102]

But Steinberg's art is an intellectual one (not for nothing did he call his drawing a "way of reasoning about the world"), and while he might provide a general example for Steig, there was little concrete that Steig could learn from Steinberg's highly idiosyncratic manner. Steinberg, drawing as an unashamed intellectual, pushed a popular art form upward toward high art. Steinberg, moreover, as we shall see, drew America from the perspective of an immigrant and a new arrival. It was important for Steig to stay in touch with the immediacy of his experience as a populist and an American.

In one respect Steig was very fortunate at this time. His work was very strongly championed by the new editor of *The New Yorker*, William Shawn, who assumed office after the death of Harold Ross in December 1951. Steig, Lillian Ross tells us, was one of the artists whose work Shawn particularly appreciated.[103] The implications of Shawn's enthusiasm are made clear by a cover count. During Ross's tenure the magazine published twenty-nine Steig covers in twenty years; under Shawn it published seventy-nine Steig covers in thirty-five years. An average of two and a quarter covers a year as opposed to fewer than one and a half is a significant difference, but the raw figures do not tell the whole story. Under Shawn's editorship Steig was a favorite cover artist for the principal seasonal events on the calendar—New Year's Day, Valentine's Day, the Fourth of July, Halloween, and above all Christmas.[104] Steig drew twenty-nine such seasonal covers, many more than the next most published artists for these occasions, Abe Birnbaum and "cem" (Charles E. Martin), who provided seventeen each. From the time of his first appearance in *The New Yorker* Steig contributed fifteen Christmas covers, almost one every two years, up to 1987 when the magazine's new owner, S. I. Newhouse Jr., removed Shawn as editor. The turning point in Steig's late career comes in the last months of 1959; from about that time Steig usually signs himself not "Wm. Steig" or "W. Steig," but "Steig," as if to mark the change of direction and a modified artistic persona. It is more than fortuitous that the three decisive works should all involve, in different ways, a dominant motif of Steig's work, that of childhood. The works in question are the four-page sequence titled "À la Recherche du Temps Perdu," published in the issue of September 26, 1959; the Halloween cover for October 31, 1959; and the Christmas cover for December 26, 1959.[105]

Steig's previous covers for Shawn, going back to 1952, had all featured his "Small Fry" characters (as did the majority of his covers). The style was, in general, consistent with the one that had evolved for these characters over the previous two decades: solid, molded faces and bodies, with the characteristically pert nose, pugnacious mouth, and popping eyes, usually set against a realistic background. Throughout the fifties Steig had played with this formula. For the issue of May 9, 1953, which shows a child holding a paintbrush and leaning against a tree, Steig superimposes his carefully drafted figure on a background that mimics a child's way of painting. For the Independence Day issue of July 2, 1955, Steig removes the background completely and sets his three patriotic boys on a dazzling white ground. The boy and toboggan featured on the January 7, 1956, cover already hint at the stylized simplification that was to become the hallmark of Steig's later style. What links these drawings, and links them with the Steig of the thirties and the forties, is the studied manner of drawing and painting, in which figures are carefully built up on an underdrawing, in a realist mode, and aim at an effect of tactile three-dimensionality. When Steig comes to draw a Halloween cover in this mode, he produces images like his cover for November 1, 1958, in which four naturalistically drawn children in Halloween makeup and costumes are shown ringing an apartment doorbell.

Compared with this, the Halloween cover for the following year, October 31, 1959, marks a dramatic departure in style. Here, in a vivacious freehand scribble, highly conventionalized Halloween figures spring out from behind a tree, with a sinister carved pumpkin shell in the foreground and a huge yellow moon looming in the sky beyond. Everything is flattened out along the picture plane, the effect of pictorial depth is minimal, and the image conveys the impression of immediacy and rapid execution. (Even Steig's previous cover, June 6, 1959, although simplified compared with earlier covers, aimed at a realistic impression of spatial depth.) The next cover, for the issue of December 26, 1959, showing Santa Claus on a rooftop, takes this much further (fig. 2.15). Here, once more, everything is laid out along the picture plane, and suggestions of depth are completely banished. The image has been quickly outlined, probably with a bamboo pen, and evidently without underdrawing; the palette is simplified (red and pink); and the figures, Santa Claus himself and the rooster atop a turret, all invoke the *art naïf* style. Here too is the emergence of the decorative impulse, an interest in pattern and texture, and a focus on the picture plane itself and on the possibilities of the medium, all of which were to become so important in Steig's later work.

But it was with the earlier four-page visual memoir "À la Recherche du Temps Perdu" that Steig had most clearly struck out in a new direction. Seen in collections,[106] the drawings lose much of the impact they have in the pages

---

Fig. 2.15. William Steig. Untitled. [Santa Claus on the roof.]

Cover illustration, *The New Yorker*, December 26, 1959. © *The New Yorker* Collection 1959 William Steig from cartoonbank.com. All rights reserved.

By the end of the fifties the emphasis in Steig's work had shifted from sociopsychology to aesthetics, as exemplified in this glowing, decorative, *art naïf* cover from the end of the decade. It is as if Steig is conceding that the real function of the artist is to give unalloyed pleasure by making beautiful works of art, period. To some extent this is a repudiation of Reich, although the underlying stress on the pleasure principle can be seen as a purer way of carrying forward the Reichian gospel. Here Steig aims at a child's spontaneity of representation, delighting in color and ornament and surrendering entirely the ambition to conquer pictorial space. Everything is laid out flat along the picture plane; there is (one surmises) no underdrawing, so the cock and Santa Claus and the turreted building are freely depicted in bamboo pen outline, and the colors are vivid and simply applied.

The Comic Worlds of Arno, Steig, Addams, and Steinberg

Dec. 26, 1959

THE NEW YORKER

Price 25 cents

of the magazine (September 26, 1959, 42–45) where, set against more conventional one-liner cartoon gags, their novelty, boldness, and freedom are exhilarating. The drawings may well have an autobiographical origin (but this should not be pushed too far — the family has four children, but one of them is a girl); certainly here is a picture of a lower-middle-class childhood just before and during the First World War, drawn in a style that recalls that of a six- or seven-year-old child. The thirteen drawings mix public and private spheres: the sequence opens and closes with placing references to the broad historical stage — the Spanish influenza epidemic and end of the Great War, October to November 1918, events immediately followed by Steig's own eleventh birthday. Interspersed are events that are important only in the context of the subjective drama of family remembrance — "Papa said that Mr. Hoffman was a genius" (Papa is stumped by a move on the chessboard), "Some European friends came to visit" (strange, flamboyant, overdressed apparitions); "Mama was very sorry for poor Mrs. Harris" (Mr. Harris lies drunk and happy under a lamppost); and so on. The central drama in the drawings, suggested in an oblique, elliptical way, is family tension. In the poignant "Sometimes Mama cried for days" we have the child's image of the mother's chronic depression; in "Mama and Papa never quarreled in front of the children" an angry scene is played out in the next room while two children clutch each other fearfully in the foreground. Beyond this there is nothing to enlighten the viewer about cause, context, or consequence. Here, then, is a pictorial version of Proustian involuntary memory: deliverance from time's unrelenting propulsion of the self into the future by remembrance and art. The drawings turn a Reichian principle (the unblocking of the body via the uninhibited gestures stabilized in the drawn line) against a Reichian credo (the futility of daydream) by celebrating and actualizing the time-transcending power of art.

Looking back over the twenty years between "À la Recherche du Temps Perdu" and Steig's psychological drawings of 1941 in *The Lonely Ones,* one is struck by how slowly, in those days, aesthetic experimentation moved from the margin into the mainstream. In only one cartoon published in the magazine over those eighteen years is there any sign that Steig had once been a very different artist outside the pages of *The New Yorker,* and this is a cartoon published in the issue for January 2, 1954 (57). It shows a dance in full swing; a man is sitting on the sidelines without a partner, his body ramrod straight, but with an agonized, distorted, decapitated head perched on his knees, in the style of his forties psychological drawings.

"À la Recherche du Temps Perdu" was the first of a series of similar visual story fragments that took inspiration from myth, legend, and story. Others included "Greek Mythology" (November 14, 1964, 54–57) and the groundbreaking "Scenes from 'The Thousand and One Nights'" (February 20, 1989, 34–37). "Scenes from 'The Thousand and One Nights'" was printed in color in the anniversary issue, the first time this had happened in *The New Yorker* since a few tentative early experiments, as one of Robert Gottlieb's modest innovations after he became editor in 1987.[107] In work like this Steig dramatically expanded the possible field of reference for comic art. His art takes a new form: although he continues to draw standard cartoons in his old style, for his more ambitious ideas he abandons the controlled line that he forged in the 1930s in favor of a much freer, more active, energetic, and exploratory line, and he becomes far more adventurous and bold in his choice of subject matter. A notable instance is the sequence of nine untitled drawings in the issue of May 14, 1960 (38–39), of types in restaurants—among them "Captain," "Righteous tipper," and "Matinée-goers"—all done in the free, spontaneous style first developed by the artist in the forties, a manner now encouraged by Steig's son, Jeremy.

Among his more ambitious visual narratives is "American Beginnings" (February 14, 1970, 36–38). *The New Yorker* published only six: "The Purchase of Manhattan Island"; "La Salle Claims the Mississippi for France"; "The Landing of the Pilgrims on Plymouth Rock"; "Henry Hudson on the River That Will Bear His Name"; "Sir Walter Raleigh's Expedition Finds Virginia in the Spring"; and "William Penn Makes a Treaty with the Indians." Like many of Steig's later drawings, the sequence reflects the artist's insatiable quest for interesting and new subjects ("What can I draw now?" he would often ask his wife, the sculptor and artist Jeanne Doron).[108] The full version of "American Beginnings" (reproduced in *William Steig: Drawings,* 1979) offers an untroubled outline of American history, from Balboa pushing through the jungle to Darien, to Washington in retirement at Mount Vernon. Native Americans are a constant presence in this story, occasionally shown with drawn bows, but Steig avoids making the clashes between them and the settlers the central event, and there are no scenes of war or violence—indeed no sense that this is a drama of contact. Native Americans are placed in the background of the Spanish conquest, as in "Balboa Struggles to Reach the Pacific" (not reproduced in *The New Yorker*) or "An Old Indian Woman Tells Ponce de León about the Fountain of Youth"; we see them hunting and swimming as Hudson explores the river he will name for himself in "Henry Hudson on the River. . ." They watch impassively as the Cavalier de La Salle asserts his rights over the Mississippi in "La Salle Claims the Mississippi for France"; the Lenapes receive wampum from Peter Minuit in 1626 in "the Purchase of Manhattan"; and, in their last appearance, a group of Delaware Indians happily accept the unarmed William Penn's treaty under the elm tree at Shackamaxon in 1682 in "William Penn Makes a Treaty with the Indians." Slavery is even more obliquely treated, surfacing only in the drawing that glances (perhaps) at the irony of Washington as a slave owner, but where the iconography (smiling slaves picking cotton) seems congruent with sentimental images of the Old South. With its charmingly naive drawings, "American Beginnings" aims to recover a child's innocent vision of the history of the Republic. But the project, with its avoidance of the problematic, is already under strain, as if such materials, whose full complexity was starting to be generally understood, can't really be handled in this way. It is certainly unduly concentrated (as the title of the series suggests) on those for whom this historical episode was indeed a beginning rather than an ending.

Steig was not an acquisitive man and lived simply, but like anyone else he had to make a living and look after his family (he married four times and had three children). In the 1930s he supported his parents after they suffered in the Depression, and in later years he helped his brother Arthur for a time and supported his children and his previous spouses.[109] To supplement his income as a cartoonist, an obvious recourse was to supply drawings to the advertising industry, which Steig had done even in his rebellious years, the early 1940s.[110] Such work was always a problem for him, and his involvement might well have made him aware of the cogency of radical critique in the 1940s. He regarded advertising commissions as an "unfitting occupation for an artist"[111] and told one interviewer, "It's always been on my conscience that I participated in huckersterism."[112] (The danger of being corrupted in this way is neatly caught in Steig's cartoon of an artist with a huge smile spread across his face settling down to paint a still life of a pile of money [October 7, 1967, 47].) In the 1960s, when the demands on Steig's income were high, he was particularly vulnerable. In the 1990s he recalled the heyday of the 1970s when "you would do ten key drawings for an animated cartoon in an evening and get $2000 — this would be worth more like $10,000 now."[113] But drawing for advertisers, Steig later told his children, "blackened the soul."[114]

The way out was offered by a fellow cartoonist at *The New Yorker,* Bob Kraus, who had started an imprint for children's books at Harper and Row. Kraus suggested that Steig write and draw a children's book. The result was *Roland the Minstrel Pig* (1968), a huge success, which was followed in the same year by *CDB!* a storybook and primer in which letters stand for words. This was followed by *Sylvester and the Magic Pebble* (1969), another hit even though (or perhaps because) it fell foul of the International Conference of Police Associations for depicting a policeman as a pig.[115] Steig was now launched on an award-winning career. He went on to publish over twenty-five children's books, including the hugely successful *Shrek* (1990). Published in a large initial edition of 100,000 copies, the book was turned into a film by Dream-

Works that became the biggest-grossing film of 2001 (taking in nearly half a billion dollars).[116] This is not the place to attempt any analysis of the children's books, since they are a large topic in their own right, but the frequency with which Steig uses anthropomorphized animals as his characters is important. One of Steig's great gifts is drawing animals, and he succeeds in making them at once animal-like, humanlike, and sympathetic. There are parallels with the later cartoons. The lost traveler in "Nobody here seems to know how I can get back on Route 22" (March 18, 1961, 40) has fetched up in a small town in the boondocks where the inhabitants are all very sympathetic animals. For Steig, animals, like children, are closer to that state of innocence uncorrupted by the demands of the social order. The frequency of animals in late cartoons and the children's books is yet another sign of the search for some sort of utopia in art, though conversely one of Steig's double-page contributions to *The New Yorker* in the late sixties was a bestiary of twenty not always sympathetic human-faced animals (March 11, 1967, 52–53).

The *art naïf* style had its dangers and ironies, as must all self-conscious attempts at naïveté. The more the drawings of an accomplished artist reproduce the untrained treatment of perspective, expression, and description characteristic of children's work, the greater the effect of technique withheld, of power deliberately checked, and of skill deployed to conceal skill. The point of the stylistic vocabulary of such drawings is obvious, but it is perhaps not surprising that (for all their charm) Steig tended not to pursue the *faux-naïf* on too many subsequent occasions. "Greek Mythology" (November 14, 1964, 54–57), which picks up in a *naïf* stylistic vein some old themes—the powers of Eros and art, the persistence of madness and violence—demonstrates the problem. The drawings are completely enchanting. A childlike Hercules, driven mad by Hera, swings his doll-like children by their arms and legs while Megara, his wife, faints on a couch holding the arm of another child who lies on the ground. Hercules' rage may look infantile—he is himself a child having a tantrum—but this is because rage itself is regressive. Similarly in other drawings, Steig gives us an image and ideal of guiltless, pre-Christian eroticism: a group of four extremely benign-looking bacchantes dance about with their tunics falling off; a puzzled "Man" discovers "Woman"; a very pleased-looking Zeus is disguised as a bull among a group of maidens. A number celebrate the artist—Pan plays his pipes to a pair of naked, Picasso-like women who sit attentively on the ground, Pygmalion embraces one of his sculptures, Orpheus charms the animals and trees and is surrounded by delighted insects, birds, reptiles, fish, and dancing mammals. The tree undulates. Again the point is partly implicit in the nostalgia of the stylistics—the style, like the world, is in its infancy. It is a time of archetypal prefigurations of man's later experience—

but everything is reembodied in shapes that are more innocent, more delight-ful, more pastoral. Even when Pandora lets evil into the world out of a box labeled "Hope," the monsters have a creative zest and charm, and in another drawing Midas is transformed into a crafted work of art. And yet there is an element of nostalgia in this simplicity that amounts to falsity, as if the artist is trying to convince us that such innocence could after all be regained—the same problem that dogs "American Beginnings." The drawings are certainly beguiling, if not quite, as Whitney Balliett has said, among some of the most beautiful done in the twentieth century.

It is in the huge numbers of occasional drawings he produced from the seventies on that Steig most frees himself from the need to *illustrate* ("to illus-trate" meaning to make the drawing serve a program that exists before the act of drawing—as, for instance, the earlier series like "Everyday Histrionics" clearly do).[117] These drawings suggest that Steig is at his best with personal rather than public themes. Following the example perhaps of the restaurant series of May 1960, he typically draws first and then (and not always then) titles the drawing. The titles—like the captions to earlier sequences—are themselves often poignant and pithy, quasi-poetical, verbal aperçus. The line is produced either with a Rapidograph pen, an instrument that permits fast, free-flowing description, or a bamboo pen, which discourages fussy, overcontrolled realist description in favor of bold sketchiness. The line is free and spontaneous. It brings the act of drawing itself to the fore, retaining the trace of the primal creative moment, the setting of pen to blank paper. The impression is truly one of drawing as a form of discovery, a mode of awareness of the external world. The drawings are sometimes amusingly wry, like the springtime caprice of a man holding a microphone up to a bird singing in a tree (May 1, 1971, 115). By the time of Steig's "Man and Woman" double-page spread (April 13, 1968, 40–41), untitled studies of various couples, the free exploratory style of the psychological drawings of the forties has finally make its appearance in the pages of *The New Yorker*.

An especially good series is "Fellow Men" (in *William Steig: Drawings*, 1979), where a virtuosic Steig draws a gallery of wondrous individuals, thirty-two in all, and then assigns to each drawing a title that off-handedly slots the individual into a general category—though these are often comically spuri-ous rather than commonly accepted. There is, for example, "Subway rider in staring duel" (a man stares at the viewer in a paranoid way), or "Officer de-scribing actions of 'perpetrator'" (which shows a television interviewer hold-ing up a microphone to an explaining policeman), or "Professor greeting new students with pleasantries" (where the professor has an all too familiar expres-sion of self-satisfaction). Both the drawing and the "category" capture familiar moments in the flow of modern city life. But everything depends on the accident of the drawing as a creation. Things like expression, gesture, and body pose carry the real weight of meaning, yet all seem truly found by the drawing. A perfect example is the expression created for "Shoplifter"—the woman has narrowed eyes compressed shiftily under her hat, not looking at what her hands are doing, and a jagged, skewed, defiant mouth. The sense of clothing is also remarkable. In later life Steig shows a predilection for nineteenth-century or Edwardian dress (earlier Arno produced drawings in a similar vein, and both artists' work here recalls *The New Yorker*'s fascination with the dandy). Many of the drawings have a retrospective air (they look like old photographs, Brendan Gill has remarked), but there is a clear interpretive thrust to them nonetheless: men are constrained and armored by the layers of clothing, the high collars, the proliferating buttons of Edwardian dress, whereas the women are all pneumatic, their full-bosomed bodies escaping from the flimsy silks and taffetas that envelop them. Here is the radical's return to one of the primary sites of repression—the authoritarian family—but usually only in order to review it nostalgically and positively.

One of these drawings rehearses Steig's long-standing doubts about marriage. It shows a slightly dopey loving couple framed by the window of a small clapboard cottage (fig. 2.16). The dominant motifs of the drawing—the heart-decorated hinges on the closed door, the chained dog, the bird in a cage, the tree in a wire frame, the flower also chained—all suggest imprisonment. Other drawings of the seventies imply the beneficent effects of unconstrained Eros and show in the comparative fluidity of the body how it expresses psychic health, a motif Steig will carry forward over the next three decades. A fanciful cover for May 24, 1993, shows a typically Steigian scene and sums up this tendency—an old woman placing roses in a jar remembers an earlier, joyous self who dances naked into the picture frame, the same roses in a garland in her hair. Nakedness—the body freed from the armor of clothing—was a central element in Reichian therapy.[118] This late image recapitulates the synthesis Steig achieved between his own temperamental instincts and Reichian therapeutics.

Steig is an extremely difficult artist to sum up. He possesses that indisputable quality of genius, the gift of abundant creativity—seemingly there was never a moment in his ninety-five years when he stopped drawing. He is all but unique, moreover, as a comic artist in having passed through at least three distinct stylistic phases—the more usual model (we shall see it in Addams) is to find an artist arriving early on at some distinctive personal pictorial style and thereafter consolidating it. Undoubtedly these phases have roots in Steig's emotionally turbulent life. He certainly becomes much harder to generalize about in his later career. The later Steig, after the crisis of the 1940s, branches out in many directions, while his drawings retain an extraordinary freshness and spontaneity and his pictorial curiosity seems boundless. From Steig one takes away the impression of an artist under the beneficent tyranny of the urge to draw—a man who continually finds new things to draw and for whom drawing is a matter of constant discovery, constant creative renewal, constant fresh vision. Yet all the time there remains the puzzle of those searing psychological drawings of the forties, the drawings that offer such a disturbing report on American society but were never admitted to the pages of *The New Yorker,* the magazine that had made Steig's career. This absence certainly qualifies the claim this book makes that *The New Yorker* tended to promote critical detachment in its readers. Given that Steig was the artist who drew images for Harold Ross that were centrally American, the magazine's reluctance to follow him into the depths in the forties, depths that were more than personal, as the popularity of the forties volumes attests, shows a failure of nerve by the magazine's editors. On the other hand, Steig himself turned away from the political protest implicit in those drawings as the fifties unfolded, and despite his sympathy for the youth revolt of the 1960s, he contributed his share of cartoons mocking long-haired youth (October 22, 1966, 53).[119]

Grasping the truth about this elusive artist requires us to notice something contradictory in his career. Steig always thought that his basic artistic impulse was optimistic, founded on the idea of innocence—that artistically speaking he was a romantic revolutionary. This is true. But his career also hints at the exact opposite. Shadowing the optimism is a pessimistic and even conservative conviction of the fallen state of human nature. Steig, like most humorists, has low expectations of human nature. He may assert that he thinks people are fundamentally "good and beautiful," but he often draws cartoons that demonstrate the reverse. It is not entirely surprising to find him announcing, in late career, that "despair is the human condition."[120] But then again, what Steig's career shows so triumphantly is that it is possible to be gloomy and still to draw and paint in a spirit of joyfulness. The lamp of art illuminates the gloom.

The importance of pleasure in the face of disappointment and unhappiness may be gauged by the experience of a member of the staff at *The New Yorker,* the British journalist Alexander Chancellor, brought to New York by Tina Brown. Chancellor's time at *The New Yorker* was, to put it at its best, a mixed one and perhaps in reality a catastrophic failure. The introduction of an Englishman to edit, of all departments, "The Talk of the Town," was quixotic to say the least. To many it was stark confirmation of how unwise it was to hand over the editorship of *The New Yorker,* of all magazines, to someone who, being British, had no long-evolved, deep personal experience of either America or

The Comic Worlds of Arno, Steig, Addams, and Steinberg

Fig. 2.16. William Steig.
Untitled. [Lovers in a
cottage, with chains.]

The New Yorker,
August 7, 1971, 72.

Steig's astonishing later flourishing is too complex to be adequately summed up in this book, but something of its range
and abundance can be glimpsed from the collection titled
William Steig: Drawings (1979), many of which appeared in *The
New Yorker.* This drawing shows that Steig (who married four
times) certainly remained a Reichian when it came to marriage. Here the perfect lovers' cottage, with dopey handcuffed
sweethearts at the window, is also a prison: the house is small
and constricting as well as cute, the door is shut, and its stout
hinges are decorated with hearts; the path is guarded by a
chained, sleeping, but no doubt ferocious watchdog (Cer-
berus?); and both the tree to the right and the canary to the
left are caged. For good measure, even the flower is chained.

New York. Chancellor himself came to have profound misgivings about it all. But in a memoir of his experiences he ends by recalling a favorite Steig cover, that of May 24 mentioned above, that so strikingly embodies Steig's own embracing of the pleasure principle. When Chancellor was asked to select a *New Yorker* cover as a farewell gift, the one he chose and received—"to my great gratitude and happiness"—was that same painting by William Steig.[121]

The Comic Worlds of Arno, Steig, Addams, and Steinberg

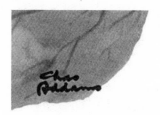

3 · CHARLES ADDAMS

Comic American Gothic

That the present changes the past is a historian's truism; but rarely has a truism been so starkly confirmed, even with reference to such a historically unimportant issue as humor, as in the case of the attacks on the World Trade Center and the Pentagon in September 2001. What jokes are possible in such times? Is it permissible to make a joke that alludes to such terrible events, however indirectly? If so, does this mean that a joke must be (as Nietzsche thought) no better than an epitaph on the death of a feeling?[1] More particularly, how do we now make sense of joking cartoons like those of Charles Addams, which frequently depict destructive and murderous acts? Can this material responsibly be made the subject of jokes? What if his jokes now seem unfunny? Worse still, what if they seem all the funnier? This last possibility prompts the thought that laughter unmasks something deeply irresponsible in us, a foolish and regressive reveling in destruction and aggression that contemporary events have rightly made shameful.

With these questions in mind, look at the 1939 cartoon of a disgruntled alumnus turned revolutionary planning to blow up the Capitol, captioned, "Dear Fellow-Alumnus: Your face was among the missing at our annual reunion last June. Won't you help us to keep 'tabs' on members of the class of '17 by telling us what you are doing now? . . ." (fig. 3.1). The unsettling implications of this drawing come into sharp focus when we discover that it was published in *The New Yorker* shortly after President Roosevelt's State of the Union address to Congress on January 4, 1939. In that speech the president, surveying the bleak international outlook, had warned of need for internal unity in the face of external aggressors.[2] Three weeks later, and in the atmosphere generated by the president's message and the grim turn of events in Europe, this cartoon appeared. There is no suggestion of a direct satiric link here, of course. Leaving aside tact and patriotism, cartoons in *The New Yorker* were never chosen as a topical response to current events, just in case events took a turn that outstripped the cartoon. The "impossible interim of magazine publication," a time lag of five days or so between an issue's closing and the magazine's appearance on the newsstands, had always made topicality, while not completely impossible, something to be avoided.[3] But if *The New Yorker*'s contributors sometimes bemoaned the lengthy editorial lead time,[4] that same time lag also opened up a situation in which they could venture sly, indirect connections without the danger of censure or criticism.[5] The least one could say of this cartoon is that if it was not intended to ricochet off Roosevelt's address, it was certainly not pulled on the grounds that such a connection might be perceived. To go further, the humor depends on its exciting just some such association in readers' minds, at however submerged a level, and it would have required an inept and insensitive editor not to anticipate this.

The cartoon was always in bad taste: after the Oklahoma City bombing it became problematic, and the events of September 11, 2001, seem to have made it callous and unconscionable. Why would anyone ever find it funny? People certainly did, and people still do. What does it really mean, what does it really imply, to laugh at such a joke? These questions raise the central issue posed by Addams's art: How "real" is it? How directly do we understand it in relation to actual events—in this example, the threat of Nazi aggression and the danger of communist subversion? On one side no less a figure than William Shawn, Harold Ross's successor as editor of *The New Yorker,* said that Addams's work "translated what is ordinarily fairly frightening into something almost cozy."[6] "Almost cozy"—it is worth repeating this as one looks at the cartoon. Many others express Shawn's subtle point with less finesse. He "steers clear of the true horrors facing us in our day-to-day living," writes one admirer. "Addams invites us to enter a world which has nothing to do with the one we live in except that, in the most glorious undeviating and giddy fashion, it turns all of its values topsy-turvy," says another.[7] On the other side are commentators like the historian of American humor Jesse Bier, who wrote feelingly of Addams's remorseless "horrification of American bourgeois living."[8] Or there is Addams's friend Wilfrid Sheed, who insists in his introduction to the most recent collection of Addams's work that Addams "really means it"—that he goes all the way with his people, "crashing them into the wall and leaving them there bleeding." It is also worth repeating this as one looks at the cartoon.

As it happens, Shawn and Sheed both have a point. The man plotting to blow up the Capitol is quite possibly living in a delusional world in which the path to action will never be taken—his energy has gone into the meticulous model, say, rather than into actual sabotage. Or the events in the cartoon take

The Comic Worlds of Arno, Steig, Addams, and Steinberg

Fig. 3.1.
Charles Addams.

The New Yorker,
January 28, 1939,
22. © 1939 Charles
Addams. Reproduced
with permission of Tee
and Charles Addams
Foundation.

"Dear Fellow-Alumnus: Your face was among the missing at our annual reunion last June. Won't you help us to keep 'tabs' on members of the class of '17 by telling us what you are doing now? . . . ."

Whether intentionally or not, as published this cartoon is in effect *The New Yorker*'s riposte to Roosevelt's call for national unity in his State of the Union address three weeks before publication. The caption, with its oblique reference to the Russian Revolution (the "class of '17"), prepares the way for Cold War hysteria over communism, although in the late thirties the patriotism of the America Marxist left was already a real issue. Like all of Addams's cartoons, the drawing overwhelms us with meticulous detail, as if the cartoon itself is his own equivalent of the saboteur's fantastically detailed model of the Capitol. A good example of Addams's "horrification" of the American middle class, the enormity of this cartoon becomes clear once we look at it with the Oklahoma bombing or September 11, 2001, in our minds.

place in the "what-if" land of comic hypothesis. Either way, the frightening becomes cozy. But no one could remain content with that interpretation, and it is impossible to expunge the thought that this man will really do what he plans. The massacre will take place. The bloodshed will be real. The frightening remains frightening. It is the ruse of the comic to dangle both possibilities before us, to force us to make a choice, and then to make us feel that whichever way we jump, we have chosen wrongly.[9]

The issue of content never really goes away, however. This is confirmed when we turn to the notorious "Boiling Oil" cartoon of 1946 (fig. 3.2), provocatively published in the Christmas issue of *The New Yorker*.[10] It is a summa of Addams's humor, pitting fallen against upright humanity.[11] It takes as its object of attack what in popular sentiment is the most important event in the Christian calendar, and it employs symbols that suggest matters deeply and centrally American. At the bottom of the drawing the carol singers embody the decent, democratic America of small town, suburb, and exurb. (The latter two are new social phenomena of the late forties and early fifties, whose comic possibilities were most strongly exploited in *The New Yorker* at that time by Robert Day—Saxon and Stevenson were not to appear in the magazine until the late fifties.) The pool of light around the group is Addams's version of the "broad and simple daylight" that Nathaniel Hawthorne said was characteristic of the American outlook on the world. The singers are gathered in the name of values central to all decent folk (peace on earth and goodwill toward men, charity, sociability, good-neighborliness, togetherness, modest artistic achievement). At the top of the drawing, bathed in a ghostly moonlight and receding into the blackness of the night sky, are four strange individuals—a ghoulish man, a vampire or witch (who both owe something to Bram Stoker's *Dracula*), a distracted madwoman, and a zombielike servant who has arrived out of Mary Shelley's *Frankenstein*. Their response to the Christian message of peace and goodwill is to pour a cauldron of boiling oil on the messengers. The cartoon reveals something essential about Addams's work: it has its origins in extremely hostile, aggressive, and antisocial feelings, which it then projects onto an imaginary group of characters who in turn enact a surrogate attack on unsuspecting ordinary folk. That Addams's popularity derives from the hostility his work expresses, from his very offensiveness, can hardly be doubted. Nor can we doubt that most people's sympathies are with the aggressors, not the victims. According to Addams, many people wrote to him seeking permission to put this cartoon on their Christmas cards.[12]

Leaving aside the people and what they are doing, the striking aspect of the cartoon's iconography is the dilapidated clapboard mansion. As Saul Steinberg once pointed out, Addams is unusual among cartoonists because of his

Fig. 3.2.
Charles Addams. Un-
captioned cartoon.
Titled: Boiling Oil.

The New Yorker,
December 21, 1946,
30. © 1946 Charles
Addams. Reproduced
with permission of Tee
and Charles Addams
Foundation.

A famous, and definitive, Addams cartoon. It was published,
for maximum provocation, in the Christmas issue of *The New
Yorker.* Addams's sadistic, ghoulish, family members (our own
dark alter egos) prepare to tip a cauldron of boiling oil over a
group of inoffensive carol singers (our own docile, socialized
selves). It is hard to imagine a more calculated attack on the
decencies of everyday communal life. The house, visually the
most striking thing in the drawing, is a staple motif of American
gothic from Poe to Hitchcock and beyond. We view the atrocity
not from the perspective of the carol singers (which would ally
us with them) but from the same level as the aggressors (as if
to confirm that it is them we really side with).

interest in architecture. This house initially appeared in Addams's cartoons in the late thirties and early forties. In the September 18, 1937, issue of *The New Yorker* a rudimentary version is towed behind a car driven by a couple of ghosts (16); in the November 10, 1945, issue the house proper is drawn with a sign in front saying "Beware of the Thing" (23); in a cartoon dating from late 1938 the house sprouts amid a riot of modernist, "democracity" architecture influenced by the plans for the World's Fair, while one onlooker says to the other, "I'm afraid Mr. Whalen will be furious" (October 22, 1938, 19). (Grover A. Whalen was president of the corporation that administered—and stylistically policed—the World's Fair of 1939–40.) The persistence of this architectural motif in Addams's work offers a promising starting point for a discussion of his humor.

The Addams "gingerbread age" house (mansard roof, shuttered windows, ornate ironwork, and a basic asymmetry of design) is in the style known as American Second Empire, recalling the France of Napoleon III, 1852–70. Old beyond its actual years, gloomy, dark, secretive, forbidding, threatening, a place of cold, darkness, and evil, the house contrasts strongly with the comfort of contemporary suburban homes or homely small-town houses. It also contrasts importantly with another kind of house, of particular relevance to the national mythology—the Jeffersonian neoclassical, Greek Revival design so favored by early American architects. This kind of house, as well as churches and civic buildings in a similar style, is characteristic of many American small towns on the East Coast. Describing one such building in a well-known passage in *The Europeans,* Henry James underscored its moral symbolism. James's Greek Revival house is "built of wood" and painted "clear, faded grey." It is "adorned along the front, at intervals, with flat wooden pilasters painted white." It has "a large white door, furnished with a highly-polished brass knocker." The front door stands wide open, "with the trustfulness of the golden age . . . of New England's silvery prime."[13] The unguarded, candid, optimistic, innocent trustingness evoked here is just the quality that Addams sets out to attack and undermine in nearly all his cartoons. Hence the very different building in Addams's carol singers cartoon. It embraces not just "the Past," or even the Old World that America has left behind, but also the dark, repressed features of the present national psychic landscape. In Addams's world the diabolical is something both as grand as an inversion of the American ideology and as everyday and commonplace as the house just around the corner. That the house in the cartoon is in part a transformation of one on East Dudley Street in Westfield, New Jersey, just around the corner from the much more ordinary house on Elm Street where Addams grew up epitomizes the argument.[14]

The Addams American Second Empire house is familiar to most people.

Fig. 3.3. Edward
Hopper (1882–1967).
House by the Railroad.
1925.

Oil on canvas, 24 by 29
inches. Gift of anony-
mous donor. Digital
image © The Museum
of Modern Art/Licensed
by SCALA/Art Re-
source NY.

Edward Hopper's *House by the Railroad* is one of the most
important images of the American Second Empire house,
a building Addams later popularized. It was also a painting
that Hitchcock knew and admired (see next illustration). But
Hopper's house is melancholy and lonely rather than menacing and evil. The railroad cuts it off from us and seems to
slice through its foundations, making the painting a pessimistic
allegory of progress.

This familiarity grows out of a series of interrelationships between painting,
cartooning, and movie making, between high art and popular culture. The
Addams house (created in the 1940s) stands halfway between Edward Hopper's *House by the Railroad,* painted in 1925 (fig. 3.3), and "Mother's House,"
the house behind the Bates Motel in Alfred Hitchcock's *Psycho,* released in
1960 (fig. 3.4).[15] We know that Hopper's painting influenced Hitchcock, because Hitchcock told Hopper so in 1960.[16] But Hitchcock was also fan of

Charles Addams: Comic American Gothic   141

Addams's work and once paid a visit to the cartoonist's studio in order, as the filmmaker is reported to have said to the cartoonist at the time, "to catch you in your own bailiwick."[17] In choosing the house in *Psycho,* was Hitchcock thinking of Hopper or Addams? The question is hard to answer, but Addams's house is more apposite to Hitchcock's needs than is Hopper's. Hopper's house, a haunting and memorable painting of a white mansion raked by the rays of the setting (or rising) sun and standing against a sky that changes from orange to cobalt blue, evokes melancholy and loneliness. Addams's house, an equally memorable image, showing a building in somber monochrome grays against a black sky, evokes mystery and fear. If Hopper put this sort of house into the national visual vocabulary, it was Addams who gave it the currency it still has, who established it in the popular imagination as a place of evil. That Hitchcock should seize on the potential of such a building, even if it was a standing set on the Universal lot and even if he knew the Hopper painting, suggests a sensibility schooled more by Charles Addams than by Edward Hopper. Hitchcock was alert to the implications of a house in the Second Empire style because he admired Addams's cartoons. There is one final, complicating detail. Hopper's house is seen from a low viewpoint (the composition has the lower part of the house sliced off by the railroad track and embankment), just as we usually see Norman Bates's house from below. Addams's house is seen from above, with the viewer's eye line slightly above the figures pouring the oil. The low viewpoint in Hopper separates the house from the viewer and makes it something apart and other. This separation between the viewer and the source of evil is taken over by Hitchcock in the early part of the film and is essential to the thriller effect, ensuring that we side with the vulnerable victims. In contrast, the high vantage point in Addams's drawing forges a link between the viewer and the diabolical figures. That link, between transgressive character and acquiescent viewer, is characteristic of Addams's art.

The connection between an Addams cartoon, a great American painting, and a seminal American gothic text reminds us that Charles Addams is not, as some people think, a grotesque sport of nature. He is not a one-off, a comic artist sui generis, a comedian whose humor is a free-floating fantasy cut off from all social and cultural referents. Addams himself once suggested, a little cryptically, that he hoped his cartoons would leave "a record of my times."[18] But since Addams, with his ghosts, ghouls, monsters, murderers, diabolical children, and sundry macabre strays out of myth, legend, and fairy tale, is hardly a cartoonist of manners, it is not obvious what he meant by such a remark. The extraordinary proliferation of gothic motifs in his cartoons does, however, suggest that Addams can be understood by placing him in the long tradition of American gothic.[19]

Fig. 3.4. "Mother's house," the house behind the Bates Motel in Alfred Hitchcock's *Psycho* (1960).

Reprinted by permission of the Film Stills Archive, Museum of Modern Art, NYC.

Hitchcock's version of the Hopper house, filtered through Addams, as it appears in *Psycho* (1960). Hitchcock wants us to identify with ordinary, everyday assailed humanity, so we typically see the house from below, as in the establishing scenes of the film. (Only toward the climax does the camera go into the house and float eerily above the investigating detective as he climbs the stairs.) Hitchcock admired Addams's work. The persistence of his house in the twentieth-century tradition of American gothic reminds us that Addams himself has to be looked at within that context.

Inaugurated in 1798 by Charles Brockden Brown's *Wieland*,[20] the genre is given currency by Edgar Allan Poe in the 1830s and carried forward in a more sophisticated form by Nathaniel Hawthorne toward the end of the nineteenth century. Subsequently it is taken up by writers as diverse as H. P. Lovecraft, Willa Cather, Carson McCullers, John Dickson Carr, Truman Capote, Ira Levin, Robert Bloch (the author of *Psycho*), Stephen King, Annie Rice, Thomas Harris, Bret Easton Ellis, Toni Morrison, and Tony Kushner (the genre is nothing if not capacious). The gothic has long held a central position in American literature (unlike England, where it has remained a marginal genre),[21] to the point where in the 1990s, as Mark Edmundson argues in his *Nightmare on Main Street,* the gothic became the preferred trope in the country's social imagination, the genre Americans have most frequently used to represent their experience. Pointing out that the major gothic modes are no longer fictive, Edmundson notes that gothic conventions have now flipped over into "ostensibly non-fictional realms" and that "American culture has become suffused with Gothic assumptions, with Gothic characters and plots."[22] Among many examples, he cites media reporting of the O. J. Simpson trial, pop therapy on *Oprah,* and the discussion of AIDS. The trend continues strongly into the twenty-first century if Martin Bashir's documentary on Michael Jackson (BBC TV, 2003) is anything to go by.

How and why American culture should become suffused with gothic tropes of demonic individuals, vampires, possession, haunting, shape changing, atrocity, and monstrosity is well understood, but the outline of the argument bears repeating because of its usefulness for a discussion of Addams's work. The character of the American nation as forged by the Founding Fathers was in large part an expression of the ideas of the European Enlightenment. These included optimistic thoughts about liberty, equality, and fraternity and perfectibilist notions of America as a country where the injustices and errors of the Old World could be erased and rectified. A belief in the value of reason went along with a conviction of the absurdity of mythology and the danger of superstition.[23] This potent intellectual heritage was buttressed by some simple facts of life. National energies throughout the nineteenth century were required for the task of nation building, meaning not abstract political theory but the nuts and bolts of the enterprise: exploration and conquest, clearing land, setting up farms, and building roads, railroads, and cities. As one historian points out, a people occupied with so momentous a task "had little time to engage in such impractical pursuits as literature and the arts."[24] Nor did they have either the surplus time or the energy to experience anxiety.[25] Nation building, moreover, requires both the ideology and the actuality of fraternity, of reliance on others' goodwill, reliability, and trustworthiness.[26] The Enlightenment heritage was bolstered by the practical teachings of the Scottish Common Sense thinkers then very popular (Dugald Stewart, Lord Kames, Adam Ferguson), whose deep mistrust of imagination was taken up by key figures like Benjamin Franklin. The consequences are well known—a high valuation of common sense and practicality, a preference for realist artistic genres, a devaluing of fantasy, mystery, and romance.[27]

The result was certainly not the absence of an art that embraces the irrational—to the contrary, in such circumstances the irrational returns as a complement of the stress on rationality.[28] Enlightenment culture is typified not just by the repression of the irrational but also by its return—the dream of reason producing monsters. In Europe the gothic novel emerges exactly when enlightened values become widespread. The same is true of America, where irrational

The Comic Worlds of Arno, Steig, Addams, and Steinberg

emphases counterpoint realist and rational ones and where the gothic tradition is supported by the armature of its very repression, as the examples of Poe and Hawthorne abundantly show. In David Lynch's *Blue Velvet* (1986), an influential contemporary reworking of gothic motifs, the daylight rational pragmatism of American life and its dark, superstitious, irrational side go together. In his comprehensive study *Redefining the American Gothic,* Louis Gross proposes that a "vision of a world of darkness, terror, oppression, and perversity, seemingly so alien from the rational bias of the Founding Fathers, is as pervasive in our national consciousness as its daylight opposite," and he adds that "the texts Americans have traditionally viewed as the reflection of national identity—the Declaration of Independence and the Constitution—have their counter-images in the long line of Gothic texts that show the land, people and institutions of this country as participants in the nightmare of history."[29]

None of this is to forget that America is a country whose national character has been built on traditions and experiences completely at variance with those of the European Enlightenment. There are two strong pre-Revolutionary elements: the Puritan settlements in New England and the slave economy of the southern plantations. Out of these comes a very different sort of ethos, not at all unfavorable to irrationalism. From Puritanism there derives a habit of introspection tending to suspicion and paranoia, attended by a strong sense of personal guilt and a conviction of the constant presence of evil, especially in the land itself, often seen as demonic (as, for example, in Hawthorne's satiric allegories like "Young Goodman Brown"). From the southern plantations, a semifeudal social system based on slavery, comes a far more dubious inheritance in which white masters fear, oppress, and demonize their black slaves. In both regions—the Northeast and the South—the historical record of white and Native American and African American contact is one of atrocity. The consequence is a dual inheritance: a sense of evil, of suspicion, and of guilt, along with a projective demonization of Native Americans and African Americans as other.[30] Such an inheritance readily coalesces with irrational modes of thought suppressed by enlightened reason.

Out of these materials and experiences the gothic artist puts together a report on the dark side of the American social imaginary, working toward the creation of states of fear and terror. The common thread is the monstrousness of the other. What the dominant culture cannot incorporate into itself it projects outward onto such a figure: both hated and desired, it is also the subject of identification and rejection. The gothic emerges, then, as a kind of double of the everyday surface life of the nation. "The Gothic," Gross says, "with its horrified fascination for points of transition between daily life and its nightmarish reflections, permits the writer and reader to stare intensely at those things hidden by more mainstream, therefore more critically respected, modes of writing."[31] A net to trap free-floating cultural anxiety, it exploits the shifting cultural bases of fear and generates an inverted demonic mirror of the American experience.[32] Central to the American version of the genre has been the way it detaches gothic horror from the exotic, bringing it into conjunction with the present time and place.

The gothic is not a constant in American literary history; it waxes in significance at the end of both the nineteenth and the twentieth centuries and wanes from the start of the First World War to the 1960s.[33] Not that it vanishes in between. But with the exception of writers like H. P. Lovecraft or John Dickson Carr, or with writers one would not ordinarily think of as full-blown gothicists, such as Willa Cather or Carson McCullers, there are no major gothic writers in those years. It is as if the troubled fifty years between the turn of the century and the Eisenhower equilibrium, like the earlier period of nation building, claimed so much of the energy and attention of those who lived through them that the "free-floating anxiety" the gothic draws on did not have a fertile soil to flourish in. Anxiety is a product of the psyche at rest and leisure, not the psyche deeply engaged with the practical affairs of life. What one does notice is the extraordinary efflorescence of the genre after this period—so that the second half of the twentieth century in America is a veritable golden age. But if this is so, then Charles Addams, the premier gothicist of midcentury America (when the genre lay dormant), is not just a humorist but a prophetic humorist, and for that reason a pivotal artist on whose work turns the whole ambivalent genre of American gothic, with its suspicious, fearful, but thrilling depiction of the other who lives next door.

Charles Addams, a comic American gothicist, whose life's work might be described as the humorous haunting of America, was himself haunted by a less than comic memory, that of the suburb. Born in 1912, he grew up in Westfield, New Jersey, "that least Transylvanian of states," as one admirer who knew him well described it, "better known for the manufacture of toys and paint than the arts"—in fact the archetypal quiet suburban town.[34] Early signs of revolt against the boredom of the suburb remain on record (with what degree of veracity it is hard to determine): the boy Addams hanging around the local cemetery, trying to imagine what it was like inside a coffin; trespassing in the Victorian house that was the original of the Addams mansion and leaving a drawing of a skeleton in its garage; finding artistic inspiration in the drawings of Arthur Rackham, Gustave Doré, and Albert Ryder.[35]

Other details are vaguer and harder to interpret. What did Addams's father do for a living? In different accounts he is said to be the manager of a music store, a piano company executive, someone who trained as an architect, the manager of a piano shop, and a naval architect. Why did Addams provide different versions of his father's career? Was having a shopkeeper for a father too suburban? Was Addams silently repairing the history of a family that had slid down the social ladder in the Depression? Or do these discrepant versions of the career of Charles Huey Addams point to nothing more than journalistic inaccuracy? What we can feel confident about is that Addams was left with a deep horror of the unfolding destiny of middle America—the comfortably furnished, manicured lawn ordinariness, blandness, and banality of suburb and exurb (much the same anywhere). The urgent need to escape that fate underlies almost everything about him, both as a man and as an artist. Hence the innumerable cartoons that turn the suburban dream of togetherness on its head. In one drawing, for example, a family is busying itself with spring cleaning (dusting off screens, tidying the lawn), while next door Uncle Fester is quietly but happily sharpening the iron spikes on his fence (April 22, 1950, 31).

Like Steig, Addams always described himself as "a normal all-American boy." But unlike Steig, Addams expects the phrase to be applied ironically. This is a matter of the art, not the life, of course. Where the life is concerned, in recent years the legend of Addams's ordinariness has supplanted the original legend of his strangeness.[36] He is "just a hell of a nice guy" (Wolcott Gibbs), "a big cheerful man who loved playing the part admirers expected of him" (W. J. Weatherby), "easy-going and pacific" (Brendan Gill), "lighthearted, urbane and civilized" (Lee Lorenz), and all attempts to prove otherwise founder "upon the rock of Charlie's manifest sanity and good nature" (Wilfrid Sheed).[37] No doubt Addams was a decent, well-behaved citizen and, in that respect at least, an all-American boy. But with Addams—so far as his art is concerned—"all-American" acquires a darker coloration: for what is important, of course, are the drawings, not the life, and the drawings offer anything but the wholesome, Forrest Gump America of the normal all-American boy.

His childhood was a perfectly happy one. But the stock market crash and the Depression of the 1930s must have affected the family and seem to have left a scar on Addams's life (he turned eighteen in 1930). This is reflected most obviously in his college education, which was sporadic and incomplete. After graduating from high school in 1929, he enrolled at Colgate University, transferring to the University of Pennsylvania the following year. In 1931 he abandoned academic studies altogether and began classes at Grand Central Art School in New York.[38] A year later, in 1932, he took a job with McFadden Publications (perhaps for financial reasons). His job was "retouching photographs for the publisher's string of 'true detective' [that is, *True Detective*] magazines" a task that involved un-Addams-like chores such as removing the blood shown in photographs of murders.[39] These fits and starts are very likely a consequence of the way middle-class incomes and careers in the early thirties were ravaged by the Depression, but then again it might just as well be the restlessness of the lonely genius who realizes that he hasn't yet found his métier. In any event, Addams stayed at McFadden's for a year and a half—probably leaving when he started publishing with *The New Yorker*. Addams later recalled these years as providing an important apprenticeship: "It was a sort of education in the technical side of drawing pictures. I learned all about rubber cement and different kinds of paper." (Saul Steinberg sounds a similar minimalist note about his architectural training: it taught him, he once said, not to bend over to pick up an eraser until it had stopped bouncing.)

Those favorite artists—Rackham, Doré, and Ryder—supplied a more useful education. He had begun drawing early, doing "a lot of sketching" when he was a child, and his characteristic comic sensibility showed itself almost immediately.[40] He was fond of recalling a cartoon that showed the kaiser run over by a Macy's truck. The drawing must coincide with the defeat of Germany in the First World War when Addams was all of six years old. The way the joke has been put together, the familiar and the threateningly strange yoked by violence (quite literally), would become the foundation of Addams's most characteristic work. At thirteen he won a competition for a children's magazine called *Ropeco* with a cartoon that again had sadistic and violent implications: a man is shown felled by a high-tension wire, and a Boy Scout arrives in rubber boots, carrying a rubber insulating mat; the caption is, "Be prepared."

It was while he was working with McFadden's that he had his first "idea drawing"—*New Yorker*ese for cartoon—accepted by *The New Yorker*.[41] It was published in the issue for February 4, 1933, and showed a bashful and embarrassed ice hockey player, one foot curled over the other, announcing to his teammates, "I forgot my skates."[42] Not exactly gothic, but the idea of what might happen if the action were to proceed is painful to contemplate—the brute fact of amputation, all those toes, blood staining the ice, seeps into the observer's mind as the drawing is contemplated. And that's to say nothing of the symbolism. For this he received payment of $30, the base rate for beginners at that time.[43]

What is striking about Addams's early contributions to *The New Yorker* is that they are invariably "reality modifying" drawings: that is, they introduce some kind of illogical modification to the fabric of everyday life. Production-line jokes are a favorite, as if Addams wants to confront Fordism head on: in one the car assembly line produces a stray horse (September 21, 1935, 23), while in another a copy of William Randolph Hearst's sensationalist *Daily Mirror*,

The Comic Worlds of Arno, Steig, Addams, and Steinberg

with the seventy-two-point headline "SEX FIEND SLAYS TOT," appears in the middle of a print run of the "all the news that's fit to print" *New York Times* (March 23, 1935, 41). The adjustment of reality was soon to become Addams's signature comic device, and—against a background of humorous art that by and large took the frame of everyday experience as fixed and gained its effects by slight exaggeration or overemphasis—his bold departures from normality stand out sharply.

Addams sold five cartoons to *The New Yorker* in 1933, only one in 1934, and twenty-one in 1935.[44] By 1936 Addams had had thirty-two drawings accepted by the magazine, suggesting he had by then become a staff contributor.[45] Payment for his drawings rose first to $35 and then to $40. These sums may have saved Addams from starving, but they are inconsequential and imply an annual income of less than $1,000. In 1934 Ralph Ingersoll reported a standard rate of $50 to $75 for a quarter-page idea drawing.[46] Addams's takings in those early years pale compared with the kind of money established artists like Arno or Steig were making in the 1930s. As we have seen, Steig reported earning $4,000 in 1930 alone, and Arno, whose publishing strike rate was often over 60 percent through much of his career, was paid at least $500 a drawing throughout the decade.[47] But no doubt Addams was paid more once his value to the magazine started to become obvious.

Addams went on to become justly famous as one of the best known, most influential, and funniest cartoonists of the twentieth century. In the forties and fifties his carefully crafted drawings appeared in *The New Yorker* at least once every two weeks, and he supplied a regular stream of cover art (sixty covers in all), particularly from the sixties onward, when his cartoons were appearing much less frequently.[48] The people he didn't reach through the magazine soon became aware of his mordant humor through the hugely successful collections of his work (ten in all), which had sold nearly half a million copies by the late seventies. In 1968 a television show based on his characters began. The bizarre group of people known as "the Addams family" soon became one of the enduring popular culture myths of the century. People now often talk about "the Addams family" as if the surname, its distinctive spelling just one more atmospheric detail like the cobwebs, the bare floorboards, and the flaking plaster, were that of the family rather than of the family's creator. Addams's influence has shown no sign of abating in recent years. There have been two feature films deriving from the television show and an animated television cartoon series for children based on the film rather than the original cartoons— a postmodern copy of a copy. Nor have the cartoons been forgotten: a new selection was published in 1994 in a handsome edition chosen by Addams's widow, to coincide with an exhibition of his cartoons at the New York Public Library.

As those early cartoons suggest, Addams began as a humorist who was highly idiosyncratic, original, and weird. Cruelty had a part in it (like the cartoon of one fakir suggesting to another, "Let's have a pillow fight" while holding up a pillow studded with nails [June 8, 1935, 28]), but Addams's comedy was never simply cruel and always had strong Dadaist qualities. Along with the unexpected use of situations involving pain and cruelty, Addams understood from the beginning how much could be gained from even the simplest challenge to the probable and the possible. In one early drawing a sheep approaches a reclining shepherd and says "Meow" (June 29, 1935, 17). A talent for devising the most startling comic contrasts, bringing together things so homely they would usually be overlooked for comic purposes and things so outré they were never thought of as within the range of comic possibility, announces itself from the start. Addams drew effortlessly on classical mythology, fairy tales, exotic South Sea Island or African locations, biblical stories, and medieval culture. He grasped that such categories exist in the public mind as a ragbag of clichés, received ideas, and stock situations, so when he defined his humor as "mauling the cliché"[49] he meant something quite precise: people's overwhelming tendency to see the world restricted by the straitjacket of such conceptions.

Once he grasped the possibilities inherent in the formula (explosion of the popular cliché plus a disjunctive association), he was on his way toward creating a new genre, the comic sublime. It is fascinating to see how quickly Addams's work moved in this direction; it took only three or four years. Soon he has Medusa sitting angrily in a hairdresser's salon, her head a mass of hissing snakes (August 15, 1936, 23); he makes a joke out of Cleopatra's barge and the University of Southern California rowing team (May 29, 1937, 27); and he produces perhaps the first cartoon to make comic use of Charon, in which two boatmen are talking before a sinister, muffled figure, with one of them asking the other, "Say, Donovan, do we have one with muffled oars?" (September 4, 1937, 13). By the mid-1930s Addams had perfected the art of creating imaginary worlds closely parallel to the real world and, in casually departing from it, making readers shiver even when the content was not explicitly transgressive.

In the first of his cartoons to make a real impact on the page, the drawing captioned "Psst. Brother Sebastian has done his room over again" (fig. 3.5), a conventional monk's cell—a bare, inhospitable, austere box—frames another cell in the background that is bright, cozy, carpeted, modern, and inviting. In it we can see a contented Brother Sebastian delicately feeding a goldfish in a bowl set on a tubular chrome table. As with so many of Addams's cartoons, the

Fig. 3.5.
Charles Addams.

"Psst. Brother Sebastian has done his room over again."

In the thirties Addams relentlessly extended the scope of comic art outward. He stretched the distance between the terms that created comic incongruity as far as possible and invented equally extreme ways to bridge that gap. How far apart could the two frames of reference be? How unbeliev-able/believable the resolution? In this instance he gives us asceticism and interior decorating as the fundamental incongruity, along with the supposedly unifying notion that a monk could plausibly be a serial redecorator. Such cartoons are in effect skeptical jokes that play with received ideas of how the world is ordered. Like all skeptical jokes they lighten, just for a moment, the burden of rationality.

idea is quirky, the realization solid, and the after-image persistent. The monk is so unlike a monk, after all: "done his room over again"—how many times has he done this? The shock is severe enough for one monk to break the code of silence (hence the "Psst"). In drawings like this Addams opened up a whole new frame of reference for comic exploitation, with an exhilarating disregard for sense and propriety.

If all humor depends on bisociation, the bringing together of seemingly incompatible frames of reference that the jokework then reconciles, Addams was one of the first cartoonists to appreciate how extreme the incompatibility could be and how precarious and unbelievable the resolution. (In this he was spurred on by the American Dadaist tradition of humor, in the work of people like Robert Benchley, Joseph Fulling Fishman, and S. J. Perelman, all of whom published in *The New Yorker*.) Addams's most memorable cartoons often hinge on the contrast between a thoroughly predictable, everyday situation and a genuinely surprising, thoroughly inappropriate event. The first term implies one set of expectations, the second triggers a wholly different set. The chasm between them is only just bridged by the jokework, as in the Brother Sebastian cartoon (fig. 3.5). The result was a comedy that was illogical, scandalous, and bizarre but wholly irresistible, partly because it liberated viewers so completely from the constraints of rationality. On this foundation Addams raised his entire oeuvre, and throughout the 1930s and the 1940s he recast graphic humor in a completely new register. In one drawing ("Can you step up here just a moment, Mr. Hodgins? I think I've found your bottleneck" [October 5, 1940, 19]) we see an old lady, pins sticking out of her mouth, sewing up the seat of a fighter plane (her right arm is pulling up the thread in a free, almost balletic, gesture) while unfinished seats pile up at the end of a conveyor belt. This collision—between Fordism and cottage industry, the production line and Grandma's quilting bee—makes us think of the whole rearmament effort's grinding to halt just because of an unaccountable oversight in the organization of the production line. The idea necessary to the joke—that a factory would ever employ someone to hand sew aircraft seats—can be maintained only with the greatest difficulty. What permits the success of the joke against the crazy improbability of the idea is the extraordinary solidity and realism of Addams's drawing.

In a similar vein, we are shown Hansel and Gretel coming across a gingerbread house in the forest and discovering a plaque on the side that reads, "Contains glucose, dry skimmed milk, oil of peppermint, dextrose and artificial coloring" (December 25, 1943, 17); a passing housewife encountering a butcher and his shop assistants wrestling with a length of sausages in the pose of the Laocoön (April 7, 1975, 39); and a hunter contentedly reading a book in his study, his equipment hung on the wall beside the stuffed animals heads —a rifle and a unicycle (*Creature Comforts,* 1981). The world of the Brothers Grimm collides with the labeling requirements of the FDA; Greek mythology resurfaces in the local strip mall;[50] big-game hunting gets mixed up with trick cycling. In the last example, the laugh is prompted not just by the idea that he has shot these animals while unicycling through the jungle but by what we infer from the startled expression in the animals' eyes at such a strange apparition—the last, and completely unintelligible, thing they see.[51]

Addams also discovered the comedy of the cliché of the exotic. Scenes in central Africa, often involving shamans, were a favorite with him. Converts to Christianity discover they can part the Red Sea (August 8, 1936, 14); an explorer laconically announces to a colleague, "Why, there's Carver now" as Carver's head is carried past on a pike (January 4, 1941, 25); a shaman, wearing a huge mask of a white MD, dances before a doubtful-looking patient (December 13, 1952, 45). The charge of racism is not unjustly leveled at such jokes, but it is important to recognize that the target of all of them is really one or another manifestation of Western complacency, as in the cartoon in which one African asks another, who is looking distinctly uncomfortable, "Now don't tell me you had anthropologist for lunch" (January 31, 1953, 21). This may well employ a derogatory cliché, but the cliché is used opportunistically rather than substantively and in some sense is recognized for what it is. It is hardly the real point of the cartoon, which rather neatly pinpoints significant stages in the history of colonialist appropriation—first explorers, then missionaries, now scientists and academics—and then makes readers participate in a comic revenge on such appropriation. That act of revenge is much more important than the cliché that enables it. What triggers the joke in Addams's exotic cartoons is always the injection of some midcentury rationalist, complacent middle-American attitude. This attitude is what these cartoon attack: the secularism that "knows" the story of Moses parting the Red Sea is just a myth; the modern world's absolute faith in medical science; the belief that the globe is completely safe for Westerners. No one could seriously offer these as examples of a benevolent politics, and they no doubt deserve a lot of the criticism they currently attract, but the cartoons are much less hegemonic that such charges imply.[52]

Because they challenge our expectations of how the world is put together, most of these jokes can be gathered into Freud's useful category of skeptical jokes, that is, jokes that attack "the certainty of our knowledge itself, of our speculative possession."[53] The wonderful drawing of the pair of unicorns (March 10, 1956, 44) left stranded on a rock as the Ark sails off into the distance derives its effect partly from the look on the unicorns' faces. (Consternation about to turn to indignation.) But the joke works so well because of the intensely realistic quality of the drawing. Its strong, rueful pathos involves us completely, not only by jolting our certitude that unicorns never existed or that the story of the Ark cannot be literally true but by linking those two incompatible mythologies. The idea of the skeptical joke in fact illuminates many of Addams's most memorable cartoons. The celebrated drawing from January 13, 1940 (13), of the skier whose tracks pass on both sides of a tree, a cartoon that has been the subject of much discussion, is at least on one level simply a skeptical joke (the two thirteens—the date and the page number—are probably not accidental).[54]

The skier cartoon makes plain something characteristic of Addams's wit. He so constructs his jokes that the path of identification for the viewer is generally not with the possessor of outraged common sense but with the agent whose actions disrupt the expected order of things. We identify with the revolutionary, not the writer of the letter; with Brother Sebastian, not his fellow monks; with the grandmother devotedly doing her sewing, not the outraged production manager; with the woman who has let the tree pass through her, not the disbelieving observer. A partial explanation of this kind of response is that maintaining a wholly rational, commonsense, sensible attitude toward the world, as is increasingly demanded of people who live in a modern industrial or postindustrial society, is extremely burdensome. The "stern stepmother reason"—the constant obligation that we abide by the standards of critical judgment—is a grim, inhibitory personage. We welcome any opportunity to escape from her clutches, to regress, and to recover, for however short a time, the playfulness of infancy and the pleasure this yields.[55]

It is understandable, then, that Addams's favorite target should be banality as represented by the ranks of ordinary, decent, law-abiding citizens. One way Addams did express his time was in his revolt against life in the suburbs, then something new. Banality, so Addams seems to imply, is emblazoned on the banner under which most lives in America were lived through the long middle reaches of the century when he flourished, from the mid-1930s to the early 1960s. Banality implies the reign of *doxa*—of received opinion, automatic expectations, clichés and stereotypes, unexamined common sense. Above all, it implies the production of boredom. Unlike Steig, Addams does not register a cryptopolitical protest about the conformism that midcentury American society imposed on its citizens, though he may have felt as keenly as Steig that things could be different, and lives fuller, if people could only throw off their chains. But Addams accepts conformity and ordinariness as given and uses them as a foil for his luxuriant comedy of transgressive compensation. Steig in some moods was a comic healer. Addams's more modest ambition was that jokes conceived as provocations would enrich the barren soil of the suburb.

Skeptical wit is tendentious wit—it produces jokes with a purpose, jokes with something to attack. Nearly all of Addams's cartoons are tendentious in this wider sense. Tendentious wit, according to Freud, manifests itself in four main ways—as sexual jokes (which indirectly bring to mind the sexual act), aggressive jokes (which make our enemy seem "small and despicable"), skeptical jokes (which attack received ideas and the certitude of our knowledge), and cynical jokes (which attack venerated social institutions).[56] These categories are all approximate, and it is perhaps simpler to say that tendentious jokes (including and perhaps especially sexual jokes) are all ultimately aggressive in character. The main feature of a tendentious joke is not just that it has a particular purpose but that it has a particular object, too. There are, Freud says, always three parties involved in a joke. There is the teller of the joke (the first person); the listener to the joke (the third person); and the person the joke is about, the butt (the second person). It is not necessary that these should be actual people: it is obvious that the listener and the second party can be the same person and not inconceivable that the teller and the second party can be the same person too. It is also obvious that the second person often features in the joke in a disguised form. A tendentious joke involves, then, an attack, usually disguised or covert, on this second person. Addams's cartoons are very frequently tendentious jokes in this sense, and Addams consequently is a joker rather than a humorist.

In Addams's cartoon of the old gentleman driving the car approaching the "Careful! Children at Play" sign, for example (fig. 3.6), the three parties that make up the joking triad are the joker, or cartoonist (the first person); the listener, or us as viewers of the cartoon (the third person); and the butt, or the man driving the car (the second person). But the old man stands for someone else. He stands for all unimaginative, literal-minded, unobservant, sentimental people who accept the myth of the innocence of childhood. He stands for anyone who, convinced that children are harmless, will not permit himself a trace of suspicion about them. (If we are honest, we will probably admit that he also stands for part of ourselves.) The joke's aim is to disabuse us of any such illusions about childhood, more particularly to mount a symbolic attack on people who hold such beliefs. Freud notes that it is "only jokes that have a purpose [that] run the risk of meeting with people who do not want to hear them."[57] Addams has run up against more than his fair share of opposition over the years. We have already come across Jesse Bier's negative assessment of Addams as a humorist who remorselessly "crosses all lines of taste" in pursuit of "his horrification of American bourgeois living."[58] Bier has a point: the man driving the car symbolizes the generality of the American middle class, whom Addams sees as incurably unimaginative, unperceptive, and complacent—predictable in their niceness, their sociability, their docility, their reasonableness, and above all their gullibility. Addams comes to associate these attitudes, as his career develops, with the suburbs of the late 1940s and the 1950s. Many of his most characteristic jokes are in fact assaults on the complacency of the suburban ethos and the banal temperateness of character it produces (hence, we might say, the very reason for his popularity in the suburbs everywhere).[59] A joke like "Careful! Children at Play" is an aggressive attempt to overcome and pay back the good citizen, an enemy who is made to appear "small, inferior, despicable or comic," but an enemy who is often simply us, reflected back in a comic distorting mirror.[60]

How deliberate this endeavor was is clear from three repeated subjects in Addams's work: his cartoons about children, marriage, and the family—tendentious jokes against three main symbols of middle-class life. Of particular interest is Addams's treatment of children, since they are so often a focus of sentimental regard. In Addams's world they are typically caged and restrained like wild beasts: we see them pushed around in carriages with metal grilles across the hood (January 22, 1949, 33), returned from summer camp safely stowed in a cage (August 30, 1947, 20), or taken out to the school bus bound and gagged (September 29, 1951, 30). Pugsley[61] is discovered standing on a child's bed with vultures' heads topping the bedposts, decorating his room with a collection of warning signs stolen from around town—"Caution! Unguarded Shaftway," "No Diving, Pool Empty," "Keep Clear, High Voltage," "Dangerous Undertow," "Spring Condemned" (August 27, 1949, 29). The temporal structure of this joke—in which an event is either about to happen or already has happened—is typical of Addams's work: the carol singers cartoon (fig. 3.2), for example, would not be funny at all had the scene been shown thirty seconds later. It is derived perhaps from Arno, who was adept at representing a scene either just before or just after the catastrophe, so that to get the joke one has to invent, prospectively or retrospectively, other stages in the narrative sequence. Here we have a lot to imagine: honest citizens falling headfirst into unmarked mine shafts, diving into empty pools, straying into electricity supply substations, swimming out into a dangerous sea, and drinking contaminated water. In another drawing Pugsley is shown gleefully staging a crash between a toy train and a toy school bus—not a greatly exaggerated idea (April 16, 1949, 21). In another he is shown guillotining his sister's doll (December 24, 1949, 27); the tree in the background and the festive wrapping tell us that both doll and guillotine are Christmas presents, though the little girl's un-

The Comic Worlds of Arno, Steig, Addams, and Steinberg

Fig. 3.6. Charles
Addams. Uncaptioned.
Titled: "Careful! Chil-
dren at Play."

The New Yorker,
December 20, 1947,
32. © 1947 Charles
Addams. Reproduced
with permission of Tee
and Charles Addams
Foundation.

The family, marriage, and children were three of Addams's
favorite targets. Here we have an aggressive, tendentious joke
in the Freudian mold with a clear butt: the man in the car, of
course, but anyone who unthinkingly and sentimentally be-
lieves—against the evidence—in the innocence of children.
Addams deploys the commonplace furnishings of everyday
life—an automobile, a quiet village street, a school, a road
sign, an old duffer, and kiddies—all effectively drawn, as usual.
But nothing is quite what it seems. The short-sighted old
gentleman is us in our blinkered, myopic view of the world.
The porcine, diabolical little boys are the old Adam within
us all, our regressive pleasure in violence. The sign, "Careful! Children at Play," is one of those phrases in which nearly
every word is an empty vessel suddenly filled with new meaning. "Careful" means not "be careful for them" but "take care
of yourself." "Play" means not the innocent play of babes but
the cruel play of the bad seed, and what they are playing with
is your safety.

resisting cooperation is disturbing. Such jokes clearly depend on an allusion to—and instant demolition of—a conventional view of children as naturally innocent and uncorrupted.[62] A drawing that sums up this theme shows Morticia and her mother chatting over a cup of tea. From her knitting we are given to understand that Morticia is pregnant. She is saying, ". . . and if it's a boy, we're going to give him a Biblical name, like Cain or Ananias" (August 9, 1958, 29). Cain is self-explanatory, but the allusion to Ananias, the man who "lied unto God" and was struck dead for punishment, shows how far Addams was prepared to send his readers in search of a joke. The contrast with Steig is striking: Steig identifies the child as radical innocent; Addams identifies the child as original sinner.[63] Addams never had children of his own, and his distance from family life possibly encouraged this lack of sentimentality: in one salient image (unpublished, dating from the late 1980s and reproduced in *The World of Charles Addams,* 1991, 295) a strange pterodactyl-like creature, a diabolical stand-in for the stork, leaves a ghastly changeling on a doorstep. Children are indeed moral changelings in Addams's world—strange goblinlike visitants from some other realm. This, no doubt, is Addams's final comment on the late twentieth-century death of childhood. In Addams's world children are never innocent and usually are the instigators of acts of evil intent. We understand perfectly why that nurse in Central Park is pushing a baby carriage equipped with a stout metal grille.

The gleeful venom shown in Addams's cartoons about children is also present in his cartoons about marriage. It is no coincidence that his most mordant cartoons on this subject are bunched together in the sixteen-year period between 1943 and 1956, the years that cover Addams's first two marriages. (These marriages were both to women who, as he himself later confessed, resembled Morticia; they shared the same first name, Barbara. After fourteen years as a bachelor he later married Marilyn "Tee" Williams in 1980, in the notorious "wedding in a pet cemetery.")[64] A large number of these cartoons are about marital homicide. Addams never shows the murder directly. Sometimes it is yet to happen: a frumpy wife packs a time bomb in her husband's lunchbox (May 14, 1949, 27) or a husband calls his wife out of their trailer, which he has stopped on the edge of a precipice: "Oh, darling, can you step out for a moment?" (December 3, 1949, 27). In other drawings the deed has already been done: a visiting couple stare at a shape suspiciously like a mummified corpse cleft in the bark of a tree in a suburban garden and wonder "if Mr. Lawrence really *did* go to South America" (June 26, 1948, 23); an attic is shown, with castoff clothes neatly stowed away in protective covers duly labeled "Maud's velvet dress," "Richard's gray jacket," "Richard's summer formals," "Richard" (*McClure Syndicate,* December 4, 1955; reproduced in *The*

World of Charles Addams, 138). The motives of the participants often show a premeditation that is breathtaking in its matter-of-factness, as with the husband at the ticket booth at Grand Central Station who orders "a round trip and a one-way to Ausable Chasm" while his foolish-looking wife stands patiently by (January 18, 1941, 28). An important variant to the motif is given by those drawings that hinge on a contrast between outer tolerance and inner hatred. A husband visiting the Colosseum with his wife has a pleasing vision of her being pursued across the arena by a lion (July 15, 1950, 26); a matron emerges from a performance of *Salome* at Carnegie Hall toying with the image of her husband's head on a platter (February 25, 1956, 37); a man out placidly canoeing with his wife is mirrored in the lake as about to hit her over the head with the paddle (July 7, 1975, 25).[65] The contrast is familiar—between the illusion of law-abiding civility and the actuality of murderous feelings. Murderous spouses connect easily with the ideals of suburban life, as in the Halloween cartoon of a dumpy middle-aged housewife surrounded by detectives who confesses to her crime in words that fuse homicidal rage with laborsaving appliances: ". . . and then I disconnected the booster from the Electro-Snuggie Blanket and put him in the deep freeze. In the morning, I defrosted him and ran him through the Handi Home Slicer and then the Jiffy Burger Grind, and after that I fed him down the Dispose-All. Then I washed my clothes in the Bendix, tidied up the kitchen, and went to a movie" (October 30, 1948, 20).

What better subject, then, than the family itself? Hence Addams's most famous series of cartoons, which make a clear transition from the criminal to the diabolical. For what are "Addams family" cartoons (twenty-four in the most comprehensive selection of Addams's work)[66] but an attack on a central value of middle America, their popularity unsurprising in an age that tiresomely insisted on the essential wholesomeness and sanity of the suburban family in its classic two-adult, two-child configuration, a configuration that the Addams family faithfully replicates and whose status as cliché he systematically explodes?[67] The link is made clear in a cartoon published in *The New Yorker* for November 4, 1950 (45), which shows the family watching television. The announcer is saying, "And now we present 'Mary and Bill,' the story of a family that might be your next-door neighbors, and of their everyday life among everyday people just like yourselves. . . ." The cliché of the perfect family was the staple of television series like "Father Knows Best," "The Nelsons," and "Leave It to Beaver"—programs that are known to have been cynically produced by people who fully admitted their falsity. In the gothic suburbs inhabited by Addams's family, "my own disreputable children" as their creator called them, Friday the thirteenth is always booked with prior engagements (April 14, 1945, 23), home improvements involve putting in a picture window to open out the view to the local cemetery (June 24, 1950, 17), and an innocent nursery rhyme like "This Little Piggy Went to Market" runs up against an extra toe (July 21, 1945, 21). In the family cartoons, the clean, safe streets, sunny lawns, and well-lit rooms of American suburbia are transformed into their opposites. The Addams family is quasi-aristocratic rather than middle class, hierarchical rather than egalitarian (it has servants and slaves), misshapen, ugly, and monstrous in a period that was well on its way to prescribing ideal faces and bodies. In an age when the new is worshipped, Addams's people inhabit a world that is decaying and moribund. Rather than a haven from evil, the house is a place that generates evil. (This is an idea that runs constantly through gothic literature and film—from Poe through Ira Levin to Stephen King, not forgetting Hollywood's contributions such as the evocative and overtly demonized houses of films such as *Dragonwyck* and *Rebecca*.) The dark, shabby interiors are drawn with relish, with the help of an eye that delights in age, ornamental excrescence, dirt, decay, and neglect. Addams's taste is the exact reverse of the burgeoning desire for clean, "form follows function" minimalism, promoted in contemporary advertisements in *The New Yorker*. These ads for silverware by Georg Jensen or furniture by Paul McCobb (the latter with its motto set in lowercase Helvetica type: "a permanent contribution to american design") radiate a stylish, bright, contemporary glow.[68] Dad has become a werewolf, Mom a witch, Grandma a hag, Uncle Fester a ghoul, and the butler a zombie. Other inhabitants suggest imprisonment, madness, slavery: a strange, scared-looking, unidentifiable figure, perhaps female, who half-wittedly overlooks the family's doings from sundry hiding places; a record player operated by skinny arms and hands angling out from its interior. Together, house and family place Addams securely in the gothic tradition.

In all these cartoons Addams encourages viewers to recognize the double-sidedness of human nature. This accords with the paranoid element in his humor. The jokes are predicated on an exaggerated suspiciousness about other people, the implication that the side they present socially is always backed up with a darker and more sinister side they never show. His conviction of the doubleness of people is laid out most plainly in his transformation drawings, of which three stand out. A simple, highly effective version of the theme is found in a drawing showing an image of stunning banality, an inoffensive man sitting in a barber's chair. But the drawing is enlivened by an eloquent rendition of the mise-en-abîme effect: several layers of reflection deep, we see a werewolf's head on the customer's shoulders (February 23, 1957, 39). An earlier version of this theme appears in 1946 in a drawing that also interlocks with the way Addams deals with the cliché of "science" as a public good. In this sequence, with allusions to Robert Louis Stevenson, a little boy playing with a child's chemistry set (evidently a Christmas present) concocts a mixture that turns him into a loathsome, animalistic monster. Hearing his mother on the stairs, he just as quickly devises the antidote and returns himself to normal — just in time for his mother to pop her head around the door and be reassured that her offspring is just having some innocent, educational fun. The happy expression on the mother's face says it all and identifies her as the butt of the joke (December 28, 1946, 20–21).

Ten years later Addams returned to the same theme, choosing another innocent, "improving" scientific setting — this time the Hayden Planetarium at Seventy-ninth Street and Central Park West. In this sequence a nobody figure finds himself turning into a werewolf as the full moon waxes on the ceiling overhead, then back to his old nobody self as it wanes (fig. 3.7). Like many of Addams's cartoons, this one assumes a viewer who is secretly skeptical about the pretensions of modern knowledge. It picks up on a change in public opinion — the replacement of prewar optimism about science by postwar dubiety, the effect largely of the atomic bomb. Addams's joke hinges, however, not so much on skepticism as on incongruity, a collision between science and superstition dramatized with great ingenuity. The transformation of man into werewolf and back again is visible to the viewer of the cartoon only because, thanks to the mechanism of the planetarium, time has been speeded up: what would normally take a month (the waxing and waning of the moon) is compressed into a few telltale minutes. The joke requires this compression of time as much as it requires the transformation itself. Medieval superstition has its veracity confirmed by the very technique, modern and scientific in character, that has supposedly banished it. Meanwhile, the audience remains unaware of the transformation, and in the end the little man (so unlike Steig's "little man") takes his hat and leaves amid everyone's pleasant chatter. The joke, like so many of Addams's, produces an unequal distribution of knowledge: a gap between the damped-down awareness of the decent folk who inhabit the drawing and the viewers' expanded consciousness. What the viewers of the cartoon savor is precisely that contrast. As we laugh we side with the nobody become werewolf (the most interesting person in the cartoon) and feel again our superiority over the unknowing generality. From such drawings we have a clear view into a world of real-life horror and evil — the sort of world that at its most extreme includes a Jeffrey Dahmer or a Fred West. Addams, we might say, suspects the existence of such people and confirms, comically, our own anxious suspicion that they might exist. The distance between cartoon and actuality is great, of course, but we see that the journey could be made. This is obviously true of the cartoon in which a squadron of detectives surrounds the suburban house of a blameless-looking little man. A plainclothes detective at the door asks, "Excuse me, sir, but are you the Arthur Johnson who lost this diary?" (September 15, 1951, 29). They might, of course, have the wrong Arthur Johnson, and that might be the joke. But they might have the right Arthur Johnson, and *that* might be the joke.

Ordinariness, then, as well as being the cartoonist's target, is the disguise people use to conceal their true—often diabolical—nature. In the attention they pay to this idea, Addams's drawings are certainly in tune with the "paranoid style" famously identified by Richard Hofstadter as a bass figure in American life in the late 1940s and the 1950s.[69] Undue suspiciousness about other people is a major feature of the paranoid style. It is usually explained in terms of projection; that is, the suspicions are about impulses that have originated in the anxious person and then been imputed to others. Projection in this sense is crucial to the paranoid style, especially in its later phase from the mid-1940s and onward, when a new uncertainty about America's role in the world, focused by the fear of international communism and the cold war, is transformed into a generalized suspicion.[70] Many of Addams's cartoons turned inside out imply a similar, if depoliticized, suspiciousness about other people ("ordinary" people are really monsters). Moreover, the general character of social reality Addams presents is one of displaced threat centering on the unnoticed monstrous stranger in our midst, like the little man in the planetarium, monsters that no doubt originate as repudiated elements of Addams's own mental life. But Addams's comedy is unique in that it deals with all this by happily taking the part of the disruptive, anxiety-provoking element. Suspicions are certainly projected onto others: hence Addams's cast of diabolical children, murderous wives and husbands, and sadistic neighbors. But these figures are imaginatively embraced and enjoyed rather than rejected and feared. Viewers (to their relief) are allowed to approve of their transgressive impulses.

Fig. 3.7. Charles Addams. Uncaptioned cartoon. Titled: Planetarium.

The New Yorker, February 18, 1956, 36–37. © 1956 Charles Addams. Reproduced with permission of Tee and Charles Addams Foundation.

Arno's and Steig's "little men" were victims: Arno's impotent Remson; Steig's harassed, sheeplike, but good-hearted carrier of the emotional plague. Charles Addams's little man is someone quite different: the innocuous person next door who also happens to be a monster. Addams drew many variants of this theme, though none, perhaps, so visually telling as this one in which the little man, on a self-improving visit to that temple of modern science, the planetarium, turns into a werewolf as the moon waxes and back to his everyday self as it wanes. It is particularly important that no one except us notices what happens. We are granted a special kind of knowledge or insight that ensures our complicity with Addams's view of humanity.

The Comic Worlds of Arno, Steig, Addams, and Steinberg

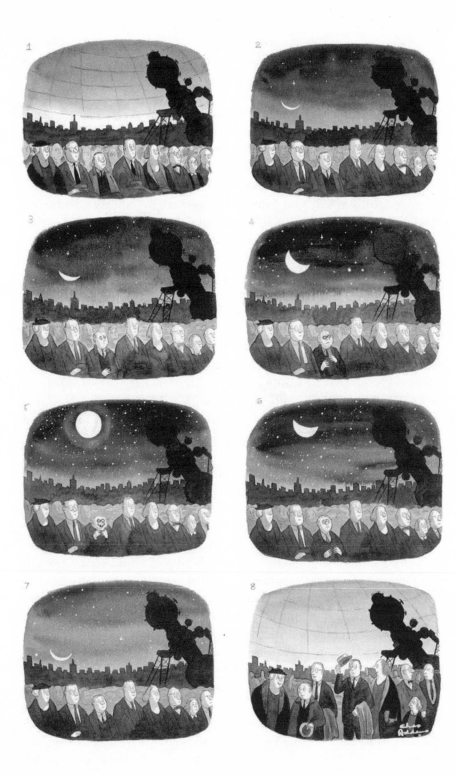

Addams, of course, never manifests the out-of-control conspiratorial delusions of the paranoid right. To the contrary, what is notable in his work is the comic neutralizing of just that sort of fantasy. We see this very clearly in Addams's treatment of one of the most obvious ways displaced anxiety manifested itself in the fifties: the fear of invasion from outer space. The classic instances are well known: Orson Welles's radio dramatization in 1938 of H. G. Wells's *The War of the Worlds* and Don Siegel's *Invasion of the Body Snatchers,* released in 1956. Although William Shawn disapproved of jokes about spacemen, Addams liked the theme. As might be expected, he takes the "invasion" as real and the skepticism inevitably shown toward it by ordinary suburbanites as a sign of their incurable stupidity and inability to make sense of what they see. A typical example is the cartoon that shows a housewife humoring a childlike figure in a spacesuit who is in fact a real extraterrestrial (November 1, 1952, 26). What is obvious if we compare this cartoon with a paranoid classic like *The Invasion of the Body Snatchers* is the way Addams's cartoon is a stabilizing gesture, reducing fearfulness in laughter rather than increasing it through horror.

Hofstadter says that the aesthetic mark of paranoia is a "distorted style,"[71] so we might expect that a "paranoid" artist would show some sign of stylistic disturbance. Is this the case with Addams? At first glance the answer appears to be no. When he was the art critic of *The New York Times,* John Russell insisted on "the sturdiness of the line, the rock-solid composition, the eye for scale and placement" in Addams's work—characteristics that signal a realist quality, the very reverse of distortion.[72] Addams's style might well be taken as a form of pictorial literalism—a naive mimetic realism, even—and thus the very opposite of any stylistic distortion that could be associated with aesthetic paranoia. It is a complicated question, however, and opens up the whole issue of the way Addams draws. Stylistically, Addams is certainly a realist and even a literalist: there is careful attention to setting (buildings, vehicles, backgrounds, furniture, clothes, and so on), and this grounds his jokes in a solid, concrete world. But that world is subject to various forms of inner distortion. Adams's literalism, for example, is a naive literalism, excessive and to that extent distorted (as the word "naive" itself implies), and his realism is hyperrealism. His draftsmanship often suggests a child's deliberateness of intent, a child's obsessive attention to detail, and a child's literal handling of scale and proportion, even where the material is adult. Because of this the final effect is often grotesque and alienating. His "ordinary" figures end up like strange, dumpy little dolls or misshapen automatons out of the uncanny world of E. T. A. Hoffmann. It is wholly characteristic of Addams that his wind-up clockwork men should be indistinguishable, except for size, from his real people (November 16, 1987, 41). His most ordinary settings have a static, deadened, nightmarish atmosphere.

The style develops slowly during his first five years at *The New Yorker*. Then, once Addams becomes aware of what he can make it do, it stabilizes and ceases to develop any further (some later drawings are done in a slightly freer style). Initially he draws in a simple ink outline. The models were probably the then influential artists working at the magazine like Rea Irvin, Gluyas Williams, and Al Frueh, who worked in an outline idiom distantly derived from Beardsley and other fin de siècle and decadent artists of the 1890s. About mid-1935 Addams begins to experiment with wash, important for that effect of verisimilitude that became essential to his comic effects. First he builds up the solidity of the figures, as in the two fakirs with the regulation beds of nails (June 8, 1935, 28). Later he develops the setting. The drawing of Brother Sebastian's cell (fig. 3.5) sets out on a stylistic path blazed by Arno (though in far more obviously stylish and theatrical manner), but also by William Steig and Robert Day, with their solid figures and closely worked drawings. From the mid-1930s a high degree of pictorial description of the mise-en-scène becomes Addams's trademark.

The importance of this move should not be underestimated. Addams's humor depends so often on the thick description of the drawing—the sheer quantity of detailed information conveyed—which establishes a comfortable yet slightly odd normality, which in turn enforces credence in a bizarre situation or locale. Credence is essential to his humor. In order to produce suspension of disbelief, the bizarre event has to be placed within a strongly believable setting. By abandoning the outline style favored by Irvin, Williams, and Frueh and the abbreviated style introduced by Thurber, Addams was able to extend the breadth, and also the extremity, of reference in his drawings. He could take graphic humor in the direction of the exotic (both geographically and historically), the bizarre, the macabre, and the supernatural because the dense realism of his art encourages suspension of disbelief. Addams's meticulous pictorialism aligns itself with his interest in the look of the mundane. He represents the blankness of everyday experience and the matter-of-fact reality of an exotic setting in a heightened manner. Addams turns this unadventurous but obsessive pictorialism back on itself by making his settings the stage for some very odd activities indeed. He is a self-conscious user of the artistic mode that he has mastered, and his aesthetic preferences should not be equated with a literal realism. The style is itself a mask, a language, an idiom, even an object of attack. The very solidity of that style is fused with the intention to create what Wolcott Gibbs called a world "terribly at variance with the observable universe," and Gibbs was right to contrast this with the "reportorial style of artists like Helen Hokinson."[73]

Addams's style is extremely prolix, and this is odd given the tendency in most comic forms toward an informal economy of means. Certainly Addams is one of those artists who are driven to pictorialize a conception fully. This is in part the artist's fascination with what Wilfrid Sheed has called "the sheer thingness of things"[74]—a fascination that underpins the extreme specificity and concreteness with which Addams creates his world. One thinks of the realism of his rooms and houses, as well as his capacity to create a mood of eeriness, desolation, loneliness, and menace. But this dense realism is also a way of accumulating the huge amount of detail necessary for the joke: not just to create a suitable setting but to make that setting rich and absorbing in itself so that within it Addams can hide the extraneous detail that will trigger the comic detonation. The viewer processes detail not instantaneously but in two stages, sorting out information from noise. When Addams has an oculist say to a customer who has his back turned to us, "Now, let's just slip it on and see how it fits" (February 3, 1945, 21), the joke requires that we finally notice, among all the clutter of the scene, one tiny detail: the monocle he is holding up has the rest for the bridge of the nose directly under the lens, showing that the customer, whose face we cannot see, must have a single Cyclopean eye. In all the crammed detail of a drawing that sets before us a solid, actual oculist's shop, this one crucial fact is to be discovered, and on that discovery the joke will depend. Addams's drawings work so well because they are remarkably free of any unwanted ambiguity. The ambiguity they do possess is functional, generated by the situation represented and essential to the joke, never a consequence of any failure of description on the part of the artist. An Addams cartoon inspires extraordinary confidence—such is its fundamental clarity. Addams's genius lies in his ability to render an idea, a conception, or a situation pictorially—to set up the elements of the joke in such a way that the viewer's attention is totally and surprisingly focused. Repletion of detail serves in a roundabout way the familiar joking principles of economy and condensation because the joke itself always depends on our noticing that one significant detail played off against an irrelevant density of context.[75]

In the 1940s Addams drew two wonderful cartoons that bring us close to the core of his humor and show very clearly how the gothic springs out of hostile feelings, suspicion, and projection. Both are set in movie houses. In the first one (fig. 3.8) we see sitting in the audience the character later known as Uncle Fester, whom Addams identified as a self-portrait of sorts.[76] Once you pick him out (he is cleverly placed just a little off center), you see he is laughing wickedly, with a superbly drawn expression of delight, hand half raised in a connoisseur's gesture of protesting admiration at whatever scene of pathos and suffering has reduced the rest of the audience to tears. The comic trope, reminiscent of the werewolf in the planetarium joke, is also a gothic trope: it

The Comic Worlds of Arno, Steig, Addams, and Steinberg

Fig. 3.8. Charles
Addams. Uncaptioned
cartoon. Titled: Sad
Movie.

The New Yorker,
March 23, 1946,
31. © 1946 Charles
Addams. Reproduced
with permission of Tee
and Charles Addams
Foundation.

Addams insisted that the captionless cartoon was the highest
example of the comic art genre, and this is a brilliantly composed and maliciously conceived example. It is common to
miss the figure who springs the trap. One's eye is drawn first
to the weeping woman in the center foreground, then to the
woman behind her, and only then, in a knight's move, to the
hunched-up, chuckling "Uncle Fester," his hand half raised in
astonished admiration at whatever misery is taking place on
the screen. It is a powerful antisentimental joke that indirectly
lets us acknowledge our own hostility toward conventional
taste and admit our enjoyment of scenes of cruelty and suffering. Addams's popularity shows how broad and deep is the
current of hostility he taps. But this is also an example of
how Addams's comedy neutralizes our aggressive instincts by
making the shameful something to be openly laughed at rather
than secretly indulged.

is that of the monster unseen in our midst. The laugh here is at the expense of the mawkishness characteristic of ordinary folk, the "tears" side of the "laughter and tears" formula, a sentimentality of which middle class people are traditionally the guardians. There is an obvious extension implied from the movie crowd shown in the drawing—all mechanically manifesting exactly the same emotional reaction, like so many obedient, well-conditioned Pavlovian dogs—to the possessors of such taste in the culture at large.

What does it mean to laugh at this joke? One does not, obviously, laugh at Uncle Fester. One laughs with him. But this implies contempt for the softhearted souls shown in the drawing. If this is true, then to laugh at this joke is once more to be drawn over to the side of the transgressor, to Uncle Fester's side, made for the moment to side with his perverse callousness. The joke is an aggressive, cynical joke at the expense of the values and habits of decent folk. It is this identification, the creation of a bond between the viewer and the transgressor at the expense of any sympathy for the unimaginative, conformist, and passive victims, that is the most characteristic feature of Addams's humor. The pleasure of such jokes derives from their mildly transgressive and regressive nature—the temporary lifting, for the viewer of the cartoon, the third person of Freud's joking triad, of the inhibitions on expressing that outright hostility we all feel more than we would ever want to admit. To laugh at this joke, and to derive pleasure from it, is to evade for a moment the rule of the superego that makes us good citizens. There is a clear element of projection in this drawing, characteristic of Addams's humor: a tendency to split off antisocial, aggressive feelings and attribute them to an imaginary character. Here Addams deals with his contempt for mawkish sentimentality and his anger toward people who indulge in it, not by expressing it directly, but by attributing it to his creation, Uncle Fester. We are all monsters in our own way, people who enjoy seeing our own negative and asocial feelings when attributed to another.

This much is virtually admitted in a second cartoon (fig. 3.9). It shows a movie where the viewer looks from the rear of the auditorium, behind the audience, toward the screen, on which a woman is screaming in horror at something or person bearing down on her. In the ordinary world we understand the terror to be confined to the film, to exist only within the screen world. (The customary reverse angle shot that often follows the closeup of a screaming face would establish this by showing whatever it was that was terrifying her.) But this drawing is an example (rare until Saul Steinberg perfected it) of ontological play in the cartoon, a shuffling or confusing of various separate levels of reality. The joke depends on our sorting out those levels—the screen world of the actor, the imaginary world created by the audience's suspension

Fig. 3.9. Charles Addams. Uncaptioned cartoon. Titled: Screen Scream.

The New Yorker, February 8, 1947, 27. © 1947 Charles Addams. Reproduced with permission of Tee and Charles Addams Foundation.

The mise-en-abîme effect in the service of American gothic. Who, or what, are they really frightened of, the actress and the audience? Something in the film? (But how can the audience see it?) Something that has invaded the theater? (But how can the actress, no more than an image on the screen, see it?) Someone over your shoulder as you look at this page? (Perhaps you should look behind you too, just to be sure?) But then we notice that most pairs of eyes in the drawing seem to be focused on us (the actress, the man second from the left, the woman second from the right). You, dear reader, are the cause of all this terror. In this drawing Addams takes the logic of his interest in the idea of the monster in our midst to its logical conclusion. The monster might not be the person sitting next to you in the planetarium after all. Instead, it could be you.

of disbelief, and the actual room in which the reader is viewing the cartoon. How complicated this is becomes clear when we try to describe what is going on. The actress sees something in the film that provokes terror. Unaccountably, the members of the audience react to her not by remaining in their seats, absorbed in her imaginary situation, but by standing up and looking behind themselves in the theater. An explanation of such odd behavior might be that her acting is so convincing that the audience members instinctively turn and look behind them to see what is causing that terror. They are "taken in" by the illusion. But no one would be satisfied with this explanation, because the people in the audience seem to have really seen something. A second attempt at explanation would add that the alarm on their faces suggests that whatever is terrifying the actress really exists and has just broken into the theater. The joke, then, is that the two planes of reality—the imaginary world of the film and the actual world of the audience—have merged (rather as they do in Woody Allen's *The Purple Rose of Cairo*).

But this game, in which separate planes of reality intersect, can go on indefinitely. What, after all, is the most probable cause of the terror—given that this cartoon takes place in a world in which the fictive and the real merge? The answer is given only if we notice that this cartoon acknowledges not two, but three planes of reality: that of the film, that of the audience, and that of the person looking at the cartoon. What strikes terror into both actress and audience, a creature whose monstrous presence is so powerful that it breaks through the boundaries separating those three planes of reality, is perhaps something over *our* shoulder. But then we notice that most pairs of eyes in the cartoon seem to be focused directly on us. Even more frightening is the idea that what everyone in the cartoon is looking at in horror is us, the viewers of the cartoon, as we hold the magazine. It is the Uncle Fester we all are, the person who laughs at suffering rather than empathizing with scenes of distress and tragedy, the person who gets pleasure out of aggression, whose real monstrousness is known to ourselves alone. The cartoon unmasks the Mr. Hyde inside the decent Dr. Jekyll, and he turns out to be us. In effect, the cartoon runs the mechanism of projection backward, showing how violence and destructiveness derive not from the other but from us. We simply project those qualities onto other people. We are the monsters in our midst. If we are Charles Addams, we invent a Pugsley, an Arthur Johnson, an Uncle Fester. If we are not Charles Addams, we let him do it for us.

Addams is obviously an aggressive joker in the Freudian sense. His cartoons single out as their butt the ordinary citizen, whom they harass and belittle. They typically express hostility and aggressiveness, impulses that civilized peo-

The Comic Worlds of Arno, Steig, Addams, and Steinberg

ple are called on to suppress daily. They aim to provide the substitutive satisfaction of such feelings, allowing us regressively to recover a long-forgone pleasure in them. Superiority and relief are important for Addams's humor, undoubtedly, but his cartoons do more than provide relief. That we end up feeling superior to ourselves means that superiority theory alone does not adequately explain his humor. Addams's cartoons strike most viewers as being the reverse of pathological, as having some kind of sanative value, and here Freudianism does not really help, perhaps because it pays too much attention to the inner drama of the self at the expense of relations between people. Freudianism lays great emphasis on the distant origins of neuroses (one's relations with one's parents in infancy, for example). It is obsessed by the past, by origins. It also puts a lot of weight on the inner drama of the psyche's development (what actually happens is important, but even more important is what the subject thinks or imagines has happened). Finally, it assumes that the repair of the disturbed mind must involve sorting out a largely internal story (the point of the therapeutic archaeological dig into the patient's psyche and the talking through of what is unearthed).

Object relations psychoanalytic theory offers the best alternative to Freud here. Object relations pays somewhat less attention to the past and rather more attention to the self's present involvement with other people. Consequently it is more useful than Freudianism in considering the idea of joking as a social transaction. In particular, because the idea of projection is so important a part of it, object relations theory offers much help in understanding Addams as a comic gothicist, in whose work this element is also very important. Louis Gross singles out projection as a key feature of American gothic. The element of projection in Addams's cartoons — roughly, attributing to other people impulses one doesn't want to acknowledge in oneself — has already been touched on. There are clear links between projection in this loose sense and the more specific concept of "projective identification" in object relations thinking, as well as the related ideas of "containing," "introjection," and "linking."[77]

It is noticeable that Addams drew many cartoons in which small children perform cruel and destructive acts, acts that, against the restraints of adult norms, the viewer surrenders to and delights in. These cartoons rely on regressive humor (the creator of the humor regresses, as does the viewer who joins in). It is a short distance from these children to the little baby as it appears in the work of object relations theorists like Melanie Klein, Donald Winnicott, and Wilfrid Bion. Unlike the Freudian baby, the object relations baby senses its relatedness to other people, especially the mother, at a very early stage, even in the first three months of life. Just as it understands its helpless dependency, it also realizes its capacity for destructiveness, and the two feelings go together.

The baby feels itself dangerously threatened by the turbulence of its emotional life, a torrent of violent, sadistic, and destructive fantasies.[78] The baby copes in two ways. It detaches the fantasies from itself (the destructiveness is not "me"), and it splits the mother into good and bad aspects (the mother who feeds the child and makes it feel secure and loved, and the mother whose absence provokes rage and anger). It is then able to pass all its rage and anger over to the bad mother.[79] This leaves the baby feeling vulnerable and guilty. Intuitively, the mother knows what the baby cannot know: that these terrible-seeming emotions are really not so destructive after all. In continuing to love and nurture the baby, she shows that she is neither injured nor destroyed by those feelings, and this ability to accept those turbulent emotions, and to scale them down, moderates their severity.[80] It is in this modified form, as emotions that have been feelingly understood and proportioned or scaled down, that the mother is able to return to the baby what the baby had thrust away from itself and onto her. The baby can accept aspects of itself that it had previously rejected. Its anxieties about its own destructive potential are allayed. A bond is made, or confirmed, between mother and child, and the child is able to take a step forward in its relations with a world of others, beyond the boundaries of its own ego. The baby can now include in its relations with its mother a realistic mixture of positive and negative attributes, of love and hate.[81] This series of transactions between mother and child can be summarized in the following way: The attribution of intense negative and destructive feelings to the mother is what object relations thinkers call "projection"; the mother's modification of those feelings is "containing"; the baby's acceptance of its own intense feelings in this modified form is "introjection"; and the way this is a paradigm for the self's relations with the outside world of others is "linking."[82]

These ideas offer a handy model for understanding the inner workings of the cartoons of a gothic humorist like Charles Addams.[83] Addams's work originates in powerful acts of imaginative projection. Intense negative feelings—anger, contempt, hostility, suspicion, destructiveness, and so on—which we all feel, are expressed for us by Addams's wilder notions. But they are not expressed directly. Rather, Addams projects them onto the outer, created world of his cartoons, turning them into suburban werewolves and murderers, amateur saboteurs and Christmas Eve sadists, Pugsleys and Uncle Festers. Everything happens at two removes: just as Addams is our representative, so his people are his. In taking up our atavistic destructive fantasies and turning them into something we can laugh at, Addams performs a role not unlike that of the baby's mother. Alarmingly turbulent and destructive impulses are accepted, absorbed, and handed back in a moderated, less destructive comic form. In these ways an Addams cartoon acts as a containing mechanism. The destruc-

The Comic Worlds of Arno, Steig, Addams, and Steinberg

tive feelings it juggles are turned into something to be laughed at rather than remaining as powerful projected emotions that threaten the very basis of our socialization. For example, which of us has not felt like visiting some act of violence on professional do-gooders, like Addams's family pouring the boiling oil on the carol singers? And who would not justly feel severe self-reproach at harboring such unworthy thoughts? Addams's cartoon accepts the impulse, turns it into something funny in its very outrageousness, and because it puts us in touch with countless other people who obviously feel the same thing, reconciles us to it at the same time. This stage in the reception of an Addams cartoon is, then, analogous to introjection. Since the feelings are acknowledged rather than ignored or denied, there are none of the dangers associated with repression. But treating them as on occasion for comedy also draws their sting. Most humor does this: recognizing whatever it is that produces pain and anxiety, but making it an occasion for pleasure. We can see in this a reconciling of the reality principle and the pleasure principle. This also involves a degree of acceptance of what we might otherwise fear, which in turn reconciles us to the other. It serves the cause of "linking." Establishing a link, a real connection, is the basis of all sociability. Whereas extreme hostility is isolating, turning everyone against everyone else, breaking links, comedy tends to promote intimacy and fellowship, to bring people together.

In projecting his unruly thoughts and impulses onto his bizarre creations, Addams is also a substitute for the reader, whose subject position flickers constantly between the first and the third (as well as quite possibly the second) person of the joking triad. Addams's readers enjoy, at one step removed, both the liberating projection and the reassuring containment of their own fearful sense of human potentiality and their darkest suspicions about human nature. They see their aggressive feelings and paranoid fears acknowledged, acted out, and transformed by the comedy. The laughter it causes signals that those impulses have been modified, turned into something we can recognize and accept rather than ignore and deny.[84] This amounts to a rueful, illusion-free acceptance of the way things are, which does not demoralize us and which also has a strange undercurrent of exhilaration—the pleasure of looking into the abyss and surviving, a triumphant struggle with monsters conducted in terms of laughter, not tragic grief.

For this is indeed a story in the comic register about gazing into the abyss, a story about a fight with monsters. The comic mode, like Perseus's reflective shield, is what prevents the monster from turning the hero to stone, what prevents the abyss from swallowing up the gazer. The quarrel about whether Addams's humor is for real signals precisely the basic ambiguity of his work, the insight of many of his deepest admirers that his humor is at the same time both really about and not really about evil. Even though the bones of the psychoanalytic skeletons rattle a bit, the process outlined above makes it possible to see how both of those alternatives are true. Addams's work triumphantly shows that the humorist can recognize something fundamentally destructive in our nature—what Freud sums up in his chilling, offhand remark that "man is a wolf to man"—and yet, by working through such material, emerge neither consumed nor deflected nor unbalanced by such a recognition. The strength of the gothic as a genre is that it recognizes the dark side of the human psyche. The genre is built on this fact. But recognizing the darkness is dangerous, as Nietzsche foresaw. Those who gaze into the abyss run the risk that the abyss will gaze back into them. Many of the films that use gothic motifs, for example, capitulate to whatever it is they disingenuously profess to inspect or use aesthetically. But the comic rearrangement of such dangerous materials shows how this danger can be both recognized and avoided. It admits the abyss yawning at our feet but steadies us by allowing us to laugh at the danger. Addams's cartoons prophetically and powerfully indicate, a quarter of a century before this became generally recognized, how potent and sanative a fusing of the gothic with the comic could be as a way of both recognizing darkness and not being engulfed by what is recognized. That the gothic has always tended toward the comic is proof—as if it has always been understood that comedy was the antidote to the draft of gothic hemlock we were all obliged to swallow.[85]

It is important to notice the constructive social activity here. If the initial content of the joke is the destruction of a link between people and a destruction of social solidarity and trust, as I suggested above, then getting the joke is the making of a link.[86] That "linking" is a crucial aspect of sociability is a point Bion makes repeatedly, and the observation has unexpected implications for something so obvious as the fact that the work of a cartoonist like Addams appears week after week. Bion's comments about the intense curiosity of the person whose own "feelings are too powerful to be contained in his personality" remind us of the serial nature of the weekly cartoonist or jokester's travails. The cartoonist is driven to produce every week a new joke that will make "it possible for him to investigate his own feelings" through a container—the jokework—powerful enough to contain them.[87] It is the special social function of comedy to act as a container in this sense—to receive our anxieties, fears, and taboo subjects and to show us how they can be braved in laughter. This requires a curious blend of courage and detachment—a standing back from the burdens of life and the capacity to use those burdens as materials for play rather than as a weight to be carried. Hence, odd as it at first appears, it makes sense to describe the cartoonist's creative state as what

Bion calls "reverie," a state of "calm receptiveness" in which something can be taken in, placed, given its comic value, and returned in a form that promotes laughter. This is the state of mind most obviously of the stand-up comic who is fully in possession of the moment—a Richard Pryor, a Robin Williams, an Eddie Izzard when the inventive fit is upon them.[88] Of course, what is said of humor here could equally well be said of all literary texts. This is all, someone might protest, a lot truer of *King Lear* than of Addams's family pouring boiling oil over some carol singers. This must be so. But the ephemeral and occasional nature of the joke—the way it is part of the flow of the everyday and the ordinary, demands no dedicated occasion, and can be absorbed with so little effort—is what lends it a special character and efficacy.

That Addams did aim to leave a record of his time, and that his cartoons are in some essential way always about the fate of America, is made clear by a handful of cartoons in which the iconography is commonplace but there is a strong effect of defamiliarization, of seeing what we always see but from a new and estranging perspective. The violent collision of "familiarity" and "unfamiliarity" is indeed the point of the cartoon in which two castaways discover that their desert island is shaped like the United States (April 27, 1957, 36). It is a cartoon that makes clear how far Addams's cartoons are always (to adapt a somewhat grandiloquent phrase of Fredric Jameson's) a comic mediation on the fate of the community. What if America really was just a desert island? The suggestion that America is buried, inundated, or obliterated is very powerfully drawn in the discovery of the Chrysler Building buried up to the top of its spire (February 20, 1965, 43—the fortieth anniversary issue, no less) or the sight of the Statue of Liberty flooded to her eyeballs (*My Crowd*, 1970, reproduced in *The World of Charles Addams*, 185). The image of unspecific social threat could hardly be clearer: the country is the site of a new flood, of burial under the detritus of eons. (As we shall see, it was Saul Steinberg who exploited to the full the joking use of national icons.) Also very telling are those drawings that register this sense of dismay directly: the little girl who comes home to find her dollhouse has been ransacked, the old man who barricades himself in his apartment while the intruder ferociously saws the floor out from under his feet.[89] But the most haunting of all is the drawing of the empty supermarket (fig. 3.10), in which plenitude, the great promise of midcentury America in an age of affluence, is turned to dearth. (An odd, menacing detail: although the shelves are empty, there is still a security guard policing the checkouts.)

Like most humorists, Addams had his special period—a time when his humor seemed peculiarly piquant, apropos, and expressive of the general mood. This period began in the 1940s and climaxed in the 1960s. A single allusion

pinpoints its zenith: Rachel Carson in 1962, seeking to describe the consequences of the overuse of systemic insecticides, chose as her metaphor "the
cartoon world of Charles Addams."[90] Carson's story taps into the vein of paranoia characteristic of the age. Her evil agents were ordinary people, who might
live next door and lead blameless lives. Or so it appeared. For they were also,
in their professional lives, agents of a terrible destruction. Carson's real subject was toxicity, and for her the idea of toxicity has metaphorical power as
well as literal applicability. Carson showed how a nation was poisoning itself,
polluting its oceans and rivers, and destroying its natural life. If Carson's book
had a moral, it was that it was people, as much as systemic insecticides, who
were weird. Where better to find a metaphor for all this than in the cartoons
of a man who specialized in weirdness and for whom toxicity was a favorite
theme, a cartoonist who had that little boy change himself into a Mr. Hyde–
like monster with a toy chemistry set, had a woman ask a neighbor if she could
borrow "a cup of cyanide" (February 8, 1941, 15), or showed a little boy making
his model tanker discharge an ugly pool of oil, to the dismay of the other children sailing their toy boats in Central Park (fig. 3.11)? This was fifteen years
before the *Exxon Valdes* disaster; but only two months before Addams's cartoon appeared, *The New Yorker* (prescient as always on environmental questions) had run a two-part "profile" by Noël Mostert on the new supertankers,
which included a long discussion of the havoc wreaked by oil spills.[91] It was
during the twenty-year period from the early forties to the early sixties that
Addams's work touched the American nerve most readily and that his comedy
was uniquely relevant. It was a comedy that acknowledged both the dominance of the banal and the undercurrent of the diabolical. This precarious balance resulted from several opposing tendencies: a knowledge of the nightmare
of recent history on one hand and a suppression of the memory of it on the
other; the continuing dominance and stability of the suburban norm along
with the emergence of a counterculture (and worse) in revolt against it; the
waning influence of both liberal humanism and Christianity and the waxing
of an intense individualism implying (beneficially) cultural pluralism and (less
beneficially) moral anarchy. In his comedy we recognize indirectly so many of
the horrors—cruel, sadistic, and diabolical—on which the modern world has
since supped fully and often.

This is the central ambiguity in Addams's work: the uncomfortable fact
that he makes laughter out of negative and dismaying situations. It is not
that destructive, irrational, and antisocial impulses have no comic value, of
course. They notoriously do. (Much emergent humor is transgressive in this
sense, kicking over the traces of good sense, decent behavior, and accepted
standards without any regard for the principles of the moral majority.) The
problem is the precise status of the transgressive in Addams's work. The idea

Fig. 3.10. Charles Addams. Uncaptioned cartoon. Titled: Empty Supermarket.

The New Yorker, September 19, 1983, 42. © 1983 Charles Addams. Reproduced with permission of Tee and Charles Addams Foundation.

In the seventies Addams drew a number of cartoons that took familiar American landmarks or scenes and subjected them to powerful estranging effects: the Statue of Liberty submerged up to her eyeballs by a high tide in New York Bay; the Chrysler Building buried to its spire in an archaeological dig; America reduced to the size of a desert island. In this "what if?" cartoon from the early eighties something as banal as the supermarket, along with a familiar mantra of customer service, is used to turn the promise of plenitude inside out. Note the security guard (some things never change).

of the joking cartoon as a container makes some sense of this, I hope—of why Wilfrid Sheed should talk of the "joyous" quality in Addams cartoons, Barbara Nicholls should praise their "beauty," and Saul Steinberg should speak of Addams's elegance "in the physical and moral sense." Along with the transgressiveness goes the intense exhilaration—the joyousness—of a humor that faces threat and anxiety and calmly turns them into humor. But it is impor-

Charles Addams: Comic American Gothic

tant not to underestimate the precariousness of what Addams is doing. The cartoons deliver, along with laughter, a definite frisson, which comes from siding with evil—siding with the threat rather than warding it off. The drawings excite a sense of elation and above all superiority by the way they encourage viewers to stand on the side of the forbidden. In a way that the pure hearted (like Rachel Carson) might not approve of or understand, the poisoning victims end up siding with the poisoners—as in that drawing of Pugsley launching his oil tanker, complete with oil spill, onto a Central Park lake full of toy boats. (That this cartoon reprises an earlier postwar cartoon [July 1, 1950, 33] showing Pugsley launching a U-boat into the same pond underscores how consistently Addams took the side of the forbidden.)[92] Addams's humor participates in the modern horrors it takes as its occasion and draws comic strength from the glee with which it folds them in its embrace. In "Of the Essence of Laughter, and Generally of the Comic in the Plastic Arts," Baudelaire proposes that "the comic is one of the clearest marks of Satan in man"[93] because laughter is prideful and comes "from a man's idea of his own superiority." The notion recalls familiar notions about laughter—that it is always, at some level, a matter of hostility, aggression, and the expression of superiority—but it has a particular applicability to Addams's work.

Addams's public persona exhibits the same dualism observable in his drawings —a middle-class stodginess that announces itself in that self-description as "an all-American boy" and then the acting out of certain dandyish, even "aristocratic" eccentricities that may or may not be serious. We encounter a carefully assembled mask of abnormality with familiar and often-paraded props and personal myths, some of which were not of Addams's devising but fitted in anyway: medieval crossbows, axes, suits of armor, the Civil War embalmer's table he used as a cocktail cabinet, the wedding in the "pet cemetery" (in reality a part of the garden where family pets had been buried), at which both bride and groom wore black, and suggestions, carefully cultivated by the tabloids if completely erroneous in fact, of periods of insanity. The trappings of medieval culture clearly signal a revolt against the ordinariness of middle-class life. Even Addams's most obvious concession to the twentieth century, his interest in vintage automobiles (he owned at various times a 1928 Mercedes that had transported, among others, Zelda and Scott Fitzgerald, Fernand Léger, and Pablo Picasso, a 1926 Bugatti, and a 1933 Aston Martin), carefully eschews the plebeian and the popular (yet when he died, on September 29, 1988, it was at the wheel of an Audi).[94] But the way Addams might be thought of as "aristocratic" contrasts with the way Arno was "aristocratic." It was the difference between a birthright and a lifestyle. What for Arno was a social manner ab-

Fig. 3.11. Charles
Addams. Uncaptioned
cartoon. Titled: Oil
Spill.

The New Yorker,
July 8, 1974, 30. © 1974
Charles Addams. Re-
produced with permis-
sion of Tee and Charles
Addams Foundation.

Addams giving deliberate offense, long before the *Exxon Valdes*
disaster of 1989, but after *The New Yorker* ran a series of
articles on supertankers that emphasized the danger of oil
spills. The point of this and similar cartoons is that we identify
with the transgressor. We are drawn over to the side of evil
and feel an antisocial and infantile pleasure in it. It makes the
burden of being a good citizen just a little easier. In this way
Addams effects the comic neutralization of gothic paranoia.

sorbed unconsciously from infancy onward as the member of a privileged social elite was for Addams a form of compensation, an antic disguise and pose. The great attraction of aristocratic humor in an age of the democratization of culture and profound social change is that is sets the individual free from the trammels of the here and now. To adopt the aristocratic pose is to open up a distance between you and contemporary culture. The humorist as aristocrat— through his contempt for the egalitarian values of a democratic society—also meshes with the figure of the dandy, so essential to *The New Yorker,* as we have seen in the case of Peter Arno.

A story often told about Addams has him removing a medieval crossbow (he was a skilled archer) from the wall of his Manhattan duplex as he launches into a bleak fantasy about defending his apartment from an intruder. "A robber breaks in and just as he comes through the door I get him—right through the neck! [smiling] In my fantasy it's *always* through the neck."[95] The anecdote stands as a good metaphor for Addams's career as a humorist. There is a threat and an invasion from the outside. He counterattacks with relish. The counterattack takes a surprising—even anachronistic—form. He clearly derives much comic pleasure from inflicting pain and violence in an unexpected way. There is a powerful sense of superiority in staging this act of aggression toward the banal realities of contemporary life. This account would not be complete if I did not add that Addams often deploys medieval armaments and accoutrements in his battle against the banal and the mundane. As a comic anecdote, the story acts out our own anxieties and aggressiveness and moderates those feelings by showing how they can be rearranged in a comically exaggerated form. Something in ourselves is thereby both recognized and neutralized. When we try to imagine the reaction of the intruder, we see that this story is just another version of the cartoon of those animals shot by a hunter on a unicycle. About here we reach the substrate of Addams's humor. Addams's jests offer, as it were, a visual equivalent to the story of the crossbow arrow piercing the flesh of the intruder—surprise and pain ending (for the spectator, at any rate) in delight and pleasure. The corpus of his cartoons is an assault, in the name of that aristocratic superiority, on a society sometimes threatening in its hostility, sometimes boring in its ordinariness; but the assault is also a temporary deliverance.

The Comic Worlds of Arno, Steig, Addams, and Steinberg

4 · SAUL STEINBERG

The Lifeline from A to B

Fame is a heady brew offered in a poisoned chalice. Just as he was starting to become famous himself, Saul Steinberg published two witty visual aphorisms on the subject in *The New Yorker*. One shows a man scurrying away from an airborne fame figure brandishing a laurel wreath (November 15, 1958, 50). The artist is terrified. Why? A second drawing provides the answer. It shows the artist buried alive under an avalanche of wreaths, ribbons, and medals, dumped out of a battered cornucopia by another fame figure, half classical goddess, half grumpy middle-class matron (fig. 4.1). The burial scene takes place before a blank canvas yet to be started—perhaps never to be started.

Over a long and productive career Steinberg studied to avoid the fate of the famous artist.[1] Fame is dangerous. It smothers you. It distracts you. It institutionalizes you. Fame stands between you and your work. You become an "Artist" ("when you do it the way others want you to") rather than an artist ("when you do it your way").[2] You end up repeating yourself, painting over and over again, like another of Steinberg's artist figures, the scene of your own coronation as a famous artist (January 6, 1962, 33). You march toward your death date, maddeningly aware of the dove of fame fluttering above you, ready to drop the laurel wreath on your balding pate just when it is all over (July 28, 1962, 20).[3] "This monumentalization of people, this freezing of life, is the terrible curse of the consciousness of fame," Steinberg said.[4] For someone as fiercely individualistic and nonconformist as he was, monumentalization was to be avoided at all costs. It was a battle from which he emerged triumphant: all the standard works on American art in the second half of the twentieth century ignore him completely.[5] But whatever the seductions of fame, the fitfulness and modesty of genuine recognition achieved without hype is something Steinberg must have regarded with pleasure. And of course he does have a place. If the soaring ambitions of high modernism made it assume a heroic, rather overblown form, a fantastic winged steed (say) in relation to the serviceable draft horse of realism or the show pony of impressionism, then Steinberg has been the gadfly under Pegasus's tail.[6]

Fame means recognition, and recognition leads to categorizing, a topic that for Steinberg is more than an art-historical note and query. As early as 1966 he observed that the critics "don't quite know where to place me."[7] Steinberg was pleased: after all, his art of observation demanded the invisibility of the observer. The dire alternative was epitomized in his anecdote about driving a Citroën DS19 in Spain in the 1950s.[8] The car was an instant sensation among the locals, and its reflected glory illuminated the owner brilliantly. Too brilliantly. "I was an object of curiosity. *They* learned something and I nothing. Now I drive a very common car, hard to recognize in a parking lot."[9] Going unrecognized was a precondition of his art. Steinberg shaved off his mustache because "it was too foreign and attracted attention" — a story told half in earnest.[10] We can call all this Steinberg's "Americanization," following Arthur C. Danto and John Hollander. This is acceptable so long as we don't take the word at face value. Steinberg's Americanization was at one level an assumption of the disguise of ordinariness, necessary because ordinariness provided that unfettered freedom of observation available only to the insider and the accepted member of the community. The person who took the trouble to counterfeit his own "plausibly implausible" Declaration of Independence (reproduced in *The Passport,* 1954) was hardly a simple patriot.[11]

Donning the cloak of ordinariness necessary to make him invisible in everyday life also made Steinberg invisible in the field of high art. The questions — whether Steinberg belongs to the cartoon world, the magazine world, or the art world; whether he is an illustrator or an artist; whether he is a "pure" artist or an "applied artist" (Robert Hughes's term) — remain unresolved. Steinberg's quizzical image of the edifice of modern art and his place within it is the cover he drew for *The New Yorker,* May 19, 1962. It shows a pair of pedestals, one on top of the other, supporting various tottering structures (a hand drawing a flourish on the pillar of fame, an eagle labeled "École de New York" perched on a cubist guitar labeled "École de Paris," and so on) with the art buyer at the very top of the pile and "Steinberg" relegated to an unobtrusive spot under the cornice of the lower pedestal. Is this "Steinberg" part of the drawing, like the other names in it, or is "Steinberg" merely the artist's signature (as we might expect) and not part of what is represented in the drawing at all? Is "Steinberg" within the system or outside it? Harold Rosenberg once said that "the genius of Steinberg is to have kept the question alive about himself for thirty-five years, and to have made it impossible for art to acknowledge

Fig. 4.1. Saul Steinberg, untitled drawing, ink on paper.

© The Saul Steinberg Foundation/Artists Rights Society (ARS), New York/Licensed by VISCOPY, Sydney 2004. Originally published in *The New Yorker*, September 15, 1962, 39.

Fame (half classical goddess, half grumpy art-loving matron) dumps a cornucopia of accolades on the artist, burying him alive. Meanwhile the next painting remains an empty canvas. It is one of a series of pictorial meditations on the danger of becoming so famous that fame stops you from doing the very thing you are famous for. In other drawings the canny artist scurries away from Fame as she attempts to crown him with a laurel wreath, and a less canny artist is reduced to drawing his own coronation as a famous artist.

his legitimacy without changing its conception of itself."[12] Another twenty-five years have passed since that comment was made, but it remains as true as ever: Adam Gopnik noted on Steinberg's death that he was an artist who found that the cartoonist's place, on the margins of art, was precisely the place he liked best.[13] A vantage point outside the frame, or in the margin, was where he could be ordinary, unnoticed, undisturbed—invisible, in a word—in his chronicling of American civilization in the years between the mid-1940s and the early 1970s and beyond. Under cover of an obscurity bought by this attitude, Steinberg was left to pursue his remarkable pictorial meditation on the appearances of America for sixty years, not exactly unnoticed but as some strange by-phenomenon of the history of modern art in America.

Not that Steinberg is a neutral chronicler. His work is about the complex fate of an Old World refugee and immigrant encountering the New World of midcentury America. It is the work of a man undergoing a personal crisis that is also an ethical and aesthetic one: In what terms do I now remake my life? How do I truly and honestly assess the civilization that I now have to live in, that has welcomed me and offered me protection and opportunity, and yet from whose deficiencies I cannot turn my eyes? How do I draw this place? These were questions Steinberg asked himself in his drawings with particular urgency in the years between 1960 and 1975. What is so absorbing is the attack, energy, and inventiveness of his wrestling with this multiple crisis. And if in the course of his career Steinberg has ended up speaking for people who are not immigrants or outsiders in any sense, speaking for Americans who recognize their own America in his drawings, this is perhaps because, by a strange quirk of history, by the turn of the twenty-first century almost all of them had begun to think of themselves as outsiders and strangers in their own country.[14]

Drawing for Steinberg is an intensely moral activity, and the investigation of the "way" a drawing is drawn is bound up with Steinberg's belief that a drawing's content should be "true" in a special sense. "The truth of the drawing's subject matter," he has said, "isn't a visible, superficial truth" but rather is a kind of absorbed "complicity" with the subject that produces a "deep knowledge" of it, a knowledge that respects appearance but also passes beyond it.[15] Consider Steinberg's comments about drawing the American scene. This presented itself to him as a problem of representation: how to draw America so that truth would be served. Steinberg's comments about his art often took the form of condensed parables, and two delivered at the beginning of the seventies—about crocodiles and Los Angeles—are pertinent.

Concerning the crocodile, he said the important thing was to work out "what sort of technique the crocodile employs to show itself."[16] The crocodile, which Steinberg had then been drawing for about ten years, "shows itself" through its mobility, its teeth, and its scales. Steinberg's crocodile walks on two legs, which gives it a human freedom of movement. It is savagely aggressive and is armored against counterattack. Drawn in this way the crocodile, sometimes crossed with a chameleon, becomes Steinberg's symbol for the commercialism and materialism of American civilization in the middle of the twentieth century.[17] (He says it represents "political power in general.") The crocodile patrols his streets, bites the timorous (September 5, 1970, 41), and jousts with stray Saint Georges. Businessmen duel within its jaws (December 10, 1960, 43), exactly the same place where the artist is obliged to set up his easel. There is no getting away from it: the ridge of its back even forms the horizon of an idyllic holiday island (April 21, 1962, 37). In Steinberg's big picture of the rise and fall of American civilization, the crocodile is what the American eagle turns into as the whole culture drops back, step by step, to the prehistoric epoch of the ammonites (November 11, 1967, cover illustration). A constant in the national landscape, it is everywhere in Steinberg's work in the sixties.

Drawing Los Angeles, on the other hand, is "a trap—like portraying clowns." Los Angeles, a topic Steinberg returned to in the mid-1960s after an assay in the early 1950s, represents for him a culminating tendency in American history: frontier individualism crossed with consumerist hedonism.[18] It is clichéd, kitsch, vulgar, ornate, self-fashioning, exuberant, and above all self-parodying, an "avant garde city of parody in architecture and even in nature (canyons and palm trees)," in Steinberg's words.[19] How do you avoid the trap of drawing something that parodies itself?[20] Since it is already a parody, it is not enough to reproduce its kitsch, its vulgar exuberance. The artist needs to find a way to draw those qualities and to suggest through a particular way of drawing how Los Angeles shows itself and what it represents in the national culture. So in Steinberg's 1966 drawing (fig. 4.2), which accompanied the first installment of Christopher Rand's three-part profile, "The Ultimate City," Los Angeles is reduced to its familiar acronym, LA, a gigantic pair of retro capitals boxed in between a hand-printed "Canada" and "Mexico" to the north and south (actually left and right in the drawing) and a copperplate "Atlantic" and "Pacific" to the east and west (upper and lower), the tall letters overshadowing the breadth of the continent, a city that humbles its rivals (San Francisco, Chicago, New York, reduced to mere dots on an empty map), the terminus of the long westward movement of American history, teetering at the edge of the continent with nowhere left to go.[21] Steinberg should not be suspected of snobbishness here, as if he were someone who recoils from what he observes: "Let's go West," he said, a few years after this drawing appeared, "that is the tradition of the American. As a matter of fact, this is the tradition of the artist—to become some one else."[22] How true this is of artists in general is debatable, but its applicability to Steinberg is obvious.

Drawing America presents the artist with a dilemma similar to the problem of drawing crocodiles or Los Angeles (which as it turns out are America for Steinberg anyway). Steinberg asks himself, What technique does America employ to show itself? He scrutinizes America for the techniques of its appearances. As it progresses, that search tries to avoid the traps set for the unwary by a culture that in its most public and self-publicizing aspects is already a parody of itself—the traps set by an America that offers itself up for pictorialization in a ready-made, clichéd, overcirculated, iconic language. Such images can be neither reproduced nor ignored. In his drawings Steinberg does not reflect passively the look of midcentury America but invents a joking way of drawing what he sees that will plainly show what is implied in the look itself, the meaning of the "techniques" the country chooses "to show itself." Not American images, but drawings of American images. Such drawings aim to open up a gap between the spectator and what is represented in the drawing and hence to promote thought and reflection in the viewer. Drawings like these, John Hollander has said, demand interpretation, meaning the active and reflective participation of the observer.[23]

Another way to put all this is to pick up a nuance from the late 1950s and say that Steinberg was fascinated by the "mythologies" of contemporary America. The word, a favorite of his, recalls Roland Barthes's essays published under that title throughout the decade, which came to grips with the appearance of a national mythology in familiar everyday customs, objects, and edifices like wrestling, steak and fries, or the Eiffel Tower. From comments he made in the 1960s it is possible that the Francophile and Francophone Steinberg knew Barthes's work before it became fashionable in an English translation in 1972.[24] Certainly Steinberg told an interviewer in the 1970s that what really interested him about America was what he then called "Americanerie," which he said was a "part of the American mythology." And Steinberg is truly a mythologist, not a mythmaker. Myth, the way the culture consciously or unconsciously represents itself, the stories it tells about itself (whether in words, pictures, buildings, or objects), and to some extend deludes itself with, is one thing. Mythology, meaning the science, or the art, of recognizing the power of those myths and at the same time making us conscious of their illusory nature, is something else. Steinberg is a visual mythologist in this latter sense, as we see from his treatment of the myth of the Native American.

A comparison with a fellow cartoonist helps clarify Steinberg's intentions. When in the 1970s James Stevenson confronts the fate of the Native American in a series called "The Indian Problem: Annals of Law and Order," he depicts certain important chapters in the tragic end of the Indian nations.[25] He draws a densely labeled map of America in 1650 followed by an empty map in 1950; he draws "Geronimo's Camp at the Time of His Capture"; he draws "The Retreat of the Nez Percés." These are rendered in freehand aquarelle outlines, a technique whose watery indistinctness mimics the fading of the way of life depicted—the near genocidal erasure. Stevenson is clearly intent on getting "behind," even exploding, the myth of the Native American (such as had been the staple of early westerns), but you would not call him a mythologist. He wants to evoke the pathos and tragedy of the destruction of an actual indigenous cul-

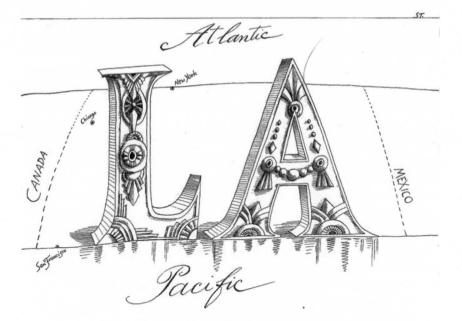

Fig. 4.2. Saul Steinberg, untitled drawing, ink on paper.

© The Saul Steinberg Foundation/Artists Rights Society (ARS), New York/Licensed by VISCOPY, Sydney 2004. Originally published in *The New Yorker*, October 1, 1966, 56.

Steinberg, showing how to avoid the trap of drawing Los Angeles. Because Los Angeles is already a parody of itself, drawing it is too easy, "like drawing clowns." In Steinberg's drawing, used for the title illustration of Christopher Rand's "profile" of the city, Los Angeles is reduced to the "way it shows itself," most commonly its initials, which here are in-filled with decorations to suggest the retro style of the city in its heyday. Seen from the "worldview" perspective favored by Steinberg and boxed in between a printed Canada and Mexico to the north and south and a copperplate Atlantic and Pacific to the east and west, it is taller than the continent is broad and completely dwarfs its rivals, Chicago, New York, and San Francisco, which are no more than dots on a map. They revolve around the colossal *L* like little moons. LA embodies the long westward drive of American history. It ends up perched precariously on the edge of the continent.

ture, largely ignored in the popular mythology of the "red Indian," a story that a newly politicized post-1960s America was just beginning to discover, and that becomes a new myth in its own right. None of this interests Steinberg, though one cannot say that his interest is any less "political" than Stevenson's. He is fascinated by the surface of the mythic image, the pull and power that Stevenson wants to circumvent. That mythic image is derived from contemporary popular culture, especially the cinema. There, Native Americans are rarely individuals. They typically appear as massed groups. So Steinberg doesn't even draw his "Indians": he goes straight to what gives them mythic life in the first place—mechanical reproduction. He has a commercial printmaker make a rubber stamp of an Indian warrior on horseback and then creates a pastiche of settler-Indian conflict by multiple stampings of the Indian along with multiple stampings of a Mormon traveler. Stevenson assuredly is seeking to represent these events in a way that is itself formally significant (the indistinct, fading, fugitive nature of the images). But what Steinberg does is confront more subtly the Indian as a persistent mythic icon in American culture. It is the appearance of the myth, not the reality it conceals, that engages him. His Indians are rubber stamped so they can be reproduced in sufficient numbers to draw the way Indians are shown in popular culture: as an anonymous, attacking horde, for example, as in his cover painting for October 15, 1966, or in the visual essay titled "Rubber Stamps" in the issue for December 30, 1966, 56–61.[26]

The originality of Steinberg's method is shown by his most famous and most often plagiarized cover for *The New Yorker*, "A View of the World from 9th Avenue" (fig. 4.3).[27] It is a remarkable drawing because although it evokes New York so perfectly it includes none of the obvious architectural features of the city—no Empire State Building, no Chrysler Building, no World Trade Center, no Statue of Liberty (an "overgrown souvenir on one of those islands on the bay without which no foreign cartoonist could be happy").[28] It also illustrates perfectly what Steinberg meant when he called *The New Yorker* "my

---

Fig. 4.3. Saul Steinberg, "View of the World from 9th Avenue."

The New Yorker cover, March 29, 1976. © 1976 The Saul Steinberg Foundation/Artists Rights Society (ARS), New York/Licensed by VISCOPY, Sydney 2004. © *The New Yorker* Collection 1976 Saul Steinberg from cartoonbank.com. All rights reserved.

Ironically (in view of Steinberg's fear of fame), the most famous magazine cover of the twentieth century, the most plagiarized image ever of a city, and one of Steinberg's most characteristic inventions. It is really a drawing of the core myth of New York, the height of its buildings. But Steinberg draws not height in the sense of tall buildings (as seen from a distance), or even the subjective and emotional experience of height (the vertiginous downward perspective), but rather the intellectual hubris associated with the elevated viewpoint, the sense that height makes you master of the universe. But is it "satire"? Not really. Although analytical and rational, the image is also entrancing. That it should have been adopted as an unofficial icon of New York shows how well Steinberg blends appreciation and critique in his drawings: the admiration is never corny, and the criticism, always intelligent, is never superior.

The Comic Worlds of Arno, Steig, Addams, and Steinberg

political world." Few of his works show so well the scrupulous mixture of criticism and appreciation, of objective distance and affectionate embrace in his work; and few show so well the subtle transactions that take place, with the publication of a Steinberg drawing, between artist and viewer. It shows a view from the middle forties, imagined perhaps from the old *New Yorker* offices themselves on West Forty-third Street, since we see a section of the West Side Highway along the Hudson in the distance, looking west. The foreground, projected from one vanishing point, shows the intersection of a cross street at Ninth and Tenth Avenues with the Hudson River beyond; the middle ground, projected from a second vanishing point, shows a compressed perspective of America from New Jersey to the West Coast, scattered with a few sporadic landmarks; and the background, using yet another vanishing point, shows an even more compressed perspective of the Pacific Ocean and the looming geopolitical masses of China, Japan, and Russia—then the chief sources of international anxiety for the United States. Those telescoped views, enabling the viewer to possess in one glance the local, the national, and the global, are daring, exhilarating, and even polemical—as if graphic art were determined here to show up in one eloquent example photography's hamstrung literalness.

This is rightly taken as a satirical view of the New Yorker's worldview ("the world as perceived by the average New Yorker" says Lee Lorenz, circumspectly).[29] It is satirical in an especially pointed way. Anyone who looks at Steinberg's other versions of this drawing (one is reproduced in Harold Rosenberg's *Saul Steinberg*, 1978, 79), in which the *New Yorker* logotype has not been laid over the image, sees something incomplete. The image is finished only when the magazine's name becomes part of the composition. Besides providing a title for the drawing, the logotype decants into the drawing all the authority of *The New Yorker* as a mouthpiece for a certain sense of New York, and indeed it is the symbolic representation of the drawing's subject. This is how the New Yorker perceives the world: the drawing is a projection of that way of looking at the world; we are seeing the world through the New Yorker's eyes. So the drawing rebounds on its implied reader, a New Yorker (any New Yorker), and perhaps even the magazine whose cover it appears on. But while the satire and hence the criticism are there, it is telling that New Yorkers should have embraced the drawing as an unofficial icon of the city's mentality and in some sense a rueful celebration of it.[30] The drawing's wit is subtle and pleasingly unstable—where it criticizes, it also approves.

The irresistible power of the drawing derives not so much from raw satire as from the new way Steinberg has discovered to depict the technique New York employs to show itself—which is at the same time a way of avoiding the trap

The Comic Worlds of Arno, Steig, Addams, and Steinberg

of drawing what is already a cliché in its very familiarity. As everyone knows, particularly people who have never been there, New York is a city of very tall buildings. That this is not true for large stretches of the city is irrelevant—we deal here not with New York, but with the myth of New York, the "New Yorkerie" of New York. The New Yorkerie of the city is bound up with the height of its buildings—of which September 2001 provided a terrible demonstration. How one draws or writes about height is a problem. A trap, Steinberg might say, "like portraying clowns." The obvious ways are precisely that—obvious and hence clichéd. Thus a cartoonist merely does his job if he simply draws very high buildings, as Carl Rose does in a cartoon captioned "They haven't got a single tenant on the fifty-fourth floor yet, Mr. Chrysler" (May 2, 1931, 27), showing a man at the top of the Chrysler Building looking with a pair of binoculars at a distant Empire State Building—both rearing high above the rest of Manhattan. Similarly, a writer makes a straightforward if poetic point about Manhattan if he writes, as E. B. White does, of the "upward thrust unmistakable . . . the great walls and towers rising . . . this vigorous spear that presses heaven hard" as seen from a railway car passing through Queens.[31] Seeking to overcome this kind of cliché, William O'Brian subjectivizes the experience of height by showing a man scaling a skyscraper (to an inquiring head popping out of a window he says, "Because it's here, that's why") seen from a viewpoint both above the climber and away from the wall of the building (September 21, 1963, 42). Similarly, Roland Barthes was moved to write about not the height but the "depth" of New York, a city experienced on foot as a series of pathways through the deep ravines of the streets.[32] These examples span a spectrum from the too obvious to the too clever. What Steinberg discovers, in his quest to find out how New York "shows itself," is that there is a way to draw height that both acknowledges what Rose and White show and encapsulates what is a little too glaring in the O'Brian cartoon, a little too clever in Barthes's essay. Steinberg draws not height, or even the subjective feeling of height, but the way the world appears to the elevated observer, fusing the actual and imaginary horizons of that observer. The drawing renders the inner complacency that accompanies a high observation point but also gives a sense of expanded vision, the imaginary quality we associate with both height and the feeling of potency: this is the world, three-quarters of the way through the American century, seen from the heady center of the new imperium.[33] The extraordinary success of a drawing that strikes every observer as exquisitely right defines the inventiveness and originality of Steinberg's genius: it discovers the means that New York City, and even the New Yorker (the magazine as well as the person), "employs to show itself," yet it does this without alienating anyone. It takes in

New York in a steady, intelligent, quietly skeptical gaze; but it does not forget the city's thrilling appeal to the imagination.

Drawings like this moved Adam Gopnik to remark, "Saul Steinberg was born in a strange place, with a strange gift."[34] But this statement, in which Romania is in effect out of sight, behind Japan and somewhere between China and Russia, is a version of the Manhattan-centered attitude that Steinberg parodied in "A View of the World from 9th Avenue." It gets everything the wrong way around. One might rewrite it thus: "Saul Steinberg was born in an ordinary place with an ordinary gift. He came to a strange place, and his gift became stranger the more he tried to draw that strange place." For Saul Steinberg, the center of the world was his childhood home, Romania, in the years during and after the First World War. Romania was what life was, what was normal. What was strange was the America he ended up in, in the 1940s — an America that grew stranger and stranger in the decades that followed, an America that changed so much that Steinberg was forced to invent new and still newer ways of drawing it.[35] It is wrong to suppose that Steinberg's "gift" was somehow immanent if not manifest "there," in Bucharest in the twenties, say.[36] In fact, Steinberg's art develops very slowly from 1942 to the early fifties; odd and intriguing in the forties, it begins to acquire the character of persuasive strangeness only toward the close of the fifties.

The drawings by Steinberg dating from the thirties in Italy that are still in print; the far more copious examples from *The New Yorker* in the early forties, including those of the Pacific war (collected in *All in Line*, 1945); and even those from the late forties (collected in *The Art of Living*, 1949) are clever "metaphysical" jokes that typically exploit the crossover between the logic of the situation the drawing is showing and the logic of how the drawing is done — like the restaurant captain who casually holds up the six fingers of one hand to signal a table for six (May 18, 1946, 19). Steinberg's first published drawing in *The New Yorker* showed a centaur, half man and half horse, except that it was the wrong half of both creatures (October 25, 1941, 15). Another early drawing was of a hand drawing a human figure drawing another figure (February 3, 1945, 22). Interestingly, in light of "A View of the World from 9th Avenue," there is a running interest in the tricks of height, but it takes a human rather than an architectural turn. Two men are perched on the edge of a cliff: one holds his hand out over the void and says to the other, "You'd hardly know my Tommy. He's about that tall now" (September 19, 1942, 13). In another, two mothers are chatting happily, while far below two minuscule daughters glare ferociously at each other (April 3, 1943, 16). In a third a man holds his little girl up to get a closer view of the moon (October 17, 1953, 29). Other cartoons show that weirdly inventive but wry imagination that first caught the eye of *The New Yorker*'s editors. A man tucked in bed has laid out his shoes, gloves, wristwatch, glasses, and hat beside him on the floor in the exact configuration of his sleeping body (March 17, 1945, 38) — a cartoon rather cheekily embedded in a profile of Norman Rockwell. An artist painting a full-length, life-size portrait of a man does it sideways on a wide, landscape canvas to save himself the trouble of reaching so high (April 13, 1946, 39). A bartender hands a drink to a man who, completely drunk, has fallen over with his stool so that he "sits" horizontally on the floor (October 27, 1965, 32).

Most of these are highly particular images that make little or no social comment — as if Steinberg were biding his time, still only intermittently interested in trying to draw his new country. But occasionally there is a foreshadowing of the way he will later make his art allude to some larger national tendency. One cartoon shows a line of office workers standing at a bar in nearly the same pose, each with his right foot resting on the bar rail. Behind them is a second row of men, all in a similar pose, with a second bar rail (fig. 4.4). Such a drawing, the first by Steinberg to notice the patterns and repetitions characteristic of a mass society, clearly prefigures his later drawings (ca. 1968) of multiple businessmen, policemen, folk singers, cowboys, and so on. In between are other similar attempts: the paper-thin married couple walking in step in the issue of December 24, 1955 (25), or the rank of marching men in the issue of June 6, 1959 (42). But Steinberg's 1947 drawing of the double row of men at the bar gestures toward, without really grasping, a crucial aspect of the national mythos: it is as if Steinberg is not yet fully able to move from a sense of incident to a sense of place — from the bar to America. Here and there we find signs of greater ambition. A modest spot drawing of the period depicts the figure of Justice with scales and sword, but instead of the traditional blindfold, she wears a pair of sunglasses (July 12, 1947, 21). And yet this, like other examples of the period, is still tentative and incidental.

So far as *The New Yorker*'s editors were concerned, throughout the forties and fifties Steinberg's skills as a witty topographer were to be confined almost completely to exotic locations. As a war correspondent, Steinberg was given double-page spreads for his drawings of North Africa (April 15, 1944, 20–21, and April 29, 1944, 22–23), Italy (June 10, 1944, 20–21, July 8, 1944, 18–19, and July 29, 1944, 18–19), India (February 24, 1945, 22–23), China (January 15, 1944, 18–19, February 5, 1944, 20–21, and March 24, 1945, 28–29), and later Berlin (March 29, 1947, 38–39, and April 12, 1947, 34–35). Under the rubric "A Reporter at Large," in the fifties he was allotted five and even six pages (the most ever devoted to a folio of drawings in *The New Yorker* at that time) for visual essays on his travels: "Samarkand, U.S.S.R." (May 12, 1956, 44–48) and "Winter in Moscow" (June 9, 1956, 30–35). These feature pages all show-case Steinberg's abilities as a visual essayist—his adeptness at getting down the essential shape of a body, a costume, a building, or a cityscape: a row of crescents along a roofline, embroidered patterns on a quilted peasant coat, the hornlike shape of a ruined arch, the geometric padded shoulders of a military greatcoat, the alien shapes of the Cyrillic alphabet, statues of robust female Soviet gymnasts, the steppelike vista of Red Square. But he was never asked to draw America.

The single exception was a four-page visual essay on Los Angeles and environs titled "The Coast" (January 27, 1951, 24–28), one of the first drawings in which Steinberg seriously asked, if he did not quite answer, the question How does America show itself? "Show itself"—so there is an emphasis, logical one might think, on the facade of the country: its architecture, strip development, the despoiling of a dramatic landscape of canyons and mountains by haphazard development, commercial exploitation, and above all advertising, most of it large-scale because it has been designed for passing motorists in an ever-expanding city built on the automobile. In the set-piece drawing the sun bursts over a road snaking around the sides of a canyon littered with huge billboards for "X-LNT Tamales," "Patio Furniture," "Eats," along with sundry "For Sale" signs and a mess of domestic architectural styles—Tudor, modern, gingerbread, feudal, art moderne, retro. A Spanish mission church has a Quonset-hut nave, an oil derrick is raised next to a dentist's office, a palm tree sprouts candelabras, and a faux baronial interior (in which the owner boasts to a guest about his Utrillo) looks newer than a patched, cracked Bauhaus dwelling. What Steinberg gets so well is the vulgar energy of the place, the sense of a buildup of extraordinary wealth that has no form through which it can adequately express itself (what we get is a crazy scallop shell facade before a swimming pool cabana, a movie house ticket box that is a marvel of sculptural swirls, a drive-in chop suey pagoda, the garishness of a highway city). But even as we admire these drawings we see the problem—the parodic impulse in the drawings has its sting drawn by the parodic quality of the place itself. The problem is Steinberg's lingering commitment to pictorial realism, a one-to-one matching of what is drawn to what is seen. He can draw Los Angeles, he can draw the show of Los Angeles, but he can't quite draw the technique Los Angeles uses to show itself.

So if in 1951 these drawings looked remarkable, they are hardly so compared with what followed once Steinberg set about trying in earnest to draw his new country. After "The Coast" lay the exploratory work of *The Passport*, published in October 1954, a transitional volume between Steinberg's metaphysical and conceptual styles. (*The Passport* reproduced about 350 drawings, two-

Fig. 4.4. Saul Steinberg, untitled drawing, ink on paper.

© The Saul Steinberg Foundation/Artists Rights Society (ARS), New York/Licensed by VISCOPY, Sydney 2004. Originally published in *The New Yorker*, January 18, 1947, 21.

One of Steinberg's early attempts to draw the look of America but also to get behind or beyond the look. Such a bar is a typical New York location, and Steinberg gets the aura of the place perfectly. But with the double row of drinkers and the double bar rail, he is aiming also at something beneath the surface: the unconscious repetitions characteristic, as he saw it, of a mass democracy. The drawing looks forward to the rows of multiple national stereotypes—protesters, organization men, drum majorettes, hard-hatted workingmen, and so on—that Steinberg drew in the late sixties.

thirds of which had never been published.)[37] As many of the drawings show, Steinberg was now beginning to wonder about the distinctive appearances of everyday America—the fantastic contortions of drum majorettes, the spider-web tracery of Manhattan's iron and steel bridges, the desolate panoramas of wide city streets (sometimes contrasting the meanness of the boroughs with the distant, heroic Manhattan skyline), brownstones made topheavy by their elaborate cornices, the messy vitality of those streets ornamented with huge advertising billboards, early fifties automobiles puffed up like metallic challahs (in one photomontage an actual challah), the languid but minatory slouch of a baseball pitcher, the desolate vistas of wide newly laid exurban streets with high skies, telegraph poles running along the undeveloped blocks, and the occasional jumble of ground-hugging buildings in a hundred and one architectural styles. Virtually none of this interrogation of the surfaces of American life made its way into the pages of *The New Yorker,* presumably because no one could quite see the value of what Steinberg was doing.

What spurred a change of heart by the magazine's editors? If there is only one cause, it is tempting to single out the four spots that Steinberg was asked to draw for a four-part profile of the Ford Foundation by Dwight Macdonald that ran in *The New Yorker* at the end of 1955. Small in size and modest in conception (a dollar sign sprouts a few leaves [November 26, 1955, 57]; a Steinberg linear businessman looks on approvingly at some copperplate-engraved Magi with their gifts [December 3, 1955, 55]; a Ford Foundation "philanthropoid" holds aloft Liberty's torch and unicycles forward grasping a cornucopia instead of a briefcase [December 10, 1955, 57]; a Model-T Ford heads up a nearly vertical cliff next to a road sign that shows the absolutely vertical path from "Aspera" to "Astra" [December 17, 1955, 40]), they have immense implications for Steinberg's art in the middle of the fifties and for what the editors thought he could do. Here, asked to illustrate a piece about a centrally American institution (commerce plus culture, the production line plus creative innovation, the philanthropic redistribution of the fabulous profits of industrial capitalism), Steinberg seems to convince *The New Yorker*'s editors that his art has greater possibilities than they had previously allowed. Drawing has to invent its own language, to become a way of reasoning about what is drawn and a form of writing as well as depicting, if it is to get at what it is that appearance both reveals and conceals. The Model-T Ford scaling the cliff face is a perfect example: if the car is a material triumph, the road sign underscores the idealistic grandeur of the conception behind it. The drawing captures both the visible achievement and the invisible ideal propelling it. These little spots are among Steinberg's first successful attempts to draw the way America shows itself, the first time he discovered that to understand appearance you had to go behind

The Comic Worlds of Arno, Steig, Addams, and Steinberg

appearance to discover the concept. They must have shown the editors of *The New Yorker* that Steinberg might become a major interpreter of the American scene. Certainly from the mid-1950s we see the appearance of many nonrealistic, conceptual drawings: the schematic boxy family groups (March 2, 1957, 28), the businessman dueling with Justice (April 7, 1956, 27), and the vicious circle of fishes labeled "Chauvinism," "Taxes," "Ambition," "Nixon" and so on, all devouring one another (December 20, 1958, 21). These works climax in Steinberg's third cover for *The New Yorker,* the magisterial "The Pursuit of Happiness" of January 17, 1959 (fig. 4.11) a work that celebrates Steinberg's emergence from the labyrinth of the midcentury United States and offers a vista of the extraordinary work that will lie ahead.

As this brief account of the evolution of Steinberg's style between the forties and the late fifties suggests, his "gift" was not there all the time but had to develop: it required opportunity, provocation, and an evolutionary niche. Personally, its fundamental occasion was the more than decade-long collision between two Steinbergs. One Steinberg was the man who had been born in Romania, was educated in Italy, and always believed he was an Eastern European with a Western European overlay ("my sort of country goes from the eastern outskirts of Milan all the way to Afghanistan," he once said).[38] The other Steinberg was the unusually receptive twenty-eight-year-old who encountered an exciting but baffling New World when he stepped onto American soil in Miami in 1942, a world he thought no one had properly described visually before. In comment after comment Steinberg insists that his work is a continuous effort to understand his experience. It is an extended autobiographical journal, a way of reasoning on paper, in the free syntax of drawing, about what he comes across next. His subject is the drama of the encounter between his eye and the strange world it cannot help seeing but constantly misrecognizes. The story of Steinberg's oeuvre is the story of his countless encounters with the manifold strangeness of his adopted country and of the constant graphic inventiveness he exercised in order to represent that strangeness, to convert the mystery of what he saw into something he could understand, the journey from perception to understanding. Hence the powerful rational element that underpins even his most inspired and fantastic creations. That is the point of the oeuvre that substitutes for a few ready-made, hand-me-down opinions a constantly changing, minute day-to-day record of his observations or inspections of that country, so the oeuvre itself is a veritable New World continually remaking itself. When Christopher Ricks says that Steinberg is "a comic announcer, not a satiric denouncer," implying an attitude in which wonder and pleasure overbalance doubt and dismay, he comes as close as anyone might to summing up Steinberg's attitude toward America in a single phrase.[39] But the antithesis is no sooner grasped than it seems too pat. In particular, insofar as Ricks's comment minimizes the steady stream of intense and demystifying ratiocinative critique in Steinberg's art, it cannot satisfy anyone familiar with this extraordinary body of work.

The question of how to draw America is inseparable from Steinberg's status as an immigrant and a refugee and the opportunities and problems that being an immigrant posed for him. This in turn is bound up with the historical moment of American culture in the twenty-five years after the Second World War. It was once said of T. S. Eliot's adoption of British citizenship, and in defense of his conservatism, that no one could decently become a national of an adopted country and then turn into its most distinguished rebel. This observation is even more pointedly true of someone like Steinberg, for whom America was a refuge from a nightmare of history far worse than anything Eliot ever experienced. The aesthetic problem America posed for Steinberg (a problem that like all aesthetic problems is at some level an ethical problem) was how to reconcile a powerful need to accept what America was with the demands of an independent critical temperament. The art needed to embody both the profound sense of security and pleasure Steinberg felt about living in America and being an American—the chance to "pursue one's tendencies freely and seek happiness as one thinks best"—and the demands of an unusually aware and uncompromising critical intelligence faced with a civilization that was occasionally difficult to absorb and sometimes impossible to identify with.[40]

Steinberg's masks of the sixties[41] and his comments on the mask and American character sum up this antithesis. Many of the masks, some of which are reproduced in the Whitney retrospective catalog (*Saul Steinberg*, 176) at first glance seem free, inventive, witty, even joyous. What Steinberg says is, "What people do, especially in America, is manufacture a mask of happiness for themselves. They put a perpetual, reassuring smile on their faces; it makes them look nice, friendly and healthy, and we don't have to worry about them."[42] When we return to the masks and remember the quotidian material they are made of (brown paper grocery bags), we see the rueful sadness they express and also the judgment they make. The duality between creative élan and penetrating critique underlies all of Steinberg's art. On the one hand, there is a person's "emotional, physical, intimate life," which is private, fluid, and unceasingly changeable, and on the other there is one's "political, social life," where a person "constantly has to appear in an expected form."[43] Steinberg's Americanization comes down to recording in generous but never uncritical ways the effect on him of his encounter with the safety and plenitude of American life, along with its leveling mass culture and material crassness. The Statue of Liberty,

The Comic Worlds of Arno, Steig, Addams, and Steinberg

which so often appears in his drawings, sometimes with the head of a Native American, sometimes with that of an American middle-class matron, is itself a piece of Americanerie, at once straightforward and ironic, profound in its symbolism yet banal in its overuse. (For example, see its appearance, along with the Chrysler Building and the Guggenheim, in "New York Totems," reproduced in *Saul Steinberg*, 91.) It was one of Steinberg's first sights of America, and it must have struck him as both wildly uplifting and crushingly ironic— the Statue of Liberty, as glimpsed from Ellis Island, on July 1, 1941, through the eyes of a man who, because he only held a transit visa, had to go on to Santo Domingo before he could enter the U.S.A.[44]

So it would be wrong to say that Steinberg's art is satiric or even parodic. The occasional examples of cosmopolitan distaste for American life—like the cartoon showing an Aunt Sally stall at a carnival with the sign "Hit the Man of Distinction" (September 20, 1947, 21)—are rare in his work and occur only in the early years. For anyone living Steinberg's life in the decades after World War II, such an attitude could hardly be maintained. Cosmopolitan distaste was a mental luxury, no longer affordable under the exigencies of the new situation. That would be the attitude of a person whose emotional loyalty was to the Old Country. Steinberg's loyalty was unambiguously to America. He despised the role of the European artist in exile, holding himself aloof from a host culture he depended on and acting as dispenser of Old World cultural values and aesthetic principles. He presented his own identification with America as an alternative to "remaining here as a refugee from Europe—a thing I detested, because you became a victim of refugee lovers." The gratitude he felt toward his adopted country was completely sincere. Once in America he embarked on a long and thorough familiarizing—traveling the country, visiting its small towns and the Civil War battlefields, absorbing himself in baseball, which he saw as the key to the American character, drawing the place tirelessly.[45] He refused both the consolation of nostalgia and the quest for an aesthetic compensation for loss, commenting mordantly that "looking back is a mistake, a taboo. The most famous example of a retrospective victim is the wife of Lot."[46] But he also rejected the obvious alternative, the assimilation that characterized an earlier generation of Eastern European Jews and their children. Unlike Steig, for example, or even Addams, Steinberg would never have called himself an "all-American boy."[47] But what remained? The third course was to find a way to live and draw when caught between two forces that threatened to crush him: roughly, Americanization versus cosmopolitanism. There is an echo of this uncomfortable predicament in Steinberg's drawing of the man walking along a road in a valley between two hills with boulders rolling down on him from both sides (July 10, 1965, 26). The situation is not as dire as it looks: "Will they crush him? They won't, because they are going to meet at the tangential point, and that point is safe enough to create something like an arch which will protect the man."[48]

Steinberg was born on June 15, 1914, in Ramnicul-Sarat, a town with a significant enough Jewish population to be called a shtetl.[49] It lies about eighty miles northeast of Bucharest, in the northern marches of the Old Kingdom province of Wallachia, at the foot of the Transylvanian Alps, the lower arc of the Carpathians. The surname "Steinberg" implies a German Jewish ethnic derivation (if not cultural orientation). The family consisted of Steinberg's father, Moritz, his mother, Rosa (née Iacobson), and his sister, Lica,[50] to whom Steinberg was deeply attached. (Lica Roman died in 1975. Photographs of the family members are reproduced in the "Chronology" section of *Saul Steinberg*.) Moritz Steinberg was a printer, a bookbinder, and a boxmaker; Rosa Steinberg, who perhaps appears in several Steinberg drawings (see the reclining figure opening the geometric Pandora's box of her womb in "Allegory, 1963," reproduced in *Saul Steinberg*, 120), a phrasemaker, a raconteur, and as her son proudly said, a cake decorator. Though not well off, the family maintained a respectable social position. In the shtetl the printer, like the local photographer and watchmaker, was middle class. Such occupations retained considerable prestige in the local scale of values.[51].

Six months after Steinberg was born the family moved to Bucharest, to a house on Palas Street with a bustling courtyard behind it, and it was there that he grew up amid a large extended family with many aunts and uncles, two of them sign painters. In a vivid passage Robert Hughes depicts the young Steinberg as a fairy tale prince in the magic toyshop of the printer's workshop — "filled with embossed paper, stamps, colored cardboard, reproductions of 'museum' Madonnas (literally, chocolate-box art) and type blocks."[52] The paraphernalia of the printing shop provided the boy's playthings. "I had from the beginning the large wooden type used for posters, so if later I made, for instance, a drawing of a man holding up a question mark by the ball, it's not such a great invention — it was something known to me."[53] As Hughes noticed, not just memories but pictorial possibilities derive from the stamps, bindings, and fonts of his father's printshop — a place where the solid external world of things is turned into signs, symbols, and representations of itself. Meanwhile the young Steinberg watched his Uncle Josef at work on his shop signs, creating "a Romania that tried to resemble the court of Versailles, with happy views of peasants in national costume, all highly suited to pastry shops, restaurants, and other such places."[54] In later years Steinberg recalled that much of René Magritte's work derives from sign painting, and he noted the importance for surrealism of the urge to show man "as a cliché." It is as if Steinberg learned effortlessly and naturally at his father's knee the kernel of ideas that a Jacques Derrida or a Jean Baudrilliard would require long careers, difficult seminars, and laborious books to explain. In the printer's workshop things turned into words, words turned into pictures, and pictures sent you back to things. It was no surprise that Steinberg should conclude that drawing was really a kind of writing and writing a kind of drawing, that the game was always a game of representation. And since writing is the realm of logos, it was also inevitable that Steinberg's visual language should be a ratiocinative and critical one.

Steinberg grew up speaking Romanian and French, and overhearing Yiddish, the latter being "the secret language of my parents." The characteristics of this "secret language," its influence on a receptive child's way of thinking, have obvious implications for someone who was a conversationalist of formidable reputation. ("He existed so memorably as a person, a speaker and a monologist, that anyone who was lucky enough to know him knew him both as Saul and as Steinberg, the talker and the drawer.")[55] Although Steinberg never spoke Yiddish in his adult life, the implications of a linguistic inheritance with a powerful cultural dimension are also pertinent for his art, which may be thought of as a joking pictorial Yiddish. Yiddish is a profoundly conversational and situational language, "replete with the gestures of the speech situation." As Benjamin Harshev explains in his study of the semiotics of Yiddish communication, Yiddish "advances not in a straight line, through affirmative statements or the logic of a problem presented in a hierarchical argument, but through many kinds of indirect or 'translogical' language." It asks a question; challenges a claim; looks for a counterexample or an alternative possibility; answers with an example, a simile, or an analogous situation; illustrates a point by telling a story, an anecdote, or a parable; quotes a holy text or a proverb; poses a riddle; tells a joke; leaps to metalanguage and metadiscourse and ponders the language used and the purpose of the whole conversation; puns on words; digresses into pseudoetymology; and shifts, by association of language, from any of those to another topic.[56] Yiddish is a perfect model, then, for an artist whose lifework will be a joking monologue on the way a host civilization unconsciously represents itself. Steinberg's art is a sequence of marginal notes glossing the artist's adopted country, a running visual commentary on the colossal "text" of midcentury America. (His many spot drawings in *The New Yorker* in the fifties are marginalia in a quite literal sense.) The form of that oeuvre is determined by its surrender to the day-to-day logic of the master text rather than by any generative logic of its own.[57] Harshav concludes his discussion of Yiddish with words that offer about as good a general description of Steinberg's oeuvre as any: "Precisely because it is devoid of clear-cut narrative structure or metaphorical density, the value of such associative talking lies in the many 'asides' it can have. Anything may be linked with anything else. From every situation, one can shift to another situation that does not explicitly relate to the problem at hand, but is rich in new experiential detail. In principle, every chain developed in a text may link it with the whole universe of discourse. Thus every trivial anecdote may attain 'metaphysical' dimensions."[58] Steinberg's mother was just this sort of talker. "She had a way of describing something verbally that was the essential thing. . . . She was terrific at making observations and describing things that were really interesting—she would add all sorts of interpretations, parentheses and footnotes." Steinberg goes on to make the link to his art, in his own version of this inconclusive, fragmentary discourse: "And this is much more a preparation for an artist than—well think of all the children of great masters who could have learned *anything*."[59]

His childhood, Steinberg later remarked, "was very strong." "It stayed like a territory, like a nation. In my childhood the days were extremely long. I was high all the time without realizing it: extremely high on elementary things, like the luminosity of the day and the smell of everything—mud, earth, humidity; the delicious smells of cellars and mold; grocers' shops."[60] In this state of mind, in 1924 Steinberg entered the Liceul Matei Basarab, "an overcrowded, tough school, devoted mostly to Latin." The Liceul was the Romanian state high school, with a demanding curriculum: Latin, literature, history, geography, French, zoology, botany, and religion. In later years students also studied Greek, German, psychology, ethics, and philosophy. Since fewer than a twentieth of all children who had finished their four compulsory years at elementary school went on to high school, and since further restrictions applied to Jews seeking entry,[61] Steinberg's attendance at the Liceul shows that he was a talented student. And yet he told Robert Hughes he was a "misfit" and that his real education came from his private reading, finding "my real world, and my real friends, in books." He read Maxim Gorky, Fyodor Dostoyevsky, Jules Verne, Émile Zola, and Anatole France. A photograph stamped "JAN.927" and "MAR.927" shows him in a schoolboy's uniform ("khaki or blue suits with peaked cap to match for boys").[62] It is one of the first of those personal images marked with the stamp of officialdom that ratifies identity in the modern world, and Steinberg would exorcize the power of such papers only with the publication in 1954 of the collection of faux documents in *The Passport*.

In 1932, after graduating from high school, he entered the University of Bucharest, "frequenting"—to use his own somewhat vague term—courses in literature, philosophy, sociology, and psychology.[63] Again this suggests that his abilities were considerable: in the 1930s the strict *numerus clausus* provisions applied to Jews entering high school also hindered them from entering universities.[64] Finding purely academic studies were not to his liking, Steinberg eventually enrolled in the Faculty of Architecture at the polytechnic in Milan in 1933. He returned to Romania each summer "by tramp steamer from Genoa to Naples, Catania, Piraeus, several Greek Islands, Istanbul and Constanza,"[65] a practice he continued perhaps as late as 1940. But the worsening situation for Jews in Romania must have impressed him deeply.[66] He was only nineteen, but it was time to leave for good.

Italy of the mid-thirties, specifically the Milan polytechnic, might well have been the seedbed of Steinberg's art, but he remembered it chiefly as a "comfortable school . . . under the influence of Cubism." Such institutions, said Steinberg, were places where people learned the clichés of the time. Modernism had already become just such a cliché. "My time was late Cubism, via Bauhaus; our clouds came straight out of Arp, complete with a hole in the middle; even our trees were influenced by the mania for the kidney shape."[67] He had no formal art-school training, which he referred to, contemptuously, as "the traditional interruption of academic training." Although Steinberg appears to have drawn from early childhood, he dates his first significant artistic experience from the time in Italy, specifically a class visit to Ferrara and Rome. It was "an important and happy memory." Later in life he explained why: "It was the first time I drew from life—in Italian, *dal vero*, 'from the true.'" In fact, one has to tell the truth in order to make a good drawing, a poetic invention of the moment, a truth that demands the elimination of all our talent (ready-made vocabulary). It demands genuine clumsiness. In fact, the best clumsy ones are Cézanne and Matisse."[68] The statement (made sometime around the end of the 1970s) postulates a clear external reality ("the true") and the idea, familiar to much modernist thought, of an antiromantic theory of creativity—art not as the expression of selfhood or personal talent but as the elimination of it.

Steinberg records publishing his first cartoon in 1936 when he was twenty-two, in an Italian satirical biweekly called *Bertoldo*, based in Milan. This was Mussolini's Italy, "where the controlled press was predictable and boring" and where humor already proposed itself as a way to unsettle accepted ways of looking at things (in this fascism appears—much as it did for Steig—as merely an intensification of the authoritarianism and conformism of much of modern life). A cartoon from this period shows a man looking in a mirror and saying, "Dammit, this isn't me! I got lost in the crowd" (the drawing is reproduced in *Saul Steinberg,* 235). The joke itself recalls the existential dramas of Eugène Ionesco, but the Steinberg touch is clearly there in the long perspective of the room, with a glimpse of a duomo (possibly that of Florence) beyond. Through his cartooning Steinberg earned enough money to live comfortably in Milan. "I had the rare, beautiful pleasure of making money out of something I enjoyed doing and then spending as soon as I made it. As I lunched I knew this was my cat—I mean my *drawing* of a cat—that I was consuming; followed by a tree, the moon and so forth."[69]

Steinberg's drawings were also a lifeline to America. His work first began appearing in American magazines from the end of the thirties onward, in *Harper's Bazaar* and *Life*.[70] But it was not until 1941 that he decided to leave Italy, a complicated process that involved getting arrested in order to gain the one remaining document, a visa, that would allow him to go.[71] He aimed for Santo Domingo.[72] A relative had already tried to interest James Geraghty, then art editor of *The New Yorker,* in sponsoring Steinberg as an immigrant, but Geraghty had never seen any of Steinberg's drawings.[73] Steinberg finally sent drawings to Geraghty, who showed them to Harold Ross, who refused to buy them. The drawings were returned, but fortunately Geraghty kept photostats, which he showed one day to Russell Maloney, the staff writer and editor. Maloney was amazed that Ross had turned them down. He confronted Ross, and in the end Geraghty was able to buy some of Steinberg's drawings for the magazine. His first published cartoon, the mixed-up centaur with a horse's head and a man's legs, captioned "But it is half man and half horse," appeared in the issue dated October 25, 1941 (15). Maloney also got in touch with "certain friends in the State Department" to assist Steinberg with his American visa.[74] The visa came through a year later, and in July 1942 Steinberg disembarked at Miami and caught the bus to New York.

That bus trip, ordinary and banal in itself, was a formative experience for Steinberg, possibly more important than the ten years in Italy. Steinberg later located the essential element, and it was, unsurprisingly, the viewpoint: "The view from the car is false, menacing; one is seated too low, as if in a living room chair watching TV in the middle of a highway. From the bus one has a much better and nobler view, the view of the horseman."[75] This was Steinberg's never to be forgotten introduction to his adopted country, and travel henceforth became an activity to which he was passionately devoted, something that structured his life and provided the leitmotif of his art.[76] The traveler's shock at seeing the familiar stripped of its familiarity, the elation at truly seeing as the phenomenologist strives to see, looking behind the taken-for-granted appearance of things, is a feeling Steinberg has written well of: "I loved to arrive in a new place and face the new situations like one newly born who sees life for the first time, when it still has the air of fiction. (It lasts one day.)"[77] Travel, he once remarked, is not for picking up ideas, it is for making the mind a tabula rasa—"by putting oneself in the uncomfortable position of the immigrant one is again like a child. . . . I cut my bridges, I am in a condition that is new to me. I suddenly have the eye that sees, the nose that sniffs. All my senses are active—I'm not taking anything for granted the way one does when living day after day in the same routine."[78] This is the moment of estrangement from the everyday that Marcel Proust called the "the annulment of the contract of habit which binds us to our familiar surroundings." It is this escape from the routine that deadens, familiarizes, and habituates that makes a Steinberg drawing possible. It allows him to draw the fictiveness of things, a fictiveness that because it is *dal vero,* records the truth that lies within appearance.[79]

Steinberg's comments on how he saw his artistic opportunity at this time are particularly worth recalling. He thought that American artists mainly drew America through the lens of European postimpressionism. "These birds were traveling to Wyoming and Nebraska and they were painting Cézanne's Mont Sainte-Victoire," whereas "fantastic things like ghost towns and American architecture—highways and diners and motels and traffic they didn't see." "When I came here I realized the American landscape was untouched. I had a great appetite to paint it, to draw it. And I did. I drew these things that hadn't been drawn before—American women, baseball games, small towns, motels and diners—but I drew them with the same carefulness that more 'noble' artists use for a nude or a still life or an apple."[80] What is also clear from Steinberg's retrospective comments is that he was able to draw as he did partly because the capacious genre of comic art, with its permeable borderlines, freed him from rigid genre expectations. Moreover, Steinberg's democratic temper of mind, his infinitely curious sensibility, his indifference to the false notions of good taste (especially of modernist decorum), also made it possible for him to draw what others, as a matter of cultural snobbism, ignored or overlooked. By the end of the sixties Steinberg understood that his art had been a pathfinder for what was then called pop art. "I was a Pop artist long before everybody, except they didn't call it art."[81] Because pop art in turn fed the larger aesthetic program of postmodernism, it is tempting to situate Steinberg's work within some such tradition—but the truth is that Steinberg cannot really be assimilated into either of these phases of taste.

Steinberg isn't a "pop artist" at all, as the following anecdote suggests. Questioned by an interviewer about a truncated wooden pyramid he had had a carpenter make for him, a pyramid with the top cut off like the one that appears on the dollar bill, Steinberg replied, "This is something for myself. I don't know what I'm going to do with it. I may make some sort of American—Americanerie—I would call it." The pyramid, Steinberg's example of "Americanerie," with its Masonic and Enlightenment pedigrees, is one of his symbols for the secular order of the New World. It symbolizes both excessive rationality and a particular application of the rational principle: the goal of perfecting mankind in a solidly based society built on strictly rational lines by human beings adhering to the plan of the great universal architect. Steinberg coined the word Americanerie on the model of *bondieuserie,* which he explained as follows: "When something becomes a powerful cliché, no matter how important, how moving it is, it deteriorates, it becomes—well the French have this word, *bondieuserie,* which comes from *bon dieu* . . . Jesuses, sweet Madonnas, and so on. So many things become *bondieuserie* in the end—respectable and beautiful, but comical because they are such clichés."[82] In this category Steinberg includes those clichés, once powerful but now debased, that are often used to symbolize American life: "Indians, pyramids, columns, symbols, rainbows, Niagara Falls, Statue of Liberty, Sphinxes, all this stuff that's part of the American mythology."[83] An advertisement in *The New Yorker* that Steinberg must have seen exemplifies the process exquisitely. It promoted Buick cars with the slogan "Life, Liberty and the Pursuit of Happiness" (issue of July 15, 1950, 43). Americanerie, then, is an ambivalent term. It embraces the highest symbols of American life (which Steinberg sincerely thinks are "respectable and beautiful"), but at the same time it holds those symbols in a debased form (they are also "comical"). Steinberg's own faux Declaration of Independence of 1952 is a good instance: Is it homage or satire?

Americanerie overlaps with the category of kitsch, a word that is essential to any understanding of Steinberg's historical moment (the late thirties to the late sixties), his sensibility, and his temper of mind, as well as the success of his art.

Used neutrally, "kitsch" describes the aesthetic chaos—the bad taste—of all democratic, capitalist, modern societies.[84] In the industrialized nations, from the middle of the nineteenth century onward, a huge class emerges, better educated than any comparable group that preceded it, eager for cultural experience, and with the desire, the money, and the leisure to consume art objects. An army of art workers springs up to meet the demand, first in the old print culture (painters and sculptors, printers, newspaper, magazine, and book publishers), then in the electronic media (radio and record producers, filmmakers, television producers). The result is a democratization of culture that brings in its train the pluralization and debasement of aesthetic standards. The proliferating forms of mechanical and electronic reproduction facilitate the circulation of "bad" art objects (the "green Asian lady"), of "good" art objects stripped of their aura because of ready availability (postcards of a Raphael Madonna), and of art in the wrong place (the Mona Lisa on a dishtowel).[85] New art objects are created that are more ambiguous in status, popular—in the sense of mass—forms. The result is a cultural and moral dilemma of the highest order. All modern societies are characterized by the emergence of an expanded and engrossing but debased aesthetic culture that people privately deplore, intermittently recognize as trivial, yet cannot ignore and finally come to accept.

Kitsch is the aesthetic accompaniment to modernity itself. The term indicates the reign of bad aesthetic experience in all realms of life—from advertisements, to dress, to television programs, to automobiles, to buildings and cityscapes—a McDonald's restaurant in a historic streetscape, a Michael Jackson video clip, computer games, a Pokemon toy, Britney Spears, the latest Harry Potter movie, *Friends,* the great cultural transformation that gets us from *Pride and Prejudice* to *Joe Millionaire,* from *1984* to *Big Brother*.[86] It sums up all these familiar aesthetic crises of everyday life, crises not large in themselves but nagging, persistent, and enervating, which involve encounters with bad pop culture objects and additionally require us to adjudicate the claims they make on us: Do we accept or reject them (all the time knowing that some degree of acceptance is inevitable, whatever the cost)?

For the responsible artist the universal, unavoidable nature of kitsch creates a dilemma. The artist can either oppose kitsch culture and risk the irrelevance of working in an alienated, minority form (roughly the path taken by high modernism and the remnant defenders of high culture) or embrace it and risk being swept away by its inconsequentiality and triviality (roughly the extreme fate of a lot of postmodernist art and theory). Steinberg's temper of mind is that of a man who is genuinely responsive to kitsch, neither horrified nor seduced by it, who is at home with its energy without being demoralized by its vulgarity and who has found a way to acknowledge and work with it that is neither disdainful nor acquiescent. Consequently he is something of a pathfinder for artists of the second half of the twentieth century. His work can be understood as a constant, vigilant struggle, waged in drawing after drawing, in the no-man's-land between late modernism and postmodernism.[87] That gap, equivalent to the historical period between the early fifties and the late sixties, constitutes Steinberg's moment of artistic opportunity. His position within it can be visualized by noting that if Steinberg is totally unlike Jackson Pollock (a heroic, high modernist, abstract expressionist), he is even more unlike Andy Warhol (the epitome of depthless, depersonalized postmodern pop art). Steinberg's drawings of New York taxis, dating from the late 1940s, show his early attempts in this territory (not published in *The New Yorker,* but reproduced in *Saul Steinberg,* 72–73). They burst onto the page with all the baroque exuberance of bad taste and accurately and prophetically pinpoint the way that the distorted but seductive style of the automobile was to become a potent universal symbol of American self-confidence and wealth in the 1950s.

We can gauge Steinberg's success in absorbing kitsch culture through two examples: his use of images derived from advertisements and his variations on one of the most characteristic visual features of popular art, the speech bubble of the strip cartoon. These both show Steinberg's critical but constructive use of kitsch materials.

Steinberg, the scion of a family of commercial artists, regularly accepted advertising commissions, like every other artist considered in this book, although in his case only in the early part of his career and no doubt with stronger reservations than most. In the 1940s he supplied panoramic vistas of Paris for a series of advertisements for Parfums d'Orsay (for example, *The New Yorker,* May 19, 1945, 9) and drawings of comically proud householders for *House and Garden* (such as the one in *The New Yorker,* April 3, 1948, 77). In 1955 he had four commissions for advertisements in *The New Yorker* alone: for Schweppes, Simplicity patterns, Emerson televisions, and Noilly Prat vermouth. The series for Simplicity patterns uses music paper pasted on for wallpaper in one advertisement (May 21, 1955, 65) and an engraving of a Victorian mirror to outline a woman's face in another (September 17, 1955, 77). The more exploratory series for Noilly Prat (October 22, 1955, 85) uses the trademark Steinberg figure of an artist drawing scrolls, flourishes, and even the compass-drawn concentric circles that will later appear in *The New Worlds* to suggest the stirring motion required to blend the vermouth into a dry martini. Since much of this work is more adventurous than his drawings that *The New Yorker* was then publishing, it is clear that Steinberg used the advertisements as an opportunity to expand his visual language beyond what *The New Yorker* was then prepared to take.[88]

Steinberg's appropriation of advertising images demonstrates a jackdaw willingness to absorb whatever lay readily to hand into his art, no matter that it is prime kitsch. The motifs of many Steinberg drawings, the linear, abstract, geometric heads, the thumbprint as symbol of the self, the image of the balance beam and fulcrum, the schematic air route, and even the grocery bag used as a mask all have probable antecedents in this or that advertising image that appeared in *The New Yorker* in the early fifties.[89] Two examples show how well Steinberg was able to reshape the empty, kitsch quality of an image into one possessing genuine content. One especially suggestive advertisement, given Steinberg's interest in Egyptian motifs, appeared in the March 12, 1955, issue (59). It was for Rand McNally maps and showed the head of Queen Nefertiti with triangles and squares, all with labeled angles, projecting out from the planes of her profile, neck, and cap. The accompanying text, noting that "geometry" meant "earth measurement," celebrated cartography as a science of stable measurement "in a world of shifting values." The idea that the power of reason could be shown as an actual geometry based on the human head strongly appealed to Steinberg. In his work it developed into an image of a person's domination by excessive rationality. His own geometries of the head—

triangles and squares with labeled angles—start to appear only after this date: the man whose conversation comes out as triangles in the page of visible conversations (June 1, 1957, 30), the two triangles in conversation with each other (October 7, 1961, 60), and the man trapped inside a square with its angles labeled (September 10, 1960, 43), among many other examples. An even more striking example is his application of a photograph used in 1953 in an advertisement for "E-Z-Eye Safety Plate" windshields (just the sort of slogan, with its neologist orthography, that delighted Steinberg). The photograph shows the view from the driver's seat, with the highway unfolding ahead through the windshield and receding in the rearview mirror (fig. 4.5). Steinberg's spot drawing (fig. 4.6) redraws the image, abstracting and emphasizing its American feel and meaning—the empty landscape, the flat horizon, the limitless possibilities of the open road, the sense of imaginative extension of self provided by the automobile along with the hollowness of the experience. (The advertisement makes it clear that the highway is in California—the approach to the Torrey Pines Grade on Highway 101 near La Jolla, to be precise—so the image harmonizes with Steinberg's conviction that America fulfills itself in the West.) Steinberg being Steinberg, what he adds is also instructive—the driver's right eye in the rearview mirror and a view of what has been left behind.

The simplest examples of the speech bubble, which Steinberg had been interested in from as early as 1958,[90] are the melancholy pictures of middle-class marriage, in which the bubbles, crammed with meaningless scribbles (the pictorialization of a conversation that has run to mere routine), collect on the floor like the pages of discarded, unread newspapers (May 8, 1965, 39). More pointed is the interview with the bank manager (or the boss, or bureaucrat) in which the speech bubble, again filled with the indecipherable scribbles representing the conversational noise of the one with power, shapes itself into the real information contained in the speech, the word "no" (November 25, 1961, 59). Steinberg's intuition that the manner of speaking, rather than the ostensible content, is the real message in a conversation is summed up in the masterly drawing of two men talking, in which the speech of one man shapes itself into a dragonlike reptile taking the meek rabbit of the other man's speech in its jaws (November 12, 1960, 47). The wit lies in the contrast between an apparent equivalence of the two speakers and a true inequality. On the surface the men mirror each other's amenable facial expressions and appear to be equals; in fact one is devouring the other. The quest for social dominance is the common drama of everyday contact in an egalitarian society and is perhaps even more exhausting and demanding than the given hierarchies of a ranked society. In an egalitarian society older oppressions and inequalities are simply replaced by new ones.

By the edge of the Pacific, approaching Torrey Pines Grade on Highway 101, near La Jolla, Calif.

THIS IS A GLARE-SHIELD

LIBBEY·OWENS·FORD SAFETY GLASS
Authorized Replacement Service

LOOK FOR THIS SIGN
when you need safety glass

Put yourself here, for extra comfort and safety.

This light blue-green *shaded* windshield of E-Z-Eye Safety *Plate* Glass does more than protect your eyes from wind and rain and dust. It shields them from the nagging strain of glare. It protects you from blinding sun and skybrightness, stabbing reflections and oncoming headlights. It makes everything look cool and clear and you feel luxuriously relaxed at the wheel.

With E-Z-Eye Safety *Plate* Glass in all your windows, you'll *feel* cooler in summer, too, because solar radiation through E-Z-Eye is much less than through regular safety glass.

For your eyes' sake—for pure pleasure and the distinguished look it gives your car—get E-Z-Eye in your next automobile. This optional feature costs very little extra. It's made only by Libbey·Owens·Ford and is available in all General Motors cars.

LIBBEY·OWENS·FORD GLASS CO., TOLEDO 3, OHIO

E-Z-EYE SAFETY PLATE
with the shaded windshield

Reduces Glare, Eyestrain, Sun Heat

ALL L·O·F SAFETY GLASS IS GRADE-MARKED
If the word PLATE isn't etched on your car windows, they aren't safety Plate glass.

Fig. 4.5. Advertisement for E-Z-Eye Safety Plate glass windshield.

The New Yorker, August 8, 1953, 3. Image reproduced by permission of the General Research Division, the New York Public Library, Astor, Lenox, and Tilden Foundations.

A dramatic advertising image, using aspects of American life that were already iconic—the car, the open highway, the road to the West. It appeared in *The New Yorker* at a time when Steinberg was accepting advertising commissions for products like Schweppes, Simplicity patterns, and Emerson televisions. As the following image suggests (fig. 4.6), Steinberg was aware of the usefulness of such images for his work.

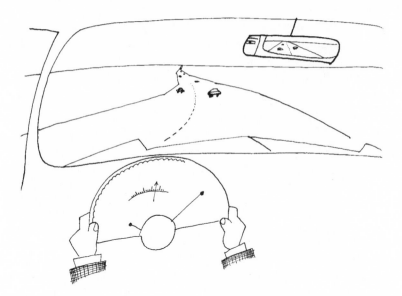

Fig. 4.6. Saul Stein-
berg, untitled drawing,
ink on paper.

© The Saul Steinberg
Foundation/Artists
Rights Society (ARS),
New York/Licensed
by VISCOPY, Sydney
2004. Originally pub-
lished in *The New Yorker*,
January 11, 1958, 22.

"How to Learn from Popular Culture—1." Impressed by
the kitsch energy and vulgarity of his New World, Steinberg
adapted images from everywhere, including advertisements
(not a huge step from drawing billboards, after all). In this
drawing, quite possibly based on the advertisement reproduced in figure 4.5, Steinberg abstracts the mythic essentials
of the scene—the wide horizon, the open highway, the speed-
ometer creeping upward, the sense of limitless extension of
self inherent in the automobile. But Steinberg adds something:
the eye that observes it all, reflected in a rearview mirror that
also shows what has been left behind.

It is a short step from here to doing without the speech bubble altogether.
The idea of everyday conversation as status contest receives a devastating expression in the drawing in which two men meet in the street and prepare for
some conversational jousting. One, whose armory consists only of a mass-
culture reference to Kim Novak, prepares to do battle with another bearing the
more elaborate weaponry of (mainly European) high culture: Rodion Raskolnikov, Emma Bovary, Julien Sorel, and Leopold Bloom, among others (fig.
4.7). Who will be the victor is uncertain. As a weapon Kim Novak, despite
the suggestion of pneumatic breasts in the fulsome scrolls of the letter *k,* is
sharp and pointy at her extremities, whereas Rodion Raskolnikov is heading
the wrong way and is rounder and probably more useful for defense than for

attack. Kim Novak (just two names) is light and maneuverable, whereas a weighty pile of nine names is awkward to deploy. (Can you counter with Candide? But he is at the back, and high up, and you read Voltaire years ago when you were in college, so he is not as easy to recall as Kim Novak, whom your opponent is obsessed with and has just seen in *Kiss Me, Stupid*.)

Last, there is Steinberg's most inventive development of the speech bubble device—his parties, drawn in the 1960s and 1970s, in which people become hieroglyphs—concentric circles, mazes, linear flourishes—representing their conversational styles (August 11, 1962, 25). Of this brilliant drawing Steinberg has commented, "A very hard outside with a soft inside sits on a straight back chair talking to a fuzzy spiral. On the sofa there is a boring labyrinth speaking to a hysterical line, a giggling, jittery bit of calligraphy. Then there is a dialogue between concentric circles and a spiral. The concentric circles represent the frozen, prudent people. The spiral can look like a series of concentric circles. Therefore these two people could seem similar in aspect. But actually the essence of spirals is different from the essence of concentric circles." Spirals move freely away from a center, concentric circles are, in the most literal sense, self-centered. Here the person has disappeared, replaced entirely by a speech bubble that in turn has lost any connection with the written word and is simply an abstract, yet concrete, line symbolizing the nature of the person speaking.

In drawings like these central elements of kitsch culture are taken over without compromising the aesthetic integrity of the artist's work. This taking over, which is not really "appropriation," is done not for the purposes of parody, denunciation, or rejection but for exploration, application, and amplification. The end is to promote understanding. Only in the last instance, as a kind of unforced totalizing of the implications of those uses, do these drawings imply a judgment on the culture that has helped produce them. The drawings are remarkable, and their wit has always been remarked on: less noticed has been the exact way they engage and take up the prevailing culture, yet distance themselves from it.

Steinberg's summing up of kitsch tendencies in the United States under the heading of Americanerie will carry us so far, but the term must be broadened if it is to be adequate to the ambitious scope of his art. We can do this by looking more closely at Steinberg's use of a particular form of Americanerie, the mythology of Freemasonry, and its association with another mythology, that of the founding ethos, rational and enlightened, of New World society. The pyramid is a good starting point because it is at the same time an example of Americanerie (lodging itself in the social imaginary via the dollar bill), a kitsch object (a debased, commonplace image loosely signifying "the exotic"), and a

Fig. 4.7. Saul Steinberg, untitled drawing, ink on paper.

© The Saul Steinberg Foundation/Artists Rights Society (ARS), New York/Licensed by VISCOPY, Sydney 2004. Originally published in *The New Yorker*, November 7, 1964, 61.

"How to Learn from Popular Culture—2." This drawing is an example of Steinberg's extension of a familiar motif of comic-book art, the speech bubble. Having drawn speech bubbles filled with meaningless scribbles (some are ejected mechanically from the mouth, some lie discarded in a pile on the floor like yesterday's newspaper, others form themselves into the shape of the real message: No), Steinberg now draws the content of a person's conversational repertoire as if it were a jousting weapon. The man on the left adroitly and aggressively brandishes his one topic, a mass-culture reference to Kim Novak. As conversational armory it looks as though it will do a good job against the unwieldy high-culture battery of the man on the right. His "Rodion Raskolnikov" is already in retreat (the *R*s point to the right, away from the action) and seems defensive rather than aggressive. He can counter with other weapons, of course. But heaped up as they are, they seem inaccessible—suppose you wanted to stab him with Candide, how would you ever reach the word in time? The pile of names also looks like a terrible burden to carry around.

profound symbol of America (the iconographic symbolism of a perfect, stabilized, Euclidean, humanly created shape). To grasp what is going on here, we need to look at Steinberg's habit of drawing rebuses of his own name.

Although Steinberg's art is abstract, it has a peculiarly concrete, even literal, cast that reminds us that the unconscious—like the child—often treats words as objects. "Steinberg" means, literally, "stone mountain."[91] Steinberg often takes up this literal meaning and plays with it to reveal its potential breadth of reference. Sometimes the "stone mountain" becomes Steinberg's icon of the predicament of the defensive self in a competitive and aggressive society. There are many drawings, for example, of the *homme moyen sensuel* actually standing on the "stone mountain" of the self—which is at once a vantage point, a fortress, a precarious resting place, a snarling face, and—as the mount with its angled axis suggests—an entire globe (September 28, 1963, 37).[92] (The self as the world, a head suspended on a globe cradle, first appears in a small spot for May 23, 1959, 40.) The petrified self then reappears in a modified form in those drawings of frozen figures standing on the edges of cliffs or on mountaintops, like the man shown peering over a stone mountain precipice into a valley littered with the passing, dead years—1946, 1953, 1958, and so on (October 23, 1965, 63). (Steinberg's repeated use of the cliff or precipice motif has often been noticed. He himself recounts being taken under police guard from Milan to the Abruzzi in 1941: "During that wonderful trip I saw perilous mountains for the first time, with the train going ever so slowly along the edge of an abyss, which was precisely my situation.")[93] Pedestals and pillars are also "stone mountains" of a kind: highly rational ones, because of their classical heritage and the way they connote disciplined, controlled, and socialized activity. Shaped to definite human meanings, they symbolize the achievement of the self-made man, the extent to which people "stand on" what they have achieved. One drawing shows four artists, their reputations graded not just by their respective sizes but also by the kinds of pedestals they have made for themselves: the really "great" artist is perched confidently on top of a high column set on a large plinth, guarded by a dour stone lion; the rest, on little plinths with no columns, are grouped haphazardly around his base (*The New World*, 1965). (Interestingly, the three largest figures are artists proper, as we see from their palettes; the smallest artist wields only a cartoonist's pen.) Another cartoon shows a complacent, stocky, besuited businessman astride his plinth, which is decorated with a profile of his wife in a medallion, with his faithful dog gazing up at him, while ordinary folk go unheedingly about their business below (June 27, 1959, 30). Steinberg constantly explores this general notion, and he digs out of it many meanings with a fine nuance. As he shows, people are comically restricted by what they have made of themselves. A particularly witty drawing on this theme shows a man leaping from the unformed stone of a cliff face to the neoclassical finish of a pedestal (November 18, 1961, 50), making the daring journey of the self-made man. The contrast here between natural and carved stone recalls Steinberg's enigmatic drawings of battered-looking cubes dreaming of a geometric perfection (July 30, 1960, 25).

A pyramid is a kind of stone mountain. In the sixties and seventies Steinberg shows a particular liking for the pyramid. He wrote in 1978: "Pyramids

The Comic Worlds of Arno, Steig, Addams, and Steinberg

are perfect; nothing surpasses their beauty and intelligence as a solemn symbol of the human presence."[94] The pyramid is Steinberg's most potent and
frequently drawn symbol of the male presence, as we see in a sketch published
in *The New Yorker,* October 17, 1964 (53), where it is counterpoised against a
decidedly feminized, not to say felinized, Sphinx.[95] Steinberg used the pyramid in one of his most worked and cryptically autobiographical drawings, "Inventory," dating from 1967, the year Steinberg turned fifty-three (fig. 4.8; not
published in *The New Yorker*). This drawing is an abstract autobiographical
halfway report on the 1960s, as seen at the end of 1967. The years from 1960
to 1966 are represented as the table and what it carries, drawn in the bottom
right-hand corner. The very prominent and annotated, lakelike 1963 (the assassination year) is recalled clearly but is separated from the years before and
after. The years 1960, 1961, and 1962 are mere notches on a line, whereas 1964
and 1965 form two new countries on an island, with inlets and a dividing river.
The year 1966 is represented as a labyrinth, its line extending to become the
meeting of the floor and the wall. From there it starts to describe the lived
space of the just completed 1967, a scene represented not only by the room
but by words said and the drawings left on the floor by the bed. Other Steinberg drawings of the decade hang on the wall. Another time scheme is given
by the chest of drawers near the door—twelve closed drawers at the bottom
(the twelve months of each year) and ten closed drawers at the top (the ten
years of the decade). The new year, 1968, is shown by the wheel at the bottom
left of the drawing, with January at the top, and also by the first week of the
new year, beginning with Monday (January 1 fell on a Monday in 1968) rolling out through the doorway at the top right. (It must be rolling out because
of the sequence of days written on it. It rolls out rather than in, because time
is always moving away from you, always a loss.) A figure we can associate with
the artist is shown as another "stone mountain," this time a pyramid, resting on
the downy bed lying beside a (perhaps) female rainbow. The scene is watched
over by the bust of a Native American, Steinberg's symbol for personal freedom (as the cowboy is the symbol for justice).

In this drawing the pyramid symbol implies a resolved, confident, and stable
self, a self in which the faculty of reason is felt as wholly beneficial. But Steinberg never ties down the meaning of the pyramid, as we see once we broaden
this line of inquiry from the personal to the public sphere. In Steinberg's drawings of the public sphere, the pyramid is a "stone mountain" symbolizing group
and national values. In this context the pyramid is no longer a symbol of the resolved and confident self but stands for the "Americanized" self, a self formed
by strictly rational, calculating, and even conformist principles. This in turn
directs us to Steinberg's interest in the way the dramatic architectural iconog-

raphy of Freemasonry can be used as a means of drawing, compactly and concretely, the American ethos itself. Steinberg pushes an interest in kitsch Americanerie outward, to the point where it becomes a complex and extensive visual symbolic language able to represent adequately not just the quirky Americanness of America but its foundational ethos and its national character as well.[96]

Freemasonry has recently begun to receive attention from historians like Margaret C. Jacob, James Stevens Curl, Keith Hetherington, and Bernard Vincent.[97] Since well-attested links existed between the European and American lodges at the end of the eighteenth century, a brief account of the situation in Europe is a useful introduction to what was happening in America. Jacob, in calling for a "textured social and political history of the Enlightenment," has identified "new enclaves of enlightened sociability" in late eighteenth-century Europe, of which the Freemasons' lodge is her prime example.[98] She argues that Freemasonry, whose language and symbols were a kind of code lingua franca for new, progressive ideas, was the route by which Enlightenment ideas and ideals passed into common currency. The class composition of the European lodges is crucial to Jacob's story. The lodges recruited aspiring, often lower-middle-class citizens, typically tradesmen and merchants and not infrequently Jews: that is, people who did not benefit from the established social structures and networks of the ancien régime. Freemasonry offered these people a coherent, largely secular social philosophy based on the ideals of rational self-improvement and social renovation. The lodges operated as a fraternal network of like-minded individuals promoting social advancement according to merit. In disseminating the cause of rational reform, society was imagined as a great edifice awaiting renovation according to the rational wisdom and principles of the universal architect. Historically speaking, the newly federalized United States was just such a world laboratory, the concrete situation in which such renovation might take place—a veritable New World, where everything could start again with reason and utility, rather than custom and tradition, determining the outcome.

It is in such a context that one has to evaluate the usefulness of the often-quoted but somewhat uncertain assertion that, of fifty-six signatories to the American Declaration of Independence, fifty-three were Masons.[99] The truth is that America was fertile soil for both Freemasonry and enlightened social perfectibilism, and the two were probably indistinguishable. Bernard Vincent has shown how the lodges, as a form of "enlightened sociability" in late eighteenth-century America, were the conduit through which ideas passed from the salons, pamphlets, and treatises of Paris into the popular political conversation of the early American Republic. He stresses the "seminal role in favor of independence, human rights, [and] the republic: a role and an influence

The Comic Worlds of Arno, Steig, Addams, and Steinberg

Fig. 4.8. Saul Steinberg, "Inventory," 1967, ink and watercolor on paper, 22 by 28 inches.

© The Saul Steinberg Foundation/Artists Rights Society (ARS), New York/Licensed by VISCOPY, Sydney 2004. Image reproduced courtesy of Chermayeff and Geismar Associates, New York.

A personal allegory showing how Steinberg's drawings often divert into autobiography. The drawing reviews the first eight years of the decade. The very prominent, lakelike 1963 (the assassination year) is recalled clearly and even has an accompanying, if indecipherable, text. It is clearly separated from the years before and after. The years 1960, 1961, and 1962 are mere notches on a line, whereas 1964 and 1965 form two new countries on an island, with inlets and a dividing river. The year 1966 is vividly present to the memory, but as a puzzling labyrinth, out of which is extruded the present year, 1967, now drawing to its close. (Ariadne's thread becomes the line depicting the walls of the labyrinth, which then becomes the base of the wall of the room of the present moment.) The drawing actually shows January 1, 1968, about to happen. The first week of the New Year is already rolling out through the door, as the sequence of the days of the week on the wheel shows. A man reclines on the bed (a pyramid, a rebus of the name "Steinberg," a "stone mountain"), beside a (perhaps) female rainbow.

that extended beyond the craft itself," and he thinks this influence "was an important factor of ideological and political transformation."[100] For Vincent, Masons are "unseen agents of social change" in eighteenth-century America, men who found in the popularized Enlightenment thought of the lodges "a ready-made philosophy that catered to all their needs."[101] America was the country where these vague ideals might finally be realized.

Such is the history, or rather the mythology, Steinberg drew on. The pyramid (to telescope Steinberg's drawings into this abbreviated account of Freemasonry in late eighteenth-century America) is a Masonic symbol of human perfection. In Steinberg's hands it becomes a convenient, ready-made, and easily drawn symbol of an ideal American character type as derived from these noble ideals. The pyramid is dressed, hewn stone. It is perfected in accordance with the universal geometric laws of a divine architect. With its wide base it is perfectly stable, it is symmetrical, and like the spire, but less precariously so, it points upward toward the divine eye in the sky, the eye that, in a moment of national hubris, actually intersects with and dwells in the pyramid on the back of the dollar bill.

A critical appreciation of the usefulness of the architectural symbolism of Freemasonry, of the usefulness of the iconography of a Freemasonry powerfully (if mythically) associated with the American ethos, underpins many of Steinberg's drawings of the late fifties through the early seventies.[102] This is what makes his constant return in drawing after drawing to street scenes, buildings, and monuments (the latter understood as a kind of Dadaist totem of America) cohere in such a meaningful fashion.[103] None of this is meant to suggest that Steinberg was a Mason. Rather, I mean to emphasize how readily he saw the opportunities Masonic iconography presented to a visual ironist like himself, an artist fascinated by symbols of all kinds and interested in drawing an America constructed as a project of the rational will, and in weighing up that ideal against the place America had actually become.[104] An early example of Steinberg's use of this symbolism is his Independence Day cover for July 4, 1964, where the pyramid sits on the horizon next to a rainbow and a stepladder reaching up to the moon. Steinberg, in whose art we have already noticed an important rationalist element (drawing as "a way of reasoning on paper," an inadequate phrase unless we follow George Eliot when she defined Dr. Johnson's wit as "reasoning raised to a higher power"), was temperamentally sympathetic to the universal, rationalist critique of the Enlightenment, of which Freemasonry is now understood to be the social wing. But, ironically, those same principles also fed Steinberg's critical temper.

The most striking instance of Steinberg's sardonic use of the iconography and symbolism of Freemasonry is the drawing commissioned by *The New Yorker* in 1967 for the title illustration of Anthony Bailey's three-part profile

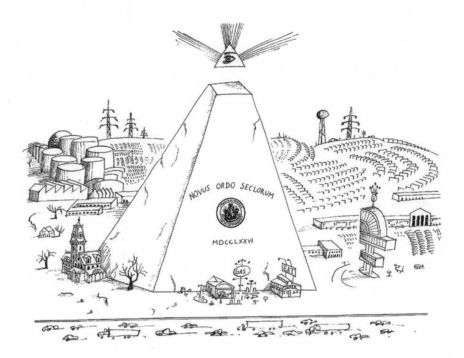

Fig. 4.9. Saul Steinberg, untitled drawing, ink on paper.

© The Saul Steinberg Foundation/Artists Rights Society (ARS), New York/Licensed by VISCOPY, Sydney 2004. Originally published in *The New Yorker,* July 22, 1967, 35.

Steinberg as "mythologist" and connoisseur of "Americanerie." The Freemasons' pyramid (lifted straight off the dollar bill), once an optimistic national image for the humanly fashioned, rational, and stable perfection of the *novus ordo seclorum* of the United States, is now a battered, cracked, and chipped structure in a fallen semiurban landscape. The past is irrelevant—Addams's gingerbread horror house is tacked on to the side, literally sidelined. The pyramid is surrounded by buildings that are the new temples of commerce—oil refineries, factories, power pylons, the suburb, motels, hotels. These are what the dollar has built or, alternatively, institutions that exist to serve the dollar. In the foreground a diner and gas station are actually build into the pyramid, while the cars on the freeway flash past as a blur. The ruled line of universal, enlightened reason, the originating but lost principle behind all this activity, is reduced to the shoulder of the freeway.

"Through the Great City," a study of the way commerce and industry were turning the northeastern corridor of the United States, the 450-mile inverted S-curve of Washington, Philadelphia, New York, and Boston, into a "megalopolis."[105] Steinberg's drawing uses the Freemasons' broken pyramid from the dollar bill as its compositional focus (fig. 4.9). The pyramid, symbolizing the visionary and utopian promise of the new secular order inaugurated in 1776, towers over the fallen landscape of the megalopolis—power pylons, oil storage tanks, factories, and anonymous suburbs, a landscape the dollar has created and is steadily degrading. To the left is the Addams house, a nineteenth-century past emptied of its haunts, forlorn, bereft, and irrelevant. To the right a confident art deco midcentury building already looks outdated. The diner and the gas station in the foreground, casually built into the side of the pyramid next to a freeway with its stream of unheeding, blurred traffic, represent the present. Significantly, the confident rational line of reason and purposive behavior is displayed only in the lines describing the shoulder of the freeway. The pyramid, which ought to be the stable element, lists to the right and has lost its pristine, clean-cut, hewn perfection: its surface is chipped and flawed, its outline irregular and imperfect.

This drawing shows how important Steinberg found architectural motifs taken from the iconography of Freemasonry. In Freemasonry, buildings were the great metaphor of society itself. Architecture fuses with geometry as a way of concretizing a philosophical view of a rational universe in which divine and human intentions coincide and the social edifice is represented as a well-made building—a symbol of something both man-made and obedient to transcendent principles. There is a direct legacy of this in Steinberg's extensive, indeed trademark, use of architectural motifs in the fifties and sixties, where they are used to describe pictorially something as abstract, huge, and unmanageable as the social order at a particular historical moment. In Freemasonry we constantly find motifs of architectural plans, drawings of buildings, monuments, statues, columns (Freemasonry devised a symbolic language for the three classical orders in which the Doric stood for strength, the Ionic for wisdom, and the Corinthian for beauty),[106] pedestals, pillars, pyramids, labyrinths, steps, sphinxes, and the tools of the trade (see fig. 4.10).[107] Most of these turn up in Steinberg's iconography. To take a key example, a lodge plan always includes a fragment of unhewn stone along with a piece of the same stone cut into a cube (sometimes surmounted by a pyramid).[108] Uncut stone is a representation of unenlightened, unperfected human material; the cube and the pyramid (a symbol in Freemasonry of perfection, ascension, and immortality) represent the shaping of rough human nature by men in accordance with the great architectural plan of the Creator. The symbolism illuminates Steinberg's recurring interest in perfected cubes as opposed to battered and patched cubes that have not quite achieved perfection (for example, in *The New Yorker*, July 30, 1960, 25), as well as unperfected stone mountains and the like, including pyramids. It also casts light on the drawing of a labeled triangle outweighing a patched-up, soft question mark on a seesaw (July 23, 1960, 16): ideology's triumph over skepticism.

The Comic Worlds of Arno, Steig, Addams, and Steinberg

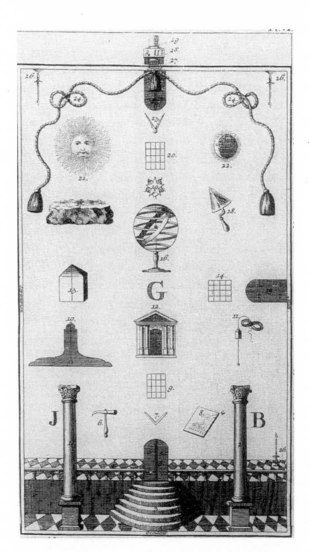

Fig. 4.10. Chart of implements and symbols associated with Freemasonry.

From Abbé Gabriel-Louis Pérau, *L'Ordre des Franc-maçons trahi et le secret des Mopses revelé* (Amsterdam, 1745). Image reproduced by permission of the General Research Division, the New York Public Library, Astor, Lenox, and Tilden Foundations.

Some of the symbols or mythology of Freemasonry (associated with the founding principles of the United States) that Steinberg seems to draw on. (Others include pyramids, palm trees, and sphinxes.) Notice in particular the globe, the unhewn and hewn pieces of stone (raw and perfected "stone mountains"), the twin pillars (Jachin and Boaz, foundations of the social order), and the tools of the mason's trade—trowel, plumb line, and callipers. As well as using some of these motifs, Steinberg paid similar homage to the tools of his trade in a series of drawings and sculptures of pencils, brushes, drawing pads, and drawing boards in the late seventies. A number of them are reproduced in *Saul Steinberg*, 31, 165, 170–71.

Not, to reiterate, that Steinberg is a propagandist for either Masonic or Enlightenment principles.[109] It is simply that his being attuned to the semiotics of the rational, perfectly straight line that gets from A to B without any peripeteia, as in the drawing of the man giving directions to an inquiring traveler (December 4, 1965, 61), opens up a world of satiric possibility in his drawings. Well in advance of other social critics, Steinberg develops a sense that a country's ethos can be drawn, and hence assayed, from its public facades—its architecture, its billboards, its cityscapes, its visual mythology—and the gap between these and a country's values and ideology. Steinberg works out the inherent logic of this intuition in those drawings of city streets that date from the 1950s. Here the universal adoption of the international style in architecture as the style of a corporate state—an architectural style that both expresses and symbolizes the principles behind it in an already ironic manner—is figured as the afterlife of enlightened rationality in American life. In such drawings (examples are to be found in *The Passport*) graph paper, cut out and stuck onto the drawing sheet, becomes the blank, anonymous, regular facade of a building, a kind of inspirational minimalism, that has been thrust down into, and towers over, the messy brownstone facades and groups of passers-by. All the life and animation is there, while the rational grid is dead and empty.

An odd development of all this is the characteristic (and hubristic) fondness of Enlightenment culture for erecting monuments to itself. This tendency is something Steinberg seizes on time and time again, usually with some amusing twist—as, for example, the drawing of the man on a pedestal that constitutes a weight he is attached to, making it impossible for the twig he is clutching to support him (October 1, 1960, 41). Adam Gopnik says that among Steinberg's greatest achievements at the end of the 1950s is the drawing of the imaginary Beaux-Arts monument titled "The Pursuit of Happiness," yet another example of an architectural edifice as symbol of the social order. Gopnik reads the drawing as a dam, the banal values of 1950s decency almost but not quite holding back the tide of hedonistic, materialistic individualism that would inundate the subsequent decades. This is just, but if it implies that Steinberg acquiesces in the culture of the 1950s, then it doesn't quite ring true. For a start, as we turn over the cover it is printed on, this satiric depiction of American materialism ironically segues into the very substance of what it is satirizing: advertisements for Johnny Walker whiskey, expensive clothes from B. H. Wragge, new Chryslers, and so on.

The "Pursuit of Happiness" (fig. 4.11), the cover of *The New Yorker* for January 17, 1959, in effect counterpoints President Eisenhower's State of the Union address of the previous week (January 9, 1959).[110] Eisenhower had summed up the American ethos as that of "freedom," and his address had made clear how important the freedom of the businessman was to his conception of that term. Steinberg's drawing shows a monument to American prosperity at the end of the fifties, with an unchained businessman at the top of the social edifice. The businessman is both a national father figure and a summation of the social evolution of the New World. He is flanked by the busts of two intercessors with nearly identical faces, stuck on pillars: Santa Claus and Sigmund Freud. (They recall Jachin and Boaz, Masonic symbols of secure foundations and strength alluding to the names of the two pillars that supposedly stood at the entrance of Solomon's temple.)[111] At first glance it all seems perfectly symmetrical and balanced, monolithic and static, its key pairings showing a neutralizing of opposites and a reconciling of traditional antagonists—art shaking hands with industry, science with commerce, labor with leisure (these abstractions are all represented by identical businessmen in hats and suits), Uncle Sam with Uncle Tom (representing the reconciliation of the North/South divide), and so on, including the balancing of Santa Claus (all you might wish for) with Sigmund Freud (in this context, all you must sublimate in order to get what you wish for). Statistics have killed the peacock of inflation, and the arrow that skewers unemployment (a skeletal-faced lion) has also pierced semantics. Metaphorically a dam, as Gopnik says. But if so there are reasons for suspecting that the dam is leaky and the Eisenhower equilibrium is trembling and unstable. Vice shakes hands with virtue, and the pursuit of happiness, which in this drawing is subordinated to prosperity, is represented by a crocodile and a snake eating each other's tails. The tutelary deities, Santa Claus and Sigmund Freud, are worrisome. Santa Claus suggests a certain infantilism in the national character. Freud, who represents the instinctual sublimation that created the 1950s social order, also heralds the dissolution of this very arrangement: the triumph of the therapeutic (hence the collapse of the remnant of other-directed character ideals that made America what it once was) and the advent of the expressive revolution of the 1960s. The dam is structurally weak. As well as being different from succeeding decades, the fifties are also the seedbed of those years.

Leaving interpretation aside, what is most remarkable about the drawing is that Steinberg has found a highly tangible and legible way to draw such a moment in history and to represent its currents and countercurrents. He does this by using the architectural symbolism of Freemasonry for the matrix of the drawing, the perfect, rational, ruled vertical and horizontal lines that embody the idea of the social edifice as an expression of utopian social ideals. Then, by recasting the whole project in comic and skeptical terms in the statuary, he ironizes the self-important and unselfconscious temper of such triumphalist monumentalizing. The drawing is a marvel, not just because of its prophetic content, not just because of the perfection of its draftsmanship, but because such an abstract and seemingly undrawable thing as the State of the Union can be so transparently registered, dissected, and held up for critical understanding.

How detached Steinberg himself is from the larger historical process that underpins the triumph of modern commercial secularism, especially in the United States, can be seen in a strip cartoon that traces the seven ages of the West, from the Dark Ages to the present day (August 30, 1958, 22–23). In the first panel the Christian knight kills the dragon of paganism. In the next the king defeats the nobleman. Then the secular state vanquishes monarchy. Then the bourgeois subdues the revolutionary republican. Then the military dictator briefly ousts the bourgeois. Then the middle-class burgher drives out the dictator. Finally the common man, with no real adversary left, history being at an end, blankly triumphs over his own intelligence: he is shown with his foot on his own decapitated head. Since this drawing may be held to show not just a temporal journey from the Dark Ages to the present but also a geographical migration from the Old World to the New, it is implicitly a severe criticism of midcentury America.

Steinberg's famous and distinctive line, the foundation of all these drawings, has been the subject of various attempts at description: "beaky," "thorny," "pizzicato," "deviously Byzantine," and so on. Harold Rosenberg has suggested that whereas the line is European, sophisticated, cosmopolitan, aware of multiple aesthetic realms and other modes of being, the America it delineates is

---

Fig. 4.11. Saul Steinberg, The Pursuit of Happiness. *New Yorker* cover, January 17, 1959.

© 1959 The Saul Steinberg Foundation/Artists Rights Society (ARS), New York/Licensed by VISCOPY, Sydney 2004. © *The New Yorker* collection 1959 Saul Steinberg from cartoonbank.com. All rights reserved.

The triumph of the American way of life, with the businessman losing his chains as its crowning achievement. The drawing shows the ironic but constructive use Steinberg made of the imagery of Freemasonry, in which the monumental edifice is the symbol of a perfectly designed society. Here everything seems stable, balanced, and secure. But there are worrying signs of disunity and conflict. The twin pillars of Jachin (strength) and Boaz (good foundations) are reduced to Santa Claus (all that you wish for) and Sigmund Freud (all that you must sublimate in order to get it). Art shakes hands prophetically with industry, vice shakes hands, more worryingly, with virtue. The pursuit of happiness, as snake and crocodile (consumer hedonism?), happily devours itself. The drawing is a counterpoint to President Eisenhower's State of the Union address, delivered the previous week.

The Comic Worlds of Arno, Steig, Addams, and Steinberg

banal, energetic, confident, supremely tolerant, and lively. But Steinberg's line
has at least two modalities (so it would be truer to speak in the plural, of his
"lines" rather than his "line"), the freehand and the ruled. These can be better
understood now we have seen how Steinberg alludes to Masonic iconography
in his drawings.[112] What is important is the contrast between the ruled straight
line and the freehand curved line—a contrast so prevalent that it could be
called a motif—found nearly everywhere in his major period (the late 1950s
through to the mid-1970s). The former is impersonal, unexpressive, geomet-
rically pure. The latter is profoundly personal, varying in thickness so that one
feels the elasticity of the nib, the pressure of the artist's hand, the bodily presence of the drawer, and is given to curves, curlicues, arabesques, and flourishes,
a line that is abundant, superfluous, self-elaborating, exploratory. The ruled
line has definite goals: it marks out the shortest distance between two points,
from A to B. The freehand line has no such destination, no established coordi-
nates: it invents itself as it goes along and brings into being not the already-
postulated points of Euclidean space but new visual territories and realms.

Both these lines are strongly motivated, and this motivation has its roots in
an antithesis deep in all cultures, a nature/culture opposition that is symbolized in the difference between the straight and the curved. Waldo Frank gives
a handy account of the American version of this dichotomy in an essay called
"Straight Streets," written in the twenties and republished in *In the American
Jungle*.[113] Frank takes as his starting point the streets and avenues of the typical city grid and asks what effect such straightness has on the American soul.

> It is plain that nature likes curves. . . . the Nature of man and near to man is a
> sinuous, rounded being. Think of our bodies and of the bodies of animals—
> not a Euclidean angle in the lot. Think of the shapes of flowers, plants, trees; of
> the configuration of hills and fields; of the sweep of waters; of the globe. Now
> think of our interior worlds. Our physical dynamo has not a straight line in it
> . . . man's mind moves in curves. His thoughts arch, vault, melt into reverie.
> . . . His heart, too, is full of arcuations. . . . From the detour of solar systems
> back upon themselves . . . to the devexities of dream, man has a universe full
> of everything but angles. And yet, the American urbanite has elected to spend
> his days in a gridiron.[114]

Whereas the towns of the Old World are "curved creatures," America is
a country that is "angularized" in almost every detail: streets, houses, laws,
morals, the "gates of Ellis Island," people's figures, and even their faces (Frank
thinks of Calvin Coolidge). Frank foresees a day when everything will accede
to the geometry of the straight line: "Perhaps the flapper of tomorrow will
have pyramidal breasts"—Madonna in one of her incarnations, of course, but

also some of Steinberg's American bodies.[115] The Manhattan grid and other straight-line rigidities of New York embody the city's crushing materialism, while the curve, epitomized by the way Broadway snakes and flexes its way up Manhattan following the old Indian pathway, is a symbol of life and growth.[116]

This early venture into semiotics has obvious implications for what Steinberg does. The straight, ruled line (along with the perfect circle) is Steinberg's graphic shorthand for those tendencies in American life that derive from the rational Enlightenment principles of the Founding Fathers and are carried over into the general spirit of rationality in American life, both utilitarian and utopian in character. This line is the straightest distance between two points. Hence the Euclidean motifs, circles, squares, lines, and angles labeled *a, b,* and *c* that turn up in Steinberg's drawings of the fifties and sixties. The journey taken by the retired couple in Steinberg's drawing of their vacation itinerary (Kansas City, via New York, to a triangle of Paris, Rome, and London, a figure adapted from the schematic air routes often seen in airline advertisements of the period) imposes a planned, prudent New World rationality over what might otherwise be a freer, more contingent summer adventure in the Old World (July 14, 1962, 23). That they have bicycle wheels for legs drives home the point: "The bicycle is the product of pure reason applied to motion," as Angela Carter wittily puts it, "geometry at the service of man."[117] Even more savagely, the suburban domestic dream is represented by the construction of absolutely unexpressive ruled lines that depict a rudimentary house with assorted triangles and squares inside and around it: all these shapes use typeset letters (not freehand) in various fonts to identify the angles. The letters spell out "House," "Man," "Wife," "son," "dog," and "car" (November 4, 1961, 55). The wife is evidently pregnant with the son, since his triangle lies within her square.

Opposed to this is the freehand, curving, varying line, Steinberg's tribute to the inventive individualism also characteristic of American civilization. This line is free-form, unpredictable, exploratory, given to flourishes and other forms of exuberant self-development, often in a kitsch manner (curlicues, arabesques, decorative and ornamental devices, faux Victorian design motifs, etc.). This kind of line, spun off arm and hand, the visible trace of the gestures of the body, is greater than the artist who has created it. In one drawing the artist is perched at one end of a balance and the flourishes he is drawing at the other; the flourishes clearly weigh more than the artist (September 21, 1963, 38). In another, the flourishes create an identity more significant than the face, simply by replacing it altogether (reproduced in *Saul Steinberg,* 36). Both sets of flourishes hint at the artist's initials, "SS," implying that it is in his expressive life that this person creates his true selfhood.

Steinberg's drawings often match one set of potentialities against the other, freehand line versus ruled line, like the rational cube that absorbs and straightens out an errant, hysterical line, turning it into a "boring labyrinth" (May 21, 1960, 37).[118] Steinberg's literal blockheads are people whose clothes are more individual and human that they are (May 5, 1962, 42–43). These are examples of how Steinberg draws the oppressive or conformist tendencies of American rationality, without forgetting what grows and flourishes in American culture.

Steinberg's interest in architecture also has consequences for his drawings of people in the 1950s and 1960s. Here Steinberg's interest lies less in faces than in bodies. Bodies, because they have the kind of architectural quality seen in the blockhead people, are a missing link between faces and buildings, between people and mise-en-scène. When Steinberg draws faces he is interested in the type, not the individual, and he gives his bland, average, characterless everyman profound significance mainly via imaginative settings. An instructive comparison here is with Ronald Searle, a near-contemporary draftsman of comparable talent whose work began appearing in *The New Yorker* from the mid-1950s onward, first in advertisements, later as cartoons.[119] For Searle, a satirist and humorist in the tradition of the great caricaturists like William Hogarth, James Gillray, Honoré Daumier, and Georg Grosz, faces are everything. Although he draws buildings effortlessly and with infinite suggestion, the visual interest lies less in the setting than in the highly individualized features, bodies, and poses of his characters. Searle's spidery, grubby wrecks of humanity are vibrant individuals from whose corrupt appearance we read off complex characterological messages; his buildings and settings, although richly evocative of mood, don't convey half as much in the way of cultural and political meaning. This tendency in British comic art is carried to its logical conclusion by a follower of Searle like Gerald Scarfe in a collection such as *Scarfe's People* (1966). A book called *Steinberg's People* would not be impossible, but it would seem an odd rationale for a collection of his drawings. We search in vain for the confronting, Dickensian individualism of Searle's or Scarfe's people in Steinberg's work.

A good example of Steinberg's treatment of people is what he does with commonplaces about conformity in a mass society. In these drawings the supposedly unique, unrepeatable human icons of American civilization are shown as anything but unique: absorbed into the American mythology, they have been cloned and stand as paper-thin simulacra in infinitely regressing rows. Multiple organization men march before rows of identical organization men. Multiple cocktail schmoozers stand before multiple protesting folksingers, about to be attacked by multiple mounted policemen. Multiple farmers march

The Comic Worlds of Arno, Steig, Addams, and Steinberg

before multiple construction workers, followed by multiple high school graduates, before multiple spacemen, multiple drum majorettes, multiple tourists, and multiple Grim Reapers (May 25, 1968, 36–41).[120] Steinberg notes that in a nascent information society dominated by the mass media, even acts of nonconformity are reproducible symptoms of a conformist tendency. In this civilization everything is a copy of some suspect or clichéd archetype: farm workers, construction workers, schoolboy graduates, spacemen, beauty queens, tourists, Grim Reapers, Abe Lincolns, Uncle Sams, American Eagles, folksingers, baton-wielding cops, dogs, children, matrons, businessmen, Native Americans, cowboys. How quick Steinberg was to understand this. What is more devastating, though with a quiet pathos of its own, than Steinberg's drawing of an infinitely regressing line of identical organization men, all stepping in unison from Monday to Tuesday (July 13, 1968, 25)? In all these drawings Steinberg is aiming at a face with minimal individual character and a generalized set of features. It is the setting and the allegorical action that are saturated with meaning.[121]

When Steinberg sets out to convey the meaning of an individual, he tends to do so less through the face (faces are impersonal, expressionless, neutral, masklike) than through body and body image. What particularly took his eye in his first decade in America were the women. He subsequently noted that in Italy "women had tremendous forms and shapes, but they were not as aggressive as American forms, because most women in Italy didn't bother to use girdles. The presence of this armor made American women look like heroic medieval knights. Shoes with spiked heels were aggressive; handbags and umbrellas looked like weapons; the women were made up in warpaint."[122] Steinberg's women are sculpted by what they wear: their clothes shape their bodies rather than the reverse. They inhabit their clothes as a hermit crab does its shell. A typical example from *The Passport* sports an ornate ten-gallon hat with a half-moon-shaped brim, flourishes of permed hair, a shelflike bust festooned with tassels, thin, tapered legs terminating in a great block of turned-up jeans cuff, and shoes with knife-edge heels and toes. It is impossible to guess what her body shape is really like, unlike the buxom Italian woman Steinberg drew in a 1970 drawing called "Milano, 1938" (reproduced in *Saul Steinberg,* 186). Steinberg's drawings of snapshot biographies often stress the startling transformation that fashion can work even on the aging body. One series charts a woman's life from infancy to old age in nine images, as a baby, a schoolgirl, a bride, and a grandmother (March 28, 1953, 30–31). The continuity makes sense until the end, when she appears wearing dramatic thick-rimmed glasses, a pointed hat, checked cowboy shirt, rolled-up jeans, and platform shoes. She is completely unrecognizable. Dress is ultimately a way of rebuilding the body.

The body and even the hair of his "Diner Girl" of 1971 (*Saul Steinberg*, 81) constitute a series of concentric segments of shiny aluminum or stainless steel, as if the same architectural principles of construction have built both diner and waitress—a perfect instance of Steinberg's architecturalizing of the body.

Each body has its own specially shaped history. The profile of that history, shown in one series of drawings as a set of steps, is different for men and women. The man attains the heights of office—the vice presidency of his company, perhaps—in five stages: infancy, childhood, adolescence, youth, young adulthood. After that comes and then the apotheosis of middle age. And after *that*, a terrible drop, right back to the level of childhood. The body, previously encased in the uniforms of all those stages but now seminaked, appears pathetic and vulnerable (*The Passport*, 1954). The woman reaches her apotheosis much earlier on, in her thirties, perhaps. Afterward, her life is a series of descending steps. When she finally regains (in widowhood?) what looks like a useful life—she is sensibly dressed, clutching a portfolio, almost as she was at an earlier stage—it is too late (*The Passport*, 1954). In such drawings Steinberg draws a Proustian self that exists in the fourth dimension of time as well as in the three dimensions of space: not a single self, but a succession of selves. What Steinberg makes us see is that men require more in the way of character armor than women. It is the men who internalize a society's ethos and who then become rigidified, trapped by what they are. The women seem freer, less anchored within the social order, more surprising and more capable of transformation—and this protean quality is often expressed through their dress. Nonetheless, the men and women share a common destiny: both sexes end up in Florida.

The most interesting gloss on Steinberg's depiction of the body in the late 1950s comes from the writings of Wilhelm Reich. How far Steinberg was acquainted with Reich is far less clear than in the case of William Steig. What is certain is that Reich's fusion of Marx and Freud, in a psychology that centered on the body, offered a telling critique of the conformist ethos of America from the late 1930s through the 1960s. And because it centered on the body, it was clearly of particular interest to cartoonists.[123] Steinberg's representations of the ordinary American body strongly recall Reich. As we have seen, for Reich character is essentially somatic—what he calls character armor and muscular armor are, he says, the same thing.[124] The habitual presentation of the body—in facial expression, posture, pose, dress, and so on—is the symptomatic and bodily expression of the compromises, adaptations, and suppressions that the ego has negotiated with the social order. The body is political. The body performs what Reich calls the "anchoring" of the social order. It is through fearful, frozen, and disciplined bodies that the social order reproduces itself. A key notion in Reich

Fig. 4.12. Saul Steinberg, untitled drawing, ink on paper.

© The Saul Steinberg Foundation/Artists Rights Society (ARS), New York/Licensed by VISCOPY, Sydney 2004. Originally published in *The New Yorker*, November 1, 1958, 41.

A Reichian drawing by Steinberg in which a timid, fluffy, loveable but knowing rabbit-ego peeps out through eyeholes cut in an erect sheet-metal carapace.

is what form of character armor individuals create in order to defend themselves. Armor rigidifies body and psyche and inhibits free relations with other people. Armoring is essential to Steinberg's sense of what happens to bodies, especially male bodies, in America in the 1950s and early 1960s. The timid but knowing rabbit ego looking out of a metallic body outline is, for example, a textbook Reichian image from the end of the 1950s (fig. 4.12). The personality has grown an exoskeleton. This new skin has the thickness and rigidity of sheet metal. The ego, a fearful, fluffy, docile, and perhaps rather lovable rabbit, peeps out anxiously, but inquiringly and sharply alert, protected by the armor.

The face, its typical structure rather than its individual features, is where such ossifications of the ego are mainly visible. One of Steinberg's most fruitful innovations was to juxtapose different drawing styles within a single drawing. The styles indicate both certain types of look or body image and certain types of personality. In the 1960s Steinberg experimented with drawing couples whose faces were reduced to the simplest and most notional linear outline, whereas the clothes were drawn in careful, realistic detail. In one such couple the bodies and the clothes are rendered in a fluent cross-hatching style that suggests the solidity but also the softness of the body and fabrics. The faces, on the other hand, are constructed out of a highly simplified geometry—tensed lines in the case of the women, geometric blocks in the case of the men (May 5, 1962, 42–43). The rigidity of the faces implies personalities similarly simplified, tensed, blocky, and sharply linear. In the end the face itself becomes a mere mask, as in the mask series of 1965–66 (some of the masks are reproduced in *Saul Steinberg*, 174–76 and 208–12).

The technique of juxtaposing one style against another is also used to suggest the hidden hierarchies of groups. In a cover drawing dating from the late sixties, for instance, the essential dynamics of the family are established entirely through the collision of drawing styles (fig. 4.13). The drawing is composed of two intersecting triangles (one inverted) an arrangement that schematizes the transmission of family power across the generations. The monochrome group (apex at the top) designates the passing, less forceful, passive members of the family. The polychrome group (the inverted triangle, apex at the bottom) are vibrant, powerful individuals on whose energies the renewal of the family will depend. Everyone appears in an appropriate drawing style. There is a firmly designated line with cross-hatching for the paterfamilias, suggesting the 1920s; a hazy scribble for his wife, whose identity has been partially obliterated by her subjugation to her husband; a sensitive pencil shading for a woman who is probably an unmarried daughter. (The family dog and an indistinct stippled female figure—perhaps a spinster aunt—go all but unnoticed.) Then there is a thick, bold line for the son in his prime; a vivacious decorative manner for his wife (the outsider); an assertive but crude kindergarten scribble for their child (the central character). The wit lies not just in Steinberg's sense

---

Fig. 4.13. (*facing page*) Saul Steinberg, untitled *New Yorker* cover, November 23, 1968.

A drawing of three generations of a family in which style itself becomes a way of "reasoning on paper" about the subject matter: the drawing is composed of two intersecting triangles, the top one inverted. The lower triangle, the grandmother, the grandfather, and the woman in the middle of the back row, depicts those members of the family in decline: the pater familias (seated, right) is the most powerful member of this group and is drawn in a style that suggests his heyday thirty years before; his wife (seated, left) is a mere hazy scribble, and their (unmarried?) daughter (standing, center) is a delicately shaded sketch. (Really unimportant figures in this grouping—the stippled family dog and a woman [rear, left] who is possibly a spinster aunt—are all but unnoticeable.) The upper inverted triangle depicts the ascendant family members. The son, pigeon-breasted with pride, the real head of the family, his vibrant but coarse wife, and their ebullient, beaming child perched on the grandfather's knee—each of these is also drawn in an appropriate style.

The Comic Worlds of Arno, Steig, Addams, and Steinberg

that the body reveals all but in the collaboration between that insight and the inventiveness and virtuosity of the pen.

The America of the seventies and eighties is rather different from the one Steinberg set about dissecting in the previous decades. America strange became America scary, in the words of Gopnik, who aptly thinks that in the unique American combination of "cruelty," "show-biz glamor," "sadism," and "affectless violence" late in the century Steinberg sees a form of contemporary fascism.[125] Steinberg's response to America toward the end of the century was to become more and more interested in the body and much less interested in architecture—even the architecturalized body. The rational line that signified the utopian hope of American civilization now dwindles to a mere background trace, marking out the edges of the curb in his horrific drawings of Greenwich Village and the view from his studio in Union Square in the seventies, for instance, or representing the wail of the police siren (as in the cover illustration for *The New Yorker,* January 16, 1971). In his later drawings of urban America, and especially New York, the city becomes a terrifying zoo without fences set against a black sky, and bodies undergo a hellish metamorphosis, becoming all heads and legs, staring eyes, and gaping mouths. Steinberg in the latter years of his career remained a very remarkable artist. If nothing in those last thirty years is quite as astonishing as the drawings of the previous twenty years, however, the years in which he truly set out to discover America, then that statement indicates as no other can what an extraordinary career his has been.

Harold Rosenberg's phrase about Steinberg's offering us the "theatre of Abstract Man" looks at first glance like a good general description of Steinberg's work.[126] But much of what this chapter has argued tends to prove the opposite. Steinberg takes ready-made, clichéd abstract propositions and renovates them through a process of concretizing and embodiment—whether in rebuses, visual riddles and puns (like "Yes, but" where "Yes" on wheels careers down a hill to meet the brick wall of "But" [November 8, 1969, 55]), or in drawings that aim to capture the ethos of the New World he discovered in America. But the notion that Steinberg offers the theater of abstract man is misleading in another way too. Steinberg inverts the usual relation between what is abstract and what is concrete.

Proust understood that it is what we usually and conventionally *expect to see* that is abstract because we substitute a dead preconception for a living perception. What is truly concrete is anything unexpected and resistant to understanding. It takes a supreme effort to really see what we don't expect to see. What is abstract is conventional perception, ingrained perception, perception simplified by habit. What is concrete is the shock of seeing something for the first time. Of people's faces, for example, Proust writes in *Within a Budding*

Grove, "We invariably forget . . . individual qualities . . . substituting for them in our mind a conventional type at which we arrive by striking some sort of mean amongst the different faces that have taken our fancy."[127] When we see this face in a new situation and our gaze is purged of habit, we hardly recognize the person. We see that person afresh, as for the first time. We are surprised but also invigorated. What is true of faces is true of places too. Places to which we are habituated appear to our consciousness as "abstract images which are lifeless and dull because they are lacking in precisely that element of novelty, different from everything we have known, that element which is proper to beauty and happiness."[128]

Steinberg aimed to produce drawings of the world in which that "element of novelty" is powerfully at work—to draw, he once said, as if he were a tourist arriving in a strange place, compelled to face "the new situation like one newly born who sees life for the first time when it still has the air of fiction."[129] This ambition is what underpins all his work. When he is successful his drawings, although not conventionally beautiful, may be said to have those elements of surprise and freshness, quite distinct from received notions of what is beautiful, that are nonetheless truly "proper to beauty and happiness." The purpose of the art is to return vividness, concreteness, and specificity to a world of which our perception has been dulled by habit. What we so readily forget, Steinberg reminds us of again, by jolting us out of our habitual, familiar modes of perception. Hence his punning wish to be seen as a novelist. "My idea of the artist, poet, painter, composer, etc., is *the novelist,*" he said.[130] The choice of the "novelist" as the type of the artist makes sense only if we ourselves overcome the habit that blinds us to the idea of the new in the phrase "the novel." It is the *novelty* of the novelist that makes us see the familiar in a new way, something that is both exhilarating and self-renewing for the viewer, and that introduces us as "an actor upon the stage of an unknown and infinitely more interesting universe" than the one we commonly inhabit. Such an unknown and infinitely more interesting universe is Steinberg's America.

Steinberg's own "novel," like Proust's, is an autobiographical fiction. Steinberg's work attempts a panoramic view of the landscape of a whole society in flux as seen from a deeply subjective viewpoint. One way to look at Steinberg's work is to see it as one continuous drawing, as if a line from one drawing simply flows into the next (what Steinberg called the continuous line of childhood). The whole forms a vast visual, autobiographical, linear collage, though not so much a confessional one as an autobiography of the self's confrontations and negotiations with the external world. Thus the jacket blurb for *The Labyrinth* says that it is "a continuation of Saul Steinberg's autobiography." This life is not a boring one (the avoidance of boredom, Steinberg once said, is a profound human duty), just as the line so described is not the infinitely predictable, Euclidean line of several of Steinberg's drawings, the shortest distance between two points. In every possible sense this line is a lifeline—the line on the palm that foreshadows a life; the line tossed to the man overboard; and, literally, the drawn or inscribed line that is a trace of an actual life lived. What this line tells of, above all, is a human presence. We have noticed Steinberg's favored contrast between a uniform, ruled, rational line that has great efficiency and decision but no personality, no possibility of growth, no chance to explore and another sort of line, the freehand line, that is exploratory and inventive. This line describes new shapes and outlines, invents new perspectives on the world, makes us see the familiar as something strange and wonderful ("as if for the first time"), conjures alternative worlds out of the blankness of the white sheet of paper. Above all, this line, as we follow its arcuations, as it grows and swells, as it waxes and wanes, reminds us of the pressure of the human hand that created it. It is hence an immediate and moving assertion of what a famous philosopher once said all forms of writing have abolished—human presence.

Steinberg's most condensed commentary on these matters is to be found in "Labyrinth, 1960," published in landscape format at the end of the "Chronology" in Harold Rosenberg's *Saul Steinberg* (fig. 4.14) and in a nearly identical version in portrait format in *The New Yorker* (October 8, 1960, 41). It shows a collection of different lifelines—conventionalized renderings of various human biographies as one or another sort of line. The drawing begins in the top left-hand corner with the two points *A* and *B*, the determining moments of birth and death, and nothing in between: a potential life, the universal framing narrative. (It is wholly typical of Steinberg's antisentimentalism that life's potential should be not *A* to *Z*, but simply *A* to *B*, birth astride a grave.) Then follow three variations on the boring, rational life that make the journey from *A* to *B* in the shortest and most efficient manner: first, a "successful" passage between them; second, a "less successful" (because less direct) but no less determined passage; third, a more varied but no less predictable journey—from *A* to *B* with regular concentric deviations. These lives, says Steinberg, "make simple, even geometric travels, tracks without surprises, lives determined by family, money, geography or even logical and normal disasters."[131] The rest of the drawing explores various other life journeys, represented by the more "disagreeable" and erratic but also more interesting lines on the drawing. These too, Steinberg insists, have their own kind of normality—perhaps that of the "neurotic or the insane," but in any case more goes on in them than in the Euclidean lifelines.

The third kind of line is that of the artist, which is unique by reason of its need to inspect all other lines and lives. It is shown by the wandering but purposive line that starts with a lowercase cursive *a* to the right above the center of

The Comic Worlds of Arno, Steig, Addams, and Steinberg

Fig. 4.14. Saul Steinberg, untitled drawing, ink on paper.

© The Saul Steinberg Foundation/Artists Rights Society (ARS), New York/Licensed by VISCOPY, Sydney 2004. Published in Saul Steinberg, *The Labyrinth*, 1960.

Another personal allegory in which Steinberg compares various kinds of lives with that of the artist. As a Beckettian pessimist, he sees life's cardinal points as only two, A and B, birth and death (top left-hand corner). This remains true no matter who you are. Normal lives get from A to B efficiently, with a minimum of fuss, like the two straight lines, one a little more ruffled than the other, also in the top left-hand corner. Others trace out boring labyrinths, erratic, formless zigzags, complicated self-crossings-out, frazzled condensed tangles, or disagreeable neurotic jerks. The artist's more complicated journeying is shown by the inquisitive line that runs between the lowercase cursive *a* just to the upper right of the center of the drawing and the typeset *B* in the same place. "The artist" says Steinberg, "(and my idea of the artist, poet, painter, composer, etc., is the novelist) investigates all other lives in order to understand the world and possibly himself before returning to his own, often for a short and dull time only." There are minuses as well as pluses, since this "accounts for the delayed (even retarded) nature of the artist." A nearly identical portrait-format version appeared in *The New Yorker*, October 8, 1960, 41.

the drawing and returns to a large typeset uppercase B in the same area. This line too has to obey the Euclidean law of death: it has to take the shortest distance between two points—at the end. But before that it has the possibility of free exploration. "The artist investigates all other lives in order to understand the world and possibly himself before returning to his own, often for a short and dull time only." In saying this Steinberg is no aesthetic snob—his gloss on the drawing concludes: "It accounts for the delayed (even retarded) nature of the artist." What motivates the line that makes this kind of life journey is not particularly any sort of faith in a happy ending. Nor is it a utopian, enlightened, planned, rational line heading toward some goal known in advance. It is always a spiraling, inquisitive, investigative, exploratory, self-inventing, and, above all, inventive line. Even so, it is always going to end up at B.

Inventiveness is the watchword of Steinberg's career—inventiveness rather than (say) inwardness. Steinberg's America is in many respects the America that strikes the visitor and the tourist. His America is not always a country he knows confidently from the inside.[132] It is perhaps at times even a little clichéd in ways that the outsider can never quite avoid. If Steinberg himself was well aware of the dense, experiential richness of American life, then, unlike the case for an Arno, this was not something that excited his imagination at the level of immediate experience and actual social transaction. Rather, his response to American life was reflective and theoretical. When Steinberg declares, "Who is American? It's a foreigner who came here and said, *tiens*! what a country. Let's go West. That is the tradition of the American."[133] His point can be granted. But the generalization is a little glib: Steinberg stands here at the end of a long line of Europeans, from Alexis de Tocqueville onward, who have made it their business to tell Americans what their country is like.[134] But in that tradition Steinberg is that rare thing, a genius. Unlike many outsider prophets, Steinberg (as his popularity shows) disclosed insights that could not be refused, and if he is a critic, he is a profoundly sympathetic one. But this depends on the inventive making-strange of his drawings. "I . . . have always thought that to express certain things I had to transform them into jokes, puns, or anyway into strangeness: so-called humor. To clothe reality so that it will be 'forgiven.'"[135] This, Steinberg's humane version of Freud's stark claim that joking is always a form of indirect criticism, perhaps explains how an intense critic of America can also be for many a favored artist. Inventiveness, not inwardness, then. But what Steinberg invents is truly exhilarating. The coherence with variety of his invented world sets up something marvelous alongside the actual world. Such a wondrous body of work, made possible only by the hospitality *The New Yorker* showed to Steinberg's talent, instances in one exceptional career the contribution to American imaginative life made by this unique magazine.

CONCLUSION

Laughing with

The New Yorker

Anyone with sufficient curiosity can now scroll through microfilm of all the back numbers of *The New Yorker* from 1925 to 1999. It will take a long time—three months for even the most cursory survey, much longer if the articles or stories waylay one to any extent. A lifetime perhaps if everything is read and looked at with the attention it deserves, and there would probably still be thousands of pages left unread. But no matter how it is done, it is a rewarding, chastening, and at times even melancholy experience. An underlying thread is the gradual loss of American innocence—what went wrong, slowly but surely, with the American century. Events that are pressing forward into a then unknown future always seem sad when one understands them backward with the blessing (if that is the right word) of hindsight. It is impossible to read about the Watergate in 1967—Washington's "newest, most luxurious residential hotel . . . the most exciting tribute to residential living in the Nation's Capital . . . eight blocks from the White House," which has "some units available on a transient basis" (*The New Yorker,* April 8, 1967, 134)—without a sense of the deep irony of things. But this is nothing compared with looking at the issue dated November 23, 1963, distributed on November 18, untouched by the events of November 22, which nonetheless cast a terrible shadow over everything in it. And as to the many cartoons in the early seventies about the newly opened World Trade Center (for example, the one by Alan Dunn in the issue for July 24, 1971, 28), none can now be contemplated in any spirit except saturnine gloom.

The breadth and variety of reading matter in *The New Yorker* quickly makes one suspicious of most ready-made generalizations about the magazine. The range of fiction, poetry, reportage, reviews, and comment suggests a readership that is anything but complacent about what is going on in the world. A reader in 1961 would be better informed about the situation in the Middle East from reading a history of Kuwait (Welles Hangen, "Our Far-Flung Correspondents—Kuwait," July 22, 1961) than most television anchors appeared to be in 1991, for example, just as a reader in 1987 would understand well what seems to mystify most people in 2003—why America was then inclined to trust Saddam Hussein and the Baathists and take Iraq's side in its war with Iran (Milton Viorst, "A Reporter at Large: The View from the Mustansiriyah," October 12, 1987, and October 19, 1987).

One consequence of even the briefest survey of these back numbers is that the reader fast-forwards year by year through the economic history of the past seventy-five years: boom, bust, depression, war, recovery, expansion, inflation, hyperinflation, uncertainty, boom and bust again. This story is told partly by the size of some of the pre-Christmas issues: 1929–132 pages; 1933–60 pages; 1937–96 pages; 1940–144 pages; 1949–156 pages; 1954–208 pages; 1962–248 pages; 1971–220 pages; 1987–194 pages; 1994–136 pages; 1998 (a double issue) —208 pages. The story is also told, in sharper focus, in the magazine's advertisements. *The New Yorker* is thick with them up to 1929; they thin out during the thirties, start to accumulate again during the war years, then take off in an unprecedented way from the late forties to the middle sixties. The numbers then flatten out and increase once more in the eighties and nineties, though never to the stupendous levels of the sixties—the issue for December 1, 1962, for instance, had no fewer than fifty full-page advertisements at the back. Abstractly, the economic history of the last three-quarters of the twentieth century is a story everyone is familiar with. Scrolling through those back numbers, however, one lives through it as a gripping narrative with an immediate personal pull.

Advertisements also write an oblique social history of the twentieth century. One can't help noticing the odd patterns in preferred luxury goods over the decades as fashions in conspicuous consumption change: cars then watches, holiday cruises then foundation garments, jewelry then designer clothes, cars then computers, casual designer clothes then perfumes . . . Technological changes are very much in the foreground. The first televisions, the first color televisions, the advent of the remote control, the first portable televisions, miniaturized televisions. An issue in the late sixties carried an advertisement for the "first portable stereo radio you can wear on your head," a cumbersome contraption with earphones the size of baseball mitts and two big aerials sticking up on each side (November 1, 1969, 47). The Bell System introduced the Bell Picturephone in the issue for July 4, 1964 ("people phone by appointment from family-type booths in attended centers"), and numerous cartoons promptly picked up on the comic opportunities. A few years later (August 30, 1969, 9), the Bell System also previewed a prototype touch-tone phone, which it said would be in every home a decade later—it was equipped with some puzzling new features, the pound and star buttons. Why would we ever need such things? And apparently there was once an era when the phrase "Where you can buy a Macintosh" did not refer to computers (September 15, 1951).

Even more profound social changes are figured in the advertisements. In the nonfeminist climate of the early sixties there is poignancy in coming across an advertisement for Betty Friedan's *The Feminine Mystique* (March 9, 1963, 171). One suddenly sees that a whole culture is on the eve of a tremendous revolution, of which it is yet entirely ignorant (it was not until *The New Yorker* for November 28, 1970, that Jane Kramer contributed a long article, "Founding Cadre," on four second-wave feminists). In such matters Madison Avenue was often quick off the mark, producing advertisements full of good intentions, if sometimes transparent and even comical. A series of advertisements for Grant's whiskey in the late fifties showed a youthful and handsome man at his desk (intellectual without being an egghead) saying to an out-of-frame woman, "As long as you're up get me a Grant's." By the middle sixties this had become a young woman in a bikini sitting on the beach (with a typewriter on her lap in a sad attempt to forestall the charge of an even more subtle sexism) and calling out the same words to an out-of-frame male (June 13, 1964, 79).

I must confess, however, that the advertisements work on readers at a much more elementary level than this. Beyond a certain point few people will escape being seduced by the world of possessions disclosed to them by the advertising copy. One emerges from a session at the microfilm reader feeling a little tarnished, very unsatisfied, and full of questions as the promise of material plenitude starts to work its magic. And along with the magic comes a sense of dissatisfaction. Why is it I'm not rich? Why don't I own more of the right sort of things? Why do I look too old (or fat, flabby, ugly, bald, white, black, Anglo, Asian, Latino, underdressed, unsophisticated, untraveled)? The list is endless. This, as we all know, is what advertising is supposed to do: create a gnawing inner unhappiness, the feeling of lack, a sharpened sense of want. It is meant to make us devalue what we have and yearn for what we don't. It happens all the time, and no one need go to the trouble of looking up the back numbers of *The New Yorker* to have the experience. I mention it only because one experiences it in a particularly acute way when looking consecutively through the back issues of a magazine. But more important, there is a particular shock in coming to realize how important the advertisements are in creating the aura of the magazine. Abstractly, one always knew this. Looking over the back issues it strikes one anew, with great force.

This last realization accounts, partly, for the reaction of dismay that so many cartoonists provided illustrations for advertisements. All four artists discussed in this book accepted advertising commissions: Arno for Stetson hats, Old Gold cigarettes, and Pepsi-Cola, among many others; Steig for *The Saturday Evening Post,* Chivas Regal whiskey, and the New York Central Residential Zone project; Addams for Remington typewriters and Shannon Rodgers clothes; and even Saul Steinberg for Parfums d'Orsay, Emerson televisions, and Noilly Prat vermouth. It is not easy to account for the sense of minor betrayal this realization produces. After all, artists have to put a roof over their heads and keep bread on the table for their families, and even the most successful artist is no success at all at the beginning of his or her career. Yet the sense of betrayal remains. The practice made the artists themselves uneasy. Arno and Steig spoke about it frequently. Arno wondered if all drawing done for sale amounted to prostitution of his talent, but then he boasted of turning down advertising work worth thousands of dollars. Steig felt guilty about his need to work for the ad man in the forties through the sixties (he gave alimony and child support as his main reasons) and confessed to severe psychosomatic torments as a result of selling his soul to Madison Avenue.[1] Addams and Steinberg rarely mentioned their advertising work (they did much less than either Arno or Steig, as it happens), but they accepted commissions nonetheless. That the artists should feel like this is understandable. But why should readers feel distressed to come across, for example, a clever set of Steinberg swirls and scrolls advertising proprietary brand vermouth? As everyone recognizes, advertisements are necessary evils. Not only artists but magazines have to pay their way: how else, unless by accepting advertising? No publication survives on subscriptions and newsstand sales alone, as Ralph Ingersoll's ill-fated *PM* demonstrated in the 1940s. *PM* did not accept any advertising but summarized advertisements as they appeared in other publications. The brave undertaking lasted less than ten years.

These thoughts lead me to propose that the advertisements need to be understood as part of the content of a magazine—that is, they affect readers' response to a magazine quite as much as editorial copy does, and there is no iron curtain separating editorial copy from advertising copy. In particular, I suggest that in *The New Yorker,* at least, because of its peculiar design principles, cartoons and advertisements vie with each other for readers' attention in an especially meaningful way. Hence the dismay we feel when our favorite artist works for an advertiser: we feel he is unexpectedly batting for the other side. In paying close attention to the work of four different cartoonists in the preceding chapters without saying much about the advertisements, I have done what art historians and critics sometimes do when, to offer a grand example, they take a Rubens out of its church or palace and consider it away from the ceremonies and practices it was once a part of. In the case of these cartoons the equivalent of that seventeenth-century church or court is *The New Yorker,* a magazine with its own distinct publishing protocols. Something of that context has to be restored and a sense given of how it operates in terms of reader response. This granted, some important questions arise. How does the particular form of publishing bear on the way the cartoons are received? How do cartoons appeal to us in everyday life, when we look at them in a magazine that contains so much besides just cartoons? Given that each of these artists invents jokes that imply a critical, sardonic, or rueful view of modern American life, how does their humor work when an important focus of American life — the luxury commodity — is present in the magazine in the form of an advertisement? (Often printed on the same page as the cartoon, so the luxury commodity is much more closely present in *The New Yorker,* within the distance of a glance, than it is in the only comparable example, the commercials in a comic television program.)

There is indeed a great difference between the weekly appearance of an artist's cartoons in a magazine and their appearance either in an anthology of that artist's work or in a general collection of cartoons. Weekly presentation is different from recapitulated presentation because in weekly presentation demand overbalances supply, whereas in recapitulated presentation supply overbalances demand. But in addition, the character of a particular magazine adds shade, nuance, and contrast to what is presented. Whether a cartoon first appeared in *Mad Magazine* or *Playboy* or *Esquire* or *The New Yorker* ought to interest us and needs to be taken into account, because what we then want to say about the reception of the cartoon will vary accordingly.

The problem is that even when the context of the cartoons is *The New Yorker,* a magazine everyone is familiar with, it is not easy to say what that context of presentation implies. What generalizations about *The New Yorker* can we rely on? And how good are they? It is easy to state the problem. The accumulated back issues of *The New Yorker* number well over 3,500 — say, 300,000 pages of text, over 250 million words, more than 68,000 drawings, published over eighty years and under five editors.[2] The numbers alone warn of the difficulty. Anyone who spends even a short time with back issues of the magazine will be constantly surprised at what appears in it. The task of generalization is daunting if not impossible. Not that there is any shortage of generalizations, usually highly critical, and the burden of many will be familiar. Josephine

Hendin: "Liberal but not democratic . . . inclusive . . . in acknowledging social issues, but exclusive in its response. . . . *The New Yorker*'s approach to political and social issues derives less from a serious engagement with the world than from a narrow esthetic, valuing neatness above all. . . . *The New Yorker* mystique calls us to the salvations of superiority. It offers the illusion that there is a vantage point, Olympian and pristine, that permits us to see difficulties while keeping a cool distance. . . . Its high elegance and magisterial voice coerce belief."[3] Dwight Macdonald: "*The New Yorker*'s position in the class war . . . is not so simple . . . its neutrality is itself a form of upper class display, since only the economically secure can afford such Jovian aloofness from the common struggle."[4] Tom Wolfe: "A great lily-of-the-valley vat full of what Lenin called 'bourgeois sentimentality.'"[5] Seymour Krim: "Middleaged, safe and increasingly divorced from the action . . . esthetically reactionary . . . the compromised [liberal] conscience . . . preaching an outworn union of fine moral discrimination and epicureanism."[6] These assertions, and many others like them, are not necessarily inaccurate, and although very unsympathetic they should be kept in mind. But they are too coat trailing to be much practical help (Tom Wolfe quoting Lenin!), and even the writers who make them with such confidence every now and then have to stop and remind themselves of the exceptions that unsettle the rule they are laying down. To reach firmer ground we need to turn to some clearly identifiable, formal features of the magazine.

Of particular importance is its remarkably consistent layout and design over the years; the absence for the greater part of its history of any editorial visual material except the artwork (that is, no photographs); a layout consisting of the pages of uninterrupted text, given additional prominence by the avoidance of tailing (printing the first part of an article at the front of a magazine with the remainder fitted in at the back, usually after a large page break—articles in *The New Yorker* always ran continuously from beginning to end) and restricted use of ad stripping (including a ban on horizontal half-page advertisements). These matters are important, though difficult to talk about, but one conclusion we can safely draw is that they give the cartoons and artwork considerable prominence. Indeed, no other magazine of its type makes the cartoon so important by virtue of its design idiom. Here we arrive at what is the most important visual aspect of *The New Yorker,* something that might help us get a handle on the way cartoons work in the magazine: the cartoons' dominance of the magazine's look and readers' experience of it. But even if that point is granted, it cannot be the whole truth. The magazine's look and readers' experience are, as I have suggested, also dominated by the advertisements, many of which use very striking images, often photographic ones, in complete contradiction of the magazine's design policy. I shall, then, focus my discussion of the cartoons by ending with some speculative thoughts about the relation between cartoons and advertisements in *The New Yorker*.

Readers' typical response to *The New Yorker* provides a warrant for such a narrowing of focus. What people always tend to notice first are the cartoons and the advertisements. The cartoons are funny, sophisticated, memorable, distracting, and so on. The advertisements are either small and weird, like the one for a sterling silver letter sealer ("your own private flap service . . . the smart, easy way to moisten envelope flaps")[7] or large and luxurious (like the sophisticated Moschino advertisements in the "Love Lessons" special double issue of *The New Yorker* of August 25/September 1, 1997). Cartoon and advertisement rivet the eye and vie for attention, which is distracted from one by the other, and vice versa. This to-ing and fro-ing identifies something essential about *The New Yorker*. It can be summed up by proposing that the magazine brings together two adversaries—the commodity as a fetish of consumerism and the release of laughter, one of the most prized of all ecstatic states of mind—and pits one against the other. The marriage of Peter Arno and Lois Long in 1927, which we might fancifully imagine as a tableau vivant titled "The Union of Laughter and Shopping," is as apt an unofficial symbol of *The New Yorker* as Eustace Tilley was the official one.

The advertisements have always been troublesome and at the back, if not the foreground, of the editors' minds. Writing about the work of his predecessor, Harold Ross (the legendary founder-editor of *The New Yorker*), William Shawn drew attention to the magazine's "chaste and lovely pages."[8] The phrase alludes both to the purity of page design and to the magazine's high editorial ideals. The "chastity" of the pages is at once an actual simplicity of design, the basically unchanging look of the page from issue to issue and year to year, and a symbolic chastity, the magazine's jealousy held reputation for journalistic integrity. Chastity also implies that refusal to entertain photojournalism of any kind, unique in a magazine of this type, and in its place promoting artwork as the sole visual feature. This ensured that the cartoons would play a very large role in readers' reception of the magazine. Underpinning the idea of chastity was an unusual separation of editorial and business powers inside *The New Yorker*. Under the editorship of Harold Ross and William Shawn, the magazine was famous for the invisible line that divided the business office from the editorial department.[9] It was a legacy of the truce struck between Ross and the original backer of the magazine, Raoul Fleischmann. From the start, as a matter of principle, Ross had refused to sit on the board of directors.[10] In return editorial matters were to proceed uninfluenced by gross business considerations. "There were two magazines, the business one and the editorial one, divided and divisive to the point of corporate schizophrenia," writes Gigi Mahon, the chronicler of *The New Yorker*'s business history. She goes on to rehearse time-honored anecdotes about this separation of powers: A. J. Russell, who rose to be president of the F-R Publishing Corporation, which owned *The New Yorker*, never daring to say good morning to Harold Ross in the elevator; John McNulty straying onto the business floor and saying "Editorial don't shoot!" Raoul Fleischmann sheepishly apologizing for his presence on the editorial floor of a magazine he effectively owned with the words, "It's all right. I have permission to be here."[11] Under Shawn this division was formalized with the appointment of a "liaison man" whose job it was to channel communications between the business and editorial departments.[12] These practical demonstrations of the "chastity" Shawn was alluding to lend to a general claim a seemingly irrefutable authority.[13]

Yet as *The New Yorker*'s first chronicler, Dale Kramer, noted many years ago, such stories contain elements of both hyperbole and myth.[14] While the conflicts and hostilities between the two sides of the magazine were real enough (the editorial veto over "unsuitable" advertising for women's underwear, for example, or the efforts to stamp out "advertorials" such as the "Water Tower" feature written by Alexander Woollcott in the thirties), they were window dressing. The two halves of the venture, editorial and business, were closely integrated, as they had to be if *The New Yorker* was to succeed as a business concern. In particular, circulation and advertising were joined in a vicious circle, each one dependent on the other. Walter Lippmann's pragmatic analysis of the newspaper business in the 1920s holds true of magazine publishing: "Circulation is a means to an end. It becomes an asset only when it can be sold to the advertiser who pays for it with revenues secured through the indirect taxation of the reader. . . . A newspaper which angers those who it pays best to reach through advertisements is a bad medium for the advertiser."[15] A magazine, like a newspaper, survives not on its cover price but on its advertising revenue. *The New Yorker* had to meet the needs not just of readers but of advertisers. As far back as 1934, Ralph Ingersoll had pointed out that *The New Yorker* was born when "the two ideas, the artistic and the commercial, joined and were one."[16] Ingersoll implies an element of good fortune here, but Jane Grant, Ross's first wife and his collaborator in founding the magazine, stresses in her memoir *Ross, "The New Yorker" and Me* how carefully she and Ross researched their market. They aimed their proposed publication not just at metropolitan readers (they were amazed to discover that no magazine existed specifically for people who lived in New York), but at local New York advertisers as well.[17]

The key to the commercial "idea" was niche-market advertising. Once established, *The New Yorker* flourished because it offered closely targeted, highly economical marketing opportunities for the advertisers of luxury goods. Ingersoll pointed out that

> its fundamental success is based on the simple mathematics that a merchant can, at $550 a *New Yorker* page, call his advertisement to the attention of some 62,000 active and literate inhabitants of the metropolitan area: while to reach the same group, either through a national medium or a local paper, would cost him several times that amount. *Vogue*'s New York circulation is 28,000 and to reach it one must buy the whole national coverage and pay $1,500. A full page in *The New York Times* reaches 389,000 but its circulation can hardly be called exclusive and the page costs $2,131.[18]

The economic sense of what *The New Yorker* offered advertisers ensured its early success and carried it through the first part of the Depression.

But an exclusively New York–oriented marketing policy could not last beyond the mid-1930s. Even in 1934, Ingersoll had noticed that half *The New Yorker*'s subscription list came from outside New York.[19] This required a new marketing strategy, and by the early 1940s, as the magazine's national circulation grew (90,000 outside New York by 1940), the business department began to capitalize on the fact that it was now a national magazine.[20] *Rebuque from Dubuque, or Where, Indeed, Are the Limits of New York?* a brochure aimed at potential advertisers and issued by *The New Yorker* in the 1940s, was designed to establish one thing: that *The New Yorker* sold luxury goods nationally. On one page it showed a huge map of the United States with the caption, "Here is where New Yorkers live." Already the ethos of New York, New York, as a token of metropolitan sophistication and personal success is treated as a marketable commodity. The copy goes on to suggest that *The New Yorker*, no longer a metropolitan magazine, is for "New York–minded people, wherever they are."[21]

> For, unlike the myriad points in which New York–minded people live, The New Yorker itself is no tack on a map, not a city, not an island nor an evening at "21." The New Yorker is a mood, a point of view. It is found wherever people are electrically sensitive to new ideas, eager for new things to do, new things to buy, new urbanities for living. Wherever you find such people you will find The New Yorker, purveying ideas and goods to people who, by their manner of living, thinking and acting, lead other people.[22]

Perhaps for the first time in history advertising executives quite deliberately transformed a city into an image of itself in order to sell things. Certainly the link between ideas and goods, art and commerce, culture and the commodity could hardly be made plainer.

By 1952 all this was so well understood that the marketing department of *The New Yorker* was able to issue a booklet of statistics titled *The Primary Markets for Quality Merchandise*. This pamphlet correlated *The New Yorker's* regional subscription levels with tables derived from the U.S. Department of Commerce, Bureau of the Census, showing income levels and spending patterns in the forty-seven primary trade areas in the United States. From it a potential advertiser could learn, for example, that the New York trade area, number one on the list, held 9.07 percent of the national population; that 197,685 families in this area had an annual income of $10,000 or more; that at $13.5 billion, retail sales in this area were 10.31 percent of the national total; that key luxury purchases such as Cadillacs or Lincolns stood at 10.74 percent of the national total; that *The New Yorker's* subscription level in this area was 94,527 copies, 29.3 percent of total circulation. In *The Primary Markets for Quality Merchandise* the artistic and literary purposes of the magazine are almost entirely submerged beneath the advertising opportunities the magazine represents. The purpose of the brochure is "to simplify selling for manufacturers of quality merchandising—to make it easier to see where to start, where to push hardest for sales, and, as a result, how to cut selling costs." Its seizing upon the selling advantages of cultural exclusiveness is shameless: "The New Yorker is itself a quality product. The magazine was conceived for intelligent, discriminating men and women who appreciate fine things and can afford them. It is edited for such people and for them alone."[23]

It is possible to remain sympathetic to Shawn's ideal of *The New Yorker's* "chaste" pages and still recognize that the magazine was as deeply implicated in a culture of consumerism as any more nakedly commercial venture.[24] Implicated nowhere more so than in the very question of its chastity. A reputation for editorial integrity is, after all, itself a marketable commodity, valuable for advertisers. As an informant to *The Wall Street Journal* noted, "What sells the magazine is its integrity, not its urbanity,"[25] something advertisers were made all too aware of. In any consideration of *The New Yorker,* the importance of advertising has to be given greater weight than is customary in standard accounts of its history and development.

Why pursue this topic in a book devoted to the discussion of humorous drawings? A starting point is given by Michel de Montaigne in words written when the New World was still very new and had yet to discover its destiny as the harbinger of modernity: "We are never 'at home': we are always outside ourselves. Fear, desire, hope, impel us towards the future; they rob us of feelings and concern for what now is, in order to spend time over what will be—even when we ourselves shall be no more."[26]

For Montaigne, "desire" is one of three constitutive but self-alienating forces within the psyche. As is well recognized, capitalism enlists desire in its service. It is built on the dream world of longing for what one does not have and depends on this longing for its existence: markets must always be extended. A major focus of desire in modern society is the commodity, the commodity that people lack and crave. The lack causes people to be not "at home" with themselves. The craving sets up a goal outside the self. Possessing the object of desire is equated to the self's happiness — whether it be an automobile, an apartment, a piece of electronic gadgetry, a pair of jogging shoes, a suntan, an activity, a vacation, a lifestyle, a look. And what creates, articulates, and directs desire for the commodity is advertising. A reader of *The Atlantic Magazine* in 1906 wrote plaintively in a letter to the editor of how "a pseudo-conscience" calls from the pages of the magazine in its advertisements, desiring readers' good — in matters of health, clothes, possessions, advice, beauty. In quoting these words, Christopher Wilson rightly remarks that this voice is prophetic of "the pathos of the modern consumer: endlessly enticed and dissatisfied, reminded of one's short-comings, set 'free' — and yet goaded by a pseudo-conscience."[27] The "pathos of the modern consumer" was well analyzed by Karen Horney in the late 1930s, when the social and economic constituents of late capitalism first began to reach critical mass: "The . . . contradiction is between the stimulation of our needs and our factual frustrations in satisfying them. For economic needs are constantly being stimulated in our culture by such means as advertisements, 'conspicuous consumption,' the ideal of 'keeping up with the Joneses.' For the great majority, the actual fulfilment of these needs is closely restricted. The psychic consequence for the individual is a constant discrepancy between his desires and their fulfilment."[28] This discrepancy is the source of much everyday discontent and unhappiness.

Advertising, as a stand-in for the commodity, is ambiguous in its effects, being at once invigorating and demoralizing. By arousing a sense of personal lack, by creating "needs" we would not otherwise know we had, advertising sets before us a reality seductively different from the one we actually inhabit. The promise is that we will be remade through the acquisition of whatever we do not yet possess. Most people have moods in which this promise is believable and even exhilarating. But if advertising excites, it also disappoints. Sooner or later demoralization sets in. Perhaps we acquire what we want and then cease to desire it, so that its meaning slips through our fingers. After a week or two even a Rolex becomes just a wristwatch, and our life is not transformed. Or the illusion collapses and reality supervenes. We are forced to admit that nothing will make us look like the models in a Chanel or Nautica advertisement. The appeal here may be shallow and crass. It may amount to no more than the most transparent of wish-fulfillment fantasies. But it is a rare person who has not experienced the gap that advertisements open up between our own messy lives and the images of perfected elegance we see in the typical advertising photograph. Who at some time or another has not been lured by the promise that our lives can be remade simply by buying something? In these ways the marketplace reaches into every aspect of our lives, and particularly into the inner, private spaces of the self.

The connection between magazines and commodities is an old one, dating from the middle of the nineteenth century. The very word "magazine" (as the French *magasin* reminds us) originally meant a warehouse where goods were stored. Subsequent meanings derive from this both metaphorically and literally. The "goods" in a magazine might well be thought of as literary goods, but just as a magazine (the building) was once a warehouse for consumer goods, so too is a magazine (the publication) a storehouse for the images of consumer goods. Certainly, before television the magazine was one of the basic forums for advertising. Hence it was an agent in that decisive moment in modern society that Tim Clark, writing about Baudelaire, has described as "the massive internal extension of the capitalist market—the invasion and restructuring of whole areas of free time, private life, leisure, and personal expression . . . a new phase of commodity production, the making-into-commodities, of whole areas of social practice which had once been referred to casually as everyday life."[29] That the first two decades of *The New Yorker* were a televisionless society merely emphasizes the point. But just because of the spread of television in the 1940s, there is no reason to suppose the role of advertising in a magazine grew any less important. On the contrary, perhaps because *The New Yorker*'s very literariness lent a special authority and cachet to products that were advertised in its pages, its advertising revenue was at its highest in the 1960s.[30] The advertising, then, is not an epiphenomenon of *The New Yorker*'s experience. The advertising is central to what the magazine is and central to the effect it produces on its readers.[31] It is through its advertising that *The New Yorker* casts its readers in the everyday drama of desire.

Humor, especially when it involves laughter, provides an everyday antidote to this common state of affairs—the seesaw of exhilaration and demoralization brought about by wanting things we can't have, the emptiness of desire satisfied, bad everyday experiences with the commodity as sign. As an antidote it is admittedly mild and limited in scope. But within those limits it is highly valuable, because it is so readily available, so modest in what it offers (happiness, in effect), and so effective in the relief it brings. Humor is, of course, a huge and nebulous topic, about which little agreement can be expected. In particular, there are disagreements between people who think that humor has a liberationist politics, those who think that humor is a form of social control, and those who think that humor manifests an indeterminacy of meaning characteristic of other literary texts from which no clear conclusions can be drawn.[32] But two crucial and recurring notions are common to all accounts: that humor is a form of play with language, and that it is an attack on rationality or a turning back of reason upon itself.[33] Both are important for the way humor countervails against the pressure of the commodity, because both involve holding the actual world at one or two removes, a distancing effect that is also steadying for the person experiencing it.

Even more important is laughter. As most writers on humor recognize, laughter is not essential to any account of humor. And yet when humor does provoke laughter we value it supremely. The reason is laughter's ecstatic nature. There are indeed many links between laughter and catharsis as a state of mind in which we literally seem to "stand outside" ourselves. Both involve transcending the ego or forgoing its claims. Various ways of explaining this characteristic effect of laughter have been advanced. What is interesting is that they all pit laughter against language and time. Thus Iris Murdoch once suggested that "laughter has no logos," meaning not just that laughter can't be explained but that laughter is "outside" language.[34] In a similar vein, Samuel Weber has proposed that laughter is "discontinuous temporality," implying that it momentarily positions us outside the Kantian category of temporality itself.[35] Drawing together the suggestions of these and similar comments, we can propose that laughter removes the ego from both the signifying and temporal frameworks within which desire is made possible. Desire requires that we see ourselves as a being projected toward some future goal. Remove the future into which we continually project ourselves, and desire itself disappears. Laughter is indeed an interruption of the signifying chain of language itself, and as Mark Weeks has argued, it is within language that the whole "cosmology of desire" of capitalism is articulated.[36]

The interruption of the signifying chain, the breaking of the enchantment of desire, the momentary standing outside both language and time can all be understood as returning ourselves to ourselves. Laughter is one of those states that enables us to live not in the past, not in the future, but in and for the present, the moment, the "now." To be able to live in the present moment is perhaps a definition of both happiness and freedom. To live in the present moment is—to return to Montaigne—to be at home with ourselves, to live if only for short while undistracted by desire, hope, or fear. (This account would not be complete if I did not add that it does not require the abolition of the desiring subject: to live without fear, desire, or hope would be a strange and not entirely welcome nirvana, even if possible.) It is the peculiar if temporary gift of laughter that it permits one to stand outside the whole cosmology of desire for a few revivifying moments, but without abolishing the very conditions of existence itself. This is one reason laughter is such a valued personal good.

These suggestions, I hope, cast some light on a general truth. They become particularly cogent when we set the cartoon, as an occasion for laughter, alongside the advertisement, as an occasion for the stimulation of desire, within the magazine considered as a material object.

The organization of the magazine page encourages a way of reading very different from that encouraged by a book.[37] When we read a book the norm is what we might call paginal sequentiality. The codex form and narrative conventions alike both encourage us to begin at the beginning and read through to the end. (Skipping forward or rereading backward is possible, of course, but not the norm.) The norm in reading a magazine, even though it is also a codex, is much more complicated and open to reader choice.[38] Readers find many points of focus on each page. As they cross over from one article to another, from an article to an advertisement, an advertisement to a cartoon, and from a cartoon back to an article, the hold of the individual worlds of the various texts they find on the page is often broken. The textual field of the magazine is by its very nature a heterogeneous or even promiscuous one—never chaste, to revert to Shawn's metaphor. The magazine is constructed on the principles of montage and collage. To read it is to encounter many textual centers that commonly command very different degrees of attention. The magazine, like the newspaper, is a truly polyphonic, dialogic form, and most of what Mikhail Bakhtin said about the newspaper and his other favorite writers (Dostoyevsky, Rabelais) is directly applicable to the magazine. As a form it offers a world organized "primarily in terms of space, not time."[39] The structural principle that the material aspect of the magazine enjoins upon the subtexts that make it up is one of "coexistence and interaction."[40] A magazine, like a newspaper (famously laid out as "front-page Cubism," "in which no single voice predominates" and where there is "no fixed point of view"),[41] is a text in which countless voices clash, compete, and quarrel. The way of reading that this sort of text encourages is one of fluctuating attention in which various centers of interest compete for attention, and the authority of any one textual center is always open to challenge by some other textual center.[42]

The focus of this contestation is the pull between the cartoons and the advertisements, between ecstatic laughter and the enchainment of desire. *The New Yorker* is a magazine of consumer values, offering, as Clement Greenberg briskly put it in the *Partisan Review* at the end of the 1930s, "high-class kitsch for the luxury trade," culture in aid of the distribution of the commodity.[43]

The Comic Worlds of Arno, Steig, Addams, and Steinberg

Nonetheless, the heteroglot character of the magazine ensures that in its pages the commodity never enjoys an absolute victory. Too much information, of too incompatible a character, is in play; and too much choice is available for readers ever to feel overwhelmed by any single textual center, any act of incorporation into the system of desire. But this would be true of many magazines, perhaps—so what, if anything, makes *The New Yorker* special? One answer is that the magazine's typical content is literary rather than entertaining and that the sort of variety one encounters in the old *New Yorker* certainly (and to a lesser extent in the current magazine) offers lots of worlds elsewhere that give readers any number of points from which the reign of the commodity can be levered aside. This is true. The additional, and I would say more important, answer is that the cartoons offer an especially potent relief from the excitation of desire promoted by the advertisements, one that is particularly able to disengage readers from their seduction by the commodity.

If advertisements activate desire, as a central principle of capitalism, and chain us to the chimera of consumption, then the cartoons, through the ecstasy of laughter, pick the lock—for a brief moment (all we can ask for). In detaching readers from futurity, for example, in returning them to the present moment, laughter helps them regain momentary self-possession. That moment of ecstasy, of time interrupted, of language balked creates a little out-of-time oasis of mastery and self-presence. The cartoons and the advertisements exist in a symbiotic but countervailing relationship. The power of the one to seduce comes up against the power of the other to detach. Against the universal empire of the commodity can be set the local revolt of laughter. And this makes possible a revaluation of the most contemned of all figures in the drama of modernity: the middle-class consciousness. Everything I have argued in this book implies a middle-class consciousness that is modestly, but encouragingly, rather more self-aware, rather more independent, rather more critical, and even a little freer than most accounts of its fortunes are prepared to concede. Humor, says Ted Cohen, is important to us because it creates intimacy. If you tell me a joke, Cohen says, "I think what you want is to reach me, and therein to verify that you understand me, at least a little, which is to exhibit that we are, at least a little, alike."[44] This is true, but, especially in the case of a magazine, it all depends on what sort of intimacy is achieved. Jean Baudrillard has attacked one kind of intimacy as a malignant, virtual community of docile consumers.[45] But with *The New Yorker* in mind, perhaps we can set against this another kind of reader and another sort of intimacy: one that creates a benevolent virtual community by virtue of the cartoons that appear in it. This is a solidarity of readers who, as connoisseurs of the incongruity, the absurdity, and the wryness of things, know the elation of living in the present

This is the life.

This is the resort that's one of a kind. With a five-star welcome and three 18-hole championship golf courses, 19 tennis courts, and superb dining. Plus horseback riding, trout fishing, skeet and trap, swimming pools, even its own Spa, all on 16,000 glorious Alleghany acres. Ask your travel agent or call us toll-free: 800-336-5771, in Virginia 800-542-5734.

𝒯𝐻𝐸 HOMESTEAD ®

HOT SPRINGS, VIRGINIA 24445

Fig. C.1.
Advertisement for the
Homestead Resort.

The New Yorker,
May 11, 1987, 88.

A typical small advertisement from *The New Yorker*. There is nothing special about it, but it is momentarily seductive—the golf courses, the horseback riding, the trout fishing, the swimming pools, the spa, the "superb dining" . . . Do we really see ourselves in the awkwardly posed models? Probably not, but then that might be the hook—you don't want to be them, you want to replace them. The small pang of desire created by advertisements like this is writ large in the more extravagant advertisements in *The New Yorker,* where the magazine truly shows itself as a warehouse for the images of consumer goods and services. Such images typically produce, if not boredom, then exhilaration followed by discontent, the familiar trajectory of consumer desire.

"This is the life, eh?"

Fortunately, we have been prepared for the image in figure C.1
by this cartoon, which appeared on the preceding page of the
same issue of *The New Yorker.* Drawn in Mankoff's characteristic broken-line style, it shows a middle-aged couple (what
the people who read the advertisement would probably be
like), sitting contentedly on their porch. Its sardonic realism
sets up a collision with the fantasy of the advertisement. The
advertisement tells us how things might be, and this cartoon
reminds us of how things usually are. The piquant intimacy of
understanding it establishes between the reader, the artist,
and the layout editor adds to the dry wit of the joke.

moment, free from an enslaving desire for the commodity, aware that at least
for a moment they are themselves and yet not alone.

I will end, then, with a small example—but the smallness is all right because everything here comes down to a series of "small examples." What I am
about to describe probably occupies the reader who notices it little more than
half a minute. And yet it is a packed thirty seconds. In *The New Yorker* dated
May 11, 1987 (88), there is a half-column advertisement for the historic Homestead resort in Hot Springs, Virginia (fig. C.1). The resort (so the copy tells

Laughing with *The New Yorker*

us) is "one of kind." It has "three 18-hole championship golf courses, 19 tennis courts, and superb dining." "Plus," the advertisement continues, "horseback riding, trout fishing, skeet and trap, swimming pools, even its own Spa, all on 16,000 glorious Alleghany acres." Then follows the invitation to "call us toll-free." A photograph of a handsome, rather anodyne, awkwardly posed couple in tennis gear accompanies the advertisement. She is blond, in her late twenties. With a towel tossed over her shoulder, she looks out of frame into the middle distance, head tilted back slightly, with a dreamy, "life is just wonderful" smile. He is a blow-dried (hair *en broussant*), thirtyish professional type. (Attorney? Doctor? Stockbroker?) He gazes too attentively into the woman's face, holding up his tennis racket, appreciative of the intimacy of the moment. It's true, we think for a moment: healthy, hardworking, unattached professionals like us do deserve to spoil ourselves just a little, and maybe more than just a little. It is by no means an extravagant advertisement and is unlikely to send readers into paroxysms of envy. But as you read the copy and look at the photograph it sounds and looks pretty good—good enough to make you feel dissatisfied with spending yet another day at the office or in the garden. It arouses just enough desire to make us feel not at home with ourselves. "This is the life"—the one that I don't have.

How fortunate, then, that we have been prepared for this advertisement by a cartoon on the previous page by Robert Mankoff (fig. C.2). Drawn in Mankoff's characteristic broken-line style (which makes solid, everyday reality seem insubstantial, permeable, and evanescent), it shows a nice boring, decent but friendly and comfortable middle-aged couple sitting contentedly in their rocking chairs on the porch, a basket of begonias hanging from the ceiling. The man is saying to the woman, "This is the life, eh?" Should we notice it, there is a little collision between this cartoon and the advertisement on the following page, between the realism of one and the fantasy of the other, joined by the repetition of the tagline. The momentary release the cartoon provides, the piquant intimacy of understanding that it establishes between the reader, the artist who drew the cartoon, and the layout editor who surreptitiously placed the advertisement just overleaf from the cartoon, adds to the dry wit of the joke (which makes its independent criticism of diminished middle-class expectations). This exchange of understandings exemplifies the way an inflated commodity can be punctured by the prick of laughter. It is a special pleasure, useful, valuable, and important: not everything, of course, but enough to get us by. "The first thing I did," says the narrator of Donald Barthelme's "The Rise of Capitalism" (*The New Yorker,* December 12, 1970, 45–47), "was make a mistake. I thought I understood capitalism, but what I had done was assume an attitude—melancholy sadness—towards it. This attitude is not correct."

An attitude of melancholy sadness certainly isn't correct, although it is very hard to say what is, and even harder now than it was in 1970 when Barthelme published that story. Anyone familiar with the tradition of cartoon art at *The New Yorker* might reasonably conclude, however, that an effective, if modest and passing, alternative is laughter.

NOTES

Introduction. The Scope of the Cartoon

1. Cartooning finally has its own research journal, *International Journal of Comic Art,* recently founded and edited by John Lent of Temple University.

2. Craig McGregor, "Cartoonists of Oz," in *Sound Track for the Eighties: Pop Culture, Australia, Politics, Suburbia, Art and Other Essays* (Sydney: Hodder and Stoughton, 1983), 156.

3. If taken as a sign that comic drawings have defied containment, of course, this is all to the good.

4. See Simon During, *The Cultural Studies Reader* (New York: Routledge, 1993), 2–7, for a brief history of the development of cultural studies.

5. Warren I. Susman, *Culture as History: The Transformation of American Society in the Twentieth Century* (New York: Pantheon, 1984), 192.

6. Although it is a study of a brilliant artist who was very important to the early *New Yorker,* Bruce Kellner's *The Last Dandy: Ralph Barton, American Artist, 1891–1931* (Columbia: University of Missouri Press, 1991) is basically biographical in character.

7. Ben Yagoda in his *About Town: "The New Yorker" and the World It Made* (New York: Scribner, 2000) prints seventeen cartoons that handily embrace the seven decades of *The New Yorker*'s existence. But the images tend to be treated in isolation, and it could not be said that Yagoda has any linking argument to make about the cartoons he does choose to mention.

8. Mary F. Corey is careful to date cartoons when she discusses them, but she does not reprint any cartoons in her thematic analysis of *The New Yorker, The World through a Monocle: "The New Yorker" at Midcentury* (Cambridge: Harvard University Press, 1999). Thomas Kunkel in his biography *Genius in Disguise: Harold Ross of "The New Yorker"* (New York: Random House, 1995) usually gives the year only. Ben Yagoda, *About Town,* is inconsistent: when the cartoons illustrate a particular decade he gives a rough date (for example, "the cartoons of the postwar period," 280), and once or twice he gives a year. Elsewhere he provides no dates at all. No cartoon is fully dated, even in the illustration credits.

9. The outstanding exception is Marilyn Addams's edition of her husband's work, *The World of Charles Addams* (New York: Alfred A. Knopf, 1991). Barbara Nicholls, the curator of the 1988 exhibition "The Art of the New Yorker," also dated the

exhibits by original date of publication. It is regrettable that the example of Addams and Nicholls has not been more generally adopted. It is a weakness of Lee Lorenz's *The Art of "The New Yorker"* (New York: Alfred A. Knopf, 1995) that—covers excepted—it does not date cartoons. More generally, chronology is handled in an incidental manner by Lorenz, who, for example, gives the date of S. I. Newhouse's announcement of the appointment of Robert Gottlieb (January 12, 1987) but not the date of his first issue with the magazine (March 2, 1987). The same is true when he deals with Tina Brown (whose editorship was announced on June 13, 1992), although readers can work out which was her first fully edited issue (October 5, 1992) from the reprint of Edward Sorel's cover.

10. *The Complete Cartoons of "The New Yorker,"* ed. Robert Mankoff, foreword by David Remnick (New York: Black Dog and Leventhal, 2004). The collection is in combined hard copy (over 2,000 cartoons) and CD ROM (68,647 cartoons) forms. The hard cover selection is arranged chronologically, decade by decade. The CD ROM collection is browsable by date, artist, and subject. The collection includes brief essays by Roger Angell, Nancy Franklin, Lillian Ross, John Updike, Calvin Trillin, Ian Frazier, Mark Singer, and Rebecca Mead.

11. See *The Primary Markets for Quality Merchandise* (New York: New Yorker, 1952). I am not implying that all its actual readers fit this prescription but am merely trying to sketch its intended demographic profile.

12. Corey, *World through a Monocle.* Corey's comments are restricted, a little disablingly perhaps, to the magazine in the forties and fifties.

13. John Updike, "Pilgrim's Progress," *New York Review of Books,* December 3, 1992, 3.

14. Apart from Yagoda's *About Town* and Corey's *World through a Monocle,* books about *The New Yorker* are Dale Kramer, *Ross and "The New Yorker"* (London: Victor Gollancz, 1952); James Thurber, *The Years with Ross* (Boston: Little, Brown, 1957); Jane Grant, *Ross, "The New Yorker" and Me* (New York: Reynall, 1968); Brendan Gill, *Here at "The New Yorker"* (New York: Random House, 1975); Gigi Mahon, *The Last Days of "The New Yorker"* (New York: McGraw-Hill, 1988); Kunkel, *Genius in Disguise;* and Lee Lorenz, *Art of "The New Yorker."* These range in character from anecdotal to historical. A more analytic treatment may be found in the following articles: [Ralph Ingersoll], "*The New Yorker,*" *Fortune,* August 1934, 73–97, 150–52; Dwight Macdonald, "Laugh and Lie Down," *Partisan Review,* December 1937, 44–53; Seymour Krim, "Who's Afraid of *The New Yorker* Now?" (1962), reprinted in *Shake It for the World, Smartass* (New York: Delta, 1971), 171–86; and Josephine Henden, "*The New Yorker* as Cultural Ideal," *Dissent* 29, no. 4 (1982): 450–54.

15. This handy phrase comes from James English's introduction to *Comic Transactions: Literature, Humor and the Politics of Community in Twentieth-Century Britain* (Ithaca: Cornell University Press, 1994), 7.

16. See the new magazine's prospectus, circulated in the fall of 1924: "*The New Yorker* will be a reflection in word and picture of metropolitan life. . . . *The New Yorker* expects to be distinguished for its illustrations, which will include caricatures, sketches, cartoons and humorous and satirical drawings in keeping with its purpose." The pro-

spectus is reprinted in full in Yagoda, *About Town*, 38–39. The interest in illustrations has to be understood alongside the magazine's long rejection of photojournalism.

17. The most obvious example is the Althusserian notion of "interpellation." In such theories "subjectivity" (a poststructuralist term emphasizing the subjection of identity to the various systems that determine or "construct" it) replaces the romantic notion of the "self" (in which people possess a deep inner core of independent identity).

18. In this paragraph I am reviving Raymond Williams's argument in *Marxism and Literature* (Oxford: Oxford University Press, 1977), 128–35. Williams proposes that works of art are often responses to what he calls a certain "structure of feeling." Structures of feeling are defined as the experiential response to, or recognition of, new social and historical situations—"practical consciousness" rather than "official consciousness," Williams calls it, or "what is actually being lived . . . not only what it is thought is being lived" (131). I am suggesting that "midway" experiences are those that typically make sense if we think of them as emerging from, or being connected to, a new "structure of feeling." Williams's case, in part, has the effect of defending the status of imaginative creation as a form of knowledge against the claims of conceptual thought then being powerfully revived by various engaged analytic systems.

19. There is indebtedness here to Hegel's notion of the "indicative" status of art.

20. Williams notes the application of this to cultural phenomena "where the true social content is . . . of an affective kind, which cannot without loss be reduced to belief systems, institutions, or explicit general relationships, though it may include all of these as lived and experienced" (Williams, *Marxism and Literature,* 133).

21. This handy phrase is also Williams's (134).

22. The historian Howard Stein uses the term "social cynosure" for the kind of popularity I have in mind here. The concept was originally coined by the psychologist Weston La Barre in the forties and taken up to great effect by Stein in his analysis of the significance of Alastair Cooke's popular history of America. A "social cynosure" is a "cultural document which receives massive sustained attention" and thus implies the existence of a broad, and once again largely intuitive, consensus of understanding within a social group or subgroup. It has an obvious applicability to humor that enjoys great popular success. See Weston La Barre, "Social Cynosure and Social Structure," *Journal of Personality* 14 (1945): 169–83, and Howard F. Stein, "Alastair Cooke's *America:* A Study in Cultural Consensus and Popular History," *Journal of American Culture* 4, no. 4 (Winter 1981): 46–54.

23. Sigmund Freud, *Jokes and Their Relation to the Unconscious,* Penguin Freud Library, vol. 6 (Harmondsworth, England: Penguin Books, 1991), 203.

24. John Harvey, "The Novel and the Cartoon," *Cambridge Quarterly* 4, no. 4 (Autumn–Winter 1969–70): 419–29, 423–25.

25. Aggressive humor is much better than aggressive behavior. Against this view, many would argue that aggressive humor is merely the trace, or the symptomatic expression, of real feelings of violence and hatred that it legitimizes.

26. *The New Yorker* was at best complacent and at worst compliant over questions of race, especially black-white relations, some early antiracist cartoons notwithstand-

ing (the George Price cartoon in which a foreman of a jury is depicted as saying," Yo' Honah, suh, afta due deliberation, we the jury is convinced that the defendant is as colored as hell, suh!" [April 29, 1933, 12], or the more famous Reginald Marsh drawing of a woman holding up a little girl in a crowd and explaining to her neighbor, "It's her first lynching" [September 8, 1934, 27]). Corey discusses race and related issues in chapter 5, "*The New Yorker* in Black and White," of *World through a Monocle,* 77–100.

27. I concede that benign humor, insofar as it promotes group solidarity, can be implicitly aggressive toward excluded groups, but this argument can be—and has been—overplayed.

28. Interview with Frank Modell, New York, July 26, 1990. Addams's phrase is actually "mauling the cliché." I quote Modell's wording.

29. Hokinson, by far the most considerable female artist in the early *New Yorker,* is a difficult case, impossible to do justice to in a few lines. I would not want to say, for instance, that Hokinson was a limited artist without adding "but only as Jane Austen is limited"—that is, not very limited at all. But it remains true that her collaboration with Parker makes her a special case, as Lee Lorenz implies when he says her cover art lacked the "grit" that came in her cartoons thanks to Parker's surgically sharp taglines. See Lorenz, *Art of "The New Yorker,"* 29.

30. Liza Donnelly is preparing a study of women cartoonists at *The New Yorker;* see *The New Yorker,* November 11, 2002, 14 and 165.

31. This last phrase, taken from a discussion of the work of George du Maurier in *Cambridge Quarterly* 4, 4 (Autumn–Winter, 1969–70): 419–20, is that of the English critic John Harvey, who has written some of the best criticism of the art of illustration and cartooning.

32. I adopt here two phrases from Stein, "Alastair Cooke's *America,*" 47.

33. The ship voyage to Australia in the 1950s took four or five weeks. Before jet travel the flight across the Pacific from Los Angeles to Sydney took thirty-five hours, to say nothing of the huge cost of an airline ticket. International phone calls were an unthought-of luxury. For a recent amusing account of postwar and fifties Melbourne see Barry Humphries's memoirs, *More Please* (London: Viking/Penguin, 1992) and *My Life as Me: A Memoir* (London: Viking/Penguin, 2002).

34. John Lardner, "Letter from the Olympics," *The New Yorker,* December 8, 1956, 153–57. Lardner had reported on the Australian side of the Pacific War, notably the Japanese bombing raids on Darwin in 1942, knew a lot about the country, and was well placed to notice changes and developments.

35. Lardner doesn't mention the other cause—Australia's postwar migration boom that brought a wave of European immigrants to the country—mainly Italians, Greeks, Yugoslavians, Latvians, Estonians, and Lithuanians—along with "ten-pound Poms" (the English). The Italians, for example, transformed the inner-city university suburb of Carlton, once a Jewish and Australian working-class neighborhood. Its main street became a concentration of Italian shops, cafés, and street life. Melbourne's large Jewish community contains one of the highest per capita populations of Holocaust survivors anywhere in the world. The architect of Australia's multicultural social policy was a Pole, Jerzy Zubrzycki, who himself arrived in Australia in 1956.

36. Barry Humphries, then a minority of minorities taste but already legendary in

theatrical and university circles, was satirizing it locally, and 45 rpm EP recordings of his work were played at late-night parties and received in a mood of hysterical rapture.

1. Peter Arno

1. "The Talk of the Town," *The New Yorker*, May 31, 1930, 11. The piece concluded: "Personally we think college education, even in its present comical setting, mixed all up as it is with Titian, Fontanne, Whiskey, Arno, Kipling, and Contacts, is a good thing; but we often pause to think what fabulous sums of money would be turned loose on the world if ever it were discovered, suddenly, that the American system of education was really wrong, and didn't actually work at all."

2. See the assessment by Charles Saxon in his introduction to the collection of Arno cartoons titled *Peter Arno* (New York: Beaufort Books, 1979).

3. I have borrowed this evocative and helpful phrase from Philip Herrera's "In Splendid Style: Peter Arno, the Cartoonist as Fine Artist, *Connoisseur*, February 1984, 65.

4. Horace Liveright and Albert Boni had formed Boni and Liveright in 1917. According to James E. Mooney's informative entry in *The Encyclopedia of New York City*, the firm published writers like Eugene O'Neill, Sherwood Anderson, and Ernest Hemingway. Along with Albert Boni's brother Charles, the firm started the Modern Library series of reprinted classics, which in turn funded the publishing of more adventurous titles. It was the target of censors and the Society for the Suppression of Vice. The firm campaigned successfully against Justice Ford's "clean books bill" of 1924. In 1918 the partners resolved a business disagreement by tossing a coin for the company. Boni lost. See Kenneth T. Jackson, ed., *The Encyclopedia of New York City* (New Haven: Yale University Press; New York: New-York Historical Society, 1995), 124 and 125. *The New Yorker* published a short obituary for William Bolitho in "The Talk of the Town," *The New Yorker*, February 28, 1931, 7.

5. On these three avatars: Arno sometimes drew in the style of Daumier; his work was often compared to that of Guys (see note 36 below); Grosz was the subject of a three-part profile by Richard O. Boyer in *The New Yorker* of November 27, December 4, and December 11, 1943, with an Arno drawing, appropriately, set in the middle of the second part.

6. William Steig, in an interview I conducted at his home in Kent, Connecticut, in June 1990, described Arno as an "aristocrat." The term is obviously metaphorical and no more, but I have adopted it because it links Arno with the dandy, also an aristocratic figure (see below). The use of the word in discussions of American culture and society is highly disputed. On this matter see Arthur R. Gold's article in *American Literary History* 2 (Summer 1990). Gold says that the aristocrat's distinguishing feature is "ease." He quotes Oliver Wendell Holmes's definition, "a provoking easy way of dressing, walking, talking, and nodding to people, as if they felt entirely at home, and would not be embarrassed in the least, if they met the Governor, or even the President of the United States, face to face." Gold stresses "the attitude of feeling at ease—aplomb, one could call it—and of exercising self-control" as the "inward mark of the American aristocrat." For an opposing view, see Louis Auchincloss, *The Vanderbilt Era: Profiles of a*

Gilded Age (New York: Scribner, 1989); the author denies that the term has any legitimacy where America is concerned, except for the planters of the antebellum South (3).

7. For varying accounts of this episode see James Thurber, *The Years with Ross* (Boston: Atlantic Press; Little, Brown, 1959), 42, and Thomas Kunkel, *Genius in Disguise: Harold Ross of "The New Yorker"* (New York: Random House, 1995), 117. On the Social Register: much cynicism was abroad about the real influence of the "400," which by 1926 had been reduced to "3.98," according to Robert Jay Misch's "Manhattan Manual" (*The New Yorker,* April 17, 1926, 32).

8. Dale Kramer, *Ross and "The New Yorker"* (London: Victor Gollancz, 1952), 81. In his *Art of "The New Yorker,"* Lee Lorenz includes a facsimile of Philip Wylie's letter of January 3, 1958, to James Thurber describing early art meetings at the magazine. See Lee Lorenz, *The Art of "The New Yorker"* (New York: Alfred A. Knopf, 1995), 16–17.

9. See Lewis A. Erenberg, *Steppin' Out: New York Nightlife and the Transformation of American Culture, 1890–1930* (Westport, CT: Greenwood Press, 1981), 231.

10. The drawing is reproduced as the frontispiece to *Peter Arno* (New York: Beaufort Books, 1979).

11. Ellin Mackay, "Why We Go to Cabarets A Post-debutante Explains," *The New Yorker,* November 14, 1925, 7–8. Her article was picked up by the *New York Times,* the *New York Herald Tribune,* and the *World* and in all accounts of the magazine's history is credited with being the contribution that first drew attention to Ross's new publication. Lee Lorenz, in *Art of "The New Yorker,"* is embarrassed that, as he puts it, "this piece of sensational fluff, not the talents of Ross, Irvin, Hokinson or Arno turned people's attention to the magazine" (35). The situation is even worse than Lorenz imagines, however, since *The New York Times* interested itself in the article only because it had been fed to the city editor, Ralph Graves, by Ross's wife, Jane Grant. See Jane Grant, *Ross, "The New Yorker" and Me* (New York: Reynall, 1968), 229–31. But as I argue, the article had a great symbolic if not sociological value. See also her follow-up piece, "The Declining Function: A Post-debutante Rejoices," *The New Yorker,* December 12, 1925, 5–16.

12. For a stimulating account of the cabaret as a new social institution, which argues that it culminates a line of development that began in the 1890s, see Erenberg, *Steppin' Out,* especially 60–142 and 233–59.

13. Mackay, "Why We Go to Cabarets," 8.

14. For the Mackays, see Laurence Bergreen, *As Thousands Cheer* (New York: Viking, 1990), 229–44 and 252–63.

15. For "understanding test" and similar terms, see James F. English, *Comic Transactions, Literature, Humor and the Politics of Community in Twentieth-Century Britain* (Ithaca: Cornell University Press, 1994), 9.

16. Thurber, *Years with Ross,* 62.

17. For another example of Arno's cheekiness in suggesting the erect penis, see the drawing in *Peter Arno's Man in the Shower* (New York: Simon and Schuster, 1944) captioned "Please! You don't understand! *I'm* the lifeguard!" [43].

18. Flanner herself was an observant chronicler of the new Manhattan, in, for example, her novel *The Cubical City* (New York, 1926), reissued in 1974.

19. William Bolitho, preface, *Peter Arno's Parade* (New York: Liveright, 1929).

20. A comparable example from *The New Yorker* might be the sketch by Kelley from *The New Yorker,* April 4, 1925, or any work by Charles Baskerville from the same period.

21. Peter Arno, foreword, *Peter Arno's Ladies and Gentlemen* (New York: Simon and Schuster, 1951), 13.

22. According to Charles Saxon, Arno would sometimes spend forty hours on a single drawing, getting it exactly right. Charles Saxon, introduction to *Seasons at "The New Yorker"* (New York: United Technologies Corporation and National Academy of Design, 1984), xv.

23. Arno in 1937, quoted in Herrera, "In Splendid Style," 66.

24. The role of gag writers and ideas men and the supplying of captions for artists are discussed by Lorenz, *Art of "The New Yorker,"* 48–49, 70–74, and 107 (the last page giving an example of Peter De Vries's editorial care); by Kunkel, *Genius in Disguise,* 325–27; and by Ben Yagoda, *About Town: "The New Yorker" and the World It Made* (New York: Scribner, 2000), 68–70. As early as 1934 Ralph Ingersoll claimed that Arno had built his reputation on a wit that wasn't his own (see [Ralph Ingersoll], *"The New Yorker," Fortune,* August 1934, 90). More bluntly, Philip Wylie says that Arno had "an idea problem" or was just "lazy" (Lorenz, *Art of "The New Yorker,"* 17).

25. For Hokinson see James Reid Parker's account of their partnership printed as a memoir at the end of *The Hokinson Festival,* with a memoir by James Reid Parker and an appreciation by John Mason Brown (New York: E. P, Dutton, 1956), and Lorenz's comments, 29. For McCallister see Kunkel, *Genius in Disguise,* 324, and Lorenz, *Art of "The New Yorker,"* 48–49. Brendan Gill mistakenly asserts that McCallister (whose name he spells McAllister) was responsible for "most of the ideas used by Helen Hokinson"; see his *Here at "The New Yorker"* (New York: Random House, 1975), 213.

26. Details supplied by Frank Modell in an interview I held at *The New Yorker* offices, New York, June 16, 1990.

27. On the size of Geraghty's payment and his difficulties in getting Arno to turn over his small percentage of the fee for the cartoon, see Lorenz, *Art of "The New Yorker,"* 70. Arno discusses the question of "ideas" in an opaque manner in the foreword to *Peter Arno's Ladies and Gentlemen:* "My ideas are produced with blood, sweat, brain-racking toil, the help of *The New Yorker* art staff, and the collaboration of keen-eyed undercover operatives" ([5]).

28. For Geraghty's care see Lorenz, *Art of "The New Yorker,"* 73.

29. Yagoda, *About Town,* 68.

30. Unlike Ross, neither William Shawn nor Robert Gottlieb had this kind of visual sensitivity, according to William Steig (interview, Kent, Connecticut, June 1990).

31. Charles Saxon notes that Arno always insisted on the priority of the drawing over the idea. Saxon, *Seasons at "The New Yorker,"* xv.

32. Provided there was reasonable lapse of time, the editors sometimes allowed different artists to use the same idea: William Galbraith drew a man saying to a woman, "Miss Wordley—Phyllis—I'm not fit to touch the hem of your gown" (*The New Yorker,* October 12, 1935, 19), an idea later used with modification by Arno (*The New Yorker,* March 20, 1943, 17).

33. Charles Baudelaire, "The Painter of Modern Life," in *The Painter of Modern Life and Other Essays*, ed. and trans. Jonathan Mayne (London: Phaidon, 1995), 9–10.

34. E. B. White, *Here Is New York* (New York: Harper, 1949), 19.

35. Baudelaire, quoted by Ellen Moers, in *The Dandy: Brummell to Beerbohm* (London: Secker and Warburg, 1960), 279.

36. As Henry McBride did in an article titled "Modern Art" in the *Dial* (February 1929). "He is the Constantin Guys of New York. I do not mean he is an imitator of Guys but a comparable artist. If you take Guys seriously you must take Arno seriously. He has that attribute we constantly look for in American art—'the wicked punch,' and he has a wider range than Guys ever dreamed of" (175). Arno mentions, as other influences, Honoré Daumier and (more credibly) Frans Masereel (see, for example, Masereel's *Passionate Journey: A Novel Told in 165 Woodcuts,* with an introduction by Thomas Mann, trans. Joseph M. Bernstein [Harmondsworth, England: Penguin Books, 1988]). Information on Arno's influences is derived from "Peter Arno by Peter Arno," *Cartoonists Profiles* 24 (December 1974): 12.

37. I owe this insight to my colleague Christopher Palmer, and it is from him that most of what I write about the dandy derives.

38. Tilley was drawn by one dandy, Rea Irvin, and named by another, the covertly gay humorist Corey Ford. See Thurber, *Years with Ross,* 42, and the Corey Ford papers held at the Dartmouth College library, Dartmouth, New Hampshire. Ross was always fearful that *The New Yorker* might appear countercultural in some way, ending up like *The Masses,* perhaps.

39. For other examples see "The Speakeasy Hostess Does Her Stuff," by C. Knapp (*The New Yorker,* March 23, 1929, 94–96), and "Speakeasy Cats," by Edmund S. Whitman (*The New Yorker,* September 14, 1929, 62).

40. Erenberg, *Steppin' Out,* 133–34. The following paragraph is a summary of Erenberg's argument about the cabaret.

41. The phrase is coined by Erenberg, who borrows Erving Goffman's term "action" to describe the cabaret world, which he calls an "action environment." See Erenberg, *Steppin' Out,* 132–34. The obvious successors for a later generation are the disco and the dance club. Whit Stillman's film *The Last Days of Disco* uses the disco both as a metaphor for the 1980s and as a focus for the behavior of an otherwise disparate social group in much the same way that I am suggesting Arno uses the cabaret.

42. The underlying assumption is that life has "fateful choices," that to live one must immerse oneself in the moment, gamble one's character and fate on that moment, and accept the unpredictable outcome of the moment.

43. Ambivalent jokes about Jews—not expressing obvious anti-Semitism yet not quite clear of it either—are everywhere in the early *New Yorker*. Arno drew one for the issue of June 5, 1926, showing a stereotypical Jew greeting some chorus girls in the dressing room of the Neighborhood Playhouse. The caption is, "One of the neighbors drops in to the Neighborhood Playhouse." The Neighborhood Playhouse, at 466 Grand Street, was obviously a little too close to the Lower East Side. One of George Price's early cartoons manifests a similar tendency: it shows a hot-dog vendor saying to another, obviously Jewish, who is invading his turf, "Go away or I'll tell Hitler"

(*The New Yorker,* June 3, 1933, 62). In general, Price was extremely liberal in his opinions, but Jews were fair game. It is hard to judge if this is defusing humor or simply covert aggression. *The New Yorker,* of course, had many Jewish contributors.

44. The Remson figure is sometimes incorrectly known as "Cadwaller." In fact, Cadwallader was the name of Arno's archetypal stockbroker, as in the cartoon captioned "Cadwallader always comes through" (*The New Yorker,* November 1, 1930, 14). The frequency with which the Remson figure crops up in Arno's work makes it plausible to think of him as an alter ego of the artist. It has been suggested to me that other artists also used this character. The only other cartoonist I know of who does (and then only once) is William Steig in a drawing that shows a similar figure in a locker room singing "Oh Mademoiselle from Armenteers" surrounded by beefy hunks (*The New Yorker,* August 23, 1930, 23). I am aware of no other artist who used the figure so regularly as Arno. In one early work the character is called "Mr. Winney"—a private joke at the expense of Ross's gay private secretary, who worked for Ross from 1930 onward and eventually embezzled thousands of dollars. In another he is called "Mr. Windle" (*The New Yorker,* January 10, 1931, 23). Elsewhere we learn that his first name is Wilmet (*The New Yorker,* January 24, 1931, 14). Another name used inappropriately for the character is "Caspar Milquetoast," who was the derby-hatted "timid soul" created by Harold Tucker Webster for the *New York World* and later the *Herald Tribune.* See Hamilton Basso, "The World of Caspar Milquetoast" *The New Yorker,* November 5, 1949, 40–61. Milquetoast, who first appeared in 1926, is closer to the Thurber/Steig "Little Man" than to Arno's hapless Remson.

45. The original caption. It was later simplified into a single sentence in some collections.

46. Different accounts exist of how fully Ross understood this cartoon. In Thurber's well-known version, Ross is a complete innocent, saying to Arno that he thought the situation had "a kind of Alice in Wonderland quality" (see Thurber, *Years with Ross,* 13 and 255). Other people remember the story rather differently: Dale Kramer says that Ross himself got the idea from Marc Connelly and passed it on to Arno, a story that, if true, is hardly compatible with Ross's not understanding the joke. See Kramer, *Ross and "The New Yorker,"* 201. Arno's early collections of drawings, such as *Peter Arno's Circus* (New York: Liveright, 1931), show that Arno was well in advance of what Ross was prepared to publish in the way of sexual jokes.

47. See Ronald Chernow, *The House of Morgan* (London: Simon and Schuster, 1990), for an account of Morgan's sexual behavior.

48. On lobster palaces, "bird and bottle bars," and the like, see Erenberg, *Steppin' Out,* 40–56.

49. Both drawings are reprinted in *"The New Yorker" Twenty-fifth Anniversary Album, 1925–1950* (New York: Harper and Brothers, 1950), [2, 5].

50. Lois Long's "On and Off the Avenue" column was one of the most obvious consequences of this (see Kramer, *Ross and "The New Yorker,"* 83). *The New Yorker* had a reasonable record in employing women in responsible positions (Katherine Angell, as fiction editor, for instance) and a good one in publishing them as both fact and fiction writers and as artists. An editorial policy that aimed *The New Yorker* at female

as well as male readers made it from the very start a very different magazine from the male-oriented *Liberty,* where Arno was, in consequence, able to publish his own more frankly "male" cartoons. See also Yagoda's comments in *About Town,* 77–78.

51. There is therefore a danger in reading back into a situation that was historically a step toward feminism a feminist critique that was possible only after that selfsame early step, the liberation of the 1920s, had taken place. Liberation, in the due process of events, uncovered the deeper structural inequalities and injustices that shaped women's lives. Arno's relation to the New Woman of the twenties was, needless to say, as ambivalent as his editor's, and he was certainly no friend of feminism. Ross was uneasily married for nine years to Jane Grant, a woman who became a founding member of the Lucy Stone League and was, along with Ruth Hale, a prominent New York feminist in the 1920s and 1930s. Her career as a singer and as a journalist at *The New York Times* took her to Paris in the years after the war, where she met Ross. Arno married the liberated Lois Long, an early contributor to *The New Yorker.* Arno and Long's unconventional sexual behavior was legendary: they were the couple found asleep naked on a sofa in the speakeasy Ross had installed in the basement of the *New Yorker* offices, an event that caused Ross to close the speakeasy down. Arno's marriage lasted even less time than Ross's. But if Arno was sexist, and no doubt misogynist as well, it should be recognized that when he showed a young woman in bed with a man, in a compromising situation with an older male, or in a state of undress, this might involve something more than oppression or victimization—though it need not exclude them. In this period sexual liberation involved risk and courage. Not to labor the point, any appreciation of Arno's interest as a social humorist is going to depend on a willingness to take the sexual element in his work with some degree of flexibility. The difficulty is that between Arno and us stand two great revolutions in sexual ethics—the liberationism of the sixties and the feminism of the late seventies and beyond. These revolutions themselves obscure the general repressiveness in sexual mores of the first half of the twentieth century and the hypocrisy that went along with it.

52. Ronald Paulson, *Figure and Abstraction in Contemporary Painting* (New Brunswick: Rutgers University Press, 1990), 83.

53. Tendentious jokes, writes Michael Neve, "derive their force from opening up the social order by freeing repressed materials and then making their comment . . . on the world." Michael Neve, "Freud's Theory of Humour, Wit and Jokes," in *Laughing Matters: A Serious Look at Humour,* ed. John Durant and Jonathan Miller (Harlow, England: Longmans, 1988), 40.

54. This was a situation Arno redrew in different versions on a number of occasions: see *The New Yorker,* May 17, 1930, 21 ("Morning, dear—what's new?"), and February 6, 1932, 14 ("Dad says if I buy any more pastels he'll cut me off"), among others.

55. A crucial qualification here is that revolt conceals strands of continuity: there is the desire to preserve the social elite and an identification with the envied older generation. Indeed, the nearness of that identification gives the clue to the intensities of Arno's sexual satire. An interesting consequence, as Arno's career progresses and he himself becomes middle-aged, is that the object of identification in the cartoons tends to slip from the younger cuckold to the older, cuckolding satyr.

56. Herrera, "In Splendid Style," 65. Patricia Arno Maxwell has said that her

father's views in politics were extremely right wing. Information provided to me by Patricia Arno Maxwell in an interview at Saratoga Springs, New York, February 11, 1989.

57. "Peter Arno, Cartoonist, 64, Dies; With *The New Yorker* 43 Years," *New York Times* (February 23, 1968), 1, 30.

58. Thomas Wolfe, *From Death to Morning* (London: Heinemann, 1936).

59. "Peter Arno by Peter Arno," 11. This could have been in either 1933 or 1935.

60. H. L. Mencken, "Totendanz," in *Prejudices,* a selection by James T. Farrell (New York: Vintage Books, 1958).

61. Mencken, "Totendanz."

62. Reprinted in Peter Arno, *Peter Arno* (New York: Beaufort Books, 1979), [105].

63. For discussion of this topic in relation to advertising, see the conclusion.

64. Malcolm Cowley, in *The Dream of the Golden Mountains,* quoted by Warren I. Susman, *Culture as History: The Transformation of American Society in the Twentieth Century* (New York: Pantheon, 1984), 187.

65. Quoted by Thurber, *Years with Ross,* 42.

66. Kunkel, *Genius in Disguise,* 324. Kunkel notes that by the forties Ross tried to grade his artists. Charles Addams and Mary Petty were "AAA." Thurber and Price, among others, were "AA." Artists like Carl Rose and Sam Cobean were "A." Then followed the lesser rankings. Arno, along with Helen Hokinson and Gluyas Williams, was considered by Ross to be so good that he was *hors de concours* and had no ranking at all. Lorenz prints the text of a letter by Ross to Hawley Truax mulling over the difficulties of this classification (Lorenz, *Art of "The New Yorker,"* 122–23).

67. Arno was accorded this privilege "because he asked for it," according to his daughter (Patricia Arno Maxwell, interview). Other artists who frequently got full-page exposure included Rea Irvin, Ralph Barton, William Galbraith (a kind of second-rate Arno), Helen Hokinson, William Steig, Mary Petty (these last two much less frequently than Arno), and later Charles Addams. Arno was not loath to exploit the privilege: Thomas Kunkel relates an anecdote in which an ideas man is sent around to Arno's apartment on Park Avenue to talk over some possible cartoons, one of which involves a game of billiards. Arno immediately rejects any idea that would require a landscape (half-page) rather than a portrait (full-page) format. The anecdote is not entirely trustworthy—it is hardly beyond the bounds of possibility for an artist to get a billiard table into a portrait format—indeed, Arno himself did just that ("Come, Osbert! No theatrics!" *The New Yorker,* January 28, 1928, 16). But the point being made has the ring of truth (see Kunkel, *Genius in Disguise,* 327). In the typical *New Yorker* running order in the forties, the week's full-page cartoon was the lead-in to the main "casual" for the week. Despite being one of Ross's favorites, Arno was never automatically given a full page for every drawing accepted. Perhaps the greatest tribute Ross paid to Arno was to allow him the longest caption of any cartoon published in *The New Yorker* (September 28, 1946, 23): it ran to 231 words.

68. [Ingersoll], "*The New Yorker,*" 90. "Idea drawings" (that is, cartoons) smaller than a half page were paid at $50 to $75, half-page drawings at $65 to $115. In 1930 Ross offered Ralph Barton a drawing account of $350 a week. Under this arrangement Barton was to be paid $250 for a full-page drawing and the same for a cover (Kellner, *Last*

Dandy, 201). Money paid for published drawings would be offset against the amount drawn and could in theory exceed it over a length of time. It is very likely that Arno worked under a similar contract, although the indications are that he received much more than $250 for a cover.

69. It is extremely difficult to find out how much was paid to anyone at *The New Yorker* at any given moment, partly because the payment system (which Thurber discusses at length in his *Years with Ross*) was very complicated and varied from contributor to contributor. In his obituary of Arno, Timothy Less in *The New York Daily Post* for February 23, 1968, 82 (Nicholls Archive) says that Arno was paid $1,000 a cartoon by 1935. This figure seems high, but if accepted it would double the annual earnings cited in the text.

70. Information from Patricia Arno Maxwell interview and "Peter Arno by Peter Arno," 11. In his 1934 article Ingersoll says Arno has been "in Hollywood for months" and implies that he is less interested in cartooning than he once was.

71. [Ingersoll], "*The New Yorker*," 74. According to Thurber in his *Years with Ross,* after Ingersoll's article appeared Ross posted a memo on *The New Yorker* notice board denying that he earned as much as Ingersoll claimed. Thurber also says that the figure of $11,000 for himself was "somewhat magnified" (Thurber, *Years with Ross,* 216). Assessing monetary value in any period is difficult, but the following figures provide some useful benchmarks as a way of gauging the purchasing power of these salaries. The average per capita income for a family of four in the United States in 1928 was $2,980. Less than 1 percent of the population earned more than $10,000 a year. A basic Plymouth cost $445 in 1933, and the Cadillac range started at about $2,695. In the early 1940s the annual rent for an eight-room apartment with three bathrooms, on Park Avenue in the eighties, began at $2,600. See Norman Ware, *Labor in Modern Industrial Society* (New York: D. C. Heath, 1935), 21, and Paul H. Douglas, *Real Wages in the United States, 1890–1926* (New York: A. M. Kelley, 1966). Car prices are as given in *The New Yorker,* August 5, 1933, and August 11, 1933. Apartment prices are quoted in *The New Yorker,* April 18, 1942, 70.

72. Rufus Jarman, "Profiles: U.S. Artist" [part 1], *The New Yorker,* March 17, 1945, 34–43, esp. 37. Apart from the example of Rockwell, it is worth recalling that F. Scott Fitzgerald famously failed to live on $36,000 in 1923 and by 1929 could command $4,000 for a single short story, a fee level he maintained well into the Depression. See André le Vot, *F. Scott Fitzgerald: A Biography,* trans. William Byron (Garden City, NY: Doubleday, 1983), 77. The cases of both Fitzgerald and Rockwell can in turn be put into perspective by recalling that Sinclair Lewis, whose *Main Street* outsold *Gatsby* four to one, was also earning nearly $40,000 a year in the early twenties, won the Nobel Prize in 1930, which came with $48,000 in cash, and in the mid-1940s made half a million dollars out of *Cas Timberlane.* See Mark Shorer, *Sinclair Lewis: An American Life* (New York: McGraw-Hill, 1961), 728.

73. A small debit against this income was the money that Arno was, in theory, supposed to pay for ideas.

74. Peter Arno, "Peter Arno by Peter Arno," 13.

75. At least one version of the Albatross was built, and it possibly still survives.

In 1983 a Mr. Bill Hill owned it and was then restoring it. See Keith Marvin's stories in *Special Interest Autos,* issues of February 1982 and February 1983. In his 1983 article Marvin quotes the figure of $75,000, which seems absurdly high for the late 1930s.

76. *New York Times,* January 2, 1941, 21.

77. It is reproduced by Gill in *Here at "The New Yorker,"* 141.

78. Bergreen, *As Thousands Cheer,* 323–24.

79. Arno later married Mary Lansing in August 1935: *New York Times,* July 19, 1935, 14; August 10, 1935, 7, and August 17, 1935, 16. The couple were divorced in 1939: *New York Times,* March 3, 1939, 44; July 5, 1939, 9.

80. The incident is reported in *New York Times* for June 17, 1931, 33; June 25, 1931, 17; June 30, 1931, 45; July 4, 1931, 4; and July 6, 1931, 5.

81. *New York Times,* January 15, 1933, 25. The Gerguson scandal ran its bizarre course and was followed over the next two years by a mesmerized readership. For an account of Gerguson's career up to 1932, see Alva Johnston's five-part profile in 1932, "The Education of a Prince," *The New Yorker,* October 29, 19–23; November 5, 28–32; November 12, 24–28; November 19, 24–28; and November 26, 24–29; reprinted in *Life Stories: Profiles from "The New Yorker,"* ed. David Remnick (New York: Random House, 2000), 245–74.

82. *New York Times,* May 11, 1934, 43.

83. *New York Times,* November 1, 1947, 32; November 2, 1947, 20; November 4, 1947, 27; March 2, 1948, 21.

84. *New York Times,* February 2, 1934, 6, col. 5; November 27, 1934, 17, col. 2.

85. "Peter Arno by Peter Arno," 11. The date of these slight but tantalizing biographical jottings is not given. They appear to have been written after Arno had given up New York and retired to his farm in Harrison, New York, possibly as notes for a talk.

86. "Peter Arno by Peter Arno," 13.

87. The name suffers all the time. Even Kunkel gets it wrong, calling him Curtis Arnaux [*sic*] Peters in *Genius in Disguise,* 124.

88. See, for example, *The New Yorker,* April 12, 1954, 13. The advertisements, which combined photograph images with line drawings, were perhaps influenced by some of Saul Steinberg's work, published in *The Passport* (1954) but in hand since the late forties.

89. "Peter Arno by Peter Arno," 10.

90. For another view on this, see Charles Saxon's remarks in his introduction to *Seasons at "The New Yorker,"* xvi.

91. "Peter Arno by Peter Arno," 11.

92. See William E. Leuchtenberg, *The Perils of Prosperity, 1914–1932* (Chicago: University of Chicago Press, 1958), 188.

93. These are the covers for March 23, 1935; July 4, 1936; November 7, 1936; April 24, 1937; October 16, 1937; October 29, 1938; June 22, 1940; February 1, 1941; August 2, 1941; October 24, 1942; April 3, 1943; July 10, 1948; December 25, 1948; January 29, 1949; and March 11, 1950. The covers are reproduced in *The Complete Book of Covers from "The New Yorker"* (New York: Alfred A. Knopf, 1989).

94. Arno himself was violent to women. Thomas Kunkel quotes *New Yorker* con-

tributor Marcia Davenport's description of Lois Long's arriving at the office with bruises or a black eye (Kunkel, *Genius in Disguise,* 165). This was also the testimony of his daughter, Patricia Arno Maxwell (interview).

95. As reported by Charles Saxon in his introduction to *Seasons at "The New Yorker,"* xvi.

96. White, *Here Is New York,* 19.

97. How alive Arno's work is can be seen by comparing him with a recent imitator, Robert Sikoryak. See the cover for *The New Yorker,* July 21, 1997.

98. For other versions of this joke see *Peter Arno's Parade:* "How am I? Amusing?" A later example from *Man in the Shower* is "Very good, Mr. Duncan! A month ago you couldn't have done this."

99. The same man shows what is either extreme sexual naïveté or extreme *pudeur,* as in "One would think she'd be subject to a series of nasty colds" (in *Peter Arno,* 107); or "What is the specialty here?" (the latter reproduced in Brendan Gill, *Here at "The New Yorker,"* 88); or "She seems to have a remarkable command of the language" (from *Peter Arno's Man in the Shower*), all said in relation to a gesticulating, half-undressed female dancer.

100. Lorenz, *Art of "The New Yorker,"* 31.

101. See, for example, Barbara Ehrenreich's *The Hearts of Men* (London: Pluto Press, 1983).

102. Patricia Arno Maxwell, interview.

2. William Steig

1. Yagoda says, "especially Jews moving into the middle class," but although he draws a few cartoons on this theme, Steig could hardly be said to embrace it enthusiastically. See Ben Yagoda, *About Town: "The New Yorker" and the World It Made* (New York: Scribner's, 2000), 67.

2. According to Steig he met Arno only once, at Ross's funeral. The characterization of Arno as an "aristocrat" is Steig's. Interview with William Steig at the artist's home in Kent, Connecticut, June 30, 1990.

3. Price's first cartoon, mildly anti-Semitic in nature, appeared in the issue for June 3, 1933; Hoff had first published a little earlier.

4. Dwight Macdonald, "Laugh and Lie Down," *Partisan Review,* December 1937, 46–47.

5. I have adapted this list from a very similar one in Christopher Lasch, *The Culture of Narcissism* (New York: Norton, 1978), xvi. Lasch's point is that these have been weakened or destroyed by "advanced capitalism" itself.

6. As a parent, Steig was liberal concerning his children's sexual morality but keen to convey to them his values, morals, and ethics. Letter from Maggie Steig, January 27, 2004.

7. William Steig, preface to *Dreams of Glory* (1955), quoted in *Contemporary Authors,* New Revision Series, vol. 21 (Detroit: Gale Research, 1987), 426.

8. According to Jeanne Steig, cited in comments made to me by the artist's daughter, Maggie Steig, December 24, 2003.

9. Steig's family disputes that Steig was particularly influenced by Horney and Reich. Interview with Maggie Steig, December 24, 2003.

10. I work into this sentence some important phrases taken from what is one of the best definitions of humor in print—that of Stephen Potter in his seemingly anecdotal, but in fact deeply reflective, essay and anthology *The Sense of Humour* (Harmondsworth, England: Penguin Books, 1964), 29, 38, 58.

11. Steig, quoted by Charles Saxon in his introduction to *Seasons at "The New Yorker"* (New York: National Academy of Design and United Technologies Corporation, 1984), xiv. Steig is referring specifically to cover illustrations, but his comment can be transferred to cartoons without any sense of strain.

12. See the drawing captioned, "Go ahead, take in Mrs. Blodgett! Let the whole Bronx be members." *The New Yorker,* June 17, 1933, 15.

13. These details are taken from Whitney Balliett's introduction, "On William Steig," to Steig's collection *Ruminations* (New York: Farrar, Straus and Giroux, 1984), n.p.; from Joshua Hammer, "William Steig," *People,* December 3, 1984; and from information supplied by Maggie Steig in a letter dated January 27, 2004.

14. Israel Shenker, "Steig, Surviving as He Nears Sixty-five, Finds Peace in Being a Depressed Cartoonist," *New York Times,* November 14, 1972, 49.

15. Quoted by Alfred Kazin, *New York Jew* (New York: Alfred A. Knopf, 1978), 9. Kazin's father was a housepainter, like Steig's.

16. The Bronx is too often viewed through its present decline, as if it has always been decayed and crime-ridden. In reality it was far from underprivileged. Between 1888 and 1939, when its population was nearly 50 percent Jewish, it was a wealthy borough with extensive commercial, cultural, and educational development. See, for example, the summary history of the Bronx in this period as given by Gary D. Hermalyn and Lloyd Ultan in Kenneth T. Jackson's *The Encyclopedia of New York City* (New Haven: Yale University Press; New York: New-York Historical Society, 1995), 142–46, esp. 144–45. See also the account of the borough, with a carefully delineated contrast between the dilapidated South Bronx and more well-to-do areas, in the Federal Writers' Project's *New York City Guide* (New York: Federal Writers' Project, 1939). Hermalyn and Ultan describe the period between 1888 and 1928 as one of "tremendous growth" and draw attention to several important features: residential developments intended for wealthy upper Manhattan residents about 1863–67; the purchase in 1888 by a specially appointed commission of large tracts of land for public parks (including what became Van Cortlandt, Crotona, Claremont, Bronx, and Pelham Bay parks); the commission for street improvements in 1890 that planned and built the Grand Concourse, "modeled after the Champs-Élysées . . . lined with trees . . . and [including] an innovative design based on the use of underpasses at major street crossings"; the establishment in 1891 of the New York Botanical Gardens in the northern section of the Bronx Park and the Bronx Zoo in the southern section; the New York University campus at University Heights ("including a Hall of Fame for Great Americans," the first Hall of Fame in the world) and the Bronx High School of Science, famous in later years for its distinguished alumni; the various subway and elevated railway extensions into the Bronx from the 1890s onward that, during the first thirty years of the century, "persuaded hundreds of thousands . . . to leave the tenements of Manhattan

for the spacious new apartments in the Bronx . . . the largest group Jews from central and eastern Europe"; the subsequent "rapid growth" of the borough's economy; the concentration and diversity of the local economy from small neighborhood businesses and shops (often highly specialized) to boutiques and large department stores (in 1938 Alexander's "made more sales per square foot than any other department store in the nation"); developments such as Loewe's Paradise Theatre built in 1929 at a cost of $4,000,000 on the Grand Concourse, with elaborate baroque decor and seating for 4,000 people; the expansion of "privately financed apartments" north of the Grand Concourse even during the Depression that "became a symbol of social and economic success"; the largest housing development of the time, Parkchester, which housed 40,000 residents and had parks, playgrounds, sculpture, convenience stores," and so on; and sporting venues such as Yankee Stadium (1923). They also quote statistics showing that by 1934 the borough had many more amenities than other boroughs did—99 percent of residences with private bathrooms, 95 percent with central heating; 97 percent with running water; and 48 percent with mechanical refrigeration. The urban environment described here had much to offer young people growing up in its midst. It was not a uniformly well-endowed place, of course—there were tenements and blighted industrial neighborhoods, and it obviously was not wealthy compared with stretches of Fifth Avenue and Park Avenue. But it was well-off compared with similar city boroughs (Queens, for example). Of course, Steig's own Bronx was the modest world of aspiring Jewish immigrants, small businessmen like his father, the world as described in detail in Ruth Gay's *Unfinished People: Eastern European Jews Encounter America* (New York: Norton, 1996). But it is important to grasp that Steig's Bronx did not constitute an impoverished or underprivileged background and not to underestimate the municipal resources or the social integrity of the Bronx in the first third of this century. Even accounts of poor Jewish lives in the Bronx in this period stress these simple facts.

17. *New York Times,* sect. 9, May 24, 1936, 8:1. Steig's mother also exhibited and was reviewed in *New York Times,* sect. 9, November 20, 1938, 10:2.

18. Family details from Balliett, introduction to *Ruminations,* and from Maggie Steig in conversation December 24, 2003. Arthur Steig "produced the best white gouache paint on the market, with great covering power. Also a line of colored inks for drawing or brushwork."

19. Henry Steig, *Send Me Down* (New York: Alfred A. Knopf, 1941), 7.

20. Henry R. Luce bought out the old *Life* magazine and in 1936 transformed it into a magazine specializing in high-quality photojournalism.

21. The sum is quoted in Steig's obituary, *New York Times,* October 5, 2003. In 1928 the average income per four-person family was $2,980 (see Norman Ware, *Labor in Modern Industrial Society* [New York: D. C. Heath, 1935], 14).

22. This is questioned by members of Steig's family, who maintain that *The New Yorker* was Steig's first publishing breakthrough. Yet the chronology suggests otherwise. Many of the drawings in *Man About Town* (New York: R. Long and R. R. Smith, 1932) did not appear in *The New Yorker.*

23. This is well above the average rate for a regular artist, few of whom would have had more than twenty-six drawings accepted in a single year. It is doubtful that

any artist except Hokinson published more—even a favored artist like Arno rarely achieved a publishing strike rate of more than 65 percent.

24. Quoted by Hammer, "William Steig." Copy from *Inside Edit: The New Yorker,* clipping in the Nicholls Archive.

25. Hammer, "William Steig."

26. [Ralph Ingersoll], *"The New Yorker," Fortune,* August 1934, 86. Irvin's long-standing lack of enthusiasm for Steig's work, and Steig's mistaken belief that it was Carmine Pepe who was against him, is discussed by Lee Lorenz in *The Art of "The New Yorker"* (New York: Alfred A. Knopf, 1995), 150.

27. A cartoon in which two Mexicans lazing in the sun debate whether "my wife can carry more wood than yours" may not escape criticism for its facile racial stereo-typing, but its humor is clearly designed to unmask the men as sexist.

28. This is not to ignore the fact that in the early thirties Steig often drew cartoons with upper-class characters in tune with *The New Yorker*'s general ethos: one shows a smart little boy offering a dime to a man asking for a handout and saying, "Are you sure it's for coffee?" (*The New Yorker,* January 16, 1932, 21). But as this example shows, the situation depicted can easily be looked at from either end of the social spectrum.

29. Margaret Mead, *Blackberry Winter: My Earlier Years* (New York: Washington Square Press, 1972), 89.

30. Others include "Dispensers of Wit" (*The New Yorker,* May 4, 1935, 18–19); "Holiday Trials" (December 26, 1936, 22–23); "A Variety of Lies" (March 27, 1937, 20–21); and "Strange People" (November 28, 1936).

31. Drawings of children with adults had appeared earlier; for example, the covers for May 7, 1932, July 2, 1932, and November 19, 1932. In the September 2, 1933, cover, however, adults are shown only in the distant background and are not part of the action.

32. William Steig, preface to *Dreams of Glory* (1955), quoted in *Contemporary Authors,* 21:426–27.

33. Diana Trilling, "Small Fry: Twenty Years Later," *New Republic,* January 25, 1943, 124.

34. There is a whole genre of cartoons in *The New Yorker* that shows children aping, or being corrupted by, adult manners, usually associated with sexual themes.

35. Cf. Kenneth Burke's observation that for the United States the positive symbol is "the people," not "the workers," and that in the case of America the doctrine of revolutionary thought cannot be extended without using "middle-class values." Steig's career is a textbook demonstration of what Burke means. See Walter I. Susman, *Culture as History: The Transformation of American Society in the Twentieth Century* (New York: Pantheon, 1984), 211, from which this remark of Burke's is drawn.

36. Obituary by Sarah Boxer, "William Steig, 95, Dies: Tough Youths and Jealous Satyrs Scowled in His Cartoons," *New York Times,* October 5, 2003.

37. Shenker, "Steig," 49.

38. Interview with William Steig, Kent, Connecticut, June 30, 1990.

39. Charles Poore, "Marriage—by Wm. Steig," *New York Times,* February 23, 1947, sec. 6, 16–17.

40. Information from Maggie Steig in conversation, December 24, 2003.

41. The Steig family rejects the idea that Steig conceptualized neurosis in the ways I am going to suggest. They believe that he was probably not thinking about neurosis when he drew and that he did not feel pressure from "society" but, as a nonacquisitive person, lived very simply. I should make it plain then that my argument about neurosis, which is sparked partly by passing remarks that Steig himself made over the years to interviewers but mainly by the nature of the drawings of the forties, is confined entirely to the decade 1939–49 and is meant not to trespass on Steig's conscious intentions (which I think are irrecoverable anyway) but to open up thought about a set of very difficult and sometimes disturbing drawings. The Steig in whose company I spent an inspiring and uplifting afternoon in 1990 was undoubtedly a completely fulfilled man, entirely at peace with himself, living for and through his work and his family. (He was, for example, far more ready to talk about the achievements of his children than his own paintings.)

42. Quoted in Jane Howard, *Margaret Mead* (London: Harvill, 1984), 199.

43. Karen Horney, *The Neurotic Personality of Our Time* (New York: Norton, 1937), 26.

44. "Neurosis" is no longer used as a diagnostic term.

45. Horney, *Neurotic Personality,* 284.

46. Horney, *Neurotic Personality,* 287.

47. Horney, *Neurotic Personality,* 289.

48. William Steig, *The Lonely Ones,* with a foreword by Wolcott Gibbs (New York: Duell, Sloan and Pearce, 1942).

49. Lorenz, *Art of "The New Yorker,"* 150.

50. In the 1980s Steig told Whitney Balliett, "I'm crazy about Picasso." See the introduction to *Ruminations.* The reluctance to see Picasso critically is typical of the period.

51. My copy is the tenth printing and has been inscribed by "H. Medill Sarkisian, Capt. MI5" to "Arthur Rothstein" as a gift, dated August 20, 1945, Kunming, China.

52. Horney, *Neurotic Personality,* 96.

53. Horney, *Neurotic Personality,* 219.

54. Horney, *Neurotic Personality,* 35–40.

55. Wolcott Gibbs, foreword to Steig's *The Lonely Ones.*

56. See W. H. Auden, "The Icon and the Portrait," in *Nation* 150, no. 2 (January 13, 1940): 48, and "New Year Letter," part 3 in *W. H. Auden: Collected Poems,* ed. Edward Mendelson (London: Faber and Faber, 1976), 186.

57. The exact date is hard to pin down. Steig told me that his first book on psychoanalytic themes (*About People* [New York: Duell, Sloan and Pearce, 1939], but perhaps *The Lonely Ones* [New York: Duell, Sloan and Pearce, 1942] as well) was not influenced by Reich. *Till Death Do Us Part: Some Ballet Notes on Marriage* (New York: Duell, Sloan and Pearce, 1947) is clearly a Reichian text. The collection that appears in between them—*Persistent Faces* (New York: Duell, Sloan and Pearce, 1945)—certainly appears to be influenced by Reich. This, then, points to a first contact somewhere between 1942 and 1945. In his biography of Reich, Myron Sharaf says that Steig was a patient of Reich's in the "mid-forties." See Myron Sharaf, *Fury on Earth: A Biography of Wilhelm Reich* (New York: St. Martin's Press, 1983), 346.

58. None of these men were actually in analysis with Reich, although Bellow was a patient of a follower of Reich.

59. Interview with William Steig. See also Steig's obituary, *New York Times,* October 5, 2003.

60. For an account of Steig's relationship with Reich, see Sharaf, *Fury on Earth,* 346 and 437.

61. Steig interviewed for *Contemporary Authors* in 1986, 21:427.

62. *Contemporary Authors,* 21:427.

63. See Hammer for one version of this anecdote. The curing of Mrs. Steig's breast cancer is frequently cited by Reich's supporters as proof of the efficacy of Reich's orgone therapy. The FBI destroyed many of Reich's orgone boxes during a 1956 raid on the Reich clinic, Organon, in New Hampshire, and the description of this by Reich's son makes distressing reading, even for the detached reader. In the context of modern alternative medicine, Reich's orgone therapy now seems run-of-the-mill stuff (if no more credible), and it requires considerable effort to understand the kind of professional paranoia that led to what is justly described as his persecution. Steig makes a reasonable point when he notes that Reich's orgone theory has affinities with other less controversial notions of cosmic energy: Newton's ether, Kepler's *vis animalis,* Bergson's *élan vital.* But these were frankly speculative entities or metaphorical terms, whereas Reich claimed to have actually observed and measured the orgone. Part of the paradox of Reich's position was that in declaring that orgone energy could be observed and measured he succumbed to the very scientism he otherwise hated—and also set the scene for his own downfall. Psychoanalysis was still trying to establish itself as a genuine science and wanted little truck with bizarre figures like Reich—hence his expulsion from the International Psychoanalytic Association in 1934. No doubt Reich's Marxism was also crucial in arousing the Eisenhower administration's suspicions about him.

64. Summarizing Reich is difficult because he never achieved an elegant syntheses of his own ideas and lacked almost completely Freud's gift for persuasive exposition.

65. Philip Rieff, *The Triumph of the Therapeutic: Uses of Faith after Freud* (New York: Harper and Row, 1966), 175.

66. Wilhelm Reich, *Character Analysis* (New York: Farrar, Straus and Giroux, 1972), xxii.

67. Reich, *Character Analysis,* xxii–xxiii.

68. Reich, *Character Analysis,* xxiv.

69. Reich, *Character Analysis,* xxiv.

70. Reich, *Character Analysis,* 186.

71. Reich, *Character Analysis,* 187.

72. Reich, *Character Analysis,* 51–52.

73. Reich, *Character Analysis,* 155–56.

74. Reich, *Character Analysis,* 353.

75. See, for example, *Character Analysis,* footnote dated 1945, 297, and also Charles Rycroft, *Reich* (London: Fontana Collins, 1971), 85. Reich's letters show that he had written to Einstein as early as December 1940, hoping to enlist his support in establishing the orgone as an observable phenomenon.

76. Reich, *Character Analysis,* 337.

77. Reich, *Character Analysis,* 340.

78. Reich, *Character Analysis,* 507.

79. Reich, *Character Analysis,* 508.

80. Wilhelm Reich, *Listen, Little Man! A Document from the Archives of the Orgone Institute* (Harmondsworth, England: Penguin, 1975), 8.

81. Lorenz, *Art of "The New Yorker,"* 151, says that Steig began this only in the 1970s, but Steig's psychoanalytic drawings from the 1940s cannot possibly have been underdrawn.

82. Thus J.-J. Sempé has remarked that he draws scores of versions freehand — at least a hundred in the case of a portrait of Duke Ellington — until he comes up with the perfect version. J.-J. Sempé, *The Musicians, by Sempé* (New York: Workman Press, 1980), jacket notes.

83. Steig continued to do underdrawing for his children's books from the late 1960s onward in order to maintain continuity. This was one of the reasons he did not like illustrating, because it was not free art. Information from Maggie Steig, letter, January 27, 2004.

84. Reich, *Character Analysis,* 366.

85. Shenker, "Steig," 49, and Steig as quoted by Lillian Ross in her introduction to *William Steig* (New York: Farrar, Straus and Giroux, 1979).

86. Steig uses the phrase of himself and his own efforts to conform in Shenker, "Steig," 49.

87. Reich, *Character Analysis,* 155.

88. Compare Ronald Searle, who used "to keep one finger awkwardly separated from his pen with tape to inhibit his natural fluency." Quoted by Alan Ross, "The Pursuit of Line," *Times Literary Supplement,* November 2–8, 1990, 1176.

89. This procedure is confirmed by Balliett, "On William Steig": "I used to start a drawing with an idea in mind, but now I draw without knowing what I am going to do."

90. Reich, *Character Analysis,* xxiv.

91. Reich, *Character Analysis,* 204.

92. Trilling, "Small Fry," 124.

93. Steig did accept advertising commissions during the period, most notably for *The Saturday Evening Post* (eighteen advertisements) in the early forties.

94. Steig now had a new publisher. *The Rejected Lovers* was published by Alfred A. Knopf in 1951. Duell, Sloan and Pearce, who had published all of Steig's previous collections, reissued seven of his books as a single volume in the 1950s.

95. William Steig, foreword to *The Rejected Lovers* (New York: Alfred A. Knopf, 1951), v.

96. Steig, *Rejected Lovers,* vi.

97. On pages 17, 37, 57, 79, 95, 113, 115, 145, 149, and 153.

98. See the drawings on pages 10, 38, and 78, for example.

99. W. H. Auden, "The Icon and the Portrait," *Nation* 150, no. 2 (January 13, 1940): 48.

100. Reich, *Character Analysis*, 354.

101. Notably D. W. Winnicott in his *Playing and Reality* (London: Tavistock, 1971). Besides attacking "day-dreaming" as uncreative, Winnicott makes a strong case that it is in play of all kinds—including cultural activity—that growth of self is possible.

102. Brendan Gill, *Here at "The New Yorker"* (New York: Random House, 1975), 235.

103. Lillian Ross, *Here but Not Here: A Love Affair* (New York: Random House, 1998), 17.

104. Steig's popularity among editors looking for seasonal covers did not wane: a cover published under the editorship of Tina Brown is on the Thanksgiving issue for November 30, 1998.

105. Since covers were generally scheduled more than six months ahead, I look at the covers first.

106. The sequence is reprinted in *"The New Yorker" Album 1955–1965: Fortieth Anniversary* (New York: Harper and Row, 1965).

107. Lorenz discusses the use of color in *Art of "The New Yorker,"* 154–55. Gottleib's first issue was that of March 2, 1987.

108. Information from Maggie Steig in conversation, December 24, 2003.

109. "Why did I want to make so much money? Because I was paying alimony. I had that type of problem." Steig, quoted by Lawrence van Gelder, ca. 1977; Nicholls Archive clipping, no source. The marriage to Elizabeth Mead ended on amicable terms, and Elizabeth asked for no alimony from her husband, although Steig provided for the children from this marriage. He paid alimony and child support for the later marriages. Information from Maggie Steig in a letter, January 27, 2004.

110. Among Steig's advertisements are drawings for Taylor Instruments (May 18, 1944) and the *Saturday Evening Post* (September 21, 1940). Steig insisted in 1990 that he had always had moral objections to advertising but confessed that the money was easy, especially for animated cartoons. He recalled artists' lunches in the 1960s, in the days when most of them lived in New York: "The artists who made money out of stocks would sit on one side, the rest on the other. I myself went into children's books." By the end of his life Steig, although well paid for his work for *The New Yorker* ($1,000 for a cartoon, $3,500 for a cover), derived most of his income from the children's books. Interview with William Steig, June 30, 1990.

111. Steig, interviewed by *Contemporary Authors,* 21:427.

112. Shenker, "Steig," 49.

113. Interview with William Steig, June 30, 1990.

114. Maggie Steig in conversation, December 24, 2003.

115. The conference attempted to get the book banned from school and public libraries by organizing a letter-writing campaign against it, which had some limited success. Steig defended himself wittily in the letters column of the *New York Times* (March 3, 1971).

116. For an account of Steig as an author of children's books, see Leonard S. Marcus, *A Caldecott Celebration: Six Artists and Their Paths to the Caldecott Medal* (New York: Walker, 1998).

117. See the discussion of this question in the chapter 1.

118. See the account in Ruth Miller, *Saul Bellow: A Biography of the Imagination* (New York: St. Martin's Press, 1990).

119. He disliked men with ponytails and beards, and though he hated suits and ties, he dressed conservatively—that is to say, in jeans with a neat button-down sports shirt, according to his daughter (letter, January 27, 2004).

120. Shenker, "Steig," 49.

121. Alexander Chancellor, *Some Times in America, and a Life in a Year at "The New Yorker"* (New York: Carroll and Graf, 2000), 305–7. It complicates this anecdote a little to know that in fact Chancellor's first choice was a painting by Saul Steinberg—but the point being made remains.

3. Charles Addams

1. For responses to these questions see the forum in the "Opinion" pages of the *Sunday Age* (Melbourne, Australia), October 29, 2000, including an opinion from me. The respondents considered whether 9/11 could ever itself be made an unforced occasion for humor, something that seemed completely impossible in the shadow of the event, certainly in mainstream popular culture. And yet, to take one example, a television special of the British comedy show *Absolutely Fabulous* set in New York and screened on ABC TV in Australia on March 10, 2003, managed to do this when the character named Edina explained to her daughter that she was worried about going to New York because "you know, honey, of all that business, that 7/11 stuff."

2. For the text of Roosevelt's speech see *New York Times,* January 5, 1939; for a summary see *Keesing's Contemporary Archives, 1937–1940,* vol. 3 (Bristol, England: Kessing's, [ca. 1941]), 3391–92. For a discussion see Kenneth Davis, *FDR, Into the Storm, 1937–1940: A History,* vol. 3 (New York: Random House, 1993), 388.

3. In exceptional circumstances copy could be altered at the last minute, as it was when Harold Ross died at 6:30 p.m. on Thursday, December 6, 1951. The next issue, datelined Saturday, December 15, but as usual to be ready for distribution by Monday, December 10, was about to close. This gave E. B. White just enough time to compose an obituary. See Thomas Kunkel, *Genius in Disguise: Harold Ross of "The New Yorker"* (New York: Random House, 1995), 429–32. The complexities of typesetting and layout in the days of Linotype and bromides, the time required to photoengrave illustrations, the fact that the magazine was not printed in New York, and the complicated distribution network all meant that the gap could never be closed to less than four or five days. Officially, *New Yorker* cartoons were not intended to comment either on current affairs or on the surrounding articles. See Charles Saxon's comments on these matters in his introduction to *Seasons at "The New Yorker"* (New York: United Technologies Corporation and the National Academy of Design, 1984), xv. The rule was not always observed: for example, after President Kennedy's very upbeat State of the Union address on January 14, 1963, James Stevenson had a cartoon published that not only mentioned it directly but made sense only if the reader recalled the gist of what Kennedy had said (see *The New Yorker,* January 26, 1963, 25).

4. The issue is discussed interestingly by E. B. White in a "Talk of the Town"

comment piece in *The New Yorker*, September 2, 1939. The phrase "the impossible interim of magazine publishing" is White's.

5. For another example see the discussion in the following chapter of Saul Steinberg's "The Pursuit of Happiness" (fig. 4.11), published as the cover for the issue dated January 17, 1959, a week after President Eisenhower's State of the Union address.

6. Quoted in *New York Times* (November 19, 1974). Shawn, a deeply phobic man (see Lillian Ross's memoir of her love affair with Shawn, *Here but Not Here: A Love Story* [New York, Random House, 1998]), was in many ways the ideal reader of Addams's work.

7. Both quoted in *Contemporary Authors New Review Series* (Detroit: Gale Research, 1984), 12:19.

8. Jesse Bier, *The Rise and Fall of American Humor* (New York: Holt, Rinehart and Winston, 1968), 292.

9. There is a third possibility. There is a real question whether this joke is literally about blowing up buildings and people. One laughs at a contrast rather than a content, and the content is put there only provisionally, to set up the contrast. The joking contrast here, the bisociation on which the joke is founded, the primary content, is the contrast between two clichés—the sedate, clubbable world of alumni associations and the violent, antisocial world of the dedicated revolutionary. This contrast is solidly grounded in the specificity with which both worlds are evoked in the drawing—the exactness of the wording of the caption and the exactness of the drawing. The quotation marks in the alumni association's letter, for example, suggest an uncertainty about the excessive use of colloquialism characteristic of communications that have to be both official and chummy. It also vividly evokes an innocence that is completely reassuring in its concern with the petty rituals of the everyday and commonplace. The staggering detail of the drawing—the rendering of the revolutionary's model of the Capitol—just as surely evokes the self-absorption and paranoid dedication of the fanatic all too familiar after September 11, 2001. What is funny is the collision between these two frames of reference, and the revolutionary is no more to be taken seriously than the alumni association secretary. For another cartoon that has a disturbing contemporary relevance, see the drawing of concertgoers, two of whom have noticed one member of the orchestra standing by a detonating handle, patiently waiting his cue (collected in *Creature Comforts* [New York: Simon and Schuster, 1981]).

10. Addams made a habit of offering a discordant view of Christmas: a cartoon in *The New Yorker*, December 23, 1939, for example, showed a group of carol singers outside a house in which we see the occupants beaten, tied up, and robbed.

11. For the importance of these terms in a discussion of American culture in the first part of the previous century, see Alfred Kazin's review of Van Wyck Brooks's *The Confident Years: 1885–1915* (New York: Dutton, 1952) in *The New Yorker*, January 26, 1952, 93–96.

12. As a comparison, see Steig's "Small Fry" cartoon of angelic child carol singers in *The New Yorker*, December 23, 1933, 22.

13. Henry James, *The Europeans*, Bodley Head Henry James, vol. 1 (London: Bodley Head, 1967), 30–35.

14. The Westfield city Web site proclaims a house on East Dudley Street as the Addams house. It is worth recording that in an interview with the *Philadelphia Inquirer* in 1976 Addams denied that the mansion was based directly on an actual house. Jack Severson, "The Man Who Gives Us the Creeps," *Philadelphia Inquirer,* November 11, 1976, 36. Clipping from Nicholls Archive.

15. Hopper's painting is in the Museum of Modern Art, New York. Hopper's house is possibly based on one in Haverstraw, just north of Nyack (see Gail Levin, *Hopper's Places* [Berkeley: University of California Press, 1998]), but Jo Hopper told a correspondent who had found this house that Hopper had seen many such buildings and had painted his house "out of his head." I am grateful to John Wiltshire for drawing Hopper's painting to my attention and telling me about its importance for Hitchcock.

16. See Gail Levin, *Edward Hopper: An Intimate Biography* (New York: Alfred A. Knopf, 1996), 536. The Hoppers learned of the link in an article by Archer Winsten in the *New York Evening Post,* June 13, 1960, and Hitchcock later confirmed the story in a letter to the Hoppers.

17. To complicate the matter even further, the house in *Psycho* is always described as a standing set—that is, already built and not constructed especially for the film—on the Universal lot, where it can be seen to this day. See Michael Haley, *The Alfred Hitchcock Album* (Englewood Cliffs, NJ: Prentice-Hall, 1981), 105.

18. Addams, quoted by Wilfrid Sheed in his introduction to *The World of Charles Addams* (London: Hamish Hamilton, 1992), x.

19. The hint is given although not developed by Wilfrid Sheed in his introduction to *World of Charles Addams,* xii. See also H. Kevin Miserocchi's catalog, *Charles Addams: American Gothic,* prepared to accompany an exhibition of Addams's cartoons at the Guild Hall, East Hampton, New York, October 2002–January 2003.

20. Charles Brockden Brown, *Wieland, or The Transformation: An American Tale* (New York, 1798). For a good discussion relevant to my argument see Jay Fliegelman's introduction to the Viking-Penguin edition of *Wieland* (New York: Viking-Penguin, 1991).

21. See Louis Gross, *Redefining the American Gothic: From Wieland to Day of the Dead* (Ann Arbor: UMI Research Press, 1989), 2.

22. Mark Edmundson, *Nightmare on Main Street: Angels, Sadomasochism, and the Culture of the Gothic* (Cambridge: Harvard University Press, 1997), xii.

23. Donald A. Ringe, *American Gothic: Imagination and Reason in Nineteenth-Century Fiction* (Lexington: University Press of Kentucky, 1982), 2. For a very different response to this inheritance, see the discussion of Saul Steinberg and Freemasonry in the following chapter.

24. Ringe, *American Gothic,* 3.

25. That is, "anxiety" in the classic sense, meaning manifestly unrealistic fears and worries, fears for which there is no apparent or objective cause.

26. Cf. the Australian value of "mateship."

27. Ringe, *American Gothic,* 2.

28. The argument that follows is drawn directly from Ringe, *American Gothic.* Ringe, stressing the centrality of the rationalist tradition, quotes Hawthorne's preface

to *The Marble Fawn,* in which the novelist complains of the commonplace prosperity of American life, where everything takes place in "the broad and simple daylight," as the summation of this state of affairs.

29. Gross, *Redefining the American Gothic,* 89.

30. Gross, *Redefining the American Gothic,* 91. The rest of this section is a summary of Gross's argument, adopting a number of his key phrases; see 89–90.

31. Gross, *Redefining the American Gothic,* 91.

32. Gross, *Redefining the American Gothic,* 76.

33. See the helpful annual summary of the gothic in F. S. Frank, *Through the Pale Door: A Guide to and through the American Gothic* (New York: Greenwood Press, 1990).

34. Severson, "Man Who Gives Us the Creeps," 37, and *New York Times,* September 30, 1974.

35. Sheed, introduction to *World of Charles Addams,* ix.

36. Sheed, introduction to *World of Charles Addams,* viii.

37. The quotations come from Wolcott Gibbs's preface to *Addams and Evil* (New York, Random House, 1947); W. J. Weather, *Guardian,* October 1, 1988; Brendan Gill, *Here at "The New Yorker"* (New York: Random House, 1975), 222; Wilfrid Sheed's introduction to *World of Charles Addams;* and Lee Lorenz, *The Art of "The New Yorker"* (New York: Alfred A. Knopf, 1995), 109.

38. Severson, "Man Who Gives Us the Creeps," 37.

39. Severson, "Man Who Gives Us the Creeps," 37. Other versions have Addams working for a "court newspaper," where his job was "to mark police photographs with the position of the corpse," as reported in the *Frankischer Anzeiger* (Rothenburg), February 27, 1971. Clipping in the Nicholls Archive.

40. Severson, "Man Who Gives Us the Creeps," 37.

41. He had already published in the issue of February 6, 1932, a spot drawing of a window cleaner seen from above, at work on a Manhattan skyscraper high above the street; reproduced in *World of Charles Addams,* x.

42. The cartoon does not appear in the UMI microfilm version of *The New Yorker* because the copy text used for the microfilm edition is the national ("star") edition rather than the metropolitan edition. There were sometimes copy differences between the two issues.

43. [Ralph Ingersoll], "*The New Yorker,*" *Fortune,* August 1934, 90.

44. Severson says Addams sold fourteen drawings, but twenty-five appear in *The Complete Cartoons of "The New Yorker"* CD ROM. See Severson, "Man Who Gives Us the Creeps," 39.

45. "A staff contributor," wrote Geoffrey Hellman, "is what is known in the Internal Revenue Department as a small businessman. He is a free-lance surrounded by such fringe benefits as a desk, a chair, a typewriter [drawing board and light box in the case of cartoonists], stationery, a pension plan, medical insurance, and two wire baskets, one for incoming mail and one for outgoing" (Geoffrey Hellman, "My Life and Times with *The New Yorker,*" *New-York Historical Society Quarterly* 52 (1968): 48–60, quotation on 48.

46. [Ingersoll], "*The New Yorker,*" 90.

47. In the mid-1970s Addams told Jack Severson that *The New Yorker* paid him

a basic rate of between $800 and $1,200 a cartoon, depending on the size, and $2,300 for a cover. A system of bonuses applied after the first ten drawings, and after the second ten, and so on. Addams originals could be bought for about $1,000 at that time. Severson, "Man Who Gives Us the Creeps," 37.

48. Addams's strike rate was never very high and was much less than one would suppose, considering the impact his work made. In the forties it hovered around 50 percent. Between 1950 and 1959, when he was at the height of his powers, it was about 38 percent (a total of 98 cartoons plus 13 covers). In the sixties it dropped to 20 percent (87 cartoons plus 14 covers). By the early seventies it had risen to 26 percent. Later (for example, July 1986 to June 1987, the last six months of Shawn's editorship and the first six of Gottleib's), it had picked up to about 32 percent.

49. Quoted by Sheed, introduction to *World of Charles Addams.*

50. It is only fair to note that William O'Brian anticipated jokes on this theme with a cartoon in *The New Yorker,* January 25, 1958, 33, and that James Stevenson carried it forward at least ten years before, with a drawing showing a middle-aged couple watching a distant group on the beach wrestling with a sea serpent: "Say, isn't that George Burckhart and his boys?" See *"The New Yorker" Album 1955–1965: Fortieth Anniversary* (New York: Harper and Row, 1965), [287].

51. An alternative reading is that the big-game hunter has also bagged the unicyclist.

52. For a discussion that takes a contrary view, see Mary F. Corey, *The World through a Monocle: "The New Yorker" at Midcentury* (Cambridge: Harvard University Press, 1999), 84. Corey concedes that certain of Addams's cartoons can be read as "a veiled critique of American imperialism," but she thinks they are implicitly racist (88). Corey has some telling criticisms of two of Addams's worst cartoons (86), but when she argues that others tend to suggest that "primitive people are just like us, but they haven't quite got it right" (85), she minimizes the disruptiveness of his humor. She pays little attention to Addams's more overtly subversive cartoons, which I think is an omission. I understand, of course, that from a poststructuralist perspective the racism is the trace of a crucial and foundational cultural paradigm. The trouble with this argument is that it emphasizes what I think is obvious and granted (that in the 1940s—or whatever decade—racism was everywhere in Western cultures) and plays down what I think is less obvious (that some mental events even then were loosening the hold of such attitudes). For a discussion of the idea that jokes often use clichés and stereotypes opportunistically rather than substantively, see Ted Cohen, *Jokes: Philosophical Thoughts on Joking Matters* (Chicago: University of Chicago Press, 1999), 21–22. Cohen argues that all such jokes are "conditional"—not on our agreeing with the stereotype but on our knowledge of it—and he also says that if we are offended by the stereotype, or reject it, then the joke will fail.

53. Sigmund Freud, *Jokes and Their Relation to the Unconscious,* Penguin Freud Library, vol. 6 (Harmondsworth, England: Penguin Books, 1991), 161.

54. This joke is discussed by Ronald Paulson, *Figure and Abstraction in Contemporary Painting* (New Brunswick: Rutgers University Press, 1990), 85.

55. See Freud, from whom the argument here is taken, on the subversion of "critical reason" as a motivation for jokes, especially *Jokes,* 176–83, 189, and 227.

56. Freud, *Jokes,* 161.

57. Freud, *Jokes,* 132.

58. Bier, *Rise and Fall of American Humor,* 292.

59. For a fascinating account of covert suburban rebelliousness in the 1950s, see Barbara Ehrenreich, *The Hearts of Men: American Dreams and the Flight from Commitment* (London: Pluto Press, 1983).

60. Freud, *Jokes,* 147.

61. The character Pugsley acquired his name, as did all the characters, only because of the television series. Addams wanted to call him Pubert, but the television executives vetoed the name because they thought it sounded obscene. Pugsley is a river in the Bronx.

62. For a discussion of notions of the angel/monster nature of children see Marina Warner, *Managing Monsters: Six Myths of Our Time* (London: Vintage Books, 1994), esp. chap. 3, and Edmundson, *Nightmare on Main Street,* passim.

63. Joyce Carol Oates dates the appearance of the bad seed (the title comes from William March's novel about an evil child) from 1954, "a curious watershed year before which, in popular culture, children were usually portrayed as angelic, and after which children might be as demonic as adults." See her article "Killer Kids," *New York Review of Books,* November 6, 1997, 20. She does not mention Addams, whose "demonic children" had been around in one form or another at least since the "Congratulations! It's a baby!" cartoon of 1940.

64. Addams married Barbara Day, a model, on May 29, 1943. The couple were divorced in 1951. Barbara Addams subsequently remarried twice, her third marriage being to John Hersey, Addams's colleague at *The New Yorker.* Addams married Barbara Barb, an attorney, on December 1, 1954. This marriage ended in 1956. That same year the second Barbara Addams married Henry Lennox d'Aubigné Hopkinson, First Baron Colyton.

65. The contrast with Steig, far more naturalistic, is instructive. His cartoon on a similar theme simply shows a grumpy middle-aged couple glaring at each other in a rowboat, with the husband snarling, "Well, you don't *look* happy" (*The New Yorker,* August 22, 1953, 24). There is no attempt here to probe what happens behind the surface amiability.

66. Charles Addams, *The World of Charles Addams,* selected by Marilyn "Tee" Addams with an introduction by Wilfrid Sheed (London: Hamish Hamilton, 1992).

67. Given the turn of the wheel and the reappearance of nostalgia for the 1950s in popular culture, it was only to be expected that a film based on the Addams characters made in the mid-1990s should be called *Addams Family Values.*

68. See *The New Yorker,* September 18, 1954, 85, and June 4, 1955, 87. For a compendium of 1950s taste, see Thomas Hine, *Populuxe* (New York: Alfred A. Knopf, 1986).

69. Richard Hofstadter, *The Paranoid Style in American Politics* (New York: Alfred A. Knopf, 1965). Hofstadter's argument, that the paranoid style has an identifiable social base, namely the failure of the "built-in social elevator in US society," is not much accepted today. But the paranoid flavor of much popular culture of the 1950s is real enough. For a recent discussion of the phenomenon in cultural terms see Timothy

Melley, *Empire of Conspiracy: The Culture of Paranoia in Postwar America* (Ithaca: Cornell University Press, 2000).

70. Hofstadter, *Paranoid Style,* 50. Other reasons, apart from the failure of the built-in status elevator in American society, are a disordered world, threatened by a great power and a powerful ideology; the growth of the mass media, which "have made it possible to keep the mass man in an almost constant state of political mobilization"; and the historical midcentury political dominance of liberal elements, which has intensified the sense of "powerlessness and victimization" among their opponents (64). To this we could add the general feeling described by E. L. Doctorow in his portrait of the period in *The Book of Daniel* (1971): a vacuum produced by the defeat of the Axis powers, a want of some enemy other that the nation could define itself against, which was filled by international communism; and the fear of invasion and of the enemy within.

71. Hofstadter, *Paranoid Style,* 6.

72. John Russell, reviewing an exhibition of Addams's cartoons at the Nicholls Gallery in *New York Times,* November 2, 1974. Clipping from the Nicholls Archive.

73. Wolcott Gibbs, preface to *Addams and Evil* (New York: Random House, 1947).

74. Sheed, introduction to *World of Charles Addams,* x.

75. Freud emphasized the necessity of condensation for the joke, seeing it as an essential part of the technique of jokes that they are "dominated by a tendency to compression." Freud, *Jokes,* 77.

76. "I've always thought of myself as Uncle Fester. We share certain attitudes, even look a little alike—although he's totally hairless, and I'm not, yet!" Quoted in Margaret Staats and Sarah Staats, "Seven Masters of Visual Wit," *Quest 79: The Pursuit of Excellence* 3, no. 4 (June 1979): 24.

77. These are tied up with other important ideas—the transition from the "paranoid-schizoid position" to the "depressive position," the importance of "play," and its relation to all forms of original and creative thinking. These ideas were developed out of the work of Melanie Klein by followers like Donald Winnicott and Wilfrid Bion in the 1940s and 1950s.

78. What follows is essentially Klein as developed by Bion.

79. See, for example, the explanation of the terms "projection" and "projection into external objects" by Bion in his essay "Attacks on Linking," in *Second Thoughts: Selected Papers on Psychoanalysis* (London: Heinemann, 1967), 93.

80. Bion's graphic figure is a baby's cry, which expresses a fear of dying: the mother who can truly contain this panicky fear instinctively recognizes what the cry means, absorbs the terror, moderates it, and returns it to the baby in a less damaging form.

81. The alternative of "projection" and "introjection" in the baby, the reassembling of the "good" and "bad" mother, marks a crucial transition in the development of the personality.

82. See, for a full account, R. D. Hinshelwood, *A Dictionary of Kleinian Thought* (London: Free Association Books, 1993), 138. Briefly, there is first a state in which the psyche is constantly splitting off anxieties and fears that cannot be mastered and projecting them onto other people (the "paranoid-schizoid position"); second, there is a

state in which "the infant . . . is psychically and emotionally mature enough to integrate his or her fragmented perceptions of mother, bringing together the separately good and bad versions (imagos) that he or she has previously experienced" (the "depressive position"). This new state, even though characterized by sadness and melancholy, is of great importance, since it is the phase in which loving and altruistic feelings can flourish and a realistic sense of the complex alterity of others is actively recognized by the psyche. For Bion these "phantasised attacks on the breast" become "the prototype of all attacks upon objects that serve as a link" (see Bion, "Attacks on Linking," 93), and hence the prototype of all forms of mental activity that work against constructive social activity—"linking" here meaning in its simplest sense all the minute interconnections between mental contents that are the symbolic basis of the means by which the social and cultural structure is "felted" together within the symbolic order. Bion, however, discerned in many of his patients a kind of recrudescence of the paranoid-schizoid position—the existence of "destructive attacks" they made "upon anything which is felt to have the function of linking one object with another." The transition from the paranoid-schizoid position to the depressive position did not necessarily take place once and for all in infancy. It might rather be a kind of permanent process within the psyche. Bion held that an alternation between the paranoid-schizoid and depressive positions was central to all forms of creative thought and invention. Forward movement in these spheres requires first a dissolution of whatever is stabilized as an internal object and a "container," and hence a reversion to the paranoid-schizoid state of splitting. The container has to be "dissolved before it can be reformed." The constructive reforming of a new thought, a new aesthetic vision, is the equivalent of setting up the depressive position, and it represents a new synthesis within the symbolic order. Bion called this alternating between the two states "Ps-D." In doing so, he depathologized the whole process, understanding that the "tolerance of a degree of disintegration," a kind of negative capability, the enduring of certain "catastrophes," is the precondition for all forms of creative symbolic activity.

83. In Bion's work it is made clear that the baby's relationship with its mother is the type of many other relationships in subsequent life.

84. The following is a technical account of the argument of this paragraph. The mother and the baby are actual people, so it is easy to see how the mother can "contain" what the baby projects, but it is not immediately apparent how a text, not being a person, can act as a container. The example of the stand-up comedian, as a kind of halfway figure between the real presence of the mother and the symbolic and seemingly inert presence of a text, may help. Stand-up comedians are experts at identifying the causes of general distress and anxiety. They have a feeling for what anxieties are ready for projection (that is, what is "around" in a society, unadmitted, repressed, and causing distress and discomfort). They absorb this projected material and transform it into a joke. But as this example shows, what contains the projected content is not really the stand-up as a person. What does the containing is the way the stand-up modifies that content—the jokework. The joke then hands that material back in a modified and indirect form to the audience, which now finds that what caused anxiety is made laughable and hence acceptable and manageable. Since we get the same relief from reading a joke as we do from hearing it told by a third party, there are good

reasons to conclude that we don't really need the stand-up at all. The joke, read as a text, allows us to be our own container (because in getting the joke we detour out of ourselves and back again, via the joke). If we harbor irrationally antagonistic feelings toward the state, for example, a cartoon like the one by Addams in which a saboteur is planning to blow up the Capitol performs a complicated set of transactions between viewer and cartoon relative to such feelings. First, it acknowledges the existence of those feelings in the figure of the saboteur (projection). Then it also shows that by our accepting such feelings (rather than denying that they exist or being so offended that we angrily repudiate them) they can be accommodated within the social order (it contains them). Finally, it returns them to us comically, in a form in which we can reaccept (introject) them, their power to disturb having been moderated. It is a process that, perhaps, helps us live a little easier with ourselves, but also with other people (linking). If someone objects that what humor does is adapt us to existing conditions (to make us feel quiescent rather than rebellious, say, or to substitute a mood for a spur to action), then the truth of this has to be acknowledged. This is why humor is never really subversive. On the other hand, because humor tends to detach us from direct involvement, to show everything at one remove, it cannot be characterized as a conservative form. If a joke can do all this, then obviously so can a cartoon. In these examples there are no longer two actual people. Just the reader, the text of the joke or cartoon, and what goes on between them—the interpretative "space" of the reader's response. Literary theory enables us to think of that space as containing something other than whatever the reader brings to the text and something other than what the text brings to the reader (for example, F. R. Leavis's "third realm," created by the meeting of text and reader, reducible to neither, as defined in *The Living Principle: English as a Discipline of Thought* [London: Chatto and Windus, 1975], 62). Another way to put this is to say a joking text requires one to take what Richard Kearney, in his introduction to the thought of Paul Ricoeur, calls the "hermeneutic detour." See Richard Kearney, "Paul Ricoeur and the Hermeneutic Imagination," in *The Narrative Path: The Later Works of Paul Ricoeur,* ed. Peter Kemp and David M. Rasmussen (Cambridge: MIT Press, 1989), 1–31, quotation on 6. Kearney refers to Ricoeur's insistence that in interpretation, that is, meaning-creating reading, a movement occurs from reader into the text and back to the reader in which the text changes the reader's self-understanding. Ricoeur argues that (especially in texts that are poetic in his terms and require some interpretive activity) this allows not just the creation of new meaning but also a kind of self-understanding that intuitive self-communing alone cannot produce. You come to "know yourself" only by taking the hermeneutic detour—by reading, and making sense of "poetic," meaning-creating texts. See, among many instances in Ricoeur's work, part 5 of "The Hermeneutical Function of Distanciation," in Paul Ricoeur, *Hermeneutics and the Human Sciences: Essays on Language, Action, and Interpretation,* ed., trans., and intro. John B. Thompson (Cambridge: Cambridge University Press, 1981). This model provides the basis for a textual version of containing that does not require the literal presence of two people. The communication of "calm and reflectiveness," a distancing from what makes one anxious, a deferral of the primary reference of the discourse, is the function of humor of all kinds.

85. The joke absorbs the projected object and modifies it, then hands it back to

the joker and his audience in a form that can be accepted and introjected, its destructive sting drawn (receiving one's "frightened personality but in a form that [one] can tolerate"). See Bion, "Attacks on Linking," 115.

86. Analogous to that between patient and analyst.

87. Bion, "Attacks on Linking," 106.

88. Hinshelwood, *Dictionary of Kleinian Thought,* 229 and 420. To take this a stage further, we could introduce at this point the idea of play, as developed by Winnicott. The importance of this is that Winnicott gets us away from the (somewhat reductive) Kleinian emphasis on symbolic play as a merely defensive (as opposed to creative) activity. See Hinshelwood, *Dictionary of Kleinian Thought,* 446. The joke is preeminently a transitional space, a third realm—something inserted between the merely internal and the simply external, in which the contents of both fantasy and reality may be allowed to mingle. Winnicott's case centers on the fundamental creativity of play as an activity in which growth can take place. There are distinct parallels between Bion and Winnicott here. See D. W. Winnicott, *Playing and Reality* (London: Routledge, 1991), especially chaps. 1, 3, 4, and 5.

89. Addams had used this image in a *New Yorker* cartoon of January 8, 1955, reprinted in *World of Charles Addams,* 133. What makes it so terrifying is the sense of speed of the sawing, the rapidity with which the catastrophe advances. See also the cartoon for April 28, 1951, *World of Charles Addams,* 110.

90. Rachel Carson, *Silent Spring* (Harmondsworth, England: Penguin, 1991), 46. The reference to Addams does not appear in the text of *Silent Spring* as published in *The New Yorker* (see the issue for June 16, 1962, 56), but to make up for this an Addams cartoon is embedded early in the article.

91. Noël Mostert, "Profiles—Supertankers," *The New Yorker,* May 13, 1974, 45–100, and May 20, 1974, 46–99. Oil spills and oil slicks are discussed in the May 20 issue (75–86).

92. Some years later the joke was parodied by Sam Gross (*The New Yorker,* June 22, 1987, 22).

93. Charles Baudelaire, *Selected Writings on Art and Artists,* trans. and intro. E. Charvet (Harmondsworth, England: Penguin, 1972), 145.

94. For information on the automobiles see Gill, *Here at "The New Yorker,"* 227–28, and Sheed, introduction to *World of Charles Addams,* x.

95. Unsourced clipping (ca. 1975), Christopher Andersen, "The Real Grisly Addams Is Cartoonist Charles Who Wants You to Get the Point," 91. Clipping in the Nicholls Archive.

4. Saul Steinberg

1. At the end of his life Steinberg was proud to be in museums but still "uncomfortable in galleries, anxious in collectors' homes," according to Adam Gopnik in his essay, "What Steinberg Saw," *The New Yorker,* November 13, 2000, 141.

2. Adapting Steinberg's own words, spoken to Harold Schonberg for an interview in *New York Times.* Harold C. Schonberg, "Artist Behind the Steinbergian Mask," *New York Times,* November 13, 1966, sect. 6, 48–51, 162–69.

3. An image perhaps based on the "tombstone tattoo" (a tombstone with the person's initials on it, followed by the date of birth and a big question mark) described by Joseph Mitchell in "The Bottom of the Harbor," *The New Yorker,* January 6, 1951, 36–52, esp. 50, an article Steinberg illustrated.

4. Jean vanden Heuvel, "From the Hand and Mouth of Steinberg," *Life,* December 10, 1965, 60.

5. Most recently Lisa Phillips, *The American Century: Art and Culture, 1950–2000* (New York: Whitney Museum of Art; Norton, 1999), and Robert Hughes, *American Visions: The Epic History of Art in America* (New York: Alfred A. Knopf, 1997). These omissions are particularly odd. Phillips's book was published to accompany an exhibition of the same name at the Whitney Museum of American Art. The Whitney sponsored the most important retrospective of Steinberg's work in 1978. In the 1970s Hughes wrote what is still perhaps the best general essay on Steinberg for *Time* magazine. Among standard studies of American art and culture in the twentieth century that ignore Steinberg are Sam Hunter, *American Art of the Twentieth Century* (New York: Abrams, 1972); Christos M. Joachimides and Norman Rosenthal, *American Art in the Twentieth Century* (London: Royal Academy of Arts, 1993); Irving Sandler, *American Art of the 1960s* (New York: Harper and Row, 1988), and idem, *American Art of the Postmodern Era: From the Late 1960s to the Early 1990s* (New York: Icon, 1996); and Barbara Rose, *American Art since 1900: A Critical History* (New York: Praeger, 1967). More specialized studies that also find no place for Steinberg include Diana Crane, *The Transformation of the Avant-Garde: The New York Art World, 1940–1985* (Chicago: University of Chicago Press, 1987); Philip Fisher, *Making and Effacing Art: Modern American Art in a Culture of Museums* (New York: Oxford University Press, 1991); Eleanor Heartney, *Critical Condition: American Culture at the Crossroads* (New York: Cambridge University Press, 1996); Christin Mamiya, *Pop Art and Consumer Culture* (Austin: University of Texas Press, 1992); Robert C. Morgan, *Between Modernism and Conceptual Art* (Jefferson, NC: McFarland, 1997); Miles Orvell, *After the Machine: Visual Arts and the Erasing of Cultural Boundaries* (Jackson: University Press of Mississippi, 1995); Howard Risati, ed., *Postmodern Perspectives: Issues in Contemporary Art,* 2d ed. (Upper Saddle River, NJ: Prentice-Hall, 1998); Terry Smith, *Making the Modern: Industry, Art, and Design in America* (Chicago: University of Chicago Press, 1993); and Paul Wood, *Modernism in Dispute: Art since the Forties* (New Haven: Yale University Press, 1993). Notable exceptions are Hilton Kramer, *The Revenge of the Philistines: Art and Culture, 1972–1984* (New York, Free Press, 1985); Harold Rosenberg, *The Anxious Object: Art Today and Its Audience* (New York: Horizon, 1964); and idem, *Art on the Edge: Creators and Situations* (New York: Macmillan, 1975). E. H. Gombrich wrote briefly, but sympathetically and admiringly, about Steinberg in his *Art and Illusion* (London: Phaidon, 1960).

6. For parallel version of this metaphor, see Steinberg's drawing of Pegasus rearing up on the back of a tortoise (*The New Yorker,* October 15, 1960, 41).

7. Quoted in Schonberg, "Artist Behind the Steinbergian Mask," 166.

8. The car as "goddess" is celebrated in Roland Barthes's essay "The New Citroën," in *Mythologies* (1957; London: Jonathan Cape, 1972). The DS19 is "a superlative *object,*" an "exaltation of glass," its elements held together "by sole virtue of their

wondrous shape," "actualizing . . . the very essence of petit-bourgeois advancement," and on and on. Barthes and Steinberg have much in common intellectually, as I shall show. The Citroën DS19 was extensively advertised in *The New Yorker* after its appearance in 1956 (for example, *The New Yorker*, March 3, 1956, 56).

9. Quoted in the autobiographical section of Harold Rosenberg, *Saul Steinberg* (New York: Alfred A. Knopf and Whitney Museum of American Art, 1978), 242.

10. Schonberg, "Artist Behind the Steinbergian Mask," 169.

11. The phrase "plausibly implausible" is Robert M. Coates's, in his review of Steinberg's large exhibition at the Parsons and Janis galleries in 1952 (*The New Yorker*, February 9, 1952, 79). Steinberg's autobiographical memoir, *Reflections and Shadows* (New York: Random House, 2002), contains many acerbic comments on American life.

12. Rosenberg, *Saul Steinberg*, 36.

13. Gopnik, "What Steinberg Saw," 141. As I point out later, the epigrammatic, joking, anecdotal cartooning form has similarities with Yiddish discourse.

14. This is the burden of people as different as Stuart Hall in "Minimal Selves," in *Identity, The Real Me: Post-modernism and the Question of Identity*, ed. Lisa Appignesi, ICA Documents, 6 (London: Institute of Contemporary Arts, 1987), 44, and Ted Cohen in *Jokes: A Philosophical Inquiry into Joking Matters* (Chicago: University of Chicago Press, 1999), 61. "I feel some of you [white Britons] surreptitiously moving towards [the] marginal identity [of blacks]," says Hall; "WASPs," says Cohen, "have become outsiders in this country of which they were once the very essence of the inside." The condition of postmodernity makes everyone an outsider. No one really "belongs" unselfconsciously anymore.

15. Steinberg, *Reflections and Shadows*, 69–70.

16. Quoted in Grace Glueck, "The Artist Speaks," *Art in America* 58, no. 6 (November–December 1970): 116.

17. A lineal descendant of John Ruskin's dragon, perhaps?

18. Rather than, say, republican austerity and self-reliance.

19. Rosenberg, *Saul Steinberg*, 238.

20. As a non-American perhaps I need to say I am not suggesting that an America described as "vulgar, kitsch, exuberant, self-parodying" is somehow America itself. As even the most casual and fleeting visitor finds, American civilization is diverse and nuanced, and of all modern cultures perhaps the one most resistant to the totalizing impression. Nonetheless, those facets of America that Steinberg was struck by, especially in the 1950s and 1960s, were, and remain, an unavoidable and dominant facet of a complex whole.

21. See Christopher Rand, "Profiles: The Ultimate City," *The New Yorker*, October 1, 1966, 56–116, October 8, 64–115, and October 15, 1966, 64–117. Steinberg's drawing allows some of Rand's pertinent comments to take shape; for instance, "Los Angeles may be the ultimate city of our age. It is the last stop, anyway, in the Protestant migration that left northern Europe three centuries ago and moved across America — the last if only because the movement reached the Pacific" (*The New Yorker*, October 1, 1966, 56). Or, noting that America has effectively had no frontier since 1890, "The frontier mystique lingers on vigorously in the south west and perhaps no where

more vigorously than in Los Angeles itself" (*The New Yorker*, October 15, 1966, 96). Rand's thesis clearly had a strong effect on Steinberg.

22. Glueck, "Artist Speaks," 117. But see my final comment on this remark below, page 238.

23. John Hollander in his introduction to a reissue of Saul Steinberg, *The Passport* (New York: Random House, 1979), [6].

24. This was certainly the case by the eighties, when the Galerie Maeght issued *All Except You*, with drawings by Steinberg and text by Roland Barthes (Paris: Maeght, 1983).

25. Published in James Stevenson, *Something Marvelous Is About to Happen* (New York: Harper and Row, 1971). These drawings were not published in *The New Yorker*.

26. See Glueck, 116, for Mormon travelers. In other drawings the Indian stands for something else. As we see in some of the later allegories, for the white imagination the Indian also symbolizes heroic, individualistic freedom, at-oneness with the natural world, the free self uncontaminated by the settling and civilizing process. The film *Dances with Wolves* (1990) was the sentimental culmination of this tendency.

27. It is usually reproduced as the cover of *The New Yorker* for March 29, 1976, but it exists in several versions. A sketch is reproduced in Rosenberg, *Saul Steinberg*, 79.

28. An apposite comment made back in the twenties by Robert Jay Misch, "Manhattan Manual," *The New Yorker*, September 4, 1926, 19.

29. Lee Lorenz, *The Art of "The New Yorker"* (New York: Alfred A. Knopf, 1995), 83.

30. A posting on *The New Yorker* Web site says that *The New Yorker* receives more requests for reproductions of this cover than any other and claims that it is "arguably the most recognized magazine cover of the 20th century." See *http://www.cartoonbank.com/steinberg.asp* (accessed January 6, 2003). Among hundreds of plagiarized versions, the most notorious was as a poster for Paul Mazursky's *Moscow on the Hudson* (1984).

31. E. B. White, *Here Is New York* (New York: Warner Books, 1988), 18.

32. Roland Barthes, "Buffet Finishes Off New York," in *The Eiffel Tower and Other Mythologies*, trans. Richard Howard (New York: Hill and Wang, 1979), 150. Barthes's essay criticizes Bernard Buffet for getting New York completely wrong, for abstracting it as a vertical grid, all facade and no life, and for ignoring what makes it the most wonderful city on earth: its street life. He also has some good remarks on the usefulness of the grid, which makes everyone an equal possessor of what the city has to offer. The essay reads as a program for Steinberg's version of the city.

33. I owe this apt phrase to Patrick McCaughey.

34. Gopnik, "What Steinberg Saw," 141.

35. Unlike Gopnik, I think Steinberg's best work was done in the two or three decades after he arrived in America. It is obvious that the later work is brilliant, but his work of the later period lacks the inventiveness of the earlier period.

36. In saying this I am aware that Steinberg himself has drawn attention to Bucharest, "in the days of my youth," as the cradle of Dada. See Steinberg, *Reflections and Shadows*, 13–14. But this is surely one of the rare moments when Steinberg is mythologizing his own life. Tristan Tzara, one of the founders of Dada, was indeed a Romanian. But he was born in 1896, a full generation before Steinberg, and Dada, founded

in 1916, was the creation of the cultural atmosphere of prewar Germany and Switzerland, especially Zurich, rather than of Romania and Bucharest.

37. Advertisement for *The Passport* in *The New Yorker,* October 23, 1954, 169.

38. Quoted in Robert Hughes, "The Fantastic World of Steinberg," *Time Magazine,* April 17, 1978, 32–36, esp. 34.

39. Christopher Ricks, "Saul Steinberg and the Law of Levity," *Bostonia: The Magazine of Culture and Ideas* 4 (Winter 1993–94): 34–35.

40. The quotation comes from Steinberg's eloquent celebration of what America offers. "The American Dream is the ideal offered to us by the Constitution, that of seeking happiness all one's life. It is an invitation to use all the facilities offered by America—this country where one has the opportunity to respect good laws—to pursue one's tendencies freely and seek happiness as one thinks best. There's no such thing as standard happiness, the same for everyone. Happiness is not imposed on Americans from outside, by the government, as happens under dictatorships" (Steinberg, *Reflections and Shadows,* 55).

41. Saul Steinberg, *Le Masque* (Paris: Maeght, 1966).

42. Steinberg to Jean vanden Heuvel, "From the Hand and Mouth of Steinberg," 70.

43. Ibid.

44. Hughes, "Fantastic World of Steinberg," 35.

45. Quoted in Kramer, *Revenge of the Philistines,* 191.

46. Kramer, *Revenge of the Philistines,* 195.

47. See Irving Howe, *World of Our Fathers: the Immigrant Jews of New York, 1881 to the Present* (London: Routledge and Kegan Paul, 1976), on the often very complicated motivations that drove assimilation. I am going to argue that this third way involved the exploration of a particular aesthetic genre, that of kitsch.

48. Saul Steinberg quoted by vanden Heuvel, "From the Hand and Mouth of Steinberg," 66. Characteristically, Steinberg continues: "Also there is no guarantee these boulders are made of rock. Maybe they are made of thin skin inflated with air; they are pasted with scotch tape, and they stay there. Perhaps there is no problem at all." One might add that Steinberg, like many midcentury artists, liked to exaggerate the interpretative indeterminacy of his work.

49. Details in this section are taken from Steinberg's autobiographical sketch in Rosenberg, *Saul Steinberg,* 234–46, and the longer account given in his autobiographical memoir *Reflections and Shadows,* supplemented by Hughes, "Fantastic World of Steinberg." Ghitta Sternberg's *Stefanesti: Portrait of a Romanian Shtetl* (New York: Pergamon Press, 1984) provides more general detail. Sternberg includes Ramnicul-Sarat in the broad category of towns with a Jewish population of between 10,000 and 50,000.

50. She later became a painter, working under the name Lica Roman.

51. Sternberg, *Stefanesti,* 50.

52. Hughes, "Fantastic World of Steinberg," 35.

53. Hughes, "Fantastic World of Steinberg," 35.

54. Steinberg, *Reflections and Shadows,* 15–16.

55. Gopnik, "What Steinberg Saw," 141.

56. I have adapted this list from Benjamin Harshav, *The Meaning of Yiddish* (Stanford: Stanford University Press, 1990), 99–100.

57. For a full discussion see Harshav, *Meaning of Yiddish*, especially the chapter "The Semiotics of Yiddish Communication," and particularly 99–102. In those pages Harshav mentions three major "modes of translogical discourse" characteristic of Yiddish that have a clear relation to Steinberg: associative digression (Steinberg's crocodile as a symbol of the aggressive side of materialist individualism); resorting to the canonized textual store (Steinberg's drawings of "Americanerie": Wild West cowboys, anonymous suited businessmen, Mickey Mouse terrorists); assuming that all frames of reference in the universe of discourse may be analogous to one another (Steinberg's businessman, Santa Claus, and Sigmund Freud as the presiding deities of the midcentury United States). He also notes that Yiddish favors short, highly condensed utterances—the proverb, the saying, the anecdote, the short story—into which list it is easy to insert the epigrammatic form of the joking drawing. These fragments of discourse are themselves part of something larger, as Steinberg's drawings are themselves part of something larger. That "something larger" is not a systematic narrative. It is a sequence of small visual anecdotes concatenating in an associative chain—a structure highly characteristic of Yiddish discourse. Harshav claims this collage technique is "protomodernist" in nature, but it might with more justice be called "proto-postmodernist." I am grateful to Den Finch-Walton for drawing my attention to this valuable book, and in particular to this chapter. For a parallel discussion see Cohen, *Jokes*, 60–67.

58. Harshav, *Meaning of Yiddish*, 102.

59. Glueck, "Artist Speaks," 114–15.

60. Hughes, "Fantastic World of Steinberg," 35.

61. Sternberg, *Stefanesti*, 136 and 39.

62. Sternberg, *Stefanesti*, 137.

63. "Biographische Daten," in *Saul Steinberg: Zeichnungen, Aquarelle, Collagen, Gemälde, Reliefs, 1963–1974* (Cologne: Kölnischer Kunstverein, 1974), 10.

64. Sternberg, *Stefanesti*, 137. The *numerus clausus* provisions were a form of negative quotas: since the Jewish population of Romania was about 5 percent, only 5 percent of school and university places were open to Jews.

65. Rosenberg, *Saul Steinberg*, 235.

66. Steinberg is reticent about his Jewishness (not observant, according to Gopnik), yet one may propose that he is in some sense a post-Holocaust artist—as Arno, Addams, and even Steig are not. One of Steinberg's early assignments for *The New Yorker* was to cover the Nuremberg trials as a war correspondent (Rosenberg, *Saul Steinberg*, 279). (No drawings on this subject were published in *The New Yorker*.) Steinberg's parents survived the war, and visited Steinberg in America (Gopnik, "What Steinberg Saw," 147). Lica Roman died in Paris in 1975.

67. Hughes, "Fantastic World of Steinberg," 35.

68. Rosenberg, *Saul Steinberg*, 235.

69. Hughes, "Fantastic World of Steinberg," 35.

70. *Saul Steinberg: Zeichnungen, Aquarelle, Collagen, Gemälde, Reliefs*, 10.

71. See Steinberg, *Reflections and Shadows,* 32.

72. Hughes, "Fantastic World of Steinberg," 35.

73. Brendan Gill, *Here at "The New Yorker"* (New York: Random House, 1975), 228.

74. Gill, *Here at "The New Yorker,"* 229. Yagoda prints a facsimile of a memo from Geraghty to Ik Shuman regarding Steinberg's predicament; see Ben Yagoda, *About Town: "The New Yorker" and the World It Made* (New York: Scribner, 2000), 178.

75. Rosenberg, *Saul Steinberg,* 236.

76. For further details on Steinberg's life in America, including his posting as a naval ensign to the Far East, see Hughes, Gopnik, and Rosenberg. On the oddity of his receiving his U.S. citizenship, commission, and overseas posting in the same year, Steinberg noted that it greatly eased the process of becoming an American.

77. Rosenberg, *Saul Steinberg,* 239.

78. Glueck, "Artist Speaks," 117.

79. Along with Marcel Proust and Samuel Beckett, Steinberg is one of the great chroniclers of the effect of habit on one's sense of the world and the enhancement of vision that comes when habit is momentarily broken.

80. Glueck, "Artist Speaks," 117.

81. Glueck, "Artist Speaks," 117.

82. Glueck, "Artist Speaks," 111–12.

83. Glueck, "Artist Speaks," 111.

84. See Norbert Elias, "The Kitsch Style and the Age of Kitsch," in *The Norbert Elias Reader: A Biographical Selection,* ed. Johan Goudsblom and Stephen Mennell (Oxford: Blackwell, 1988).

85. Notions of "good" and "bad" are used here in a provisional sense because such valuations depend for their validity on that long-lost solid social base. Elias suggests that the disappearance of the court culture of the ancien régime and its system of patronage effectively destroyed the "objectivity" of any such terms.

86. For an early polemical view see Bernice Martin, *A Sociology of Contemporary Cultural Change* (Oxford: Blackwell, 1981).

87. The sense of being caught between two opposing forces is really another version of being caught between Americanization and cosmopolitanism.

88. Cf. "My development started at the bottom, with cartoons. I learned by working and I managed to get out of a number of culs-de-sac, some of the vulgarities of humorous drawing and the banalities of commercial art, while still preserving a little of that element of mediocrity—I'd almost say vulgarity—that I wouldn't care to give up, since I consider it something necessary; like a man who, in changing his social class, still wouldn't want to break up with his wife and old friends" (Steinberg, *Reflections and Shadows,* 71–72).

89. For the abstract head see the advertisement for Austin, Ltd., January 24, 1953, 73; for the thumbprint see the advertisement for General Electric, November 14, 1953, 59; for the balance beam see the advertisement for Capitol records, September 29, 1956; for the schematic air route see (among many examples) the advertisement for United Airlines, May 26, 1951, 128; and for the paper-bag mask see the advertisement

for the *Ladies Home Journal,* October 8, 1960, 119. Each of these examples anticipates the appearance of the motif in Steinberg's work: his abstract heads first appear about 1956, the thumbprint in 1954, the balance beam in 1961, the schematic air route in 1962, and the masks in 1965.

90. See the drawings titled "Comic Strip" in Rosenberg, *Saul Steinberg,* 46–47. Steinberg noted René Magritte's interest in speech bubbles; see Steinberg, *Reflections and Shadows,* 58.

91. A location surname, meaning "a person who lives on or near a stony mountain." It is explained in this way in *The Oxford Dictionary of Surnames,* under "Stein."

92. For Masonic interest in the globe, see fig. 4.10.

93. Steinberg, *Reflections and Shadows,* 35.

94. Saul Steinberg, "Chronology," in Rosenberg, *Saul Steinberg,* 245.

95. Compare Steinberg's comment about a drawing in the "Hotel Plaka" series, which he called a "parody of eroticism," and which shows a "Pythagorean triangle" transfixing "a question mark." "One could say that the question mark, fat and voluptuous, is the woman, while the triangle, precise, geometric, the symbol of logic, is the man. But this exposes our prejudices, because one always thinks of the man as the logical part, while the woman is the question mark with all the insecurity implicit in this symbol. It could be in fact an affair between a fat man and a smart woman" (Rosenberg, *Saul Steinberg,* 13n). We may admit that Steinberg's symbolism is not easily pinned down, but I at least start to wonder here whether—because the image of penetration is so obvious—Steinberg isn't deliberately muddying the waters with such a comment.

96. See Rosenberg, *Saul Steinberg,* 21–22. Steinberg deployed Masonic imagery quite deliberately. In the sixties he advised a young correspondent inquiring about his iconography to "look at the dollar bill—see Annvit Coeptis etc—part of the Great Seal of USA—An interesting seal, Masonic symbols (13 stars, 13 olives, 13 arrows . . .)." Steinberg to Andrew Sunshine, January 21, 1969. Copy at the Saul Steinberg Foundation.

97. I recognize that "Freemasonry and America" is not a topic to inspire confidence and is even likely to set alarm bells ringing. This phase of the argument does not, however, offer Freemasonry as the key to all Steinberg's mythologies, nor does it suggest that Steinberg had any but the most passing connection with Freemasonry. I aim only to show that Steinberg uses certain motifs derived from the iconography of Freemasonry to help him draw America. The purpose of these paragraphs is to see what light can be cast on Steinberg's work by recent scholarship in this area.

98. See Margaret C. Jacob, *The Radical Enlightenment: Pantheists, Freemasons and Republicans* (London: Allen and Unwin, 1981), and idem, *Living the Enlightenment: Freemasonry and Politics in Eighteenth-Century Europe* (New York: Oxford University Press, 1991). For a more general and theoretical account of the relation between Freemasonry and utopian thinking, see Keith Hetherington, *The Badlands of Modernity: Heterotopia and Social Ordering* (London: Routledge, 1997), especially chapter 5, "Secret Virtues, Euclidean Space: Freemasonry, Solomon's Temple and the Lodge."

99. For a discussion of this claim see Bernard Vincent, "Masons as Builders of the Republic: The Role of Freemasonry in the American Republic," in *The Early Repub-*

lic: The Making of a Nation, the Making of a Culture, ed. Steve Ickringill (Amsterdam: Free University Press, 1988).

100. Vincent, "Masons as Builders of the Republic,"140–41. For a monograph on Freemasonry at the time of the Republic, see Dorothy Lipson, *Freemasonry in Federalist Connecticut, 1789–1835* (Princeton: Princeton University Press), 1977.

101. Vincent, "Masons as Builders of the Republic," 139.

102. For an account of the architectural symbolism and iconography of Freemasonry see James Stevens Curl, *The Art and Architecture of Freemasonry* (London: Batsford, 1990).

103. Gopnik has some brief but pertinent comments about American totemism and Steinberg's appreciation of its role in the national imaginary. Gopnik does not note that as Steinberg becomes less interested in Americanness and more horrified by the social Balkanization of America in the late seventies and beyond, there is a shift of interest in his drawings away from buildings and toward people. Of course, another factor here is Steinberg's training as an architect. This undeniably sensitized him to the importance of drawing the built environment. Thus he praised Charles Addams for being the first cartoonist to draw architecture intelligently. But there are obvious links between architecture and Freemasonry.

104. Along with the social history of Freemasonry already discussed I reemphasize here the historical associations of eighteenth-century speculative Freemasonry with Enlightenment thought more generally. As we have seen, throughout the eighteenth century Freemasonry was one of the principal social institutions through which Enlightenment ideas of human perfectibility were circulated. These ideas involved notions of the reconstitution of the ancien régime on egalitarian and rational principles, of universal brotherhood (as opposed to established privilege) and enlightened nationalism, and of rational systems of thought more generally, including the theistic idea that the cosmos was the work of a divine architect. Freemasonry was also linked socially with both dissent and lower-middle-class ambition, and—despite having aristocratic patronage—it found its constituency very much among the politically conscious and socially impatient lower middle class. It is the link between speculative Freemasonry, conversation in the lodges, and Enlightenment thought that explains the appearance of the Freemasons' pyramid on the dollar bill.

105. *The New Yorker,* July 22, 1967, 35–69, July 29, 1967, 35–69, and August 5, 1967, 32–63. The term "megalopolis," to denote the woodland/urban sprawl of commuter/light-industrial development of lands adjacent to the great cities of the northeastern seaboard of the United States, was popularized by Jean Gottman's 1961 book of the same title. ("Woodland" implies the decline in tillage.)

106. See Curl's *Art and Architecture of Freemasonry.* Curl discusses the classical orders on 54.

107. Curl gives numerous examples on 70–77.

108. See, for example, the lodge plans reproduced in Curl, *Art and Architecture of Freemasonry,* 70–71, 75.

109. Nor is this to imply that Freemasonry is strictly rational. There is a coincidence of temper between the characteristic mingling of the rational and the occult in Freemasonry and the same mingling of the rational and the cryptic in Steinberg. Re-

cent historians of Freemasonry are particularly interested in its occult side, and this theme could be profitably explored in relation to Steinberg.

110. The drawing cannot be an actual response simply because of the time frame within which *The New Yorker* was printed (the Saturday, January 17 issue would have been at the printers by the previous weekend, January 10). But Shawn must have chosen the painting quite deliberately with the State of the Union address in mind, and it would not have been hard to guess at the likely drift of the president's address. See the discussion of fig. 3.1.

111. The Masonic allusion is more obvious in a much later version of this drawing, where the monument has become a three-dimensional building, a veritable Solomon's temple of Commerce, sandwiched between Lexington and Madison avenues. This 1991 version is reproduced in *The Discovery of America* (New York: Alfred A. Knopf, 1992).

112. A third variant, found in most of his drawings in the forties and fifties, is an unexpressive, neutral, reportorial line, whose properties I do not consider here.

113. Waldo Frank, best known for his association with *The New Masses,* also wrote a column for *The New Yorker* in the 1920s under the pseudonym "Searchlight."

114. Waldo Frank, *In the American Jungle* (1937; Freeport, NY: Books for Libraries Press, 1968), 123–24.

115. Frank, *In the American Jungle,* 125.

116. This train of thought makes sense of the appeal of the feminine curves of *The New Yorker* icon Eustace Tilley.

117. Angela Carter, "The Lady of the House of Love," in *The Bloody Chamber* (Harmondsworth, England: Penguin, 1979), 97.

118. Steinberg's phrase, from *Life,* 62.

119. Searle's first cartoon did not appear until November 12, 1966 (59).

120. The businessmen remind us of the legacy of the fifties: the period of the organization man in the gray flannel suit lost in the lonely crowd—as well as the title of a famous film starring Gregory Peck. I run together here some titles of popular sociological books of the decade, David Riesman's *The Lonely Crowd* (1956), and William H. Whyte's *The Organization Man* (1957). Paul Goodman's *Growing Up Absurd* (1960) reminds us that such figures were often assessed from the vantage point of the now forgotten category of the absurd.

121. One might need to make an exception of his "Romanian," or Eastern European, figures, who I suspect are often drawings based on his mother.

122. Steinberg, *Life,* 64–66.

123. As we have seen, William Steig, Steinberg's colleague at *The New Yorker* and the one other artist there whose ambitions as a social analyst were as serious and broad as Steinberg's, was a follower and patient of Reich's. Steinberg's friend Saul Bellow was in analysis with a pupil of Reich's.

124. See the fuller discussion of Reich in chapter 2.

125. Gopnik, writing in 1987 in a Pace Gallery catalog introducing a selection of Steinberg's work, quoted by John Updike, "Pilgrim's Progress," *New York Review of Books,* December 3, 1992, 4.

126. Rosenberg, *Saul Steinberg,* 11.

127. Marcel Proust, *Within a Budding Grove,* in *Remembrance of Things Past,* trans. C. K. Scott Moncrieff (London: Chatto and Windus, 1976), 3:326.

128. Proust, *Within a Budding Grove,* 3:326–27.

129. Rosenberg, *Saul Steinberg,* 239. "It lasts one day," Steinberg mordantly adds.

130. Rosenberg, *Saul Steinberg,* 243.

131. Rosenberg, *Saul Steinberg,* 243.

132. Brendan Gill records one small, though probably not uncharacteristic, lapse of Steinberg's intuition in *Here at "The New Yorker,"* 233–34.

133. Quoted by Glueck, "Artist Speaks," 117.

134. I am probably no exception to this rule.

135. Steinberg, *Reflections and Shadows,* 84.

Conclusion. Laughing with *The New Yorker*

1. Joshua Hammer, "William Steig," *People,* December 3, 1984.

2. Apart from the cartoons these figures are indicative only, for obvious reasons. I have calculated based on an eighty-six-page issue, at 413 words per column (560 for listings), about 130 full columns per issue. When she was editor, Tina Brown reduced the magazine to forty-six issues (including six double issues).

3. Phrases taken from Josephine Hendin, "*The New Yorker* as Cultural Ideal," *Dissent* 29, no. 4 (1982): 450, 451–52, 454.

4. Phrase taken from Dwight Macdonald, "Laugh and Lie Down," *Partisan Review,* December 1937, 50.

5. Tom Wolfe, "Lost in the Whichy Thicket: *The New Yorker*—II," *New York Herald Tribune,* April 18, 1965, 20; quoted in Mary F. Corey, *The World through a Monocle: "The New Yorker" at Midcentury* (Cambridge: Harvard University Press, 1999), 139.

6. Phrases taken from Seymour Krim, "Who's Afraid of the *New Yorker* Now?" reprinted in *Shake It for the World, Smartass* (New York: Delta, 1971), 171, 184–85.

7. *The New Yorker,* October 4, 1969, 120.

8. Quoted in Brendan Gill, *Here at "The New Yorker"* (New York: Random House, 1975), 389.

9. For an account of the separation of editorial and business departments at *The New Yorker,* see James Wood, *Magazines in the United States* (New York: Ronald Press, 1971), 271–72.

10. In his autobiography, Ingersoll drew attention to Ross's dislike of the business side of things, especially his hatred of speculative newspaper proprietors. Ralph Ingersoll, *Points of Departure: An Adventure in Autobiography* (New York: Harcourt, Brace, and World, 1961), 154.

11. Gigi Mahon, *The Last Days of "The New Yorker"* (New York: McGraw-Hill, 1988), 7 and 40. Wood, *Magazines in the United States,* 272.

12. "Urbanity, Inc.," *Wall Street Journal,* June 30, 1958, 6.

13. Ross was particularly incensed about the magazine's dependence on advertis-

ing, and the sincerity of his indignation cannot be doubted. See the excellent account in Thomas Kunkel, *Genius in Disguise: Harold Ross of "The New Yorker"* (New York: Random House, 1995), 196–202. Kunkel notes that Ross considered all advertising "inherently dishonest."

14. Dale Kramer, *Ross and "The New Yorker"* (Garden City, NY: Doubleday, 1951), 167.

15. Walter Lippmann, *Public Opinion* (New York: Macmillan, 1922), 323–24.

16. [Ralph Ingersoll], "*The New Yorker,*" *Fortune,* August 1934, 80. Ingersoll's own daily newspaper, *PM,* started in the 1940s, was an attempt to produce a paper without advertisements, because, as Ingersoll wrote, "advertising, as currently organized, tends to limit editorial freedom" (advertisement in *The New Yorker,* June 8, 1940, 36–37). See Jane Grant, *Ross, "The New Yorker" and Me* (New York: Reynal, 1968), 212–13.

17. Grant, *Ross, "The New Yorker" and Me,* 212–13.

18. [Ingersoll], "*The New Yorker,*" 73.

19. [Ingersoll], "*The New Yorker,*" 73. Ingersoll says that the 62,000 metropolitan subscribers were matched by a further 63,000 from outside New York.

20. Eventually the magazine published two editions: a metropolitan one and a national one, charging advertisers an extra $300 a page for the latter.

21. *Rebuque from Dubuque, or Where, Indeed, Are the Limits of New York?* ([New York?]: New Yorker, [ca. 1940]). Copy held in the New York Public Library, stamped 246923B.

22. *Rebuque from Dubuque,* 25.

23. *The Primary Markets for Quality Merchandise* (New York: New Yorker, 1952), 5.

24. For a skeptical view of what "being a subscriber" means, see Jean Baudrillard, "Mass Media Culture," in *Revenge of the Crystal,* ed. Paul Foss and Julian Pfanis (Leichardt, Australia: Pluto Press, 1990), 72–73.

25. "Urbanity Inc.," *Wall Street Journal,* June 30, 1958, 6.

26. Michel de Montaigne, "3: Our emotions get carried away beyond us," *The Complete Essays,* trans. and ed. with an introduction and notes by M. A. Screech (Harmondsworth, England: Penguin, 1993), 11.

27. Christopher Wilson, "The Rhetoric of Consumption: Mass Market Magazines and the Demise of the Gentle Reader, 1880–1920," in *The Culture of Consumption: Critical Essays in American History, 1880–1980,* ed. R. W. Fox and T. J. Lears (New York: Pantheon, 1981), 64.

28. Karen Horney, *The Neurotic Personality of Our Time* (London: Norton, 1937), 288–89.

29. T. J. Clark, *The Painter of Modern Life: Paris in the Art of Manet and His Followers* (London: Thames and Hudson, 1985), 9.

30. See Mahon, *Last Days of "The New Yorker,"* 62. Even as late as 1983, *The New Yorker* stood third in a table of magazines ranked according to how many pages of advertising they sold (Mahon, 177).

31. I am chary of saying it "constructs" its readers, because this overused term betrays the hubris of the cultural studies approach. An alternative word—"interpellates"—meaning the way a text "hails" its readers or requires a certain response, a response that in effect does construct a certain social role for those readers, is a term

deriving from the brief heyday of Althusserian Marxism. In this context it is appropriate enough to be worth recalling if not reviving.

32. As an example of the first of these three positions, see D. H. Munro, *Argument of Laughter* (Melbourne: Melbourne University Press, 1951): "If we want a convenient single word for [a theory of humor], we may call it inappropriateness," (235). For examples of the second, see, classically, Henri Bergson's *An Essay on the Meaning of the Comic,* trans. Cloudesley Brereton and Fred Rothwell (London: Macmillan, 1935), and, in this context, MacDonald, "Laugh and Lie Down": "Laughter is . . . a defense of the social order, like the police force" (48). As an example of the third, see James F. English, *Comic Transactions: Literature, Humor and the Politics of Community in Twentieth-Century Britain* (Ithaca: Cornell University Press, 1994): "The politics of a joke has to be understood in terms of the joke-work (the socialized dream-work) it performs or enables—the redistribution of energies and repositioning of subjects it effects through processes of 'condensation, displacement and indirect representation and so on' . . . and not in terms of a stable and altogether 'serious' partisanship" (16). It is hard to escape the thought, however, that much depends on where and how one places the emphasis. This book argues for the first position, with a modified leaning toward English's arguments.

33. Thus Freud says that a joke is "developed play," while Kant asserted that the comic was "a strained expectation that comes to nothing."

34. Iris Murdoch, *The Fire and the Sun: Why Plato Banished the Artists* (Oxford: Oxford University Press, 1977), 74.

35. Samuel Weber, *The Legend of Freud* (Minneapolis: University of Minnesota Press, 1982), 90.

36. For this original suggestion I am indebted to Mark C. Weeks, "Laughter and *Indifférance:* The Predicament of Laughter in the Age of Fast Capitalism," (PhD diss., University of Western Australia, 1997). Weeks's case deserves to be much better known than it is. An article that covers some of the essential ground is Mark Weeks, "Thailand: A Time and Motion Study," *Meridian: The La Trobe University English Review* 16, no. 2 (October 1997): 117–22.

37. And even more different from that encouraged by watching television.

38. In this respect the material and physical aspects of *The New Yorker* have set themselves against the general trend of photojournals in the twentieth and no doubt the twenty-first century. But without turning away from graphics, the magazine has forged a highly distinctive (and remarkably stable) graphic style that has attracted to it, over the decades, all the associations that make up the mystique of the magazine.

39. Pam Morris, ed., *The Bakhtin Reader* (London: Arnold, 1994), 90.

40. Morris, *Bakhtin Reader,* 90.

41. These terms are Marshall McLuhan's, quoted by Christopher Brookeman. As Brookeman puts it, "the lay-out of the page, in which a whole range of disconnected stories and features simultaneously seek the attention of the reader, creates the same kind of landscape as that envisioned by avant-garde painting and science." See Christopher Brookeman, *American Culture and Society since the 1930s* (London: Schocken Books, 1984), 131.

42. Brookeman, *American Culture and Society,* 131.

43. Clement Greenburg, "Avant-Garde and Kitsch" (1939), in *Clement Greenburg: The Collected Essays and Criticism,* ed. John O'Brian (Chicago: University of Chicago Press, 1986), 1:13.

44. Ted Cohen, *Jokes: Philosophical Thoughts on Joking Matters* (Chicago: University of Chicago Press, 1999), 29–30.

45. In Baudrillard, "Mass Media Culture," 91. Baudrillard calls this a "retribalization" of the consumer.

ESSAY ON SOURCES

The following pages offer suggestions for background and further reading about comic art at *The New Yorker* and, more selectively, about *The New Yorker* itself. There is no bibliography of comic art or artists at *The New Yorker*. Comprehensive bibliographies relevant to the magazine can be found in Thomas Kunkel, *Genius in Disguise: Harold Ross of "The New Yorker"* (New York: Random House, 1995), and Ben Yagoda, *About Town: "The New Yorker" and the World It Made* (New York: Scribner, 2000). Mary F. Corey's *The World through a Monocle: "The New Yorker" at Midcentury* (Cambridge: Harvard University Press, 1999) does not include a bibliography, but since her reading of scholarly material is much wider than either Kunkel's or Yagoda's, the extensive footnotes are particularly worth consulting. Relevant indexes to *The New Yorker* are Janet R. Utts, *Index to Cartoons of "The New Yorker" Magazine with Artist, Date, Page and Keyword Citations, 1975–1985* (Evanston, IL: J. G. Burke, 1986); Robert Owen Johnson, *An Index to Literature in "The New Yorker" Volumes I–XV* (Metuchen, NJ: Scarecrow Press, 1961–71), and, by the same author, *An Index to Profiles in "The New Yorker"* (Metuchen, NJ: Scarecrow Press, 1972). Yagoda's book doubles as a particularly helpful reader's companion to *The New Yorker*, while Kenneth T. Jackson, ed., *The Encyclopedia of New York City* (New Haven: Yale University Press; New York: New-York Historical Society, 1995), is a valuable adjunct.

Comic Drawings in *The New Yorker*

The best way to become acquainted with the tradition of graphic humor in *The New Yorker*, whether as a scholar or as an interested general reader, is through the UMI (University of Michigan, Ann Arbor) microfilm series of back issues of the magazine, which now runs from the first issue in February 1925 to February 1999. Nothing can replace the direct contact with the primary material given by looking through the back issues in chronological order and seeing the development of an artist's work, the rhythms of his or her appearance, the sense of what other cartoonists are doing, and of course what else was going on. Historical developments, social changes, economic conditions, literary events, and advertising trends are all to hand. A few words of warning. The quality of both editorial supervision and reproduction in the UMI microform series is variable. It is not always clear whether the issue being copied is the metropolitan or the national "star" edition. (Before 1960, items that were considered of local New York interest only—along with cartoons that happened to appear on the same pages—were cut from star editions. Sometimes the UMI copy text is the star edition.) On a few occasions pages of advertisements are removed, although other inserts—subscription blanks and even the series of pamphlets to advertisers that appeared in the magazine at the end of the sixties—are usually included. A real problem is that the microfilm is in high-contrast black and white (possibly not even panchromatic film), and the cover images (reproduced in black and white) are sometimes very hard to discern. Furthermore, the microfilming is done in a shoddy way (not even presentation is uniform), and the intensity of the printed image is inconsistent (some issues are in strong black and white, others are underexposed and pale). If possible, view the microfilm in a library that has recent, well-serviced microform readers, ideally with photocopy or scanning and Internet facilities (this will obviate the need for photocopying, since scans can be e-mailed direct to your address). This may seem a trivial point, but it makes the difference between a chore and a pleasure. There are some positives. The series is widely available at good libraries; the cartoons are easily identifiable as one scrolls through; the captions are at least quick to read; and scrolling through a microfilm is easier than turning the same number of physical pages. The curious can get through issues at a good pace, if necessary, but it still it takes three or four months to view the whole run.

The New Yorker keeps individual pasted-in folios of each current artist's work (I have seen only Frank Modell's), and these would be of considerable help in tracking the development of an individual artist and gauging the published corpus, but the price you pay for ease of reference is the absence of context. In 1991, when *The New Yorker* moved offices from 25 West Forty-third Street across the road to 20 West Forty-third Street, its archives (about five hundred cartons) were given to the rare books and manuscripts division of the New York Public Library (see *New York Times,* February 19, 1991, B1 and B8, and Tuesday, March 26, 1991, C13 and C14). Some records were lost or destroyed in the transfer. The archives include thirteen boxes (1940–83) of the papers of James M. Geraghty, mainly from when he was art editor of *The New Yorker.* The Smithsonian Institution also acquired memorabilia and furnishings at this time with a view to recreating the original offices of Calvin Trillin and Edward Koren. For this book I was fortunate in being able to use the private archive of clippings and other material (including an excellent library of collections of cartoons) of Barbara Nicholls, for many years the assistant to James Geraghty when he was art editor of *The New Yorker.*

Comic Drawings in *The New Yorker:*
Collections, Survey, and Criticism

All 68,647 cartoons published in *The New Yorker* between 1925 and 2004 are collected in *The Complete Cartoons of "The New Yorker,"* edited by Robert Mankoff, foreword by David Remnick (New York: Black Dog & Leventhal, 2004) published in combined hard copy and CD ROM form. The hard cover selection of over 2,000 representative cartoons is arranged chronologically, decade by decade. The complete CD ROM collection of 68,647 cartoons is browsable by date, artist, and subject. The collection includes brief (1,000-word) essays on each decade by Roger Angell, Nancy Franklin, Lillian Ross, John Updike, Calvin Trillin, Ian Frazier, Mark Singer, and Rebecca Mead. There are also thumbnail sketches of selected artists. The collection, naturally enough, does not include spot drawings and illustrations not classifiable as cartoons. The creates minor problems, especially with an artist like Steinberg who on occasion contributed an important drawing as the title illustration to an article. The drawings in the hard cover selection are not dated except by decade and there are no page numbers so it is impossible to know where in the magazine the cartoons appeared. Nor are we told in what size they were reproduced. The quality of reproduction is generally good, although not always. The lettering on a road sign, crucial to a Sam Cobean cartoon (p. 194), is barely decipherable. In the case of Charles Addams, the reproduction of the "Carol Singers" cartoon of 1946 (p. 171), although reproduced full-page, is greatly inferior to the version in *The World of Charles Addams*. All cartoons in CD ROM form are dated, but no page number is given and once again there is no indication of size. To view the CDs and navigate through them successfully requires Adobe 6 (downloadable from the CDs). In his introduction to the collection Mankoff writes that "pixels and computer screens can't do justice to the lush washes of an Arno or Addams, the delicate charcoals of a Robert Weber or a Charles Saxon, or the eloquent line of a Saul Steinberg." This is a way of saying that, depending on a number of variables such as the size of the original, the degree of detail in it, the original scanning settings and the screen size and screen settings on the computer being used to view the images, the appearance of a particular cartoon on the screen is unlikely to be very satisfactory. Details can be indistinct, even at optimal size on the screen: the expressions on the faces of the people in Addams's "Carol Singers" are unreadable at all degrees of magnification, for example. Few of the cartoons will tolerate being viewed at even two or three stages of magnification and beyond a certain point the images collapse completely. For the scholar of the form whose interests extend beyond the caption to the drawing itself, this makes *The Complete Cartoons of "The New Yorker,"* extraordinary achievement as it is, of more value as a visual index than as a primary document. But while it does not replace looking at the cartoons as they originally appeared, either in the microfilm version or (best of all) in the bound back issues, it does for the first time make it possible to locate images with very little trouble. And, as the CD ROM is fully browsable, the collection immediately expands the possibilities inherent in the comparative, thematic study of cartoons, of particular interest to sociologists of popular culture and students of cultural studies.

Before the publication of *The Complete Cartoons of "The New Yorker,"* the magazine reprinted only a small proportion of its cartoons—less than 3 percent—in various selections. There was a lot of repetition, and earlier selections were frequently cannibalized for later ones. Between 1928 and 1942, nine such *"New Yorker" Albums* were published. These collections are now interesting chiefly as examples of editorial tastes in humorous drawings. The most important is *The Seventh "New Yorker" Album* (1935), which has two contending introductions, one critical by Lewis Mumford and one positive by Wolcott Gibbs. There are also a number of retrospective collections covering a longer time span. The most useful is the twenty-fifth anniversary selection, *"The New Yorker" Twenty-fifth Anniversary Album, 1925–1950* (New York: Harper and Brothers, 1951), which arranges about 700 cartoons (out of some 20,000 then published) in a loose chronological sequence by half decades but does not date drawings more exactly. Also valuable are "*The New Yorker*" *1950–1955 Album* (New York: Harper and Brothers, 1955) and "*The New Yorker*" *Album 1955–1965: Fortieth Anniversary* (New York: Harper and Row, 1965). In the following decade a fiftieth anniversary edition (drawing very heavily on the twenty-fifth anniversary edition with later additions) was published as "*The New Yorker*" *Album of Drawings, 1925–1975* (New York: Viking Press, 1975), with the cartoons again arranged in roughly chronological order but with no actual dates. This was followed ten years later by *The New Yorker Cartoon Album, 1975–1985* (New York: Viking Penguin, 1985). Subsequently many collections of cartoons have appeared in thematic volumes — "*The New Yorker*" *Book of Lawyer Cartoons* (1993), "*The New Yorker*" *Book of Business Cartoons* (1998), and so on, following on from "*The New Yorker*" *Album of Art and Artists* (Greenwich, CT: New York Graphic Society, 1970), a very good collection on an important theme.

The covers up to the anniversary issue of February 20, 1989, have been collected in *The Complete Book of Covers from "The New Yorker," 1925–1989* (New York: Alfred A. Knopf, 1989), with a foreword by John Updike. It reprints all 3,226 covers from this period (the anniversary cover once at the beginning and once at the end with 51 other images per year) in three formats: one large featured image for each year (reproduced at about $6^7/_8$ by $9^7/_8$ inches, although the size varies from year to year), a reduction of about 82 percent on the actual cover dimensions; two or three selected images for each year in a smaller format (about 3 by 4 inches), and the remainder in a greatly reduced format (about $2^1/_2$ by $3^3/_8$ inches). This way of republishing the covers has attracted criticism, with suggestions that the last two formats were too tiny to be of any use. And yet it is hard to see what else could have been done without making the book prohibitively expensive. The resolution of the smaller images is high, and details can be picked up with the help of a good magnifying glass. Color values appear to be good (but see below). The magazine's actual dimensions are noted where appropriate — originally $8^1/_2$ by $11^7/_8$ inches, it changed slightly in 1928, 1943 (twice), 1946, 1956, 1964, 1980 and 1988, and ended up $8^1/_4$ by $10^7/_8$ inches. The names of all artists and the dates of issues are clearly given. There is a good index. At least once an image has been placed out of sequence and the 142 cover illustrations by Abe Birnbaum (1899–1966) are misattributed to Aaron Birnbaum (1895–1998).

In 1984 the United Technologies Corporation in association with the National Academy of Design published the very handsome *Seasons at "The New Yorker": Six Decades of Cover Art,* a selection of eighty covers, all reproduced at full published size without the *New Yorker*'s logo superimposed. Charles Saxon contributed an introduction. The book is admirable in giving the medium and original dimensions of all cover artwork, most of which was done to a size of about 12 by 17 inches, giving a reduction of about 60 percent to the printed cover page. (This means that the smallest images in *The Complete Book of Covers* are reduced to about 17 percent of their original size, which lends weight to the complaints of those who thought they were reproduced at far too small a scale.) Color values are excellent, and a comparison between the original artwork and the actual cover (reproduced in a small format on each opposite verso page) sometimes reveals variation between the original treatment of color and the way a painting was reproduced on the cover (for example, George Price's Father Christmases, December 25, 1965).

Lee Lorenz's *The Art of "The New Yorker"* (New York: Alfred A. Knopf) is a lavishly illustrated history of cartooning at the magazine, at once authoritative, informative, and entertaining. Lorenz, himself a cartoonist, was art director until Robert Mankoff took over. The book is brillintly designed. Ronald Paulson's *Figure and Abstraction in Contemporary Painting* (New Brunswick: Rutgers University Press, 1990) refers interestingly to several *New Yorker* cartoonists' work in pursuing its larger argument, as does E. H. Gombrich's much earlier *Art and Illusion* (London: Phaidon, 1960). For anyone interested more generally in the academic discussion of graphic humor, there is now a dedicated research journal, the *International Journal of Comic Art* (edited from Temple University by John Lent), and the journal of the International Society for Humor Studies, *Humor: International Journal of Humor Research* (edited by Salvatore Attardo, Youngstown State University), frequently carries articles on cartooning. Bruce Kellner's biography *The Last Dandy: Ralph Barton, American Artist, 1891–1931* (Columbia: University of Missouri Press, 1991) covers the career of one of the most important artists at the early *New Yorker,* the talented and tormented Ralph Barton, who committed suicide in 1931. John Updike has written extensively and stimulatingly in a series of fugitive pieces on cartooning at *The New Yorker,* and his comments are particularly worth seeking out. His lengthy appreciation of Ralph Barton is reprinted as "A Case of Melancholia" in his *Just Looking: Essays on Art* (New York: Alfred A. Knopf, 1989), and his own reflections on a career in cartooning that didn't happen, "Lost Art," can be found in the "Cartoon Issue" of *The New Yorker* for December 15, 1997 (75–80). The same issue includes a good article by Roger Angell, "'Congratulations! It's a Baby'" (132–39), and a large three-fold photograph of current and past cartoonists by Arnold Newman (104–7). The double issue of *The New Yorker* for December 7 and 14, 1998, has a piece by Hendrik Hertzberg on sex in *New Yorker* cartoons (144–49), along with many other relevant articles and features.

Individual Artists

Peter Arno

Arno's early work is collected in three important volumes that print some drawings not taken by *The New Yorker.* These are *Peter Arno's Parade* (New York: Liveright, 1929) with a good introduction by William Bolitho; *Peter Arno's Hullabaloo,* with "A Note on Pictorial Humor" by Robert Benchley (New York: Simon and Schuster, 1931); and *Peter Arno's Circus* (New York: Liveright, 1931). Arno also published a novel based on the adventures of the Whoops Sisters, *Whoops Dearie!* (New York: Simon and Schuster, 1927). Although Arno is given as both author and illustrator, the text was by Philip Wylie. Later albums of Arno's work are *Peter Arno's Favorites* (New York: Simon and Schuster, 1932); *Peter Arno's For Members Only* (New York: Simon and Schuster, 1935); *Peter Arno's Cartoon Revue* (New York: Simon and Schuster, 1941); *Peter Arno's Man in the Shower* (New York: Simon and Schuster, 1944); *Peter Arno's Sizzling Platter* (New York: Simon and Schuster, 1949); *Peter Arno's Hell of a Way to Run a Railroad* (New

York: Simon and Schuster, 1956); and *Peter Arno's Lady in the Shower* (New York: Simon and Schuster, 1967). *Peter Arno's Ladies and Gentlemen* (New York: Simon and Schuster, 1951) is a selection of Arno's drawings to the date of publication prefaced by an interesting account by Arno himself of his drawing techniques. *Peter Arno* (New York: Beaufort Books, 1979), a posthumous collection, reprints 248 of Arno's best drawings (236 from *The New Yorker*) spanning his career, selected by Patricia Arno (the artist's daughter) and A. Halsey Cowan, with a brief introduction by Charles Saxon. The selection is good, but the sequence of drawings is only intermittently chronological, and no dates are given.

Background information on Arno and comments on his work can be found in "Peter Arno by Peter Arno," *Cartoonists Profiles* 24 (December 1974); Henry McBride, "Modern Art", *The Dial,* February 1929; and Philip Herrera, "In Splendid Style: Peter Arno, the Cartoonist as Fine Artist," *Connoisseur,* February 1984. The background to Arno's cabaret world is described in Lewis A. Erenberg, *Steppin' Out: New York Night-life and the Transformation of American Culture, 1890–1930* (Westport, CT: Greenwood Press, 1981).

There is no scholarly account of Arno's career, and no biography.

William Steig

William Steig's extraordinarily prolific and varied career continued to his death in October 2003. His very early work is gathered in *Man About Town* (New York: R. Long and R. R. Smith, 1932). Steig's psychological volumes of the late thirties and forties are *About People: A Book of Symbolical Drawings,* with an introduction by Arthur Steig (New York: Duell, Sloan and Pearce, 1939); *The Lonely Ones,* with a foreword by Wolcott Gibbs (New York: Duell, Sloan and Pearce, 1942); *All Embarrassed,* with a foreword by Arthur Steig (New York: Duell, Sloan and Pearce, 1944); *Persistent Faces* (New York: Duell, Sloan and Pearce, 1945); *Till Death Do Us Part: Some Ballet Notes on Marriage* (New York: Duell, Sloan and Pearce, 1947); and *The Rejected Lovers* (New York: Alfred A. Knopf, 1951). Also of interest in relation to these drawings is Wilhelm Reich's *Listen Little Man! A Document from the Archives of the Orgone Institute,* with illustrations by William Steig (New York: Orgone Institute Press, 1948). The drawings about children are gathered in *Small Fry* (New York: Duell, Sloan and Pearce, 1944 [1951]); *The Agony in the Kindergarten,* with a foreword by Arthur Steig (New York: Duell, Sloan and Pearce, 1950); and *Dreams of Glory* (New York: Duell, Sloan and Pearce, 1953). Later collections, including many drawings not published in *The New Yorker,* are *Continuous Performance* (New York: Duell, Sloan and Pearce, 1963); *Male/Female* (New York: Farrar, Straus and Giroux, 1971); *William Steig: Drawings,* with an introduction by Lillian Ross (New York: Farrar, Straus and Giroux, 1979); *Ruminations,* with a preface by Whitney Balliett (New York: Farrar, Straus and Giroux, 1984); *Our Miserable Life,* with a foreword by Alfred Hubbell (New York: Noonday Press, 1990); *Sick of Each Other* (New York: HarperCollins, 2001); and *When Everybody Wore a Hat* (New York: Joanna Cotler Books, 2003). Musical settings of Steig's work include *Small Fry: A Collection of Songs about "Small Fry"* by Bing Crosby ([New York]: Decca, [1941], a five-record 78 rpm set; and Norman Cazden's published score of "The Lonely

Ones: For piano: Opus 44a" (Bangor, ME: Andrews Music House, 1944), "based on the cartoons of William Steig," later a ballet choreographed by Ann S. Halprin. Collections of Steig's work are *Collected Drawings* (Wakefield, RI: Moyer Bell, 1994) and *The World of William Steig,* edited by Lee Lorenz with an introduction by John Updike (New York: Artisan Press, 1998). William Steig's daughter, Maggie Steig, has a home video recording of the artist drawing.

Background and comment on Steig's work include W. H. Auden, "The Icon and the Portrait," in *Nation* 150, no. 2 (January 13, 1940); Israel Shenker, "Steig Surviving as He Nears Sixty-five, Finds Peace in Being a Depressed Cartoonist," *New York Times,* November 14, 1972; and Joshua Hammer, "William Steig," *People,* December 3, [1984?]. For a discussion of Wilhelm Reich see Philip Rieff, *The Triumph of the Therapeutic: Uses of Faith after Freud* (New York: Harper and Row, 1966), and Charles Rycroft, *Reich* (London: Fontana Collins, 1971).

There is no scholarly account of Steig's cartoons, although his children's books (not covered here) are discussed in Leonard S. Marcus, *A Caldecott Celebration: Six Artists and Their Paths to the Caldecott Medal* (New York: Walker, 1998). Biographical details are given in *The World of William Steig,* but there is no full biography.

Charles Addams

Charles Addams has been well served posthumously by *The World of Charles Addams* (New York: Alfred A. Knopf, 1991), a wide selection of his work mainly from *The New Yorker* made by his widow, Marilyn "Tee" Addams (now deceased), with a good introduction by Wilfrid Sheed. The format is very handsome, and the reproductions are generally first rate (the Carol Singers cartoon of 1948 is reproduced here much better than in Addams's earlier collection, *Addams and Evil*). Cartoons are dated by appearance in *The New Yorker*. Principal collections of Addams's work are *Drawn and Quartered,* with a foreword by Boris Karloff (New York: Random House, 1942); *Addams and Evil* (New York: Random House, 1947); *Monster Rally* (New York: Simon and Schuster, [1950]); *Homebodies* (New York: Simon and Schuster, 1954); *Nightcrawlers* (New York: Simon and Schuster, 1957); *Dear Dead Days* (New York: Putnam, 1959); *Black Maria* (New York: Simon and Schuster, 1960); *The Groaning Board* (New York: Simon and Schuster, 1964); *My Crowd* (New York: Simon and Schuster, 1970); *Favorite Haunts* (New York: Simon and Schuster, 1976); and *Creature Comforts* (New York: Simon and Schuster, 1981). In 1964 an exhibition of paintings and sculpture selected by Charles Addams under the title *The Dark Mirror* was sponsored by the American Federation of Arts (see the catalog, 1964). Other books Addams has contributed to include John Kobler, *Afternoon in the Attic,* with pictures by Charles Addams (New York: Dodd, Mead, 1950), and *Think Small* (New York: Golden Press, 1967), with text and cartoons by Addams and others, introduced by Herb Valen.

Addams's work is discussed interestingly by Jesse Bier, *The Rise and Fall of American Humor* (New York: Holt, Rinehart and Winston, 1968), 292. (Bier criticizes Addams for what Van Wyck Brooks would call the fallen image of man in his drawings.) See also among the more journalistic but nonetheless useful accounts Jack Severson, "The Man Who Gives Us the Creeps," *Philadelphia Inquirer,* November 11, 1976, and Margaret

Staats and Sarah Staats, "Seven Masters of Visual Wit," *Quest 79: The Pursuit of Excellence* 3, no. 4 (June 1979): 22–29. Robert Mankoff (the current cartoon editor of *The New Yorker*) discusses some recently unearthed and unpublished cartoons by Charles Addams in the double issue of *The New Yorker* for December 7 and 14, 1998 (150–51).

For the gothic background to Addams's work, Louis Gross, *Redefining the American Gothic: From Wieland to Day of the Dead* (Ann Arbor: UMI Research Press, 1989), and Donald A. Ringe, *American Gothic: Imagination and Reason in Nineteenth-Century Fiction* (Lexington: University Press of Kentucky, 1982), are informative. Mark Edmundson, *Nightmare on Main Street* (Cambridge: Harvard University Press, 1997), brings the picture up to the present. For an introduction to object relations theory and further leads, see R. D. Hinshelwood, *A Dictionary of Kleinian Thought* (London: Free Association Books, 1993). A retrospective exhibition of Addams's work at the Guild Hall, East Hampton, New York (October 2002–January 2003), curated by H. Kevin Miserocchi, was accompanied by a catalog titled *Charles Addams: American Gothic,* edited and with an introduction by Miserocchi.

There is no scholarly account of Addams's work. A biography by Linda H. Davis is close to being published. The Tee and Charles Addams Foundation has recently been established under the trusteeship of H. Kevin Miserocchi (director) and Michael Solomon to further the appreciation of Addams's work. The Foundation's address is the Tee and Charles Addams Foundation, PO Box 248, Wainscott, NY 11975, e-mail *festerthing@addamsfoundation.org.*

Saul Steinberg

Steinberg's own recollections of his childhood and youth (including his time in Italy), his impressions of America, and reflections on his art can be found in Saul Steinberg with Aldo Buzzi, *Reflections and Shadows,* trans. from the Italian by John Shepley (New York: Random House, 2002). Steinberg's letters to Aldo Buzzi have been published as *Lettere a Aldo Buzzi* (Milan: Adelphi, 2002). In the 1970s Steinberg recorded an interview with Raymond Rosenthal and Moishe Ducovny that has been transcribed and is held in the New York Public Library in the American Jewish Committee Oral History Collection (Oral Histories, box 74, no. 4).

Although there are several good retrospective volumes of Steinberg's work (see below), there is no comprehensive collection that surveys his entire career. The main collections of Steinberg's work are *All in Line* (New York: Duell, Sloan, and Pearce, 1945); *The Art of Living* (New York: Harper and Brothers, 1949); *The Passport* (New York: Harper and Brothers, 1954); rev. ed. with a new introduction by John Hollander (New York: Random House, 1979); *The Labyrinth* (New York: Harper and Brothers, 1960); *The New World* (New York: Harper and Row, 1965); *Le Masque,* with text by Michel Butor and Harold Rosenberg, photographs by Inge Morath (Paris: Maeght, 1966); *The Inspector* (New York: Viking Press, 1973); *Steinberg at the Smithsonian* (Washington, DC: Smithsonian Institution Press, 1973); *Saul Steinberg,* with an introduction by Harold Rosenberg and a useful pictorial chronology and autobiographical sketch (New York: Alfred A. Knopf and Whitney Museum of American Art, 1978);

Dal Vero: Portraits by Saul Steinberg, text by John Hollander (New York: Whitney Museum of American Art, 1983); Canal Street, text by Ian Frazier and drawings by Steinberg (New York: Whitney Museum of American Art, 1990); The Discovery of America, with an introduction by Arthur C. Danto (New York: Alfred A. Knopf, 1992); and Saul Steinberg Masquerade, photographs by Inge Morath (New York: Viking Studio, 2000). There are also a number of editions published outside America. From France there are six editions of Derrière le miroir, among them #205 (Paris: Maeght, 1973), with 44 works by Steinberg and an essay by Hubert Damisch, and #224 (Paris: Maeght, 1977), with 105 works and an introduction by Italo Calvino. These publications give the title, size, and medium of the originals, although there is no key to the illustrations and sometimes a location if the work is in private hands or a gallery. The same publisher has also issued All Except You, with drawings by Steinberg and text by Roland Barthes (Paris: Maeght, 1983), and Repères: Cahiers d'art contemporain, no. 30, with 62 works by Steinberg (Paris: Maeght Lelong, 1986). From Holland there are Steinberg (Rotterdam: Museum Boymans–Van Beuningen, 1967) and LSD25 (The Hague: Bakker/Daamen, 1970). From Germany, the exhibition catalog Saul Steinberg: Zeichnungen, Aquarelle, Collagen, Gemälde, Reliefs, 1963–1974 (Cologne: Kölnischer Kunstverein, 1974) has essays by Tilman Osterwold, Wilhelm Salber, and Gertrud Textor, an excellent chronology (better in some respects than the one in Rosenberg's Whitney Museum Saul Steinberg), and a bibliography. Documents/Saul Steinberg is a short catalog of a Steinberg exhibition at the Serpentine Gallery in London, organized by the Arts Council of Great Britain in 1979. A U.S. exhibition catalog, Still Life and Architecture (New York: Pace Gallery, 1982), publishes Italo Calvino's essay from Derrière le miroir #224 in English as "The Pen in the First Person." Also published in the United States are Saul Steinberg: Fifty Works from the Collection of Sivia and Jeffrey Loria (New York: Jeffrey H. Loria, 1995), with an appreciation by Jean Leymarie and an introduction by John Updike, and Bernice Rose, Steinberg: Drawing into Being (New York: Pace Wildenstein, 1999).

Critical writing on Steinberg is voluminous (a good bibliography up to 1978 is given in Saul Steinberg). Besides the introductory essays mentioned above by Danto, Hollander, and Rosenberg, I have found the following especially useful: Jean vanden Heuvel, "From the Hand and Mouth of Steinberg," Life, December 10, 1965, 59–70; Harold C. Schonberg, "Artist Behind the Steinbergian Mask," The New York Times Magazine, November 13, 1966, sec. 6; Hilton Kramer, The Revenge of the Philistines: Art and Culture, 1972–1984 (New York: Free Press, 1985); Harold Rosenberg, The Anxious Object: Art Today and Its Audience (New York: Horizon, 1964), and idem, Art on the Edge: Creators and Situations (New York: Macmillan, 1975); E. H. Gombrich in his Art and Illusion (London: Phaidon, 1960); Grace Glueck, "The Artist Speaks," Art in America 58, no. 6 (November–December 1970): 110–17; Robert Hughes, "The Fantastic World of Steinberg," Time Magazine, April 17, 1978, 32–36; John Updike, "Pilgrim's Progress," New York Review of Books, December 3, 1992, 3–4; Christopher Ricks, "Saul Steinberg and the Law of Levity," Bostonia: The Magazine of Culture and Ideas 4 (Winter 1993–94): 34–45; Adam Gopnik, "What Steinberg Saw," The New Yorker, November 13, 2000, 140–47 (Gopnik also contributed an introduction to a Pace Gallery show of Steinberg's work in 1987). Joel Smith's *Steinberg at "The New Yorker,"* which, along with a scholarly text, reproduces all Steinberg's *New Yorker* covers and over 130 other drawings, appeared as this book was going to press.

For Steinberg's Romanian background a fascinating study is Ghitta Sternberg's *Stefanesti: Portrait of a Romanian Shtetl* (New York: Pergamon Press, 1984). On the properties of Yiddish, Benjamin Harshav, *The Meaning of Yiddish* (Stanford: Stanford University Press, 1990), is very useful. The classic account of kitsch is Norbert Elias's "The Kitsch Style and the Age of Kitsch," in *The Norbert Elias Reader: A Biographical Selection,* ed. Johan Goudsblom and Stephen Mennell (Oxford: Blackwell, 1988). For recent relevant work on Freemasonry see Margaret C. Jacob, *Living the Enlightenment: Freemasonry and Politics in Eighteenth-Century Europe* (New York: Oxford University Press, 1991); Bernard Vincent, "Masons as Builders of the Republic: The Role of Freemasonry in the American Republic," in *The Early Republic: The Making of a Nation, The Making of a Culture,* ed. Steve Ickringill (Amsterdam: Free University Press, 1988); James Stevens Curl, *The Art and Architecture of Freemasonry* (London: Batsford, 1990); and Keith Hetherington, *The Badlands of Modernity: Heterotopia and Social Ordering* (London: Routledge, 1997).

The Saul Steinberg Foundation (executive director Sheila Schwartz) was established by the artist's will. Its mission is to promote the study and appreciation of Saul Steinberg's contribution to twentieth-century art. Anyone interested in Steinberg's work should consult the Foundation's informative Web site, www.saulsteinbergfoundation .org, which includes a brief introduction to the artist's work, a bibliography, and a list of one-man shows. On his death Saul Steinberg's own collection of his works was divided between the Saul Steinberg Foundation and the Beinecke Rare Book and Manuscript Library, Yale University, which also received Steinberg's archives. There is no full scholarly account of Steinberg's career, nor is there a biography.

Books and Articles on *The New Yorker*

Books and articles on *The New Yorker* can be divided into those that are mainly anecdotal and those that aim at a critical or historical perspective. The following selection mainly concentrates on the early years.

Anecdotal memoirs and descriptive portraits of *The New Yorker* still make a good introduction to the magazine for anyone unfamiliar with its genesis, history, and character: they provide a historical outline, introduce the dramatis personae, and convey a sense of the magazine's ethos. Chief among them is James Thurber's *The Years with Ross* (Boston: Little, Brown, 1957). It was much criticized on publication, most famously by E. B. White and Katherine White, who thought Thurber exaggerated his importance to the magazine and portrayed Harold Ross, the magazine's founding editor, disrespectfully ("a sly exercise in denigration, beautifully concealed in words of sweetness and love," as White wrote to Howard Cushman, October 26, 1959; see *Letters of E. B. White,* collected and edited by Dorothy Lobrano Guth [New York: Harper and Row, 1976], 465). Yet it remains one of Thurber's best books, perhaps because Thurber envied Ross, the sort of man Thurber wanted to be but wasn't. This perhaps unconscious envy produces a book with flair and humor as well as the spice of malice. It has many evocative touches, as even White admits ("Jim could always reproduce Ross's mannerisms and general demeanour, and vividly"). It is essential reading and a fine introduction to the magazine. Something of the flavor of the social milieu *The New Yorker* sprang from can be gleaned from Margaret Chase Harriman's *Vicious Circle* (New York: Rinehart, 1951). Jane Grant's autobiography, *Ross, "The New Yorker" and Me* (New York: Reynal, 1968), is less gripping than Thurber's book but still engrossing. Grant was Ross's first wife, and her autobiography is informative on the background to the founding years of *The New Yorker.* Brendan Gill's *Here at "The New Yorker"* (New York: Random House, 1975), written to coincide with the magazine's fiftieth anniversary, is readable and appealingly opinionated. More worldly than Thurber, surer of himself and more detached, Gill is interested in *The New Yorker* as a cultural phenomenon with many facets: what it published, of course, and its personalities, but also its offices, the artists, the people who produced it, their public life, the mystique and mythology of the institution. He cares about the art, and his book contains many fascinating thumbnail sketches of the artists along with much else including photographs. Gill is also said by some to be hostile to Ross, but he reprints in full William Shawn's generous tribute to him. Useful articles in this vein include Allen Churchill, "Ross of *The New Yorker,*" *American Mercury,* August 1948; A. J. Liebling, "Harold Ross — the Impresario," *Nieman Reports,* April 1959; Russell Maloney, "Tilley the Toiler," *Saturday Review of Literature,* August 30, 1947.

In recent years there has been a revival in the memoirs of writers associated with *The New Yorker.* E. J. Kahn Jr.'s two books of recollections, *About "The New Yorker" and Me: A Sentimental Journey* (New York: G. P. Putnam's Sons, 1979) and *Year of Change: More about "The New Yorker" and Me* (New York: Viking, 1988), are disappointing. Of genuine interest is Ved Mehta's four-hundred-plus-page *Continents of Exile: Remembering Mr. Shawn's "New Yorker": The Invisible Art of Editing* (New York: Overlook Press, 1998). As Mehta presents him, Mr. Shawn (Mehta always scrupulously preserves the title) is the dream editor, father figure, and mentor, and the book details at great length the truly astonishing particularity of interest that Shawn showed in his blind protégé. Lillian Ross's *Here but Not Here: A Love Affair* (New York: Random House, 1998), a moving but sometimes discordant account of her long-standing love affair with William Shawn, written while she was still grieving and close to the pain, is often revealing. Alexander Chancellor's entertaining *Some Times in America and a Life in a Year at "The New Yorker"* (New York: Carroll and Graf, 2000) explains some of the things that went wrong with Tina Brown's editorship of *The New Yorker.* (His account of editing "The Talk of the Town" opens with the disarming if unsettling words, "I have not yet confessed that until I came to New York I had rarely read the *New Yorker.*") Renata Adler's opinionated and acerbic *Gone! The Last Days of "The New Yorker"* (New York: Simon and Schuster, 1999) is well worth reading. Adler, a contrarian firebrand, was an admirer of Shawn, but unlike Mehta she offers some cogent and convincing criticisms of his style as editor. Her book is dedicated in part to the memory of Saul Steinberg.

Critical and historical accounts of *The New Yorker* (usually but not always by people from an academic background) begin with Dale Kramer's *Ross and "The New Yorker"*

(Garden City, NY: Doubleday, 1951). On its appearance it was anonymously criticized by *The New Yorker* in a severe, not to say patronizing, manner in the issue for November 17, 1951. Gigi Mahon's, *The Last Days of "The New Yorker"* (New York: McGraw-Hill, 1988) is a business history of the magazine written after the takeover of F-R Publishing (the magazine's original owners) by S. I. Newhouse's Advance Publications. It is completely fascinating, though written with more than a touch of schadenfreude.

The forty-four-year gap between Kramer's book and the appearance of the first scholarly treatment of similar material (but with a biographical focus), Thomas Kunkel's *Genius in Disguise: Harold Ross of "The New Yorker"* (New York: Random House, 1995), is in retrospect very surprising. Kunkel's brilliant and readable book is a canny, pathfinding study, based on much original material. It convincingly rehabilitates Ross's reputation as an editor of genius. Kunkel does not especially concentrate on the cartoons, but he does discuss them in passing and conveys a great deal of useful information.

Mary F. Corey's *The World through a Monocle: "The New Yorker" at Midcentury* (Cambridge: Harvard University Press, 1999) is still the only scholarly book that engages with *The New Yorker* at a level other than that of historical narrative: it is done enterprisingly and very thoroughly. She treats *The New Yorker* as though it is greater than the sum of the articles and drawings, as though it forms a megatext that transmits a certain "vision of reality" or "version of the real world" or "road map" to its readers. In making this assumption she ducks the difficult question of whether so heterogeneous a production as *The New Yorker* can seriously be thought of as offering a single "version" of anything, let alone the real world. Corey wants to describe and criticize that vision of reality in terms that owe something to a mixture of new historicism, cultural studies, and critical theory. In doing so she is often unwilling to recognize how some of the writing *The New Yorker* published was itself unsettling to prevailing attitudes. Divided about whether it wants to praise or bury the magazine, the book tries to do both. Concentrating on the magazine about 1950 is certainly a good idea because it makes discussion focused and manageable, but it is also a problem. Corey's book encounters the magazine at its quietist and most conventional period. If it is true as Antonio Gramsci said, that in ideological conflict we need to take on our opponents at their point of strength, not just their point of weakness, then Corey's book shies away from doing this. She is right to point out sexist or racist elements in the cartoons, for example, yet she never mentions someone like Steinberg who was publishing throughout her period but doesn't fit in with her argument. (What she would do with Donald Barthelme, two decades later, is a puzzle.)

Ben Yagoda's *About Town: "The New Yorker" and the World It Made* (New York: Scribner, 2000) is a straightforward but masterly publishing, biographical, social, and intellectual history of *The New Yorker* up to the end of Tina Brown's editorship. It does in scholarly depth what Kramer did more superficially in 1951. Yagoda has digested a huge amount of primary and fugitive material and is often the first person to have done so. The book is essential reading.

Mary Corey is a historian and Kunkel and Yagoda both have backgrounds mainly in journalism, but the large, complex questions *The New Yorker* raises offer an unusual opportunity for a scholar familiar with twentieth-century literature, recent literary theory, cultural history, and critical theory. The magazine awaits a treatment by someone from such a background, but the task is formidable.

Articles that deal with *The New Yorker* in an analytical or a critical spirit begin with Ralph Ingersoll's anonymous piece in *Fortune,* August 1934, 73–152, which is well worth reading but mainly concerned with the business side of things. Ingersoll, who had briefly worked with Ross at *The New Yorker,* was a canny and worldly man who understood both magazine publishing and editing inside out. Dwight Macdonald's "Laugh and Lie Down," *Partisan Review,* December 1937, 44–53, was the first article to attempt a serious ideological critique of the magazine. In the same left-liberal tradition are the following pieces: Seymour Krim, "Who's Afraid of *The New Yorker* Now?" first published in 1962 and reprinted in *Shake It for the World, Smartass* (New York: Delta, 1971); Tom Wolfe, "Lost in the Whichy Thicket: *The New Yorker,*" *New York Herald Tribune,* April 11 and April 18, 1965 (very hard to get hold of); and Josephine Hendin, "*The New Yorker* as Cultural Ideal," *Dissent* 29, no. 4 (1982): 450–54. Among much comment on the death of the old *New Yorker* (that is, the editorship of Tina Brown), Joseph Epstein's review of the reissue of Joseph Mitchell's *Up in the Old Hotel* in *The Times Literary Supplement,* September 4, 1992, 6–8, is worth reading (con), alongside (pro) Robert McCrumm's feature article in *The Guardian,* October 1, 1992, 23.

INDEX

Page numbers in *italics* denote cartoons. Artists are identified by their initials.

America (*cont.*)

lightenment values and, 144, 216–18; Great Depression and, 60, 147; and loss of innocence, 239; national ethos of, 144, 145, 198, 216–18, 222–23, 291n20; New Deal and, 75; postwar cultural influence of, 15–16; Puritanism and, 24, 145; Scottish Common Sense philosophers and, 144; slavery and, 145; southern plantations and, 145; Steinberg's metaphor for, 223; values and ideals of, 138. *See also* American gothic; Freemasonry

American Beginnings (WS), 127–28, 130

American gothic, 144–46, 174; Addams and, 142, 146; anxiety and, 145; Louis Gross on, 145–46, 171; history of, 146

. . . and if it's a boy (CA), 158

And now, Miss Evans (PA), 48

Arno, Patricia Maxwell, 269n67

ARNO, PETER (1904–68), 2, 75, 76, 82, 84, 96, 165, 238, 263–64n6, 268–69n56, 271–72n94; advertising commissions and, 54–55, 242; cabaret and, 29, 41, 43–46, 64; as dandy, 21, 39, 41–43, 61, 74, 263n6; father and, 22, 50–52, 56–58, 60; feminism and, 47–49, 268n51; gag writers and, 36, 265nn24,27,31&32, 269n67; historical moment of, 21, 24–27, 32, 52, 74, 75; humor, characteristics of, 14–15, 17, 21–22, *23*, 24, 25, 42, 61–62, 70, 71–74; influence of, 30; legal troubles, 55–56; marriages: —to Mary Lansing, 271n79; —to Lois Long, 26, 27, 47, 56, 245; masculinity and, 25, 46, 50, 64, 70–71, 74, 267n44, 268n55; money and, 53, 54–55, 58, 149, 242, 269n67; Ross and, 54; sexual themes and, 29–32, 34, 46–50, 70, 271–72n94; technique of, 23, 34–36, 66, 68, 156; as type of his generation, 24, 26, 27, 28, 50, 75

[*Artist, buried alive by Fame*] (SS), 181, *183*

Artist and Model (WS), 86, *88*

Atlantic Magazine, 249

Auden, W. H., 103, 120

Balliett, Whitney, 130

Barlow, Perry, 12, 91

[*Bar scene*] (SS), 193, *195*

Barthelme, Donald, 256–57

Barthes, Roland, 186, 191, 290–91n8

Barton, Ralph, 26, 91, 269n67, 269–70n68

basic biophysical attitude of the *unarmored* and *armored* organism (Reich), 108, *109*, 114, *117*

Baudelaire, Charles, 39–40 *passim*, 64; on the comic, 178; *flâneur* defined by, 40; on Guys, 41

Baudrillard, Jean, 201, 253

Beardsley, Aubrey Vincent, 165

Bedtime Story (unattributed), 34, *35*

Berlin, Irving, 28, 56

Bertoldo, 203

Bion, Wilfrid, 171, 174

Birnbaum, Abe, 123

Boiling Oil (CA), 138, *139*, 175

Bolitho, William, 34

Bombing of Civilians (WS), 88, *89*

Boni and Liveright, 21, 263n4

Brown, Tina, 132, 279n104

But it is half man and half horse (SS), 192, 204

By all means, dear—buy it (PA), 71–74

By golly, Miss Eppis (PA), 41

cabaret, 27, 29, 43–44, 64, 71–72, 264n11

Can you step up here just a moment? (CA), 152

capitalism: commentary on, 21, 196, 249, 256–57; Horney and, 98–100, 249; Reich and, 103–5, 109, 113, 116

[*Careful! Children at Play*] (CA), 155, *157*

Carson, Rachel, 176, 178
cartoonists: advertisements and, 242; dandy and, 41; as image makers, 6; selection principles, 3, 14. *See also individual artists*
cartoons in *New Yorker:* advertisements and, 252–53; dating of, 4, 259nn7&8, 259–60n9; detachment encouraged by, 10, 12; drawing style, importance of, 8; editing of, 37; effect on reader, 245; and examples, 8; features of, 1, 5, 7; full-page drawings, 54, 269n67; gag writers, 36–38, 265n24; historical epoch and, 6–7, 10, 14–15, 261n18; idea and drawing, 38–39; middle class and, 5–6; modesty of, as form, 10; new social experiences and, 6–7; numbers published, 3; payment for, 54–55, 269n67, 269–70n68, 270n69; racist themes, 12, 266–67n43; recapitulated presentation of, 243; repeated motifs, 4, 59–60, 265n32; sexual themes in, 47–50; as social cynosure, 261n22; weekly presentation of, 243
Carver, Raymond, 18
cem (Charles E. Martin), 123
Cette . . . and cette . . . (PA), 61, 68–70, *69*
Chancellor, Alexander, 132–34
[Chanteuse and diner] (PA), 71, *73*
Chast, Roz, 13, 18
Coast (SS), 194
Cobean, Sam, 269n66
Colliers, 82
Connelly, Marc, 267n46
Coolidge, Calvin, 226
[Crocodile, artist with easel in jaws] (SS), 185

Dada, 17, 152, 218, 292–93n36
dandy: aristocrat and, 263–64n6; Baudelaire and, 39; as cartoonist, 41; described, 40, 41; humor and, 41; idea

of, and NYC, 39; middle classes and, 41–42; modernity and, 39; politics of, 42; Eustace Tilley as, 43; Whitman and, 39
Darrow, Whitney, Jr., 37, 48
Daumier, Honoré, 34, 68, 116, 228, 263n5, 266n36
Day, Robert, 91, 138
Dear Fellow-Alumnus (CA), 135–38, *137*
Decker, Richard, 91
de Montaigne, Michel, 248
de Tocqueville, Alexis, 238
De Vries, Peter, 18; as caption writer, 37
doxa, 13, 154
Do you realize who I am? I am Morton P. Ipplehart (WS), 96
Dreams of Glory [boy arrests Hitler] (WS), 86
[Driver's view of highway] (SS), 209, *211*

Empty Supermarket (CA), 175, *177*
Enlightenment, 216–18, 222. *See also* Freemasonry
Europeans, The (Henry James), 140
Excuse me, sir, but are you the Arthur Johnson? (CA), 161–62
E-Z-Eye Safety Plate (advertisement), 209, *210*

[Family in automobile on map collage] (WS), 92, *95*
[Family in various styles] (SS), 232–34, *233*
feminism, 241, 268n51
Fishman, Joseph Fulling, 152
Fitzgerald, F. Scott, 178, 270n72
flâneur, 40, 64. *See also* dandy
Flanner, Janet, 32, 43, 100, 264n18
Fleischmann, Raoul, 245, 246
Ford, Corey, 82, 266n38
[Ford Foundation illustrations] (SS), 196
Frank, Waldo, 226–27
Freemasonry: commentary on, 205, 216–24; iconography and symbolic

theories of, 301n32. *See also* jokes; laughter

Humphries, Barry, 262n33, 262–63n36

illustration: Ross on, 37–38; Steig and, 130

I love this old place (PA), 71

I'm the luckiest man in the world (WS), 113, *115*

Indian Problem (Stevenson), 186–87

Ingersoll, Ralph McAllister, 22, 82; on *New Yorker,* 246; *PM* and, 242

Inventory (SS), 215, *217*

Ionesco, Eugène, 203

Irvin, Rea, 26, 91, 165, 266n38, 269n67

I was discussing the Mexican situation (PA), 38, 50, *51,* 60, 70

James, Henry, 140

jokes: aggressive, 138, 155, 168, 170, 178, 261n25; cynical, 155, 168; sexual, 155; skeptical, 153–54, 155; tendentious, 48; —defined, 155; —examples of, 155–60, 268n53; triadic structure of, 155, 156, 168, 173. *See also* Addams, Charles

Kael, Pauline, 18

[Kim Novak and Rodion Raskolnikov conversation] (SS), 211–12, *213*

Klein, I., 83

Klein, Melanie, 171

Krim, Seymour, 244

[*L.A.*] (SS), 185, *187*

[*Labyrinth*] (SS), 236–38, *237*

Lardner, John, 16, 19, 262n34

laughter, 2, 135; commodity and, 251, 253, 256; language and, 251; self-possession and, 251–52; temporality and, 251

Levin, Arnie, 18

Levin, Ira, 160

Life (1883–1936), 22, 81, 82, 274n20; *The*

Bedtime Story (cartoon) discussed, 34, *35*

Life (1936–72), 16, 204

[*Life history, infant to businessman*] (SS), 230

[*Life history, infant to businesswoman*] (SS), 230

[*Life history, infant to grandmother*] (SS), 229

Lippmann, Walter, 246

Liveright, Horace, 21, 263n4

loiterer, 64; E. B. White and, 40. *See also* dandy

Long, Lois, 26–27; marriage of, 245

Look, 16

Look what I've brought you (WS), 118, *119*

Lorenz, Lee, 3, 71, 100, 108, 147

[*Lovers in cottage with chains*] (WS), 131, *133*

Macdonald, Dwight, 196, 244

Mackay, Ellen: *The Declining Function,* 264n11; and marriage to Irving Berlin, 28; *Why We Go to Cabarets,* 27–28, 264n11. *See also* cabaret

magazine: desire and, 253; etymology of, 250; textual field of, 252–53

Maloney, Russell, 204

Man in the Shower (PA), 24, *25,* 71

Mankoff, Robert, 256

Marsh, Reginald, 261–62n26

[*Masks*] (SS), 198, 232

Master (WS), 109, *110*

McAllister, Ward, 22

McCallister, Richard, 37

McNulty, John, 246

McPhee, John, 18

Mead, Margaret, 84

Mencken, H. L., 53

middle class: Addams and, 147, 154–55, 156, 159, 160; American history and, 2, 275n35; dandy and, 41–42; history of, 2; *New Yorker* and, 4, 41; selected cartoonists and, 15; values of, 76

Mitchell, Joseph, 14

Modell, Frank, 1, 13, 18; as caption writer for Whitney Darrow Jr., 37

modernism: abstract expressionism, 207; Hans Arp, 203; Bauhaus, 203; Cubism, 203; Ferdinand Léger, 178; René Magritte, 200; Frans Masereel, 266n36; Henri Matisse, 203; Pablo Picasso, 100, 178; Jackson Pollock, 207; postmodernism and, 207; Steinberg and, 181–83, 290n5; Andy Warhol, 207

Mother's House (*Psycho,* film still), 141–42, *143*

[*Multiple marchers*] (SS), 229

My true love will come some day, (WS), 101, *102*

My youngest is a terror (WS), 75

Newhouse, S. I., Jr., 123

New Woman, 47

New York City: Barthes description of, 191, 292n32; cityscape of, 17–18; dandy and, 39–41; ethos of Manhattan: —in 1920s, 52–54; —in 1980s, 17–18; myth of, 191; Steig's psychological portraits and, 110; E. B. White on, 40, 191; World Trade Center, 9/11 attack on, 135, 239

New Yorker, 3; achievement of, 18; Addams and, 2, 135–36, 148–49; advertisements, 2, 240–41, 242, 244, 246–47 (*see also* advertising); Arno and, 21, 22, 26, 29, 43; art meetings at, 264n8; cartoonists and, 3 (*see also individual artists*); cartoons in, 2–3, 136, 242; —and payment for, 54–55, 269n67, 269–70n68, 270n69; —and prominence of, 244; character of, 5, 17–18; circulation and distribution of, 247; commodity and, 243; consumerism and, 54; contents of, 239–40; dandy and, 39–43; Depression and, 60; descriptions of, 243–44; design and layout of, 242–43, 244, 301n41;

—Shawn on, 245; drawing accounts, 269–70n68; editorial and business departments, 245–46; ethos of, 82; female employees and, 267–68n50; and gag writers, 265n24; generalizations about, 243–44; as guide to NYC, 17–18; humor of, 3, 10, 12, 262n27; —racist aspects of, 12, 261–62n26, 272n3; image of New York and, 247; integrity of, 248; issues: —contents aggregated, 243; —size of, 240; marketing to advertisers, 247–48; —and *Primary Markets for Quality Merchandise,* 248; —and *Rebuque from Dubuque, or Where, Indeed, Are the Limits of New York?* 247; microform version of, 239–42; production and distribution schedule of, 136, 280n3, 298n110; prospectus of, 5, 260–61n16; as publishing forum, 17, 243; reader response to, 18, 244, 245; readership of, 3, 4, 18, 253; running order, 60; salaries at, 54, 270n71; sophistication of, 43; Steig and, 75, 78–80, 82, 83, 91, 92, 96–97, 132, 275n28; Steinberg and, 3, 238; studies of, 260n14. *See also* magazine

Notice, class, how Angela (Darrow), 48

Now, let's just slip it on (CA), 166

object relations: applied to Addams, 171–73; baby in, 171–72; comedy and, 174; commentary on, 286–87n82, 287–88n84, 288–89n85; containing, 171, 172, 174, 287–88n84; and emotional life, 172; joke as social transaction, 171, 287–88n84; key concepts of, 171–72; as model for joker, 172; projection, 162, 171, 172; regression and, 171; reverie, 175

O'Brian, William, 191

Oh, Hortense (PA), 30, 32

Oil Spill (CA), 176, 178, *179*

paranoid style: cold war period and, 162, 286n70; projection and, 162

Pardon me, young man (Hokinson with WS), 75, *77*

Parker, James Reid, 13, 36

Partisan Review, 252

Peck, Gus, 83

[*Pedestal, businessman on*] (SS), 214

[*Pedestal, man leaping to, from cliff face*] (SS), 214

[*Pedestals, artists on*] (SS), 214

Perelman, S. J., 152

Peters, Curtis Arnoux, Jr. *See* Arno, Peter

Peters, Curtis Arnoux, Sr., 22, 50, 56–57; punishment of Arno as child, 58

Petty, Mary, 269nn66&67

Phenomena (WS), 86, *87*

photojournalism, *New Yorker* and, 260–61n16, 301n38

Planetarium (CA), 161, 162, *163*

Price, Garrett, 91

Price, George, 38–39, 75, 91, 261–62n26, 266–67n43, 272n3; graded by Ross, 269n66

Primary Markets for Quality Merchandise, 248

Proust, Marcel, 126; on habit, 205; on self in time, 230; Steinberg and, 234–35

Psst. Brother Sebastian (CA), 150–52, *151,* 165

Psycho (dir. Hitchcock), 141

[*Purilia*] (PA), 59, *59*

Pursuit of Happiness (SS), 197, 222–24, *225*

[*Pyramid by the freeway*] (SS), 218–20, *219*

[*Rabbit ego in boilerplate skin*] (SS), 231, *231*

Rea, Gardner, 91

Ready Marcel (PA), 62

Rebecca (dir. Hitchcock), 160

Rebuque from Dubuque, or Where, Indeed, Are the Limits of New York? 247

Reich, Wilhelm, 76, 97, 126, 230, 277n75; diagram, *109;* dreaming and fantasy, 120–21; ideas discussed, 103–8, 277n63; —applied to Steig, 107–21; —applied to Steinberg, 230; oceanic feeling, 120; and Steig drawing, 113–14, *117. See also under* Steig, William; Steinberg, Saul

Ricks, Christopher, 197

Ricoeur, Paul, 288n84

Rieff, Philip, 103

Rockwell, Norman, 54, 193

Roman, Lica (sister of Saul Steinberg), 200, 293n50

Romania, 192, 202–3

Romanoff, Prince Michael Obolensky. *See* Gerguson, Harry

Roosevelt, Franklin Delano, 135, 136

Rose, Carl, 191, 269n66

Rosenberg, Harold, 182

Ross, Harold, 2, 123; advertising, attitude toward, 299–300n13; Arno and, 22, 54, 269n67; death of, 280n3; editorial and business separation in *New Yorker* and, 245–46; as editor of cartoons, 37–38, 265n30; grades artists, 269n66; Ingersoll hired by, 22; salary of, 54; sex in cartoons, attitude toward, 32, 46, 267n46; Steig and, 78; Steinberg and, 204

Ross, Lillian, 123

Sad Movie (CA), 166–78, *167*

Sandlot Baseball (WS), 90

[*Santa Claus on roof*] (WS), 124, *125*

Saturday Evening Post, 53, 54

Saxon, Charles, 13, 17, 138

Scarfe, Gerald, 228

Screen Scream (CA), 168–70, *169*

Searle, Ronald, 228, 278n88

Sempé, Jean-Jacques, 278n82

Shawn, William, 2, 18, 265n30; Addams and, 136, 164; editorial and business

203, 204, 214; —relation to his art, 204–5; Yiddish and, 201–2, 294n57
Stern, Bert, 58, 271n88
Stevenson, James, 13, 18, 186–87, 280n3
[*Stone mountain selves*] (SS), 214

They're discussing sex (Alice Harvey), 47
This has gone a bit too far, Remson! Someone purloined my Burberry (PA), 21–22, *23*
This is the life (Robert Mankoff), *255,* 256
Thurber, James, 7–10, 13, 60, 80, 91, 96, 103, 165; daydream and, 120; graded by Ross, 269n66; income of, 54; popularity of, 10
Tilley, Eustace, 43, 82, 245, 266n38
Trilling, Diana, 15, 90–91, 116

Updike, John, 18
[*Upper class couple in restaurant*] (PA), 65–66, *67*

View of the World from 9th Avenue (SS), 188–92, *189*
Visiting hours are over (PA and Price), 38–39

Webster, Harold Tucker, 84–85, 267n44
[*Werewolf at barbershop*] (CA), 160

White, E. B., 36–37, 40, 54, 64, 191, 280n3, 280–81n4
Williams, Gluyas, 165, 269n66
Williams, Marilyn "Tee": as editor, 259–60n9; marriage to Charles Addams, 158
Williams, Raymond, 6, 261n18
Winchell, Walter, 27, 56
Winnicott, Donald W., 171, 279n101, 289n88
Wolfe, Tom, 244
Woollcott, Alexander, 246
Wylie, Philip G., caption writer for Arno, 37

Yagoda, Ben, 3, 37
You cad! You're not fit (PA), 66–68
You do give such perfect parties, Alice (PA), 28, 61
Young woman, do you realize my time is worth thirty dollars a minute? (PA), 48, *49*
You're like a lovely flower tonight (PA), 29–30, *31, 34*, 61
You're so kind to me (PA), 43
You wait here and I'll bring the etchings down (James Thurber), 7–10, *11*

Ziegler, Jack, 18